T0344272

The Arithmetic of
Z-Numbers

Theory and Applications

The Arithmetic of

Z-Numbers

Theory and Applications

Rafik A Aliev
Azerbaijan State Oil Academy, Azerbaijan

Oleg H Huseynov
Azerbaijan State Oil Academy, Azerbaijan

Rashad R Aliyev
Eastern Mediterranean University, Turkey

Akif A Alizadeh
Azerbaijan University, Azerbaijan

World Scientific

NEW JERSEY · LONDON · SINGAPORE · BEIJING · SHANGHAI · HONG KONG · TAIPEI · CHENNAI

Published by

World Scientific Publishing Co. Pte. Ltd.
5 Toh Tuck Link, Singapore 596224
USA office: 27 Warren Street, Suite 401-402, Hackensack, NJ 07601
UK office: 57 Shelton Street, Covent Garden, London WC2H 9HE

British Library Cataloguing-in-Publication Data
A catalogue record for this book is available from the British Library.

THE ARITHMETIC OF Z-NUMBERS
Theory and Applications

ISBN 978-981-4675-28-4

Printed in Singapore

Dedication

Dedicated to the memory of my wife Aida Alieva

Rafik Aliev

To my parents and grandparents

Oleg Huseynov

To my parents and family

Rashad Aliev

To the memory of my father Vali Alizadeh

Akif Alizadeh

Preface

Real-world information is imperfect and we often use natural language (NL) in order to represent this feature of the former. On the one hand, such information is often characterized by fuzziness. This implies that we often impose soft constraints on values of variables of interest. On the other hand, what is very important is that it is not sufficient to take into account only fuzziness when dealing with real-world imperfect information. The other essential property of information is its partial reliability. Indeed, any estimation of values of interest, be it precise or soft, are subject to the confidence in sources of information we deal with – knowledge, assumptions, intuition, envision, experience – which, in general, cannot completely cover the whole complexity of real-world phenomena. Thus, fuzziness from the one side and partial reliability form the other side are strongly associated to each other. In order to take into account this fact, L.A. Zadeh suggested the concept of a Z-number as a more adequate formal construct for description of real-world information. A Z-number is an ordered pair $Z = (A, B)$ of fuzzy numbers used to describe a value of a variable X, where A is an imprecise constraint on values of X and B is an imprecise estimation of reliability of A and is considered as a value of probability measure of A.

The concept of a Z-number has a potential for many applications, especially in the realms of computation with probabilities and events described in NL. Of particular importance are applications in economics, decision analysis, risk assessment, prediction, anticipation, planning, biomedicine and rule-based manipulation of imprecise functions and relations.

Thus, real-world information is often represented in a framework of Z-number based evaluations. Such information is referred to as Z-information. The main critical problems that naturally arises in processing Z-information are computation and reasoning with Z-information. The existing literature devoted to computation with Z-numbers is quite scarce. Unfortunately, there is no general and computationally effective approach to computations with Z-numbers. There is a need in development of a universal approach to computations with Z-numbers which can be relatively easily applied for solving a wide spectrum of real-world problems in control, decision analysis, optimization and other areas. Computation and reasoning with Z-information are characterized by propagation of restrictions, that is, they are restriction-based computation and reasoning. As it is mentioned by L.A. Zadeh, the principal types of restrictions are probabilistic restrictions, possibilistic restrictions and combinations of probabilistic and possibilistic restrictions. Indeed, Z-information falls within the category of possibilistic-probabilistic restrictions. Nowadays, the existing literature devoted to computation and reasoning with restrictions includes well-developed approaches and theories to deal with pure probabilistic or pure possibilistic restrictions. For computation with probabilistic restrictions as probability distributions, the well-known probabilistic arithmetic is used. Fuzzy arithmetic deals with possibilistic constraints, which describe objects as classes with "unsharp" boundaries.

Unfortunately, up to day there is no approach to computation and reasoning with objects described by combination of probabilistic and possibilistic restrictions, such as Z-numbers. Arithmetic of Z-numbers is a basis of a future mathematical formalism to process Z-information. Arithmetic of Z-numbers is greater than just "mechanical sum" of probabilistic arithmetic and fuzzy arithmetic, it is a synergy of these two counterparts. Consequently, development of this arithmetic requires generalization of the extension principle to deal with a fusion of probabilistic and possibilistic restrictions. In turn, computation of restrictions is computation of functions and functionals that involves optimization problems, particularly, mathematical programming and variational problems.

Nowadays there is no arithmetic of Z-numbers suggested in the existing literature. The suggested book is the first to present a comprehensive and self-contained theory of Z-arithmetic and its applications. Many of the concepts and techniques described in the book are original and appear in the literature for the first time.

This book provides a detailed method in arithmetic of continuous and discrete Z-numbers. We also provide the necessary knowledge in its connections to other types of theories of uncertain computations. In addition, we discuss widely application of Z-numbers in variety of methods of operations research, economics, business and medicine.

Let us emphasize that many numbers, especially, in fields such as economics and decision analysis, are in reality Z-numbers, but they are not treated as such, because it is much simpler to compute with numbers than with Z-numbers. Basically, the concept of a Z-number is a step toward formalization of the remarkable human capability to make rational decisions in an environment of imprecision and uncertainty.

The book is organized into 7 chapters. The first chapter includes papers of L.A. Zadeh: *L.A. Zadeh. Toward a restriction-centered theory of truth and meaning (RCT). Information Sciences, 248, 2013, 1–14*; and *L.A. Zadeh, A note on Z-numbers, Information Sciences, 181, 2011, 2923-2932.* In the first section, the restriction centered theory, RCT, is considered which may be viewed as a step toward formalization of everyday reasoning and everyday discourse. Unlike traditional theories— theories which are based on bivalent logic—RCT is based on fuzzy logic. In the second section, the general concepts of a Z-number and Z^+-number are suggested which have a potential for many applications. Also, sound theoretical foundation of computation of different functions of Z-numbers are suggested.

For the present book to be self-containing, foundations of fuzzy sets theory, fuzzy logic and fuzzy mathematics which are used as the formal basis of the suggested theory of computation with Z-numbers are given in Chapter 2. We would like to mention that this chapter contains a material on a spectrum of computations with uncertain and imprecise information including the basics of interval arithmetic, probabilistic arithmetic, and fuzzy arithmetic. In this chapter we also give properties of continuous and discrete Z-numbers.

Operations on continuous Z-numbers are explained in Chapter 3. Arithmetic operations such as addition, standard subtraction, multiplication and standard division are considered. Also, square and square root of a continuous Z-number are given. Chapter 4 provides a method of computation with discrete Z-numbers. Taking into account the fact that real problems are characterized by linguistic information which is, as a rule, described by a discrete set of meaningful linguistic terms, in this book we consider also discrete Z-numbers. This chapter includes original methods for performing all arithmetic operations: addition, standard subtraction, Hukuhara difference, multiplication and standard division of discrete Z-numbers; computation methods for square of a discrete Z-number, square root of a discrete Z-number, maximum and minimum of discrete Z-numbers, and ranking of discrete Z-numbers are also suggested. Algebraic system of Z-numbers is described in Chapter 5. Here, distance between two discrete Z-numbers, functions of discrete Z-numbers, equations with discrete Z-numbers, derivative of a function of discrete Z-numbers, t-norm and t-conorm of discrete Z-numbers, aggregation of discrete Z-numbers, and functions as discrete Z-numbers-based IF-THEN rules (Z-rules) are considered. Different methods of aggregation of Z-numbers, mainly, T-norm, T-conorm, weighted average and Choquet integral-based aggregations are given. In this chapter, a special emphasis is put on Z-rules and interpolation procedures for reasoning.

All the methods in Chapters 1-5 are illustrated by a vast spectrum of examples.

Chapters 6, 7 deal with applications of Z-numbers in different areas. In Chapter 6 we suggest a new approach to solving a Z-valued linear programming problem and construction of Z-linear regression models, We also consider Z-restriction based multicriteria choice problem. A special emphasis is done on decision making under Z-information and computing with words in Z-information framework.

Chapter 7 is devoted to application of the methods suggested in Chapters 1-6 to real-world problems in economics, business and planning problems.

This book is intended to offer comprehensive coverage of the methods for computation with Z-numbers. It is written to be suitable to different groups of readers, mainly for senior college students, graduate students and for researchers and practitioners with advanced knowledge in statistics, fuzzy logic and the Z-number theory.

Our goal was set to write a complete introductory and comprehensive book on Z-number based uncertain computation. We hope that this book has led to a good foundation for learning computation with Z-numbers, as well as being a stepping stone to farther research in this new and very important theory and practice.

The book will be helpful for professionals, academicians, managers and graduate students in fuzzy logic, decision sciences, artificial intelligence, mathematical economics, and computational economics.

We would like to express our thanks to Professor Lotfi Zadeh, the founder of the fuzzy set and Soft Computing theories and a creator of the idea of Z-number, for his permanent support, invaluable ideas and advices for our research.

R.A. Aliev
O.H. Huseynov
R.R. Aliyev
A.V. Alizadeh

Contents

Chapter 1

The General Concept of a
Restriction and Z-numbers

This chapter includes the papers of L.A. Zadeh: 1. *L.A. Zadeh, Toward a restriction-centered theory of truth and meaning (RCT). Information Sciences, 248, 2013, 1–14*; 2. *L.A. Zadeh, A note on Z-numbers, Information Sciences, 181, 2011, 2923-2932.*

1.1. Z-restriction

1.1.1. *Introduction*

The concepts of truth and meaning are of fundamental importance in logic, information analysis and related fields. The restriction-centered theory outlined in this paragraph, call it RCT for short, is a departure from traditional theories of truth and meaning, principally correspondence theory, coherence theory, Tarski semantics, truth-conditional semantics and possible-world semantics [42, 43, 83, 105, 115, 119, 131, 134].

In large measure, traditional theories of truth and meaning are based on bivalent logic. RCT is based on fuzzy logic. Standing on the foundation of fuzzy logic, RCT acquires a capability to enter the realm of everyday reasoning and everyday discourse — a realm which is avoided by traditional theories of truth and meaning largely because it is a realm that does not lend itself to formalization in the classical tradition.

In RCT, truth values are allowed to be described in natural language. Examples.Quite true, very true, almost true, probably true, possibly true, usually true, etc. Such truth values are referred to as linguistic truth values. Linguistic truth values are not allowed in traditional logical systems.

The centerpiece of RCT is the deceptively simple concept—the concept of a restriction. The concept of a restriction has greater generality than the concept of interval, set, fuzzy set and probability distribution. An early discussion of the concept of a restriction appears in [153]. Informally, a restriction, *R(X)*, on a variable, *X*, is an answer to a question of the form: What is the value of *X* ? Example. Robert is staying at a hotel in Berkeley. He asks the concierge, ''How long will it take me to drive to SF Airport?'' Possible answers: 1 h, 1 h plus/minus fifteen minutes, about 1 h, usually about 1 h, etc. Each of these answers is a restriction on the variable, driving time. Another example. Consider the proposition, p: Most Swedes are tall. What is thetruth value of p? Possible answers: true, 0.8, about 0.8, high, likely high, possibly true, etc. In RCT, restrictions are preponderantly described as propositions drawn from a natural language. Typically, a proposition drawn from a natural language is a fuzzy proposition, that is, a proposition which contains fuzzy predicates, e.g., tall, fast, heavy, etc., and/or fuzzy quantifiers, e.g., most, many, many more, etc., and/or fuzzy probabilities, e.g., likely, unlikely, etc. A zero-order fuzzy proposition does not contain fuzzy quantifiers and/or fuzzy probabilities. A first-order fuzzy proposition contains fuzzy predicates and/or fuzzy quantifiers and/or fuzzy probabilities. It is important to note that in the realm of natural languages fuzzy propositions arethe norm rather than exception. Traditional theories of truth and meaning provide no means for reasoning and computation with fuzzy propositions.

Basically, *R(X)* may be viewed as a limitation on the values which *X* can take. Examples.

> *X = 5; X* is between 3 and 7; *X* is small; *X* is normally
> distributed with mean m and variance σ^2 ; It is likely that
> *X* is small
> Summers are usually cold in San Francisco
> (*X* is implicit)
> Robert is much taller than most of his friends
> (*X* is implicit)

As a preview of what lies ahead, it is helpful to draw attention to two key ideas which underlie RCT. The first idea, referred to as the meaning postulate, MP, is that of representing a proposition drawn from a natural language, p, as a restriction expressed as

$$p \rightarrow X \text{ isr } R,$$

where X is the restricted variable, R is the restricting relation, and r is an indexical variable which defines the way in which R restricts X. X may be an n-ary variable, and R may be an n-ary relation. Generally, X and R are implicit in p. Basically, X is the variable whose value is restricted by p. X is referred to as the focal variable. In large measure, the choice of X is subjective, reflecting one's perception of the variable or variables which are restricted by p. However, usually there is a consensus. It should be noted that a semantic network representation of p may be viewed as a graphical representation of an n-ary focal variable and an n-ary restricting relation. The expression on the right-hand side of the arrow is referred to as the canonical form of p, CF(p). CF(p) may be interpreted as a generalized assignment statement [161]. The assignment statement is generalized in the sense that what is assigned to X is not a value of X, but a restriction on the values which X can take. Representation of p as a restriction is motivated by the need to represent p in a mathematically well-defined form which lends itself to computation.

The second key idea is embodied in what is referred to as the truth postulate, TP. The truth postulate equates the truth value of p to the degree to which X satisfies R. The degree may be numerical or linguistic. As will be seen in the sequel, in RCT the truth value of p is a byproduct of precisiation of the meaning of p.

To simplify notation in what follows, in some instances no differentiation is made between the name of a variable and its instantiation. Additionally, in some instances no differentiation is made between a proposition, p, and the meaning of p.

1.1.2. The Concept of a Restriction – A Brief Exposition

A restriction $R(X)$ on variable X may be viewed as information about X. More concretely, $R(X)$ may be expressed in a canonical form, $CF(R(X))$,

$$CF(R(X)) : X \text{ isr } R.$$

A restriction is precisiated if X, R and r are mathematically well defined. Precisiation of restrictions plays a pivotal role in RCT. Precisiation of restrictions is a prerequisite to computation with restrictions. Here is an example of a simple problem which involves computation with restrictions.

Usually Robert leaves his office at about 5 pm.

Usually it takes Robert about an hour to get home from work.

At what time does Robert get home?

Humans have a remarkable capability to deal with problems of this kind using approximate, everyday reasoning. One of the important contributions of RCT is that RCT opens the door to construction of mathematical solutions of computational problems which are stated in a natural language.

There are many types of restrictions. A restriction is singular if R is a singleton. Example. $X = 5$. A restriction is nonsingular if R is not a singleton. Nonsingularity implies uncertainty. A restriction is direct if the restricted variable is X. A restriction is indirect if the restricted variable is of the form $f(X)$. Example.

$$R(p): \int_a^b \mu(u)p(u)du \text{ is likely,}$$

is an indirect restriction on p.

In the sequel, the term restriction is sometimes applied to R.

The principal types of restrictions are: possibilistic restrictions, probabilistic restrictions and Z-restrictions.

Possibilistic restriction (r = blank)

$$R(X): X \text{ is } {}^{A,}$$

where A, is a fuzzy set in a space, U, with the membership function, μ_A. A plays the role of the possibility distribution of X,

$$\text{Poss}(X = u) = \mu_A(u).$$

Example.

$$\underset{\uparrow}{X} \quad \text{is} \quad \underset{\uparrow}{\text{small}}$$

restricted variable   restricting relation (fuzzy set).

The fuzzy set small plays the role of the possibility distribution of X (Fig. 1.1).

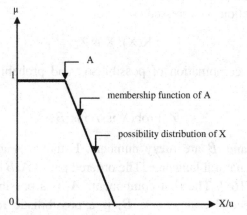

Fig. 1.1. Possibilistic restriction ox X.

Example.

Leslie is taller than Ixel →
(Height (Leslie), Height(Ixel)) is $\underset{\uparrow}{\text{taller}}$

     restricted variable   restricting relation (fuzzy relation)

The fuzzy relation taller is the possibility distribution of ((Height (Leslie), Height (Ixel)).

Probabilistic restriction (r = p)

$$R(X) : X \text{ isp } p,$$

where p is the probability density function of X,

$$\text{Prob}\,(u \le X \le u + du) = p(u)du.$$

Example.

$$X \ isp \ \frac{1}{\sqrt{2\pi}} \exp(-(X-m)^2/2\sigma^2).$$

↑   ↑

restricted variable   restricting relation (probability density function)

Z-restriction (r = z)
A Z-restriction is expressed as

R(X): X is Z,

where Z is a combination of possibilistic and probabilistic restrictions defined as

Z: Prob(X is A) is B,

in which A and B are fuzzy numbers. Usually, A and B are labels drawn from a natural language. The ordered pair, (A, B), is referred to as a Z-number [168]. The first component, A, is a possibilistic restriction on X. The second component, B, is a possibilistic restriction on the certainty (probability) that X is A, X is a real-valued random variable. A Z-interval is a Z number in which the first component is a fuzzy interval.
Examples.
　　　Probably Robert is tall → Height(Robert) is (tall; probable)
　　　Usually temperature is low → Temperature is (low; usually)
　　　Usually X is A,
is a Z-restriction when A is a fuzzy number.
　　A Z-valuation is an ordered triple of the form (X, A, B), and (A, B) is a Z-number. Equivalently, a Z-valuation (X, A, B), is a Z-restriction on X,

(X,A,B) → X is (A,B).

Examples.
　　　　　(Age(Robert), young, very likely)
　　　　　(Traffic, heavy, usually).
　　A natural language may be viewed as a system of restrictions. In the realm of natural languages, restrictions are predominantly possibilistic.

For this reason, in this paragraph we focus our attention on possibilistic restrictions. For simplicity, possibilistic restrictions are assumed to be trapezoidal.

Example. Fig. 1.2 shows a possibilistic trapezoidal restriction which is associated with the fuzzy set middle-age.

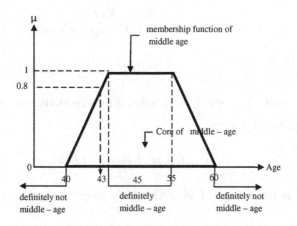

Note. Parameters are context-dependent.

Fig. 1.2. Trapezoidal possibilistic restriction on age.

Computation with restrictions

Computation with restrictions plays an essential role in RCT. In large measure, computation with restrictions involves the use of the extension principle [149,155]. A brief exposition of the extension principle is presented in the following. The extension principle is not a single principle. The extension principle is a collection of computational rules in which the objects ofcomputation are various types of restrictions. More concretely, assume that Y is a function of X, $Y = f(X)$, where X may be an n-ary variable. Assume that what we have is imperfect information about X, implying that what we know is a restriction on X, $R(X)$. The restriction on X, $R(X)$, induces a restriction on Y, $R(Y)$. The extension principle is a computational rule whichrelates to computation of $R(Y)$ given $R(X)$. In what follows, we consider only two basic versions of the extension principle. The simplest version [149] is one in which the restriction is possibilistic and direct. This version of the extension principle reduces computation of $R(Y)$ to the solution of a variational problem,

$$Y = f(X)$$
$$R(X) : X \text{ is } A$$
$$R(Y) : \mu_Y(v) = \sup_u (\mu_A(u))$$

subject to

$$v = f(u),$$

where μ_A and μ_Y are the membership functions of A and Y, respectively. Simply stated,

If X is A then Y is f(A),

where $f(A)$ is the image of A under f. A simple example is shown in Fig. 1.3.

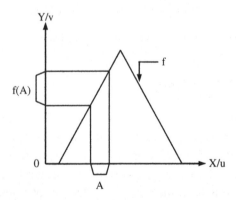

Fig.1.3. Possibilistic version of the basic extension princible. f(A) is the image of A under f. What is shown is a trapezoidal approximation to f(A).

An inverse version of this version of the extension principle is the following.

$$Y = f(X)$$

$$R(Y) : Y \text{ is } B$$
$$R(X) : \mu_A(u) = (\mu_B(f(u)))$$

Simply stated, A is the preimage of B under f (Fig. 1.4).

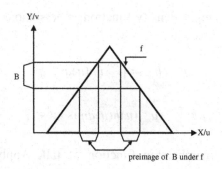

Fig. 1.4. Inverse version of the basic possibilistic extension principle. The induced restriction on X is the preimage of B, the restriction on Y.

A slightly more general version [155] is one in which $R(X)$ is possibilistic and indirect.

$$Y = f(X)$$
$$R(X) : g(X) \text{ is } A$$
$$R(Y) : \mu_Y(v) = \sup_u (\mu_A(g(u)))$$

subject to

$$v = f(g(u)).$$

Example.

Given, p: Most Swedes are tall.
Question, q: What is the average height of Swedes?

The first step involves precisiation of p and q. For this purpose, it is expedient to employ the concept of a height density function, h.

$h(u)du=$*fraction* of Swedes whose height lies in the interval
$[u, u +du]$.

If h_{min} and h_{max} are, respectively, the minimum and maximum heights in the population, we have

$$\int_{h_{\min}}^{h_{\max}} h(u)\,du = 1.$$

In terms of the height density function, precisiations of q and p, q^* and p^*, may be expressed as

$$q^*:? h_{ave} = \int_{h_{\min}}^{h_{\max}} u h(u)\,du,$$

$$p^*: \int_{h_{\min}}^{h_{\max}} \mu_{tall}(u) h(u)\,du \text{ is most,}$$

where μ_{tall} is the membership function of tall. Applying the basic, indirect, possibilistic version of the extension principle, computation of h_{ave} is reduced to the solution of the variational problem

$$\mu_{h_{ave}}(v) = \sup{}_h \, \mu_{most} \left(\int_{h_{\min}}^{h_{\max}} \mu_{tall}(u) h(u)\,du \right),$$

subject to

$$v = \int_{h_{\min}}^{h_{\max}} u h(u)\,du,$$

and

$$\int_{h_{\min}}^{h_{\max}} h(u)\,du = 1.$$

In RCT, for purposes of reasoning and computation what are needed—in addition to possibilistic versions of the extension principle—are versions in which restrictions are probabilistic restrictions and Z-restrictions. These versions of the extension principle are described in [175].

1.1.3. *Truth and Meaning*

It is helpful to begin with a recapitulation of some of the basic concepts which were introduced in the Section 1.1.1.

There is a close relationship between the concept of truth and the concept of meaning. To assess the truth value of a proposition, p, it is necessary to understand the meaning of p. However, understanding the meaning of p is not sufficient. What is needed, in addition, is precisiation of the meaning of p. Precisiation of the meaning of p involves representation of p in a form that is mathematically well defined and lends itself to computation. In RCT, formalization of the concept of truth is a byproduct of formalization of the concept of meaning. In the following, unless stated to the contrary, p is assumed to be a proposition drawn from a natural language. Typically, propositions drawn from a natural language are fuzzy propositions, that is,propositions which contain fuzzy predicates and/or fuzzy quantifiers and/or fuzzy probabilities.

The point of departure in RCT consists of two key ideas: the meaning postulate, MP, and the truth postulate, TP. MP relates to precisiation of the meaning of p. More concretely, a proposition is a carrier of information. Information is a restriction. Reflecting these observations, MP postulates that the precisiated meaning of p — or simply precisiated p — may be represented as a restriction. In symbols, p may be expressed as

$$p \xrightarrow{} X \text{ isr } R,$$

where X, R and r are implicit in p. The expression Xisr$R$ is referred to as the canonical form of p, CF(p). In general, X is ann-ary variable and R is a function of X. Basically, X is a variable such that p is a carrier of information about X. X is referred to as a focal variable of p. In large measure, the choice of X is subjective.
Examples.

p: Robert is young Age (Robert) is young
$\uparrow\uparrow$
XR
p: Most Swedes are tall $\rightarrow$
Proportion(tall Swedes /Swedes) is most
$\uparrow\uparrow$
XR
p: Robert is much taller than most of his friends $\rightarrow$ Height (Robert) is

much taller than most of his friends

p: Usually it takes Robert about an hour to get home from
  work → Travel time from office to home is (approximately 1 h.,
  usually).

The truth postulate, TP, relates the truth value of p to its meaning. More concretely, consider the canonical form

$$CF(p) : X \text{ isr } R.$$

TP postulates that the truth value of p is the degree to which X satisfies R.

In RCT, truth values form a hierarchy: First-order (ground level), second order, etc. First order truth values are numerical. For simplicity, numerical truth values are assumed to be points in the interval (Fig. 1.5).

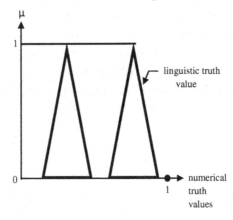

Fig. 1.5. Hierarchy of truth values. A numerical truth value is first-order (ground level) truth value. A linguistic truth value is a second-order truth value. A linguistic truth value is a restriction on numerical truth values. Typically, a linguistic truth value is a fuzzy set or, equivalently, a possibility distribution.

A generic numerical truth value is denoted as *nt*. Second order truth values are linguistic.

Examples. Quite true, possibly true. A generic linguistic truth value is denoted as lt. In RCT, linguistic truth values are viewed as restrictions on numerical truth values. In symbols, $lt = R(nt)$. A generic truth value is denoted as t. t can be nt or lt.

Precisiation of X, R and p

Typically, X and R are described in a natural language. To compute the degree to which X satisfies R it is necessary to precisiate X and R. In RCT, what is used for this purpose is the concept of an explanatory database, ED [160,172]. Informally, ED is a collection of relations which represent the information which is needed to precisiate X and R or, alternatively, to compute the truth value of p. Example. Consider the proposition, p: Most Swedes are tall. In this case, the information consists of three relations, TALL[Height; μ], MOST[Proportion; μ] and POPULATION[Name;Height]. In TALL, μ is the grade of membership of Height in tall. In MOST, μ is the grade of membership of Proportion — a point in the unit interval — in most. In POPULATION, Height is the height of Name, where Name is a variable which ranges over the names of Swedes in a sample population. Equivalently, and more simply, ED may be taken to consist of the membership function of tall, μ_{tall} , the membership function of most, μ_{most} , and the height density function, h. h is defined as the fraction, h(u)du, of Swedes whose height is in the interval [u,u+du].

X and R are precisiated by expressing them as functions of ED. Precisiated X, R and p are denoted as X^*, R^* and p^*, respectively. Thus,

$$X^*=f(ED), \ R^*=g(ED).$$

The precisiated canonical form, $CF^*(p)$, is expressed as $X^*isr^*R^*$. At this point, the numerical truth value of p, nt_p, may be computed as the degree to which X^* satisfies R^*. In symbols,

$$nt_p=tr(ED),$$

in which tr is referred to as the truth function (Fig. 1.6).

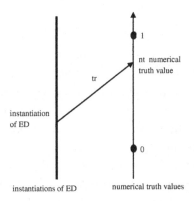

Fig. 1.6. A numerical truth value, nt, is induced by an instantiation of ED. tr is the truth function.

What this equation means is that an instantiation of ED induces a value of nt_p. Varying instantiations of ED induces what is referred to as the truth distribution of p, denoted as Tr(p|ED). The truth distribution of p may be interpreted as the possibility distribution of ED given p, expressed as Poss(ED|p). Thus, we arrive at an important equality

$$Tr(p|ED)=Poss(ED|p).$$

In RCT, the precisiated meaning of p is expressed in three equivalent forms. First, as the precisiated canonical form, CF*(p). Second, as the truth distribution of p, Tr(p|ED). Third, as the possibility distribution, Poss(ED|p). These representations of the precisiated meaning of p play an essential role in RCT. The precisiated meaning of p may be viewed as the computationalmeaning of p. Of the three equivalent definitions stated above, the definition that is best suited for computational purposes is that which involves the possibility distribution of ED. Adopting this definition, what can be stated is the following.

Definition 1.1. The precisiated (computational) meaning of p is the possibility distribution of ED, Poss(ED|p), which is induced by p.

Example. Consider the proposition, p: Robert is tall. In this case, ED consists of Height(Robert) and the relation TALL[Height; μ] or, equivalently, the membership function μ_{tall}. We have,

$$X = \text{Height(Robert)}, \quad R = \text{tall}.$$

The canonical form reads

$$\text{Height(Robert) is tall}.$$

The precisiated X and R are expressed as

$$X^* = \text{Height(Robert)}, \quad R^* = \text{tall},$$

where tall is a fuzzy set with the membership function, μ_{tall}.
The precisiated canonical form reads

$$\text{Height(Robert) is tall}.$$

Note that in this case the unprecisiated and precisiated canonical forms are identical. The truth distribution is defined by

$$nt_p = \mu_{tall}(h),$$

where h is a generic value of Height(Robert).
The basic equality reads

$$Tr(p|h) = Poss(h|p).$$

More specifically, if $h = 175$ cm and $\mu_{tall(175cm)} = 0.9$, then 0.9 is the truth value of p given h=175 cm, and the possibility that h=175 cm given p (Fig. 1.7).

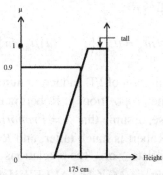

Fig. 1.7. 0.9=Truth value of the proposition Robert is tall, given that Robert's height is 175 cm. 0.9=possibility that Robert's height is 175 cm, given the proposition Robert is tall.

Example. Robert is *handsome*. In this case, assume that we have a sample population of men, Name$_1$, . . ., Name$_n$ with μ_i being the grade of membership of Name$_i$ in the fuzzy set *handsome*. The meaning of p is the possibility distribution associated with the fuzzy set *handsome* — the possibility distribution which is induced by p. The possibility that Name$_i$ is *handsome* is equal to the grade of membership of Name$_i$ in *handsome*.

Example. Consider the proposition, p: Most Swedes are tall. In this case, X = Proportion(tall Swedes/Swedes) and R = most. The canonical form of p is

Proportion(tall Swedes/Swedes) is most.

The precisiated X and R may be expressed as

$$X^* = \int_{h_{min}}^{h_{max}} h(u)\mu_{tall}(u)du,$$

$$R^* = \text{most},$$

where most is a fuzzy set with a specified membership function, μ_{most}.
The precisiated canonical form reads

$$CF^*(p): \int_{h_{min}}^{h_{max}} h(u)\mu_{tall}(u)du \text{ is most.}$$

The truth distribution, Tr(p|ED), is defined by computing the degree, nt_p, to which X^* satisfies R^*,

$$nt_p = \mu_{most}\left(\int_{h_{min}}^{h_{max}} h(u)\mu_{tall}du\right).$$

Note that an instantiation of ED induces a numerical truth value, nt$_p$.

Example. Consider the proposition, p: Robert is much taller than most of his friends. In this case, assume that X = *Proportion* of friends of Robert in relation to whom Robert is much taller, and R=*most*. The explanatory database, ED, consists of the relations FRIENDS[Name; μ], HEIGHT[Name;Height], MUCH.TALLER[Height$_1$;Height$_2$; μ], and Height(Robert). Equivalently, ED may be expressed as μ_F (Name$_i$), h$_i$, and μ_{MT} (h,h$_i$), *i=1,.., n*. In this ED, h = Height(Robert), h$_i$ =Height

(Name$_i$), μ_F (Name$_i$)= grade of membership of Name$_i$in the fuzzy set of friends of Robert, and μ_{MT} (h,h$_i$) = grade of membership of (h,h$_i$) and the fuzzy set much taller. Precisiated X and R are expressed as,

$$X* = \left(\frac{1}{n}\sum_i \mu_{MT}(h,h_i) \wedge \mu_F(Name_i) \right), \ R* = \text{most},$$

The precisiated meaning of p is expressed as,

$$Poss(ED \mid p) = \mu_{most}\left(\frac{1}{n}\sum_i \mu_{MT}(h,h_i) \wedge \mu_F(i) \right),$$

where $\wedge$ denotes conjunction.

The concept of an instantiated ED in RCT is related to the concept of a possible world in traditional theories. Similarly, the concept of a possibility distribution of the explanatory database is related to the concept of intension.

Precisiation of meaning is the core of RCT and one of its principal contributions. A summary may be helpful.

Summary of Precisiation

The point of departure is a proposition, p, drawn from a natural language. The objective is precisiation of p.

1. Choose a focal variable, X, by interpreting p as an answer to the question: What is the value of X ? Identify the restricting relation, R. R is a function of X. At this point, X and R are described in a natural language.

2. Construct the canonical form, $CF(p) = X \ isr \ R$.

3. Construct an explanatory database, ED. To construct ED, ask the question: What information is needed to express X and R as functions of ED? Alternatively, ask the question: What information is needed to compute the truth value of p?

4. Precisiate X and R by expressing X and R as functions of ED. Precisiated X and R are denoted as $X*$ and $R*$, respectively.

5. Construct the precisiated canonical form, $CF*(p): X* \ isr* R*$.

6. Equate precisiated p to *CF*(p)*.

7. *CF*(p)* defines the possibility distribution of ED given *p*, *Poss(ED|p)*.

8. *CF*(p)* defines the truth distribution of the truth value or p given ED, *Tr(p|ED)*.

9. *Poss(ED|p) = Tr(p|ED)*.

10. Define the precisiated (computational) meaning of p as the possibility distribution of ED given p, *Poss(ED|p)*. More informatively, the precisiated (computational) meaning of *p* is the possibility distribution, *Poss(ED|p)*, together with the procedure which computes *Poss(ED|p)*.

Truth qualification. Internal and external truth values

A truth-qualified proposition is a proposition of the form t p, where t is the truth value of p. t may be a numerical truth value, nt, or a linguistic truth value, lt. Example. It is quite true that Robert is tall. In this case, t=quite true and p=Robert is tall. A significant fraction of propositions drawn from a natural language are truth-qualified. An early discussion of truth-qualificationis contained in [157]. Application of truth-qualification to a resolution of Liar's paradox is contained in [156].

In a departure from tradition, in RCT a proposition, p, is associated with two truth values—internal truth value and external truth value. When necessary, internal and external truth values are expressed as Int(truth value) and Ext(truth value), or *Int(p)* and *Ext(p)*.

Informally, the internal numerical truth value is defined as the degree of agreement of p with an instantiation of ED. Informally, an external numerical truth value of p is defined as the degree of agreement of p with factual information, F. More concretely, an internal numerical truth value is defined as follows:

Definition 1.2.

$$Int(nt_p) = tr(ED).$$

In this equation, ED is an instantiation of the explanatory database, *Int(nt$_p$)* is the internal numerical truth value of *p*, and *tr* is the truth function which was defined earlier.

More generally, assume that we have a possibilistic restriction on instantiations of ED, *Poss(ED)*. This restriction induces a possibilistic restriction on nt$_p$ which can be computed through the use of the extension principle. The restriction on *nt$_p$* may be expressed as *tr(Poss(ED))*. The fuzzy set, *tr(Poss(ED))*, may be approximated by the membership function of a linguistic truth value. This leads to the following definition of an internal linguistic truth value of *p*.

Definition 1.3.

$$Int(lt_p) \approx tr(Poss(ED)).$$

In this equation, ≈ should be interpreted as a linguistic approximation. In words, the internal linguistic truth value, *Int(lt$_p$)*, is the image — modulo linguistic approximation — of the possibility distribution of ED under the truth function, tr. It is important to note that the definition of linguistic truth value which was stated in the previous subsection is, in fact, the definition of internal linguistic truth value of *p* (Fig. 1.8).

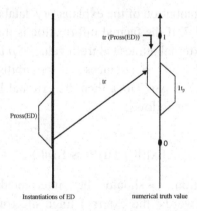

Fig. 1.8. A linguistic truth value, lt$_p$, is induced by a possibilistic restriction on instantions of ED, Poss(ED). lt$_p$ is a linguistic approximation to the image of Poss(ED) under tr.

Poss(ED), tr(Poss(ED)) and lt_p are fuzzy sets. For simplicity, denote these fuzzy sets as A, B and C, respectively. Using the extension principle, computation of lt_p reduces to the solution of the variational problem,

$$\mu_B(\text{v}) = \sup_u \mu_A(u)$$

subject to

$$v = tr(u)$$

$$\mu_C \approx \mu_B.$$

The external truth value of p, $Ext(p)$, relates to the degree of agreement of p with factual information, F. In RCT, factual information may be assumed to induce a possibilistic restriction on ED, $Poss(ED|F)$. In particular, if F instantiates ED, then the external truth value is numerical. This is the basis for the following definition.

Definition 1.4. The external numerical truth value of p is defined as

$$\text{Ext}(nt_p) = tr(ED|F),$$

where ED is an instantiation of the explanatory database induced by F.

Example. In Fig. 1.7, if the factual information is that Robert's height is 175 cm, then the external numerical truth value of p is 0.9.

More generally, if F induces a possibilistic restriction on instantiations of ED, $Poss(ED|F)$, then the external linguistic truth value of p may be defined as follows:

Definition 1.5.

$$\text{Ext}(lt_p) \approx tr(Poss(ED|F)).$$

In this equation, $\approx$ should be interpreted as a linguistic approximation. In words, the external linguistic truth value of p is — modulo linguistic approximation — the image of $Poss(ED|F)$ under tr.

Example. Consider the proposition, p: Most Swedes are tall. Assume that the factual information is that the average height of Swedes is around 170 cm. Around 170 cm is a fuzzy set defined by its membership function, $\mu_{\text{ar.170cm}}$. In terms of the height density function, h, the average height of Swedes may be expressed as

$$h_{\text{ave}} = \int_{h_{\text{min}}}^{h_{\text{max}}} uh(u)du.$$

The explanatory database consists of μ_{tall}, μ_{most} and h. Assuming that μ_{tall} and μ_{most} are fixed, the possibilistic restriction on ED is induced by the indirect possibilistic restriction

$$\int_{h_{\text{min}}}^{h_{\text{max}}} uh(u)du \text{ is around 170 cm,}$$

which is equivalent to the possibility distribution of h expressed as

$$\text{Poss}(h|h_{\text{ave}}) = \mu_{\text{ar.170cm}} \left(\int_{h_{\text{min}}}^{h_{\text{max}}} uh(u)du \right).$$

An important observation is in order. An internal truth value modifies the meaning of p. An external truth value does not modify the meaning of *p*; it places in evidence the factual information, with the understanding that factual information is a possibilistic restriction on the explanatory database.

How does an internal truth value, *t*, modify the meaning of *p*? Assume that the internal truth value is numerical. The meaning of *p* is the possibility distribution, *Poss(ED|p)*. The meaning of nt_p is the preimage of *nt* under the truth function, tr. In other words, the meaning of *p*, expressed as the possibility distribution, *Poss(ED|p)*, is modified to the possibility distribution *Poss(ED|nt_p)*. If the internal truth value is linguistic, lt_p, the modified meaning is the preimage of lt_p, *Poss(ED|lt_p)*, under tr. (Fig. 1.9). More concretely, using the inverse version of the basic extension principle, we can write

$$\mu_{\text{Poss(ED|}lt_p)}(u) = \mu_{\text{tr(Poss(ED|}lt_p))}(\text{tr}(u)),$$

where$u$ is an instantiation of ED, $\mu_{\text{Poss(ED|}lt_p)}$ and $\mu_{\text{tr(Poss(ED|}lt_p))}$ are the membership functions of *Poss(ED|lt_p)* and *tr(Poss(ED|lt_p))*, respectively.

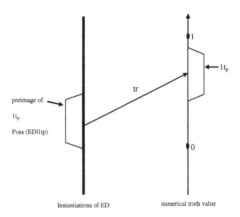

Fig. 1.9. Modification of meaning of p. Modified meaning of p is the preimage of 1tp under tr.

Example. In Fig. 1.7, the preimage of 0.9 is 175 cm. The meaning of *p* is the possibility distribution of tall. The truth value 0.9 modifies the possibility distribution of tall to *Height(Robert)=175 cm*. More generally, when the truth value is linguistic, lt_p, the modified meaning of *p* is the preimage of lt_p under *tr* (Fig. 1.10).

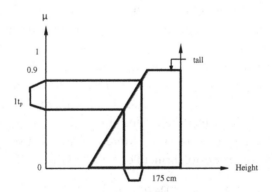

preimage of $1t_p$ (modified meaning of p)

Fig. 1.10. An internal linguistic truth value modifies the meaning of p.

There is a special case which lends itself to a simple analysis. Assume that It is of the form h true, where h is a hedge exemplified by quite, very, almost, etc. Assume that p is of the form X is A, where A is a fuzzy set. In this case, what can be postulated is that truth-qualification modifies the meaning of p as follows.

$$h \text{ true}(X \text{ is } A) = X \text{ is } h \ A.$$

$h A$ may be computed through the use of techniques described in early papers on hedges [91,151].

Example.

(usually true) snow is white = snow is usually white.

Example. (Fig. 1.11)

It is very true that Robert is tall = Robert is very tall.

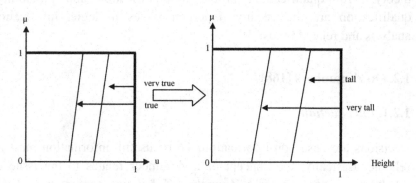

Fig. 1.11. Meaning –modification induced by truth-qualification.

A word of caution is in order. Assume that there is no hedge. In this case, the equality becomes

$$\text{true}(X \text{ is } A) = X \text{ is } A.$$

If truth is bivalent, and true is one of its values, this equality is an agreement with the school of thought which maintains that propositions p and p is true have the same meaning. In RCT, p and p is true do not have the same meaning. There is a subtle difference. More concretely, the meaning of p relates to the agreement of p with a possibilistic restriction on ED. The meaning of p is true relates to a possibilistic restriction which is induced by factual information.

When lt_p is an external truth value, the meaning of p is not modified by lt_p. In RCT, a simplifying assumption which is made regarding the factual information, F, is that F may be described as a possibility distribution of instantiations of ED, *Poss(ED|F)*. The external truth value, lt_p, identifies the factual information as the preimage of lt_p under *tr*,

$$\text{Ext(ltp)=tr(Poss(ED|F))}$$

$$\text{F=Poss(ED|Ext(ltp)).}$$

Truth-qualification in RCT is paralleled by probability-qualification in probability theory and by possibility-qualification in possibility theory. Truth-qualification, probability-qualification and possibility-qualification are intrinsically important issues in logic, information analysis and related fields.

1.2. On Z-numbers [168]

1.2.1. *Introduction*

Decisions are based on information. To be useful, information must be reliable. Basically, the concept of a Z-number relates to the issue of reliability of information. A Z-number, Z, has two components, Z=(A, B). The first component, A, is a restriction (constraint) on the values which a real-valued uncertain variable, X, is allowed to take. The second component, B, is a measure of reliability (certainty) of the first component. Typically, Aand B are described in a natural language. The concept of a Z-number has a potential for many applications, especially in the realms of economics, decision analysis, risk assessment, prediction, anticipation and rule-based characterization of imprecise functions and relations.

In the real world, uncertainty is a pervasive phenomenon. Much of the information on which decisions are based is uncertain. Humans have a remarkable capability to make rational decisions based on information which is uncertain, imprecise and/or incomplete. Formalization of this capability, at least to some degree, is a challenge that is hard to meet. It is this challenge that motivates the concepts and ideas outlined in this note.

The concept of a restriction has greater generality than the concept of a constraint. A probability distribution is a restriction but is not a constraint [146]. A restriction may be viewed as a generalized constraint [166]. In this note, the terms restriction and constraint are used interchangeably.

The restriction

$$R(X): X \text{ is } A;$$

is referred to as a possibilistic restriction (constraint), with A playing the role of the possibility distribution of X. More specifically,

$$R(X): X \text{ is } A \to Poss(X = u) = \mu_A(u)$$

where μ_A is the membership function of A and u is a generic value of X. μ_A may be viewed as a constraint which is associated with R(X), meaning that $\mu_A(u)$ is the degree to which u satisfies the constraint.

When X is a random variable, the probability distribution of X plays the role of a probabilistic restriction on X. A probabilistic restriction is expressed as:

$$R(X): X \text{ isp } p$$

where p is the probability density function of X. In this case,

$$R(X): X \text{ isp } p \to Prob(u \le X \le u + du) = p(u)du$$

Generally, the term "restriction" applies to X is R. Occasionally, "restriction" applies to R. Context serves to disambiguate the meaning of "restriction."

The ordered triple (X, A, B) is referred to as a Z-valuation. A Z-valuation is equivalent to an assignment statement, X is (A, B). X is an uncertain variable if A is not a singleton. In a related way, uncertain computation is a system of computation in which the objects of computation are not values of variables but restrictions on values of variables. In this note, unless stated to the contrary, X is assumed to be a random variable. For convenience, A is referred to as a value of X, with the understanding that, strictly speaking, A is not a value of X but a restriction on the values which X can take. The second component, B, is referred to as certainty. Closely related to certainty are the concepts of sureness, confidence, reliability, strength of belief, probability, possibility, etc. When X is a random variable, certainty may be equated to probability. Informally, B may be interpreted as a response to the question: How sure are you that X is A? Typically, A and B are perception-based and are described in a natural language. A collection of Z-valuations is referred to as Z-information. It should be noted that much of everyday reasoning and decision-making is based, in effect, on Z-information. For purposes of computation, when A and B are described in a natural language, the meaning of A and B is precisiated (graduated) through association with membership functions, μ_A and μ_B, respectively (Fig. 1.12). The membership function of A, μ_A, may be elicited by asking a succession of questions of the form: To what degree does the number, a, fit your perception of A? Example: To what degree does 50 min fit your perception of about 45 min? The same applies to B. The fuzzy set, A, may be interpreted as the possibility distribution of X. The concept of a Z-number may be generalized in various ways. In particular, X may be assumed to take values in R^n, in which case A is a Cartesian product of fuzzy numbers. Simple examples of Z-valuations are:

(anticipated budget deficit, close to 2 million dollars, very likely)
(price of oil in the near future, significantly over 100 dollars/barrel, very likely)

If X is a random variable, then X is A represents a fuzzy event in R, the real line. The probability of this event, p, may be expressed as[150]:

$$p = \int_R \mu_A(u) p_X(u) du,$$

where p_X is the underlying (hidden) probability density of X. In effect, the Z-valuation (X, A, B) may be viewed as a restriction (generalized constraint) on X defined by:

$$\text{Prob(X is } A) \text{ is } B.$$

What should be underscored is that in a Z-number, (A, B), the underlying probability distribution, p_X, is not known. What is known is a restriction on p_X which may be expressed as:

$$\int_R \mu_A(u) p_X(u) du \text{ is } B.$$

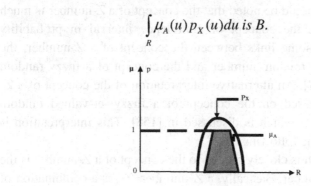

Fig. 1.12. Membership function of A and probability density function of X.

A subtle point is that B is a restriction on the probability measure of A rather than on the probability of A. Conversely, if B is a restriction on the probability of A rather than on the probability measure of A, then (A, B) is not a Z-number.

In effect, a Z-number may be viewed as a summary of p_X. It is important to note that in everyday decision-making most decisions are based on summaries of information. Viewing a Z-number as a summary is consistent with this reality. In applications to decision analysis, a basic problem which arises relates to ranking of Z-numbers. Example: Is (approximately 100, likely) greater than (approximately 90, very likely)? Is this a meaningful question?

An immediate consequence of the relation between p_X and B is the following. If $Z=(A, B)$ then $Z'=(A', 1-B)$, where A' is the complement of A and Z' plays the role of the complement of Z. $1-B$ is the antonym of B [132]. Example: The complement of $Z=(A;$ likely$)$ is $Z'=($not $A;$ unlikely$)$.

An important qualitative attribute of a Z-number is informativeness. Generally, but not always, a Z-number is informative if its value has high specificity, that is, is tightly constrained [141], and its certainty is high. Informativeness is a desideratum when a Z-number is a basis for a decision. A basic question is: When is the informativeness of a Z-number sufficient to serve as a basis for an intelligent decision?

The concept of a Z-number is based on the concept of a fuzzy granule [158,166,177]. It should be noted that the concept of a Z-number is much more general than the concept of confidence interval in probability theory. There are some links between the concept of a Z-number, the concept of a fuzzy random number and the concept of a fuzzy random variable [35,80,107]. An alternative interpretation of the concept of a Z-number may be based on the concept of a fuzzy-set-valued random variable – a concept which is discussed in [158]. This interpretation is not considered in the following.

A concept which is closely related to the concept of a Z-number is the concept of a Z^+-number. Basically, a Z^+-number, Z^+, is a combination of a fuzzy number, A, and a random number, R, written as an ordered pair $Z^+=(A,R)$. In this pair, A plays the same role as it does in a Z-number, and R is the probability distribution of a random number. Equivalently, R may be viewed as the underlying probability distribution of X in the Z-valuation (X, A, B). Alternatively, a Z^+-number may be expressed a (A, p_X) or (μ_A, p_X), where μ_A is the membership function of A. A Z^+-valuation is expressed as (X, A, p_X) or, equivalently, as (X, μ_A, p_X), where p_X is the probability distribution (density) of X. A Z^+-number is associated with what is referred to as a bimodal distribution, that is, a distribution which combines the possibility and probability distributions of X. Informally, these distributions are compatible if the centroids of μ_A and p_X are coincident, that is,

$$\int_R up_X(u)du = \frac{\int_R u\mu_A(u)du}{\int_R \mu_A(u)du}.$$

The scalar product of μ_A and p_X, $\mu_A \cdot p_X$, is the probability measure, P_A, of A. More concretely,

$$\mu_A \cdot p_X = P_A = \int_R \mu_A(u)p_X(u)du.$$

It is this relation that links the concept of a Z-number to that of a Z^+-number. More concretely,

$$Z(A,B) = Z^+(A, \mu_A \cdot p_X \text{ is } B).$$

What should be underscored is that in the case of a Z-number what is known is not p_X but a restriction on p_X expressed as: $\mu_A \cdot p_X$ is B. By definition, a Z^+-number carries more information than a Z-number. This is the reason why it is labeled a Z^+-number. As will be seen in the sequel, computation with Z^+-numbers is a portal to computation with Z-numbers.

The concept of a bimodal distribution is of interest in its own right. Let X be a real-valued variable taking values in U. For our purposes, it will be convenient to assume that U is a finite set, $U=\{u_1,...,u_n\}$. We can associate with X a possibility distribution, μ, and a probability distribution, p, expressed as:

$$\mu = \mu_1/u_1 + \cdots + \mu_n/u_n$$
$$p = p_1 \setminus u_1 + \cdots + p_n \setminus u_n$$

in which μ_i/u_i means that μ_i, $i=1,...,n$, is the possibility that $X=u_i$. Similarly, $p_i \setminus u_i$ means that p_i is the probability that $X=u_i$.

The possibility distribution, μ, may be combined with the probability distribution, p, through what is referred to as confluence. More concretely,

$$\mu : p = (\mu_1, p_1)/u_1 + \cdots + (\mu_n, p_n)/u_n.$$

As was noted earlier, the scalar product, expressed as $\mu \cdot p$, is the probability measure of A. In terms of the bimodal distribution, the Z^+-valuation and the Z-valuation associated with X may be expressed as:

$$(X, A, p_x)$$
$$(X, A, B), \quad \mu_A \cdot p_x \text{ is } B,$$

respectively, with the understanding that B is a possibilistic restriction on $\mu_A \cdot p_X$.

Both Z and Z^+ may be viewed as restrictions on the values which X may take, written as: X is Z and X is Z^+, respectively. Viewing Z and Z^+ as restrictions on X adds important concepts to representation of information and characterization of dependencies. In this connection, what should be noted is that the concept of a fuzzy if-then rule plays a pivotal role in most applications of fuzzy logic. What follows is a very brief discussion of what are referred to as Z-rules – if-then rules in which the antecedents and/or consequents involve Z-numbers or Z^+-numbers.

A basic fuzzy if-then rule may be expressed as: if X is A then Y is B, where A and B are fuzzy numbers. The meaning of such a rule is defined as:

if X is A then Y is $B \rightarrow (X, Y)$ *is* $A \times B$

where $A \times B$ is the Cartesian product of A and B[162]. It is convenient to express a generalization of the basic if-then rule to Z-numbers in terms of Z-valuations. More concretely,

if (X, A_X, B_X) then (Y, A_Y, B_Y).

Examples:

if (anticipated budget deficit, about two million dollars, very likely) then (reduction in staff, about ten percent, very likely)

if (degree of Robert's honesty, high, not sure) then (offer a position, not, sure)

if $(X$, small) then $(Y$, large, usually).

An important question relates to the meaning of Z-rules and Z^+-rules. The meaning of a Z^+-rule may be expressed as:

if (X, A_X, p_X) then $(Y, A_Y, p_Y) \rightarrow (X, Y)$ is $(A_X \times A_Y, p_X p_Y)$,

where $A_X \times A_Y$ is the Cartesian product of A_X and A_Y.

The meaning of Z-rules is more complex and will not be considered in this note. Z-rules have the potential for important applications in decision analysis and modeling of complex systems, especially in the realm of economics.

A problem which plays a key role in many applications of fuzzy logic, especially in the realm of fuzzy control, is that of interpolation. More concretely, the problem of interpolation may be formulated as follows. Consider a collection of fuzzy if-then rules of the form:

$$\text{If } X \text{ is } A_i \text{ then } Y \text{ is } B_i, \quad i = 1,...,n$$

where the A_i and B_i are fuzzy sets with specified membership functions. If X is A, where A is not one of the A_i, then what is the restriction on Y?

The problem of interpolation may be generalized in various ways. A generalization to Z-numbers may be described as follows. Consider a collection of Z-rules of the form:

$$\text{If } X \text{ is } A_i \text{ then usually } Y \text{ is } B_i, \quad i = 1,...,n$$

where the A_i and B_i are fuzzy sets. Let A be a fuzzy set which is not one of the A_i. What is the restriction on Y expressed as a Z-number? An answer to this question would add a useful formalism to the analysis of complex systems and decision processes.

Representation of Z-numbers is facilitated through the use of what is called a Z-mouse[170]. Basically, a Z-mouse is a visual means of entry and retrieval of fuzzy data. A different system of visual entry and retrieval of fuzzy data was employed by Buisson for balancing meals[37].

The cursor of a Z-mouse is a circular fuzzy mark, called an f-mark, with a trapezoidal distribution of light intensity. This distribution is interpreted as a trapezoidal membership function of a fuzzy set. The parameters of the trapezoid are controlled by the user. A fuzzy number such as "approximately 3" is represented as an f-mark on a scale, with 3 being the centroid of the f-mark (Fig. 1.13a). The size of the f-mark is a measure of the user's uncertainty about the value of the number. As

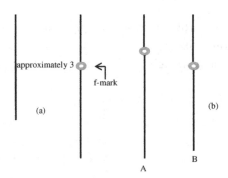

Fig. 1.13. (a) f-mark of approximately 3 ; (b) f-marks of a Z-number.

was noted already, the Z-mouse interprets an f-mark as the membership function of a trapezoidal fuzzy set. This membership function serves as an object of computation. AZ-mouse can be used to draw curves and plot functions.

A key idea which underlies the concept of a Z-mouse is that visual interpretation of uncertainty is much more natural than its description in natural language or as a membership function of a fuzzy set. This idea is closely related to the remarkable human capability to precisiate (graduate) perceptions, that is, to associate perceptions with degrees. As an illustration, if I am asked "What is the probability that Obama will be reelected?" I would find it easy to put an f-mark on a scale from 0 to 1. Similarly, I could put an f-mark on a scale from 0 to 1 if I were asked to indicate the degree to which I like my job. It is of interest to note that a Z-mouse could be used as an informative means of polling, making it possible to indicate one's strength of feeling about an issue. Conventional polling techniques do not assess strength of feeling.

Using a Z-mouse, a Z-number is represented as two f-marks on two different scales (Fig. 1.13b). The trapezoidal fuzzy sets which are associated with the f-marks serve as objects of computation.

1.2.2. Computation with Z-numbers

What is meant by computation with Z-numbers? Here is a simple example. Suppose that I intend to drive from Berkeley to San Jose via Palo Alto. The perception-based information which I have may be expressed as Z-valuations: (travel time from Berkeley to Palo Alto, about 1 h, usually) and (travel time from Palo Alto to San Jose, about 25 min, usually.) How long will it take me to drive from Berkeley to San Jose? In this case, we are dealing with the sum of two Z-numbers (about 1 h, usually) and (about 25 min, usually.) Problems involving computation with Z-numbers are easy to state but far from easy to solve. Example: What is the square root of *(A,B)?* Computation with Z-numbers falls within the province of Computing with Words (CW or CWW) [163]. In large measure, computation with Z-numbers is a move into an uncharted territory. What is described in the following is merely a preliminary step toward exploration of this territory.

Computation with Z^+-numbers is much simpler than computation with Z-numbers. Assume that * is a binary operation whose operands are Z^+-numbers, $Z_X^+ = (A_X, R_X)$ and $Z_Y^+ = (A_Y, R_Y)$. By definition,

$$Z_X^+ * Z_Y^+ = (A_X * A_Y, R_X * R_Y)$$

with the understanding that the meaning of * in $R_X * R_Y$ is not the same as the meaning of * in $A_X * A_Y$. In this expression, the operands of * in $A_X * A_Y$ are fuzzy numbers; the operands of * in $R_X * R_Y$ are probability distributions.

Example: Assume that * is sum. In this case, $A_X + A_Y$ is defined by:

$$\mu_{(A_X + A_Y)}(v) = \sup_u(\mu_{A_X}(u) \wedge \mu_{A_Y}(v - u)), \quad \wedge = \min. \tag{1.1}$$

Similarly, assuming that R_X and R_Y are independent, the probability density function of $R_X * R_Y$ is the convolution, $\circ$, of the probability density functions of R_X and R_Y. Denoting these probability density functions as p_{R_X} and p_{R_Y}, respectively, we have:

$$p_{R_X + R_Y}(v) = \int_R p_{R_X}(u) p_{R_Y}(v - u) du$$

Thus,

$$Z_X^+ + Z_Y^+ = (A_X + A_Y, p_{R_X} \circ p_{R_Y}).$$

It should be noted that the assumption that R_X and R_Y are independent implies worst case analysis.

More generally, to compute $Z_X * Z_Y$ what is needed is the extension principle of fuzzy logic [141,150]. Basically, the extension principle is a rule for evaluating a function when what are known are not the values of arguments but restrictions on the values of arguments. In other words, the rule involves evaluation of the value of a function under less than complete information about the values of arguments.

Originally, the term "extension principle" was employed to describe a rule which serves to extend the domain of definition of a function from numbers to fuzzy numbers. In this note, the term "extension principle" has a more general meaning which is stated in terms of restrictions. What should be noted is that, more generally, incompleteness of information about the values of arguments applies also to incompleteness of information about functions, in particular, about functions which are described as collections of if-then rules.

There are many versions of the extension principle. A basic version was given in [149]. In this version, the extension principle may be described as:

$$Y = f(X)$$

$$\frac{R(X) : is\ A\,(\text{constraint on } u \text{ is } \mu_A(u))}{R(Y): \quad \mu_Y(v) = \sup_u \mu_A(u) \quad (f(A) = R(Y))}$$

subject to

$$v = f(u)\,,$$

where A is a fuzzy set, μ_A is the membership function of A, μ_Y is the membership function of Y, and u and v are generic values of X and Y, respectively. A discrete version of this rule is:

$$Y = f(X)$$
$$\frac{R(X): X \ is \ (\mu_1 / u_1 + \cdots + \mu_n / u_n)}{R(Y): \quad \mu_Y(v) = \sup_{u_1,\ldots,u_n} \mu_i}$$

subject to

$$v = f(u_i)$$

A more general version was described in [155]. In this version, we have

$$Y = f(X)$$
$$\frac{R(X): g(X) \ is \ A \ (\text{constraint on } u \ is \ \mu_A(g(u)))}{R(Y): \quad \mu_Y(v) = \sup_u \mu_A(g(u))}$$

subject to

$$v = f(u).$$

For a function with two arguments, the extension principle reads:

$$Z = f(X,Y)$$
$$R(X): g(X) \ is \ A(\text{constraint on } u \ is \ \mu_A(g(u)))$$
$$\frac{R(Y): h(Y) \ is \ B(\text{constraint on } v \ is \ v_B(h(v)))}{R(Z): \quad \mu_Z(w) = \sup_{u,v}(\mu_X(g(u)) \wedge (\mu_Y(h(v)))), \wedge = \min}$$

subject to

$$w = f(u,v).$$

In application to probabilistic restrictions, the extension principle leads to results which coincide with standard results which relate to functions of probability distributions [21]. Specifically, for discrete probability distributions, we have:

$$Y = f(X)$$
$$\frac{R(X): X \ is \ p \ p, p = p_1 \backslash u_1 + \cdots + p_n \backslash u_n}{R(Y): \quad p_Y(v) = \sum_i p_i \quad (f(p) = R(Y))}$$

subject to

$$v = f(u_i).$$

For functions with two arguments, we have:

$$Z = f(X, Y)$$
$$R(X): X \ isp \ p, \ p = p_1 \backslash u_1 + \cdots + p_m \backslash u_m$$
$$\frac{R(Y): Y \ isp \ q, \ q = q_1 \backslash v_1 + \cdots + q_n \backslash v_n}{R(Z): \quad p_Z(w) = \sum_{i,j} p_i q_j \quad (f(p,q) = R(Z))}$$

subject to

$$w = f(u_i, v_j).$$

For the case where the restrictions are Z^+-numbers, the extension principle reads:

$$Z = f(X, Y)$$
$$R(X): X \ is \ (A_X, p_X)$$
$$\frac{R(Y): Y \ is \ (A_Y, p_Y)}{R(Z) = (f(A_X, A_Y) \ f(p_X, p_Y))}.$$

It is this version of the extension principle that is the basis for computation with Z-numbers. Question: Is $f(p_X, p_Y)$ compatible with $f(A_X, A_Y)$?

Turning to computation with Z-numbers, assume for simplicity $* =$ sum. Assume that $Z_X = (A_X, B_X)$ and $Z_Y = (A_Y, B_Y)$. Our problem is to compute the sum $Z = X + Y$. Assume that the associated Z-valuations are $(X, A_X, B_X), (Y, A_Y, B_Y)$, and (Z, A_Z, B_Z).

The first step involves computation of p_Z. To begin with, let us assume that p_X and p_Y are known, and let us proceed as we did in computing the sum of Z^+-numbers. Then

$$p_Z = p_X \circ p_Y$$

or more concretely,

$$p_Z(v) = \int_{\mathcal{R}} p_X(u) p_Y(v-u) du.$$

In the case of Z-numbers what we know are not p_X and p_Y but restrictions on p_X and p_Y

$$\int_{\mathcal{R}} \mu_{A_X}(u) p_X(u) du \text{ is } B_X,$$

$$\int_{\mathcal{R}} \mu_{A_Y}(u) p_Y(u) du \text{ is } B_Y.$$

In terms of the membership functions of B_X and B_Y, these restrictions may be expressed as:

$$\mu_{B_X}\left(\int_{\mathcal{R}} \mu_{A_X}(u) p_X(u) du\right),$$

$$\mu_{B_Y}\left(\int_{\mathcal{R}} \mu_{A_Y}(u) p_Y(u) du\right).$$

Additional restrictions on p_X and p_Y are:

$$\int_{\mathcal{R}} p_X(u) du = 1,$$

$$\int_{\mathcal{R}} p_Y(u) du = 1,$$

$$\int_{\mathcal{R}} u p_X(u) du = \frac{\int_{\mathcal{R}} u \mu_{A_X}(u) du}{\int_{\mathcal{R}} \mu_{A_X}(u) du} \text{ (compatibility)},$$

$$\int_{\mathcal{R}} u p_Y(u) du = \frac{\int_{\mathcal{R}} u \mu_{A_Y}(u) du}{\int_{\mathcal{R}} \mu_{A_Y}(u) du} \text{ (compatibility)}.$$

Applying the extension principle, the membership function of p_Z may be expressed as:

$$\mu_{p_Z}(p_Z) = \sup_{p_X, p_Y} \left(\mu_{B_X} \left(\int_{\mathcal{R}} \mu_{A_X}(u) p_X(u) du \right) \wedge \mu_{B_Y} \left(\int_{\mathcal{R}} \mu_{A_Y}(u) p_Y(u) du \right) \right) \quad (1.2)$$

subject to

$$p_{R_X + R_Y}(v) = \int_{\mathcal{R}} p_{R_X}(u) p_{R_Y}(v - u) du \quad (1.3)$$

$$\int_{\mathcal{R}} p_X(u) du = 1, \quad (1.4)$$

$$\int_{\mathcal{R}} p_Y(u) du = 1, \quad (1.5)$$

$$\int_{\mathcal{R}} u p_X(u) du = \frac{\int_{\mathcal{R}} u \mu_{A_X}(u) du}{\int_{\mathcal{R}} \mu_{A_X}(u) du}, \quad (1.6)$$

$$\int_{\mathcal{R}} u p_Y(u) du = \frac{\int_{\mathcal{R}} u \mu_{A_Y}(u) du}{\int_{\mathcal{R}} \mu_{A_Y}(u) du}. \quad (1.7)$$

In this case, the combined restriction on the arguments is expressed as a conjunction of their restrictions, with $\wedge$ interpreted as min. In effect, application of the extension principle reduces computation of p_Z to a problem in functional optimization. What is important to note is that the solution is not a value of p_Z but a restriction on the values of p_Z, consistent with the restrictions on p_X and p_Y.

At this point it is helpful to pause and summarize where we stand. Proceeding as if we are dealing with Z^+-numbers, we arrive at an expression for p_Z as a function of p_X and p_Y. Using this expression and applying the extension principle we can compute the restriction on p_Z which is induced by the restrictions on p_X and p_Y. The allowed values of p_Z consist of those values of p_Z which are consistent with the given information, with the understanding that consistency is a matter of degree.

The second step involves computation of the probability of the fuzzy event, Z is A_Z, given p_Z. As was noted earlier, in fuzzy logic the probability measure of the fuzzy event X is A, where A is a fuzzy set and X is a random variable with probability density p_X, is defined as:

$$\int_{\mathcal{R}} \mu_A(u) p_X(u) du$$

Using this expression, the probability measure of A_Z may be expressed as:

$$B_Z = \int_{\mathcal{R}} \mu_{A_Z}(u) p_Z(u) du, \tag{1.8}$$

where

$$\mu_{A_Z}(u) = \sup_{v} \left(\mu_{A_X}(v) \wedge \mu_{A_Y}(u - v) \right). \tag{1.9}$$

It should be noted that B_Z is a number when p_Z is a known probability density function. Since what we know about p_Z is its possibility distribution, $\mu_{P_Z}(p_Z)$, B_Z is a fuzzy set with membership function μ_{B_Z}. Applying the extension principle, we arrive at an expression for μ_{B_Z}. More specifically,

$$\mu_{B_Z}(w) = \sup_{p_Z} \mu_{P_Z}(p_Z)$$

subject to

$$w = \int_{\mathcal{R}} \mu_{A_Z}(u) p_Z(u) du$$

where $\mu_{P_Z}(p_Z)$ is the result of the first step. In principle, this completes computation of the sum of Z-numbers, Z_X and Z_Y.

In a similar way, we can compute various functions of Z-numbers. The basic idea which underlies these computations may be summarized as follows. Suppose that our problem is that of computing $f(Z_X, Z_Y)$, where Z_X and Z_Y are Z-numbers, $Z_X = (A_X, B_X)$ and $Z_Y = (A_Y, B_Y)$, respectively, and $f(Z_X, Z_Y) = (A_Z, B_Z)$. We begin by assuming that the underlying probability distributions p_X and p_Y are known. This assumption reduces the computation of $f(Z_X, Z_Y)$ to computation of $f(Z_X^+, Z_Y^+)$, which can be carried out through the use of the version of the extension principle which applies to restrictions which are Z^+-numbers. At this point, we recognize that what we know are not p_X and p_Y but restrictions on p_X and p_Y. Applying the version of the extension principle which relates to probabilistic restrictions, we are led to $f(Z_X, Z_Y)$. We can compute the restriction, B_Z, on the scalar product of $f(A_X, A_Y)$ and $f(p_X, p_Y)$. Since $A_Z = f(A_X, A_Y)$, computation of B_Z completes the computation of $f(Z_X, Z_Y)$.

It is helpful to express the summary as a version of the extension principle. More concretely, we can write:

$$Z = f(X, Y)$$

X is (A_X, B_X) (restriction on X)

Y is (A_Y, B_Y) (restriction on Y)

Z is (A_Z, B_Z) (induced restriction on Z)

$A_Z = f(A_X, A_Y)$ (application of extension principle for fuzzy numbers)

$$B_Z = \mu_{A_Z} \cdot f(p_X, p_Y)$$

where p_X and p_Y are constrained by:

$$\int_{\mathcal{R}} \mu_{A_X}(u) p_X(u) du \text{ is } B_X$$

$$\int_{\mathcal{R}} \mu_{A_Y}(u) p_Y(u) du \text{ is } B_Y.$$

In terms of the membership functions of B_X and B_Y, these restrictions may be expressed as:

$$\mu_{B_X}\left(\int_{\mathcal{R}}\mu_{A_X}(u)p_X(u)du\right),$$

$$\mu_{B_Y}\left(\int_{\mathcal{R}}\mu_{A_Y}(u)p_Y(u)du\right).$$

Additional restrictions on p_X and p_Y are:

$$\int_{\mathcal{R}}p_X(u)du=1,$$

$$\int_{\mathcal{R}}p_Y(u)du=1,$$

$$\int_{\mathcal{R}}up_X(u)du=\frac{\int_{\mathcal{R}}u\mu_{A_X}(u)du}{\int_{\mathcal{R}}\mu_{A_X}(u)du}\quad\text{(compatibility)},$$

$$\int_{\mathcal{R}}up_Y(u)du=\frac{\int_{\mathcal{R}}u\mu_{A_Y}(u)du}{\int_{\mathcal{R}}\mu_{A_Y}(u)du}\quad\text{(compatibility)}.$$

Consequently, in agreement with earlier results we can write:

$$\mu_{P_Z}(p_Z)=\sup_{p_X,p_Y}\left(\mu_{B_X}\left(\int_{\mathcal{R}}\mu_{A_X}(u)p_X(u)du\right)\wedge\mu_{B_Y}\left(\int_{\mathcal{R}}\mu_{A_Y}(u)p_Y(u)du\right)\right)$$

subject to

$$p_Z=p_X\circ p_Y,$$

$$\int_{\mathcal{R}}p_X(u)du=1,$$

$$\int_{\mathcal{R}}p_Y(u)du=1,$$

$$\int_{\mathcal{R}} u p_X(u)du = \dfrac{\displaystyle\int_{\mathcal{R}} u \mu_{A_X}(u)du}{\displaystyle\int_{\mathcal{R}} \mu_{A_X}(u)du},$$

$$\int_{\mathcal{R}} u p_Y(u)du = \dfrac{\displaystyle\int_{\mathcal{R}} u \mu_{A_Y}(u)du}{\displaystyle\int_{\mathcal{R}} \mu_{A_Y}(u)du}.$$

What is important to keep in mind is that A and B are, for the most part, perception-based and hence intrinsically imprecise. Imprecision of A and B may be exploited by making simplifying assumptions about A and B – assumptions that are aimed at reduction of complexity of computation with Z-numbers and increasing the informativeness of results of computation. Two examples of such assumptions are sketched in the following. Briefly, a realistic simplifying assumption is that p_X and p_Y are parametric distributions, in particular, Gaussian distributions with parameters m_X, σ_X^2 and m_Y, σ_Y^2, respectively. Compatibility conditions fix the values of m_X and m_Y. Consequently, if b_X and b_Y are numerical measures of certainty, then b_X and b_Y determine p_X and p_Y, respectively. Thus, the assumption that we know b_X and b_Y is equivalent to the assumption that we know p_X and p_Y. Employing the rules governing computation of functions of Z^+-numbers, we can compute B_Z as a function of b_X and b_Y. At this point, we recognize that B_X and B_Y are restrictions on b_X and b_Y, respectively. Employment of a general version of the extension principle leads to B_Z and completes the process of computation. This may well be a very effective way of computing with Z-numbers.

Another effective way of exploiting the imprecision of A and B involves approximation of the trapezoidal membership function of A by an interval-valued membership function, A_b, where A_b is the bandwidth of A (Fig. 1.14). Since A is a crisp set, we can write:

$$(A_X^b, B_X) * (A_Y^b, B_Y) = (A_X^b * A_Y^b, B_X \times B_Y)$$

where $B_X \times B_Y$ is the product of the fuzzy numbers B_X and B_Y. Validity of this expression depends on how well an interval-valued membership function approximates to a trapezoidal membership function.

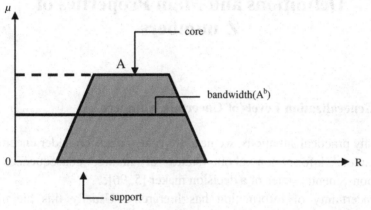

Fig. 1.14. Interval-valued approximation to a trapezoidal fuzzy set.

Chapter 2

Definitions and Main Properties of Z-numbers

2.1. Generalization Levels of Uncertain Numbers

In many practical situations, we need to make a decision under uncertain, incomplete information about states of nature, consequences of decisions, mental states of a decision maker [5, 96].

Uncertainty of information has hierarchy. Usually this hierarchy includes the following levels of restrictions that describe uncertain information: interval uncertainty; set-valued uncertainty; type-1 fuzzy uncertainty; type-2 fuzzy uncertainty and Z-number valued uncertainty (Fig. 2.1).

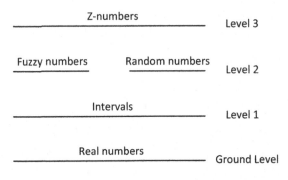

Fig. 2.1. Levels of uncertain numbers (restrictions).

A new theory of decision making under uncertainty – based on the extension of the notion of utility to interval, fuzzy, and Z-number uncertainty – is described in [3]. Let us characterize uncertain numbers that are used for description of information in different levels of hierarchy[96].

Interval uncertainty: description. Let us start with a simple case of uncertainty in decision making, in which, instead of knowing the exact gain x of selecting an alternative, we only know the lower bound $\underline{x}$ and the upper bound $\overline{x}$ on this gain – and we have no information on which values from the corresponding interval $[\underline{x}, \overline{x}]$ are more probable or less probable. This situation, in which the only information that we have about the gain x is that this gain belongs to the interval $[\underline{x}, \overline{x}]$, is called interval uncertainty and is described by interval number $[\underline{x}, \overline{x}]$.

Case of Set-valued Uncertainty

Description of the case. In some cases, in addition to knowing that the actual gain belongs to the interval $[\underline{x}, \overline{x}]$, we also know that some values from this interval cannot be possible values of this gain. For example, if we gamble on a situation with an unknown probability, we either get the price or lose the money but we cannot gain any value in between. In general, instead of a (bounded) interval of possible values, we can consider a more general bounded set of possible values. It makes sense to consider closed bounded sets, i.e., bounded sets X that contain all their limits points. Indeed, if $x_n \in X$ for all n and $x_n \to x$, then, for any given accuracy, x is undistinguishable from some possible value x_n – thus, in effect, the value itself is possible.

Case of Fuzzy Uncertainty

Fuzzy numbers: In the classical decision theories they usually considered situations when about each value of gain x, the expert is either absolutely sure that this value is possible or absolutely sure that this value is not possible. Then, they took into account that the expert may not be absolutely sure about that. It is assumed that the expert either knows the exact probability p describing his/her degree of certainty, or that the expert is absolutely sure which probabilities can describe his/her uncertainty and which cannot.

In reality, an expert is often uncertain about the possible values, and uncertain about possible degrees of uncertainty.

To take this uncertainty into account, L. Zadeh introduced the notion of a *fuzzy set* [84,108,149] where, to each possible value of x, we assign a degree $\mu(x) \in [0,1]$ to which this value x is possible. Similarly, a fuzzy set $\mu_p : [0,1] \rightarrow [0,1]$ can describe the degrees to which different probability values are possible.

Fuzzy Type 2 sets possess more expressive power to create models adequately describing uncertainty. The three- dimensional membership functions of Type-2 fuzzy sets provide additional degrees of freedom that make it possible to directly and more effectively model uncertainties.

In this book, we restrict ourselves to *type-1 fuzzy numbers A*, i.e., fuzzy sets for which the membership function is different from 0 only on a bounded set, where it first monotonically increases until it reaches a point x at which $\mu_A(x) = 1$, and then monotonically decreases from 1 to 0.

Cases of Crisp Interval and Set-valued Numbers with Certainty Degree

Description of the case. Previously, when considering the interval and set-valued uncertainty, we assumed that we are 100% certain that the actual gain is contained in the given interval (or set). In reality, mistakes are possible, and usually, we are only sure that u belongs to the corresponding interval or set with some probability $0 < p < 1$. In such situations, to fully describe our knowledge, we need to describe both the interval (or set) *and* this probability p.

We will call a pair consisting of a (crisp) number and a (crisp) probability a *crisp number with certainty*; We will call a pair consisting of an interval and a probability a *interval number with certainty*.

We will call a pair consisting of a set and a probability a *set valued number with ceratinty*.

When we have two independent sequential decisions, and we are 100% sure that the first decision leads to gain x_1 and the second decision leads to gain x_2, then the user's total gain is equal to the sum $x_1 + x_2$. When we consider the situation in which: for the first decision, our degree of confidence in the gain estimate x_1 is described by some probability p and for the second decision, our degree of confidence in the gain estimate x_2 is described by some probability q the estimate $x_1 + x_2$ is valid only if both gain estimates are correct. Since these estimates are independent, the probability that they are both correct is equal to the product $p \cdot q$ of the corresponding probabilities. Thus: for numbers $(x_1,\ p)$ and $(x_2,\ q)$, the sum is equal to $(x_1 + x_2, p \cdot q)$, for intervals $([\underline{x_1}, \overline{x_1}], p)$ and $([\underline{x_2}, \overline{x_2}], q)$, the sum is equal to $([\underline{x_1} + \underline{x_2}, \overline{x_1} + \overline{x_2}], p \cdot q)$, and for sets (S,p) and (S',q), the sum is equal to $(S + S', p \cdot q)$.

We arrive at the following definitions.

Definition 2.1. A crisp number with confidence. By a crisp number with known confidence, we mean a pair *(u,p)* of two real numbers such that $0 < p < 1$.

The same can be formulated for intervals and sets.

Definition 2.2. An interval with confidence. By a interval, we mean a pair $([\underline{x}, \overline{x}], p)$ consisting of an interval $[\underline{x}, \overline{x}]$ and a real number p such that $0 < p \leq 1$.

Definition 2.3. A set-valued number with certainty. By a set-valued number with certainty, we mean a pair *(S, p)* consisting of a closed bounded set S and a real numbers p such that $0 < p \leq 1$.

Now we consider a crisp number, an interval number, and a set-valued number, when probabilities are known with interval or set-valued uncertainty. When we know the exact probabilities p and q that the corresponding estimates are correct, then the probability that both estimates are correct is equal to the product $p \cdot q$.

Similarly to the fact that we often do not know the exact gain, we often do not know the exact probability p. Instead, we may only know the interval $[\underline{p}, \overline{p}]$ of possible values of p, or, more generally, a set P of possible values of p. If we know p and q with such uncertainty, what can we then conclude about the product $p \cdot q$?

For positive values p and q, the function $p \cdot q$ is increasing as a function of both variables: if we increase p and/or increase q, the product increases. Thus, if the only information that we have about the probability p is that this probability belongs to the interval $[\underline{p}, \overline{p}]$, and the only information that we have about the probability q is that this probability belongs to the interval $[\underline{q}, \overline{q}]$, then the smallest possible of $p \cdot q$ is equal to the product $\underline{p} \cdot \underline{q}$ of the smallest values, the largest possible of $p \cdot q$ is equal to the product $\overline{p} \cdot \overline{q}$ of the largest values; and the set of all possible values $p \cdot q$ is the interval $[\underline{p} \cdot \underline{q}, \overline{p} \cdot \overline{q}]$.

For sets P and Q, the set of possible values $p \cdot q$ is the set

$$P \cdot Q \stackrel{def}{=} \{p \cdot q : p \in P \ \text{ and } \ q \in Q\}.$$

Definition 2.4. A crisp number under interval valued p-uncertainty. By a crisp number under interval valued p-uncertainty, we mean a pair $(x, [\underline{p}, \overline{p}])$ consisting of a real number x and an interval $[\underline{p}, \overline{p}] \subseteq (0,1]$.

Definition 2.5. A crisp number under set-valued p-uncertainty. By a crisp number under set-valued p-uncertainty, we mean a pair (x, P) consisting of a real number x and a bounded closed set $P \subseteq (0,1]$ for which in f $P > 0$.

Definition 2.6. A set-valued number under set-valued p-uncertainty. By a set-valued number under set-valued p-uncertainty, we mean a pair (S,P) consisting of a bounded closed set S and a bounded closed set $P \subseteq (0,1]$ for which $\inf P > 0$.

The Case of Z-number uncertainty. In the general context, after supplementing the information about a quantity with the information of how certain we are about this piece of information, we get what L. Zadeh calls a *Z-number* [168]. In this case, we have two fuzzy numbers: the fuzzy number A which describes the values and the fuzzy number B which describes our degree of confidence in the piece of information described by A. In this book we will mainly consider operations at high level of uncertainty hierarchy, a level of a Z-number.

2.2. Interval Arithmetic

Intervals are special cases of fuzzy numbers. Interval analysis is frequently used in decision theories, in decision making with imprecise probabilites. We will consider operations over intervals of real line[4,52,106]. It is easy to see that a result of operations over closed intervals is also a closed interval. Due to this fact, the bounds of the resulting closed interval are to be expressed by means of the bounds of the given intervals.

Below we introduce the basic operations over closed intervals. Assume that the following intervals of the real line $\mathcal{R}$ are given:

$$A=[a_1,a_2], B=[b_1,b_2].$$

Addition. If

$$x \in [a_1,a_2] \text{ and } y \in [b_1,b_2] \tag{2.1}$$

then

$$x+y \in [a_1+b_1, a_2+b_2]. \tag{2.2}$$

This can symbollically be expressed as

$$A+B=[a_1, a_2]+[b_1, b_2]=[a_1+b_1, a_2+b_2]. \tag{2.3}$$

The image of A. If $x \in [a_1, a_2]$ then $-x \in [-a_2,-a_1]$. This is symbolically expressed as

$$-A = [-a_2,-a_1]$$

Let us consider the result of $A + (-A)$. According to the operations given above, we can write:

$$A + (-A) = [a_1, a_2] + [-a_2, -a_1] = [a_1 - a_2, \ a_2 - a_1].$$

Note that $A + (-A) \neq 0$.

Subtraction. If $x \in [a_1, a_2]$ and $y \in [b_1, b_2]$, then

$$x - y \in [a_1 - b_2, a_2 - b_1] \tag{2.4}$$

$$A - B = [a_1, a_2] - [b_1, b_2] = [a_1 - b_2, a_2 - b_1]. \tag{2.5}$$

Multiplication. The production of intervals $A, B \subset \mathcal{R}$ is defined as follows:

$$A \cdot B = [\min(a_1 \cdot b_1, a_1 \cdot b_2, a_2 \cdot b_1, a_2 \cdot b_2), \ \max(a_1 \cdot b_1, a_1 \cdot b_1, a_2 \cdot b_1, a_2 \cdot b_2)]. \tag{2.6}$$

For the case $A, B \subset \mathcal{R}_+$ the result is obtained easily as

$$A \cdot B = [a_1, a_2] \cdot [b_1, b_2] = [a_1 \cdot b_1, a_2 \cdot b_2]. \tag{2.7}$$

The multiplication of an interval A by a real number $k \in \mathcal{R}$ is defined as follows:

if $k > 0$ then $k \cdot A = k \cdot [a_1, a_2] = [ka_1, ka_2]$,

if $k < 0$ then $k \cdot A = k \cdot [a_1, a_2] = [ka_2, ka_1]$.

Division. Under assumption that the dividing interval does not contain 0 and $A, B \subset \mathcal{R}_+$ one has

$$A : B = [a_1, a_2] : [b_1, b_2] = [a_1 / b_2, \ a_2 / b_1]. \tag{2.8}$$

Based on (2.8), the inverse of A can be defined as follows:

If $x \in [a_1, \ a_2]$ then

$$\frac{1}{x} \in \left[\frac{1}{a_2}, \frac{1}{a_1}\right]$$

and

$$A^{-1} = [a_1, a_2]^{-1} = [1/a_2, 1/a_1].\qquad(2.9)$$

In a general case the ratio of A and B can be done as follows

$$[a_1, a_2]:[b_1, b_2]$$
$$=[a_1, a_2]\cdot[1/b_2, 1/b_1]$$
$$= [\min\{a_1/b_1, a_1/b_2, a_2/b_1, a_2/b_2\}, \max\{a_1/b_1, a_1/b_2, a_2/b_1, a_2/b_2\}]$$

$$(2.10)$$

Note that,

$$A\cdot A^{-1} = [a_1/a_2, a_2/a_1] \neq 1.$$

The division by a number $k > 0$ is equivalent to multiplication by a number $1/k$.

2.3. Operations on Random Variables

The problem of operations on random variables arises in a wide range of applications where calculation of functions of random variables are required. In some cases analytical solutions exist, but in other cases numerical methods are used. In this section we will consider both analytical and numerical methods for arithmetic operations on random variables.

Usually determination of distributions of functions of random variables was based on search for analytical solutions. For some restricted classes of problems a formula for the required distributions can be tabulated, but in general it is not practicable to give such results. Exact analytical techniques for determining distributions arising in statistics is described in [101]. An alternative approach is to use numerical methods for calculating the required distributions.

General solution to the distribution of functions of random variables in terms of the Jacobian of transformation is given in [139]. In this chapter we will consider calculation for a function of only one and two random variables. It is very easy to extend the results to functions of n random variables.

Definition 2.7. Random variables and probability distributions[126]. A random variable, X, is a variable whose possible values x are numerical outcomes of a random phenomenon. Random variables are of two types: continuous and discrete.

A continuous random variable X is a variable which can take an infinite number of possible values x. A discrete random variable is a variable which can take only a countable number of distinct values.

To determine a probability that a continuous random variable X takes any value in a closed interval $[a,b]$, denoted $P(a \le X \le b)$, a concept of probability distribution is used. A probability distribution or a probability density function is a function $p(x)$ such that for any two numbers a and b with $a \le b$:

$$P(a \le X \le b) = \int_a^b p(x)dx,$$

where $p(x) \ge 0$, $\int_{-\infty}^{\infty} p(x)dx = 1$.

Consider a discrete random variable X with outcomes space $\{x_1,...,x_n\}$. A probability of an outcome $X = x_i$, denoted $P(X = x_i)$ is defined in terms of a probability distribution. A function p is called a discrete probability distribution or a probability mass function if

$$P(X = x_i) = p(x_i),$$

where $p(x_i) \in [0,1]$ and $\sum_{i=1}^{n} p(x_i) = 1$.

Adding Constant to Random Variable[126]

Let X be a random variable and $Y = X + c, \quad c \in R$. Then the probability density function (pdf) of Y, p_Y, will be

$$p_Y(y) = p_X(y - c).$$

It is obvious that the density function is simply shifted c units to the right $(c > 0)$ or left $(c < 0)$.

Scalar Product of Random Variable[126]

X is a random variable and $Y = aX, \quad a \in R$. Density function $p_Y(y)$ is determined as

$$p_Y(y) = \frac{1}{a} p_X(y/a) \quad if \ a > 0$$

$$p_Y(y) = -\frac{1}{a} p_X(y/a) \quad if \ a < 0.$$

Linear Transformation of Random Variable [126]

Let Y be a continuous random variable, which is linear function of a continuous random variable X. For

$$Y = aX + b \tag{2.11}$$

a density function $p_Y(y)$ is determined as

$$p_Y(y) = \frac{1}{a} p_X\left(\frac{y - b}{a}\right). \tag{2.12}$$

If X is a normal random variable with

$$p_X(x) = \frac{1}{\sqrt{2\pi}} e^{-(x - \mu)^2 / 2}, \tag{2.13}$$

then

$$p_Y(y) = \frac{1}{a\sqrt{2\pi}} e^{-(\frac{y-b}{a} - \mu)^2 / 2}. \tag{2.14}$$

A linear function of a normal random variable is

$$X \sim \mathcal{N}(\mu, \sigma^2) \;\Rightarrow\; Y \sim \mathcal{N}(a\mu + b, a^2\sigma^2).$$

Square of a Random Variable[126]

X is a random variable and $Y = X^2$. The density function is determined as

$$p_Y(y) = \frac{1}{2\sqrt{y}} \left[p_X(\sqrt{y}) + p_X(-\sqrt{y}) \right], \; y \geq 0. \tag{2.15}$$

Example. Square of a Gaussian random variable is a Chi-square random variable

$$X \sim \mathcal{N}(0,1) \;\Rightarrow\; Y \sim X_2^2, \;\; p_Y(y) = \frac{e^{-y/2}}{\sqrt{2\pi y}}, \; y \geq 0.$$

Square Root of a random variable[126]

Assume that X is a continuous random variable with density function p_X. It is required to find the pdf p_Y for

$$Y = \sqrt{X}. \tag{2.16}$$

If $y \geq 0$ then

$$p_Y(y) = 2y p_X(y^2). \tag{2.17}$$

Example. Square root of a random variable with exponential distribution. Suppose that X is random variable with density function

$$p_X(x) = \lambda e^{-\lambda x} (x \geq 0)$$

and consider the distribution of $Y = \sqrt{X}$. The transformation

$$y = g(x) = \sqrt{x}, \quad x \geq 0$$

gives

$$p_Y(y) = p_X(y^2)2y = 2\lambda ye^{-\lambda y^2}, \quad y \geq 0.$$

Consider two independent random variables X and Y with probability distributions p_X and p_2 respectively [48,138]. Let $Z = X * Y$, $* \in \{+,-,\cdot,/\}$. Suppose we would like to determine a probability distribution p_{12} of X_{12}.

If the considered function f of the two random variables X and Y is one of the four arithmetic operations, we have the four convolution equations [112,126,139]

$$Z = X + Y: \quad p_Z(z) = \int_{-\infty}^{\infty} p_{XY}(z - x, x)dx, \tag{2.18}$$

$$Z = X - Y: \quad p_Z(z) = \int_{-\infty}^{\infty} p_{XY}(z + x, x)dx, \tag{2.19}$$

$$Z = X \times Y: \quad p_Z(z) = \int_{-\infty}^{\infty} \frac{1}{|x|} p_{XY}(z/x, x)dx, \tag{2.20}$$

$$Z = X / Y: \quad p_Z(z) = \int_{-\infty}^{\infty} |x| p_{XY}(zx, x)dx. \tag{2.21}$$

In case X and Y are independent we can obtain

$$Z = X + Y: \quad p_Z(z) = \int_{-\infty}^{\infty} p_X(z - x, x)p_Y(x)dx, \tag{2.22}$$

$$Z = X - Y: \quad p_Z(z) = \int_{-\infty}^{\infty} p_X(z + x, x)p_Y(x)dx, \tag{2.23}$$

$$Z = X \times Y: \quad p_Z(z) = \int_{-\infty}^{\infty} \frac{1}{|x|} p_X(z/x, x)p_Y(x)dx, \tag{2.24}$$

$$Z = X / Y: \quad p_Z(z) = \int_{-\infty}^{\infty} |x| p_X(zx, x)p_Y(x)dx. \tag{2.25}$$

Equations (2.22)–(2.25) are basic for calculation probability distributions of sum, subtraction, product and quotient of two independent random variables.

For calculation of distributions of sums and subtractions of two normal random variables exact formulae do exist. If $Z = f(X_1, X_2) = X_1 \pm X_2$ [139]

$$\mu_Z = \mu_{X_1} \pm \mu_{X_2},\qquad(2.26)$$

$$\sigma_Z^2 = \sigma_{X_1}^2 + \sigma_{X_2}^2.\qquad(2.27)$$

If $X_i, \ i = \overline{1, n}$ are normal independent random variables such that $X_i \sim N(\mu_i, \sigma_i^2)$, then $Y = \sum_{i=1}^{n} X_i$ is normally distributed with [69]

$$\mu = \sum_{i=1}^{n} \mu_i \text{ and } \sigma^2 = \sum_{i=1}^{n} \sigma_i^2.$$

$$Y \sim N(\mu, \sigma^2).$$

If $a_i, \ i = \overline{1, n}$ are real constants, then $Y = \sum_{i=1}^{n} a_i X_i$ is normal distributed with

$$\mu = \sum_{i=1}^{n} a_i \mu_i \text{ and } \sigma^2 = \sum_{i=1}^{n} a_i^2 \sigma_i^2.$$

$$Y \sim N(\mu, \sigma^2).$$

Unfortunately, exact formulae for moments of products and quotients do not exist. In this case approximations are useful for application in applied probability theory. For an arbitrary function of n independent random variables $Z = f(X_1, ..., X_n)$ approximate formulae is [68]

$$\mu_Z \approx f(\mu_{X_1}, ..., \mu_{X_n}) + \frac{1}{2} \sum_{i=1}^{n} \frac{\partial^2 f}{\partial X_i^2} \sigma_{X_i}^2 \qquad(2.28)$$

$$\sigma_Z^2 \approx \sum_{i=1}^{n} \left(\frac{\partial f}{\partial X_i}\right)^2 \sigma_{X_i}^2 + \left(\frac{\partial f}{\partial X_i}\right)\left(\frac{\partial^2 f}{\partial X_i^2}\right)^2 \mu_{X_i}^3. \tag{2.29}$$

Let's consider product and quotient of two independent normal random variables X_1 and X_2.

If $Z = h(X_1, X_2) = X_1 X_2$,

$$\mu_Z \approx \mu_{X_1}\mu_{X_2}, \tag{2.30}$$

$$\sigma_Z^2 \approx \mu_{X_1}^2 \sigma_{X_2}^2 + \mu_{X_2}^2 \sigma_{X_1}^2 + \sigma_{X_1}^2 \sigma_{X_2}^2. \tag{2.31}$$

If $Z = f(X_1, X_2) = X_1 / X_2$,

$$\mu_Z \approx \frac{\mu_{X_1}}{\mu_{X_2}} + \frac{\mu_{X_1}\sigma_{X_2}^2}{4\mu_{X_2}^3}, \tag{2.32}$$

$$\sigma_Z^2 \approx \frac{\sigma_{X_1}^2}{\mu_{X_2}^2} + \frac{\mu_{X_1}^2 \sigma_{X_2}^2}{\mu_{X_2}^4} - \frac{\mu_{X_1}^2 \mu_{X_2}^3}{2\mu_{X_2}^5}. \tag{2.33}$$

A different approach to calculation of distribution of product of random variables is given in [65]. Random variables X and Y have supports on the intervals (a,b) and (c,d) respectively. In [65] they prove that the pdf of $Z = XY$ is

$$h(z) = \begin{cases} \int_a^{z/c} g\left(\frac{z}{x}\right) p(x)\frac{1}{x}dx, & ac < z < ad, \\ \int_{z/d}^{z/c} g\left(\frac{z}{x}\right) p(x)\frac{1}{x}dx, & ad < z < bc, \\ \int_{z/d}^{b} g\left(\frac{z}{x}\right) p(x)\frac{1}{x}dx, & bc < z < bd, \end{cases}$$

when $ad < bc$,

$$h(z) = \begin{cases} \int_a^{z/c} g\left(\dfrac{z}{x}\right) p(x) \dfrac{1}{x} dx, \ ac < z < ad, \\ \int_{z/d}^b g\left(\dfrac{z}{x}\right) p(x) \dfrac{1}{x} dx, \ ad < z < bd, \end{cases}$$

when $ad = bc$,

$$h(z) = \begin{cases} \int_a^{z/c} g\left(\dfrac{z}{x}\right) p(x) \dfrac{1}{x} dx, \ ac < z < ad, \\ \int_a^b g\left(\dfrac{z}{x}\right) p(x) \dfrac{1}{x} dx, \ bc < z < ad, \\ \int_{z/d}^b g\left(\dfrac{z}{x}\right) p(x) \dfrac{1}{x} dx, \ ad < z < bd, \end{cases}$$

when $ad > bc$.

It is possible to apply this approach to different members of distributions family as uniform, Triangular, Gaussian and others.

Example [65]. For the random variable $X \sim U(1,2)$ and the random variable $Y \sim U(3,4)$. A distribution of $Z = XY$ is obtained as

$$h(z) = \begin{cases} \ln z - \ln 3, & 3 < z < 4, \\ \ln 4 - \ln 3, & 4 < z < 6, \\ 3\ln 2 - \ln z, & 6 < z < 8. \end{cases}$$

Example [65]. For the random variables $X \sim$ Triangular $(1,2,3)$ and $Y \sim$ Triangular $(-2,1,2)$ the pdf of $Z = XY$ is obtained as

$$
h(z) = \begin{cases}
-4z/3 + (2/3)\ln z + (2z/3)\ln z + 4/3, & 1 < z < 2, \\
\begin{aligned}&-8 + (14/3)\ln 2 + (7z/3)\ln 2 + 10z/3 - 4\ln z \\ &-(5z/3)\ln z,\end{aligned} & 2 < z < 3, \\
\begin{aligned}&-4 + (14/3)\ln 2 + (7z/3)\ln 2 + 2z - 2\ln z \\ &-z\ln - 2\ln 3 - (2z/3)\ln 3,\end{aligned} & 3 < z < 4, \\
\begin{aligned}&44/3 - 14\ln 2 - (7z/3)\ln 2 - 8z/3 - 2\ln 3 \\ &+(22/3)\ln z - (2z/3)\ln 3 + (4z/3)\ln z,\end{aligned} & 4 < z < 6, \\
\begin{aligned}&8/3 - 8\ln 2 - (4z/3)\ln 2 - 2z/3 + (4/3)\ln z \\ &+(z/3)\ln z + 4\ln 3 + (z/3)\ln 3,\end{aligned} & 6 < z < 8, \\
\begin{aligned}&-8 + 8\ln 2 + (2z/3)\ln 2 + 2z/3 + 4\ln 3 \\ &-4\ln z + (z/3)\ln 3 - (z/3)\ln z,\end{aligned} & 8 < z < 12.
\end{cases}
$$

For the random variables $X \sim N(0,1)$ and the random variable $Y \sim N(0,1)$, pdf of $Z = XY$ is [65]

$$
h(z) = \begin{cases}
\dfrac{\mathrm{BesselK}(0,\, z \cdot \mathrm{signum}(z))}{\pi}, & -\infty < z < 0, \\[2mm]
\dfrac{\mathrm{BesselK}(0,\, z \cdot \mathrm{signum}(z))}{\pi}, & 0 < z < \infty,
\end{cases}
$$

which relies on Maple's BesselK and signum functions.

In [75] it is considered different numerical solution methods of the problem of calculation of distributions of product and subtractions of tow random variables. It is considered families which contain practically all distributions used in practice and which are closed under the four arithmetic operations [75]. The families include distributions with infinite supports and a finite number of singularities [75]. Wide class of distributions is embraced by software PaCAL [75].

Convolution $p_{12} = p_1 \circ p_2$ of probability distributions p_1 and p_2 is defined as follows:

$$p_{12}(z) = \frac{b(z) \cdot c(z)}{a^3(z)} \frac{1}{\sqrt{2\pi}\sigma_x\sigma_y} \left[2\Phi\left(\frac{b(z)}{a(z)}\right) - 1 \right]$$

$$+ \frac{1}{a^2(z) \cdot \pi\sigma_x\sigma_y} e^{-\frac{1}{2}\left(\frac{\mu_x^2}{\sigma_x^2} + \frac{\mu_y^2}{\sigma_y^2}\right)}$$

(2.34)

where

$$a(z) = \sqrt{\frac{1}{\sigma_x^2} z^2 + \frac{1}{\sigma_y^2}}$$

$$b(z) = \frac{\mu_x}{\sigma_x^2} z + \frac{\mu_y}{\sigma_y^2}$$

$$c(z) = \exp\left(\frac{1}{2}\frac{b^2(z)}{a^2(z)} - \frac{1}{2}\left(\frac{\mu_x^2}{\sigma_x^2} + \frac{\mu_y^2}{\sigma_y^2}\right)\right)$$

(2.35)

$$\Phi(z) = \int_{-\infty}^{z} \frac{1}{\sqrt{2\pi}} e^{-\frac{1}{2}u^2 du}.$$

For the case $\mu_X = \mu_Y = 0$ and $\sigma_X = \sigma_Y = 1$, (2.34) is reduced to

$$p_{12}(z) = \frac{1}{\pi}\frac{1}{1+z^2}.$$

Let X_1 and X_2 be two independent discrete random variables with the corresponding outcome spaces $X_1 = \{x_{11},...,x_{1i},...,x_{1n_1}\}$ and $X_2 = \{x_{21},...,x_{2i},...,x_{2n_2}\}$, and the corresponding discrete probability distributions p_1 and p_2. The probability distribution of $X_1 * X_2$, where $*$ is some binary operation, is the convolution $p_{12} = p_1 \circ p_2$ of p_1 and p_2 which is determined as follows:

$$p_{12}(x) = \sum_{x = x_{1i} * x_{2j}} p_1(x_{1i}) p_2(x_{2j}),$$

for any $x \in \{ x_1 * x_2 | x_1 \in X_1, x_2 \in X_2 \}$.

Below we provide formulas for convolution $p_{12} = p_1 \circ p_2$ as a probability distribution of $X = X_1 * X_2$ for several typical binary operations.

Addition $X = X_1 + X_2$:

$$p_{12}(x) = \sum_{x = x_{1i} + x_{2j}} p_1(x_{1i}) p_2(x_{2j}). \tag{2.36}$$

Subtraction $X = X_1 - X_2$:

$$p_{12}(x) = \sum_{x = x_{1i} - x_{2j}} p_1(x_{1i}) p_2(x_{2j}). \tag{2.37}$$

Multiplication $X = X_1 X_2$:

$$p_{12}(x) = \sum_{x = x_{1i} \cdot x_{2j}} p_1(x_{1i}) p_2(x_{2j}). \tag{2.38}$$

Division $X = X_1 / X_2$:

$$p_{12}(x) = \sum_{x = x_{1i} / x_{2j}} p_1(x_{1i}) p_2(x_{2j}). \tag{2.39}$$

Minimum $X = \min(X_1, X_2)$:

$$p_{12}(x) = \sum_{x = \min(x_{1i}, x_{2j})} p_1(x_{1i}) p_2(x_{2j}). \tag{2.40}$$

Maximum $X = \max(X_1, X_2)$:

$$p_{12}(x) = \sum_{x = \max(x_{1i}, x_{2j})} p_1(x_{1i}) p_2(x_{2j}). \tag{2.41}$$

Functions of a discrete random variable[126]

Assume that X is a discrete random variable with probability distribution p_X. Let f be a function $f : \mathcal{R} \to \mathcal{R}$. The probability distribution p_Y for the discrete random variable $Y = f(X)$ is defined as follows:

$$p_Y(y) = \sum_{x \in f^{-1}(y)} p_X(x).$$

Linear transformation of a discrete random variable. For a discrete random variable X with probability distribution p_X, the probability distribution p_Y of its linear transformation

$$Y = aX + b,$$

where $a, b \in \mathcal{R}$, is defined as follows:

$$p_Y(y) = p_X\left(\frac{y-b}{a}\right). \tag{2.42}$$

Square of a discrete random variable. For a discrete random variable X with probability distribution p_X, the probability distribution p_Y of its square

$$Y = X^2,$$

is defined as follows:

$$p_Y(y) = \sum_{x \in \{\sqrt{y}, -\sqrt{y}\}} p_X(x) = p_X(-\sqrt{y}) + p_X(\sqrt{y}). \tag{2.43}$$

Square root of a discrete random variable. For a discrete random variable X with probability distribution p_X, the probability distributions p_{Y_1} and p_{Y_2} of its square roots

$$Y_1 = \sqrt{X} \text{ and } Y_2 = -\sqrt{X}$$

are defined as follows:

$$p_{Y_1}(y_1) = p_X(y_1^2) \text{ and } p_{Y_2}(y_2) = p_X(y_2^2). \tag{2.44}$$

Absolute value of a discrete random variable. For a discrete random variable X with probability distribution p_X, the probability distribution p_Y of its absolute value

$$Y = |X|,$$

is defined as follows:

$$p_Y(y) = \sum_{x \in \{|y|, |-y|\}} p_X(x) = p_X(|-y|) + p_X(|y|). \tag{2.45}$$

Exponential of a discrete random variable. For a discrete random variable X with probability distribution p_X, the probability distribution p_Y of its exponential

$$Y = e^X,$$

is defined as follows:

$$p_Y(y) = p_X(\ln(y)). \tag{2.46}$$

Natural logarithm of a discrete random variable. For a discrete random variable X with probability distribution p_X, the probability distribution p_Y of its natural logarithm

$$Y = \ln(X),$$

is defined as follows:

$$p_Y(y) = p_X(e^y). \tag{2.47}$$

2.4. Fuzzy Arithmetic

In this paragraph we consider arithmetic operations on fuzzy numbers. Fuzzy sets, introduced by Zadeh in 1965, provide us a new mathematical tool to deal with uncertainty of information. A fuzzy number is a special case of a fuzzy set used to account for uncertainty and imprecision of values of variables of interest. We will consider operations on two main types of fuzzy numbers: continuous and discrete fuzzy numbers. Before explanation of fuzzy arithmetic we give some preliminary information on fuzzy sets.

2.4.1. *Main Definitions*

Definition 2.8. Type-1 fuzzy sets. Let X be a classical set of objects, called the universe, whose generic elements are denoted x. Membership in a classical subset A of X is often viewed as a characteristic function μ_A from X to $\{0,1\}$ such that

$$\mu_A(x) = \begin{cases} 1 & \textit{iff } x \in A \\ 0 & \textit{iff } x \notin A \end{cases}$$

where $\{0,1\}$ is called a valuation set; 1 indicates membership while 0 - non-membership. If the valuation set is allowed to be in the real interval $[0,1]$, then A is called a Type-1 fuzzy set A [4,14,84,149,181]. $\mu_A(x)$ is the grade of membership of x in A

$$\mu_A : X \to [0,1].$$

As closer the value of $\mu_A(x)$ is to 1, so much x belongs to A. $\mu : X \to [0,1]$ is referred to as a membership function (MF).

A is completely characterized by the set of pairs:

$$A = \{(x, \mu_A(x)),\ x \in X\}.$$

Example: The representation of temperature within a range $[T_1, T_2]$ by Type-1 fuzzy and crisp sets is shown in Fig. 2.2a, and 2.2b, respectively.

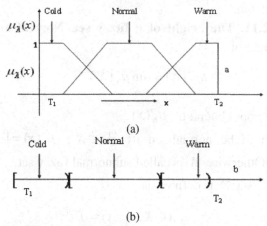

(a)

(b)

Fig. 2.2. Representation of temperature by (a) Type-1 fuzzy and (b) crisp sets.

In the first case we use membership function $\mu:[T_1, T_2] \to [0,1]$ for describing linguistic concepts *"cold"*, *"normal"*, *"warm"*. In the second case right-open intervals are used for describing of traditional variable by crisp sets.

Fuzzy sets with crisply defined membership functions are called ordinary fuzzy sets or Type-1 fuzzy sets.

Properties of Type-1 fuzzy sets [4]

Definition 2.9. Equality of fuzzy sets. Two fuzzy sets A and B are said to be equal denoted $A = B$ if and only if

$$\forall x \in X, \quad \mu_A(x) = \mu_B(x)$$

Definition 2.10. The support and the crossover point of a fuzzy set. The singleton. The support of a fuzzy set A is the ordinary subset of X that has nonzero membership in A :

$$\text{supp(A)} = A^{+0} = \{ x \in X, \mu_A(x) > 0 \}.$$

The elements of x such as $\mu_A(x) = 1/2$ are the crossover points of A.

A fuzzy set that has only one point in X with $\mu_A = 1$ as its support is called a singleton.

Definition 2.11. The height of a fuzzy set. Normal and subnormal sets. The height of A is

$$hgt(A) = \sup_{x \in X} \mu_A(X)$$

i.e., the least upper bound of $\mu_A(x)$.

A is said to be normalized iff $\exists x \in X$, $\mu_A(x) = 1$. This implies $hgt(A) = 1$. Otherwise A is called subnormal fuzzy set.

The empty set $\varnothing$ is defined as

$$x \in X, \mu_\varnothing(x) = 0.$$

The universe of discourse X is defined as

$$\forall x \in X, \mu_X(x) = 1.$$

One of important way of representation of fuzzy sets is α-cut method. Such type of representation allows us to use properties of crisp sets and operations on crisp sets in fuzzy set theory.

Definition 2.12. α-level fuzzy sets. The (crisp) set of elements that belongs to the fuzzy set A at least to the degree α is called the α-level set:

$$A^\alpha = \{x \in X, \mu_A(x) \ge \alpha\}. \tag{2.48}$$

$A^\alpha = \{x \in X, \mu_{\bar{A}}(x) > \alpha\}$ is called "strong α-level set" or "strong α-cut".

Now we introduce fuzzy set A_α, defined as

$$A_\alpha(x) = \alpha A^\alpha(x). \tag{2.49}$$

The fuzzy set A may be defined in terms of its α-cut as $A = \bigcup\limits_{\alpha \in [0,1]} A_\alpha$,

where $\bigcup$ denotes union of classical sets.

Definition 2.13. Convexity of fuzzy sets. A fuzzy set A is convex iff

$$\mu_A(\lambda x_1 + (1-\lambda)x_2) > \min(\mu_A(x_1), \mu_A(x_2)) \qquad (2.50)$$

for all $x_1, x_2 \in R$, $\lambda \in [0,1]$, min denotes the minimum operator.

Alternatively, a fuzzy set A on $\mathcal{R}$ is convex iff all its α-level sets are convex in the classical sense.

Definition 2.14. The cardinality of a fuzzy set. When X is a finite set, the scalar cardinality $|A|$ of a fuzzy set A on X is defined as

$$|A| = \sum_{x \in A} \mu_A(x).$$

Sometimes $|A|$ is called the power of A. $\|A\| = |A|/|X|$ is the relative cardinality. When X is infinite, $|A|$ is defined as

$$|A| = \int_X \mu_A(x)\,dx.$$

Definition 2.15. Fuzzy set inclusion. Given fuzzy sets A, B, A is said to be included in B $(A \subseteq B)$ or A is a subset of B if $\forall x \in X$,

$$\mu_A(x) \leq \mu_B(x).$$

When the inequality is strict, the inclusion is said to be strict and is denoted as $A \subset B$.

Representations and constructing of Type-1 fuzzy sets

It was mentioned above that each fuzzy set is uniquely defined by a membership function. In the literature one can find different ways in which membership functions are represented.

List representation. If universal set is a finite set $X = \{x_1, x_2, \ldots, x_n\}$, membership function of a fuzzy set A on X, $\mu_A(x)$, can be represented as a table. Such a table lists all elements in the universe X and the corresponding membership grades as shown below

$$A = \mu_A(x_1)/x_1 + \ldots + \mu_A(x_n)/x_n = \sum_{i=1}^{n} \mu_A(x_i)/x_i.$$

Here symbol /(slash) does not denote division, it is used for correspondence between an element in the universe X (after slash) and its membership grade in the fuzzy set A (before slash). The symbol + connects the elements (does not denote summation).

If X is a finite set then

$$A = \int_X \mu_A(x)/x.$$

Here symbol $\int_X$ is used for denoting a union of elements of set X.

Graphical representation. Graphical description of a fuzzy set A on the universe X is suitable in case when X is one or two-dimensional Euclidean space. Simple typical shapes of membership functions are usually used in the fuzzy set theory and practice (Table 2.1).

Fuzzy n cube representation. All fuzzy sets on universe X with n elements can be represented by points in the n-dimensional unit cube – n-cube.

Assume that universe X contains n elements $X = \{x_1, x_2, \ldots, x_n\}$. Each element $x_i, i = \overline{1, n}$ can be viewed as a coordinate in the n dimensional Euclidean space. A subset of this space for which values of each coordinate are restricted in $[0,1]$ is called n-cube. Vertices of the cube, i.e. bit list $(0, 1, \ldots, 0)$ represent crisp sets. The points inside the cube define fuzzy subsets.

Table 2.1. Typical membership functions of A.

Type of Membership function	Craphical Representation	Analytical Representation
triangular MF		$\mu_{\tilde{A}}(x) = \begin{cases} \dfrac{x-a}{a_2-a_1}r, & if\ a_1 \leq x \leq a_2, \\ \dfrac{a_3-x}{a_3-a_2}r, & if\ a_2 \leq x \leq a_3, \\ 0, & otherwise \end{cases}$
trapezoidal MF		$\mu_{\tilde{A}}(x) = \begin{cases} \dfrac{x-a}{a_2-a_1}r, & if\ a_1 \leq x \leq a_2, \\ r, & if\ a_2 \leq x \leq a_3 \\ \dfrac{a_4-x}{a_4-a_3}r, & if\ a_3 \leq x \leq a_4, \\ 0, & otherwise \end{cases}$
S – shaped MF		$\mu_{\tilde{A}}(x) = \begin{cases} 0, & if\ x \leq a_1 \\ 2\left(\dfrac{x-a_1}{a_3-a_2}\right)^2, & if\ a_1 < x < a_2, \\ 1-2\left(\dfrac{x-a_1}{a_3-a_1}\right), & if\ a_2 \leq x \leq a_3, \\ 1, & if\ a_3 \leq x \end{cases}$
Gaussian MF		$\mu_{\tilde{A}}(x) = c\exp\left(-\dfrac{(x-a)^2}{b}\right)$

Analytical representation. In case if universe X is infinite, it is not effective to use the above considered methods for representation of membership functions of a fuzzy sets. In this case it is suitable to represent fuzzy sets in an analytical form, which describes the shape of membership functions.

There are some typical formulas describing frequently used membership functions in fuzzy set theory and practice.

For example, bell-shaped membership functions often are used for representation of fuzzy sets. These functions are described by the formula:

$$\mu_A(x) = c \exp\left(-\frac{(x-a)^2}{b}\right)$$

which is defined by three parameters, a, b and c.

Definition 2.16. Type-2 fuzzy set [3-5,102]. Type-2 fuzzy set (T2 FS) in the universe of discourse X can be represented as follows:

$$A = \{((x,u), \mu_A(x,u)) | \forall x \in X, \forall u \in J_x \subseteq [0,1]\} \tag{2.51}$$

where $0 \le \mu_{\tilde{A}}(x,u) \le 1$. The Type-2 fuzzy set A also can be represented as follows:

$$A = \int_{x \in X} \int_{u \in J_x} \mu_A(x,u) / (x,u)$$
$$= \int_{x \in X} \left[\int_{u \in J_x} \mu_A(x,u) / u \right] / x \tag{2.52}$$

where x is the primary variable, $J_x \subseteq [0,1]$ is the primary membership of x, u is the secondary variable. $f(x) = \int_{u \in J_x} \mu_A(x,u) / u$ is the secondary membership function at x. $\iint$ denotes the union over all admissible x and u.

If X is a discrete set with elements $x_1, ..., x_n$ then Type-2 fuzzy set A can be as follows:

$$A = \sum_{x \in X} \left[\sum_{u \in J_x} f_x(u) / u \right] / x = \sum_{i=1}^{n} \sum_{u \in J_x} [f_x(u) / u] / x_i \tag{2.53}$$

2.4.2. Operations on Continuous Fuzzy Numbers

Definition 2.17. Type-1 Continuous fuzzy number. A fuzzy number is a fuzzy set A on $\mathcal{R}$ which possesses the following properties: a) A is a normal fuzzy set; b) A is a convex fuzzy set; c) α-cut of A, A^α is a closed interval for every $\alpha \in (0,1]$; d) the support of A, supp(A) is bounded.

There is an equivalent parametric definition of fuzzy number [24,66]. A fuzzy number A is a pair $(\underline{\mu_A}, \overline{\mu_A})$ of functions $\underline{\mu}_A(\alpha), \overline{\mu}_A(\alpha)$; $0 \le \alpha \le 1$ with following requirements:

1) $\underline{\mu}_A(\alpha)$ is a bounded monotonic increasing left continuous function; 2) $\overline{\mu}_A(\alpha)$ is a bounded monotonic decreasing left continuous function; 3) $\underline{\mu}_A(\alpha) \le \overline{\mu}_A(\alpha), 0 \le \alpha \le 1$.

There are different methods for developing fuzzy arithmetic [149]. In this section we present two methods.

Method based on the extension principle [4,149]. By this method basic arithmetic operations on real numbers are extended to operations on fuzzy numbers. Let A and B be two fuzzy numbers and $*$ denote any of four arithmetic operations $\{+, -, \cdot, : \}$.

A fuzzy set $A * B$ on $\mathcal{R}$ can be defined by the equation

$$\forall z \in \mathcal{R}, \quad \mu_{(A*B)}(z) = \sup_{z = x*y} \min\{\mu_A(x), \mu_B(y)\}. \tag{2.54}$$

It is shown in [84] that $A * B$ is a fuzzy number and the following theorem has been formulated and proved. Let us mention that a fuzzy number with continuous membership function is referred to as a continuous fuzzy number.

Theorem 2.1. Let $* \in \{+, -, \cdot, : \}$, and let A, B denote continuous fuzzy numbers. Then, the fuzzy set $A * B$ defined by (2.54) is a continuous fuzzy number.

Then for four basic arithmetic operations on fuzzy numbers we can write

$$\mu_{(A+B)}(z) = \sup_{z=x+y} \min[\mu_A(x), \mu_B(y)] \tag{2.55}$$

$$\mu_{(A-B)}(z) = \sup_{z=x-y} \min[\mu_A(x), \mu_B(y)] \tag{2.56}$$

$$\mu_{(A \cdot B)}(z) = \sup_{z=x \cdot y} \min[\mu_A(x), \mu_B(y)] \tag{2.57}$$

$$\mu_{(A:B)}(z) = \sup_{z=x:y} \min[\mu_A(x), \mu_B(y)]. \tag{2.58}$$

Method based on interval arithmetic and α-cuts. This method is based on representation of arbitrary fuzzy numbers by their α-cuts and use interval arithmetic to the α-cuts. Let $A, B \subset \mathcal{R}$ be fuzzy numbers and $*$ denote any of four operations. For each $\alpha \in (0,1]$, the α-cut of $A*B$ is expressed as

$$(A*B)^\alpha = A^\alpha * B^\alpha. \tag{2.59}$$

For $* = /$ we assume $0 \notin \text{supp}(B)$.

The resulting fuzzy number $A*B$ can be defined as (see section 2.4.1)

$$A*B = \bigcup_{\alpha \in [0,1]} \alpha (A*B)^\alpha. \tag{2.60}$$

Next using (2.59), (2.60) we illustrate four arithmetic operations on fuzzy numbers.

Addition. Let A and B be two fuzzy numbers and A^α and B^α be their α cuts

$$A^\alpha = \left[a_1^\alpha, a_2^\alpha \right]; B^\alpha = \left[b_1^\alpha, b_2^\alpha \right]. \tag{2.61}$$

Then we can write

$$A^\alpha + B^\alpha = [a_1^\alpha, a_2^\alpha] + [b_1^\alpha, b_2^\alpha] = [a_1^\alpha + b_1^\alpha, a_2^\alpha + b_2^\alpha] \qquad (2.62)$$

here

$$A^\alpha = \{x / \mu_A(x) \geq \alpha\}; B^\alpha = \{x / \mu_B(x) \geq \alpha\}. \qquad (2.63)$$

Subtraction. Subtraction of given fuzzy numbers A and B can be defined as

$$(A - B)^\alpha = A^\alpha - B^\alpha = [a_1^\alpha - b_2^\alpha, a_2^\alpha - b_1^\alpha], \forall \alpha \in [0,1]. \qquad (2.64)$$

We can determine (2.64) by addition of the image B^- to A, where α-cut of the former is

$$\forall \alpha \in [0,1], B^{\alpha^-} = [-b_2^\alpha, -b_1^\alpha]. \qquad (2.65)$$

Multiplication. Let two fuzzy numbers A and B be given. Multiplication $A \cdot B$ is defined as

$$(A \cdot B)^\alpha = A^\alpha \cdot B^\alpha = [a_1^\alpha, a_2^\alpha] \cdot [b_1^\alpha, b_2^\alpha] \forall \alpha \in [0,1]. \qquad (2.66)$$

Multiplication of fuzzy number A in $\mathcal{R}$ by ordinary numbers $k \in \mathcal{R}_+$ is performed as follows

$$\forall A \subset \mathcal{R} \quad kA^\alpha = [ka_1^\alpha, ka_2^\alpha], \forall \alpha \in [0,1].$$

Division. Division of two fuzzy numbers A and B is defined by

$$A^\alpha : B^\alpha = [a_1^\alpha, a_2^\alpha] : [b_1^\alpha, b_2^\alpha] \quad \forall \alpha \in [0,1]. \qquad (2.67)$$

Definition 2.17. Absolute value of a fuzzy number[1]. Absolute value of fuzzy number is defined as:

$$[abs(A)]^\alpha = \begin{cases} A^\alpha & if \ \mathrm{supp}(A) \subset [0, \infty) \\ -A^\alpha & if \ \mathrm{supp}(A) \subset (-\infty, 0] \\ [0, \max(-A_1^\alpha, A_2^\alpha)] & if \ 0 \in (A_1^\alpha, A_2^\alpha) \end{cases} \qquad (2.68)$$

In terms of a membership function[4]:

$$\mu_{abs(A)} = \begin{cases} \max(\mu_A(x), \mu_{-A}(x)), & \text{for } \mathcal{R}_+ \\ 0, & \text{for } \mathcal{R}_- \end{cases}$$

Square of a Continuous Fuzzy Number

The square of fuzzy number A denoted by μ_{A^2}, is a continuous fuzzy number defined by

$$\mu_{A^2}(y) = \max(\mu_A(\sqrt{y}), \mu_A(-\sqrt{y})). \tag{2.69}$$

Example[24]. If A is the continuous fuzzy number defined by:

$$\mu_A(x) = \begin{cases} \dfrac{x+1}{3}, & -1 \le x \le 2 \\ 3-x, & 2 \le x \le 3 \\ 0, & \textit{otherwise} \end{cases}$$

then A^2 is defined as

$$\mu_{A^2}(x) = \begin{cases} \dfrac{5 - \sqrt{16-3x}}{3}, & -3 \le x \le 0 \\ \dfrac{1+\sqrt{x}}{3}, & 0 \le x \le 4. \\ 3 - \sqrt{x}, & 4 \le x \le 9 \\ 0, & \textit{otherwise} \end{cases}$$

Denote $\mathcal{R}_{\mathcal{F}}$ the set of fuzzy numbers defined on $\mathcal{R}$, and $\mathcal{R}_{U\mathcal{F}}$ the set of fuzzy numbers defined on $U = [0, \infty)$.

Square Root of a Continuous Fuzzy Number

The square root of a fuzzy number X is a function $F : \mathcal{R}_{\mathcal{F}} \to \mathcal{R}_{U\mathcal{F}}$ denoted by $F(X) = \sqrt{X}$ with α-cut $[\sqrt{X}]^{\alpha} = \{\sqrt{x} \mid x \in X^{\alpha}\}$. Since $f(x) = \sqrt{x}$ is a continuous function on $U = [0, \infty)$, we get $F(X) = \sqrt{X}$ is a continuous function on $\mathcal{R}_{U\mathcal{F}}$. Because f is increasing on U, we have

$$[\sqrt{X}]^{\alpha} = \left[\sqrt{X_1^{\alpha}}, \sqrt{X_2^{\alpha}} \right].$$

Example. Let $A \in \mathcal{R}_{\mathcal{F}}$ with $A^{\alpha} = [\alpha, 2 - \alpha]$ for each $\alpha \in [0,1]$. Then

$$\left(\sqrt{A^{\alpha}} \right)^{\alpha} = [\sqrt{\alpha}, \sqrt{2 - \alpha}]. \qquad (2.70)$$

Let $A \in \mathcal{R}_{\mathcal{F}}$, then we have $\sqrt[n]{A^n} = |A|$ if n is an even positive integer, $\sqrt[n]{A^n} = A$ if is n an odd positive integer [1].

If A is a continuous fuzzy number and there exists a fuzzy number X such that $X^2 = A$ then A is said to have a square root and X is called a square root of A, i.e. $\sqrt{A}$.

Example[24]. Consider a fuzzy number A defined by

$$\mu_A(x) = \begin{cases} \dfrac{x+2}{2}, & -2 \leq x \leq 0 \\[2mm] \dfrac{3-x}{3}, & 0 \leq x \leq 3 \\[2mm] 0, & \textit{otherwise} \end{cases}$$

Then

$$\sqrt{A}^1(x) = \begin{cases} 1 - \dfrac{1}{3}x^2, & -\sqrt{3} \le x \le 0 \\[2mm] 1 - \dfrac{3}{4}x^2, & 0 < x \le \dfrac{2}{\sqrt{3}} \\[2mm] 0, & otherwise \end{cases} \qquad \sqrt{A}^2(x) = \begin{cases} 1 - \dfrac{3}{4}x^2, & -\dfrac{2}{\sqrt{3}} \le x < 0 \\[2mm] 1 - \dfrac{1}{3}x^2, & 0 \le x \le \sqrt{3} \\[2mm] 0, & otherwise \end{cases}$$

The Exponential of a Fuzzy Number

The exponential of a fuzzy number $X \in \mathcal{R}_{\mathcal{F}}$ is a function $F : \mathcal{R}_{\mathcal{F}} \to \mathcal{R}_{U\mathcal{F}}$ denoted by $F(X) = e^X$ with α-cut $(e^X)^\alpha = \left\{ e^x \,\middle|\, x \in X^\alpha \right\}$.

Since $f(x) = e^x$ is a continuous function on $\mathcal{R}$, we get $F(X) = e^X$ is a continuous function on $\mathcal{R}_{\mathcal{F}}$. Because f is increasing on R, we get $(e^X)^\alpha = [e^{X_1^\alpha}, e^{X_2^\alpha}]$.

The Logarithm of a Fuzzy Number

The natural logarithm of a fuzzy number $X \in \mathcal{R}_{\mathcal{F}}$ is a function F: $\mathcal{R}_{U\mathcal{F}} \to \mathcal{R}_{\mathcal{F}}$ denoted by $F(X) = \ln X$ with α-cut $(\ln X)^\alpha = \left\{ \ln x \,\middle|\, x \in X^\alpha \right\}$.

Since $f(x) = \ln x$ is a continuous function on $[\varepsilon, \infty)$, $\varepsilon > 0$, we get $F(X) = \ln X$ is a continuous function on $\mathcal{R}_{U\mathcal{F}}$. Because f is increasing on $[\varepsilon, \infty)$, $\varepsilon > 0$, we have $(\ln X)^\alpha = \left[\ln X_1^\alpha, \ln X_2^\alpha \right]$.

For positive fuzzy numbers $A, B \in \mathcal{R}_{U\mathcal{F}}$, we have
$\ln 1 = 0$; $\ln AB = \ln A + \ln B$; $\ln A / B = \ln A - \ln B$; $\ln A^\alpha = \alpha \ln A$ [1].

Let $A \in \mathcal{R}_{\mathcal{F}}$ and $B \in \mathcal{R}_{U\mathcal{F}}$, then we have $\ln(\exp A) = A$; $\exp(\ln B) = B$.

2.4.3. *Arithmetic Operations on Discrete Fuzzy Numbers*

Definition 2.19. A discrete fuzzy number [5,9,44,45,56]. A fuzzy subset A of the real line $\mathcal{R}$ with membership function $\mu_A : \mathcal{R} \rightarrow [0,1]$ is a discrete fuzzy number if its support is finite, i.e. there exist $x_1, ..., x_n \in \mathcal{R}$ with $x_1 < x_2 < ... < x_n$, such that $\text{supp}(A) = \{x_1, ..., x_n\}$ and there exist natural numbers s, t with $1 \leq s \leq t \leq n$ satisfying the following conditions:

1. $\mu_A(x_i) = 1$ for any natural number i with $s \leq i \leq t$
2. $\mu_A(x_i) \leq \mu_A(x_j)$ for each natural numbers i, j with $1 \leq i \leq j \leq s$
3. $\mu_A(x_i) \geq \mu_A(x_j)$ for each natural numbers i, j with $t \leq i \leq j \leq n$.

In general, the extension of arithmetical or lattice operations, $\mathcal{O}$, to fuzzy numbers A, B [104] can be approached either by the direct use of their membership function $\mu_A(x)$, $\mu_B(x)$ as fuzzy subsets of $\mathcal{R}$ with Zadeh's extension principle:

$$\mu_{\mathcal{O}(A,B)}(z) = \sup\{\mu_A(x) \wedge \mu_B(y) \mid O(x,y) = z\}$$

or by the equivalent use of the α-cuts representation [104,125]:

$$\mathcal{O}(A,B)^\alpha = O(A^\alpha, B^\alpha) = \{O(x,y) \mid x \in A^\alpha, y \in B^\alpha\}$$

and

$$\mu_{\mathcal{O}(A,B)}(z) = \sup\{\alpha \in [0,1] \mid z \in \mathcal{O}(A,B)^\alpha\}.$$

Nevertheless, in the discrete case, this process can yield a fuzzy subset that does not satisfy the conditions to be a discrete fuzzy number [44,137].

In order to overcome this drawback, several authors [44,45,137] have proposed other methods to get a closed addition in the set DFN:

Definition 2.20. Addition of discrete fuzzy numbers [44,45,136,137]. For discrete fuzzy numbers A_1, A_2 their addition $A_{12} = A_1 + A_2$ is the discrete fuzzy number whose α-cut is defined as

$$A_{12}^{\alpha} = \{x \in \{\text{supp}(A_1) + \text{supp}(A_2)\} \mid \min\{A_1^{\alpha} + A_2^{\alpha}\} \le x \le \max\{A_1^{\alpha} + A_2^{\alpha}\}\},$$

where

$$\text{supp}(A_1) + \text{supp}(A_2) = \{x_1 + x_2 \mid x_j \in \text{supp}(A_j), j = 1, 2\}, \min\{A_1^{\alpha} + A_2^{\alpha}\}$$
$$= \min\{x_1 + x_2 \mid x_j \in A_j^{\alpha}), j = 1, 2\},$$

$\max\{A_1^{\alpha} + A_2^{\alpha}\} = \max\{x_1 + x_2 \mid x_j \in A_j^{\alpha}, j = 1, 2\}$ and   the   membership
function is defined as

$$\mu_{A_1 + A_2}(x) = \sup\{\alpha \in [0,1] \mid x \in \{A_1^{\alpha} + A_2^{\alpha}\}\}. \tag{2.71}$$

Below we provide several definitions of the suggested arithmetic of discrete fuzzy numbers (Definitions 2.21-2.30). In these definitions, as well as in Definition 2.20, non-interactive fuzzy numbers are considered.
Definition 2.21. Standard subtraction of discrete fuzzy numbers [5,9]. For discrete fuzzy numbers A_1, A_2 their standard subtraction $A_{12} = A_1 - A_2$ is the discrete fuzzy number whose α-cut is defined as

$$A_j^{\alpha} = \{x \in \{\text{supp}(A_1) - \text{supp}(A_2)\} \mid \min\{A_1^{\alpha} - A_2^{\alpha}\} \le x \le \max\{A_1^{\alpha} - A_2^{\alpha}\}\},$$

where

$$\text{supp}(A_1) - \text{supp}(A_2) = \{x_1 - x_2 \mid x_j \in \text{supp}(A_j), j = 1, 2\},$$

$$\min\{A_1^{\alpha} - A_2^{\alpha}\} = \min\{x_1 - x_2 \mid x_j \in A_j^{\alpha}, j = 1, 2\},$$

$$\max\{A_1^{\alpha} - A_2^{\alpha}\} = \max\{x_1 - x_2 \mid x_j \in A_j^{\alpha}, j = 1, 2\}$$

and the membership function is defined as

$$\mu_{A_1 - A_2}(x) = \sup\{\alpha \in [0,1] \mid x \in \{A_1^{\alpha} - A_2^{\alpha}\}\}. \tag{2.72}$$

For the standard subtraction one has:

$$A_2 + (A_1 - A_2) \ne A_1.$$

Definition 2.22. Hukuhara difference of discrete fuzzy numbers [5,9].
For discrete fuzzy numbers A_1, A_2 their Hukuhara difference denoted
$A_1 -_h A_2$ is the discrete fuzzy number A_{12} such that

$$A_1 = A_2 + A_{12}. \tag{2.73}$$

Hukuhara difference exists only if $n \geq m$. The conditions on the
existence of Hukuhara difference $A_1 -_h A_2$ are given in Chapter 4.

Definition 2.23. Multiplication of discrete fuzzy numbers [5,9]. For
discrete fuzzy numbers A_1, A_2 their multiplication $A_{12} = A_1 \cdot A_2$ is the
discrete fuzzy number whose α-cut is defined as

$$A_j^\alpha = \{ x \in \{ \mathrm{supp}(A_1) \cdot \mathrm{supp}(A_2) \} \mid \min\{ A_1^\alpha \cdot A_2^\alpha \} \leq x \leq \max\{ A_1^\alpha \cdot A_2^\alpha \} \},$$

where

$$\mathrm{supp}(A_1) \cdot \mathrm{supp}(A_2) = \{ x_1 \cdot x_2 \mid x_j \in \mathrm{supp}(A_j), j = 1, 2 \},$$
$$\min\{ A_1^\alpha \cdot A_2^\alpha \} = \min\{ x_1 \cdot x_2 \mid x_j \in A_j^\alpha, j = 1, 2 \},$$
$$\max\{ A_1^\alpha \cdot A_2^\alpha \} = \max\{ x_1 \cdot x_2 \mid x_j \in A_j^\alpha, j = 1, 2 \}$$

and the membership function is defined as

$$\mu_{A_1 \cdot A_2}(x) = \sup\{ \alpha \in [0,1] \mid x \in \{ A_1^\alpha \cdot A_2^\alpha \} \}. \tag{2.74}$$

Definition 2.24. Standard division of discrete fuzzy numbers [5,9].
For discrete fuzzy numbers A_1, A_2 given that $0 \notin \mathrm{supp}(A_2)$ their
standard division $A_{12} = {A_1}/{A_2}$ is the discrete fuzzy number whose α-cut is
defined as

$$A_{12}^\alpha = \{ x \in \{ \mathrm{supp}(A_1)/\mathrm{supp}(A_2) \} \mid \min\{ A_1^\alpha / A_2^\alpha \} \leq x \leq \max\{ A_1^\alpha / A_2^\alpha \} \},$$
where

$$\mathrm{supp}(A_1)/\mathrm{supp}(A_2) = \{ x_1/x_2 \mid x_j \in \mathrm{supp}(A_j), j = 1, 2 \},$$

$$\min\{ A_1^\alpha / A_2^\alpha \} = \min\{ x_1/x_2 \mid x_j \in A_j^\alpha, j = 1, 2 \},$$

$$\max\{ A_1^\alpha / A_2^\alpha \} = \max\{ x_1/x_2 \mid x_j \in \mathrm{supp}(A_j), j = 1, 2 \}$$

and the membership function is defined as

$$\mu_{A_1/A_2}(x) = \sup\{\alpha \in [0,1] \mid x \in \{A_1^\alpha/A_2^\alpha\}\}. \tag{2.75}$$

For the standard division one has:

$$A_2 \cdot (A_1/A_2) \neq A_1.$$

Definition 2.25. A square of a discrete fuzzy number [5,9]. For a discrete fuzzy number A its square A^2 is the discrete fuzzy number whose α-cut is defined as

$$\left[A^2\right]^\alpha = \{y \in \text{supp}(A^2) \mid \min((A^\alpha)^2) \leq y \leq \max((A^\alpha)^2)\}$$

where

$$\text{supp}(A^2) = \{y \mid y = x^2, x \in \text{supp}(A)\},$$

$$\min(A^\alpha)^2 = \min\{y \mid y = x^2, x \in A^\alpha\},$$

$$\max(A^\alpha)^2 = \max\{y \mid y = x^2, x \in A^\alpha\}.$$

Thus, $\left[A^2\right]^\alpha = \left(A^\alpha\right)^2$. The membership function of A^2 is defined as

$$\mu_{A^2}(y) = \sup\{\alpha \in [0,1] \mid y \in \left[A^2\right]^\alpha\}. \tag{2.76}$$

Definition 2.26. A square root of a discrete fuzzy number [5,9]. For a discrete fuzzy number A, where $\text{supp}(A) \subset [0,\infty)$, its square root $\sqrt{A}$ is the discrete fuzzy number whose α-cut is defined as

$$\left[\sqrt{A}\right]^\alpha = \{y \in \text{supp}(\sqrt{A}) \mid \min\sqrt{A^\alpha} \leq y \leq \max\sqrt{A^\alpha}\}$$

where

$$\text{supp}(\sqrt{A}) = \{y \mid y = \sqrt{x}, x \in \text{supp}(A)\},$$

$$\min \sqrt{A^\alpha} = \min\{y \mid y = \sqrt{x}, x \in A^\alpha\},$$

$$\max \sqrt{A^\alpha} = \max\{y \mid y = \sqrt{x}, x \in A^\alpha\}.$$

Thus, $\left[\sqrt{A}\right]^\alpha = \sqrt{A^\alpha}$. The membership function of $\sqrt{A}$ is defined as

$$\mu_{\sqrt{A}}(y) = \sup\{\alpha \in [0,1] \mid y \in \left[\sqrt{A}\right]^\alpha\}. \tag{2.77}$$

Definition 2.27. Minimum and maximum of discrete fuzzy numbers [46]. For discrete fuzzy numbers (DFNs) A_1, A_2, $A_1 = \{x_1^\alpha, ..., x_p^\alpha\}$ $A_2 = \{y_1^\alpha, ..., y_k^\alpha\}$, their minimum $A_{12} = MIN(A_1, A_2)$ is the DFN whose α-cut is defined as

$$A_{12}^\alpha = \{x \in \{\text{supp}(A_1) \wedge \text{supp}(A_2)\} \mid \min\{x_1^\alpha, y_1^\alpha\} \leq z \leq \min\{x_p^\alpha, y_k^\alpha\}\}$$

where

$$\text{supp}(A_1) \wedge \text{supp}(A_2) = \{z = \min(x, y) \mid x \in \text{supp}(A_1), y \in \text{supp}(A_2)\}.$$

Then

$$MIN(A_1, A_2)(z) = \sup\{\alpha \in [0,1] \mid z \in A_{12}^\alpha\}. \tag{2.78}$$

For DFNs A_1, A_2, $A_1 = \{x_1^\alpha, ..., x_p^\alpha\}$, $A_2 = \{y_1^\alpha, ..., y_k^\alpha\}$ their maximum $A_{12} = MAX(A_1, A_2)$ is the DFN whose α-cut is defined as

$$A_{12}^\alpha = \{x \in \{\text{supp}(A_1) \vee \text{supp}(A_2)\} \mid \max\{x_1^\alpha, y_1^\alpha\} \leq z \leq \max\{x_p^\alpha, y_k^\alpha\}\},$$

where

$$\text{supp}(A_1) \vee \text{supp}(A_2) = \{z = \max(x, y) \mid x \in \text{supp}(A_1), y \in \text{supp}(A_2)\}.$$

Then

$$MAX(A_1, A_2)(z) = \sup\{\alpha \in [0,1] \mid z \in A_{12}^{\alpha}\}. \tag{2.79}$$

Denote $\mathcal{D}$ the set of DFNs defined on $\mathcal{R}$. As it shown in [46], the triple $(\mathcal{D}, MIN, MAX)$ is a distributive lattice.

Definition 2.28. An absolute value of a discrete fuzzy number. For a discrete fuzzy number A its absolute value $abs(A)$ is the discrete fuzzy number whose α-cut is defined as

$$[abs(A)]^{\alpha} = \{y \in \text{supp}(abs(A)) \mid \min(abs(A^{\alpha})) \le y \le \max(abs(A^{\alpha}))\}$$

where

$$\text{supp}(abs(A^{\alpha})) = \{y \mid y = abs(x), x \in \text{supp}(A)\},$$

$$\min abs(A^{\alpha}) = \min\{y \mid y = abs(x), x \in A^{\alpha}\},$$

$$\max abs(A^{\alpha}) = \max\{y \mid y = abs(x), x \in A^{\alpha}\}.$$

Thus, $[abs(A)]^{\alpha} = abs(A^{\alpha})$. The membership function of $abs(A)$ is defined as

$$\mu_{abs(A)}(y) = \sup\{\alpha \in [0,1] \mid y \in [abs(A)]^{\alpha}\}. \tag{2.80}$$

Definition 2.29. A discrete fuzzy exponential function. The discrete fuzzy exponential function is a function $f : \mathcal{D} \to \mathcal{D}$ denoted $f(A_X) = e^{A_X}$ whose α-cut is defined as

$$\left[e^{A_X}\right]^{\alpha} = \{y \in \text{supp}(e^{A_X}) \mid \min(e^{A_X^{\alpha}}) \le y \le \max(e^{A_X^{\alpha}})\}$$

where

$$\text{supp}(e^{A_X}) = \{y \mid y = e^{x}, x \in \text{supp}(e^{A_X})\},$$

$$\min(e^{A_X^{\alpha}}) = \min\{y \mid y = e^{x}, x \in A_X^{\alpha}\},$$

$$\max(e^{A_X{}^\alpha}) = \max\{y \mid y = e^x, x \in A_X{}^\alpha\}.$$

Thus, $\left[e^{A_X}\right]^\alpha = e^{A_X{}^\alpha}$. The membership function of e^{A_X} is defined as

$$\mu_{e^{A_X}}(y) = \sup\{\alpha \in [0,1] \mid y \in \left[e^{A_X}\right]^\alpha\}. \tag{2.81}$$

Definition 2.30. A discrete fuzzy natural logarithm. A discrete fuzzy exponential function is a function $f : D \to D$ denoted $f(A_X) = \ln(A_X)$ whose α-cut is defined as

$$\left[\ln(A_X)\right]^\alpha = \{y \in \mathrm{supp}(\ln(A_X)) \mid \min(\ln(A_X{}^\alpha)) \le y \le \max(\ln(A_X{}^\alpha))\}$$

where

$$\mathrm{supp}(\ln(A_X)) = \{y \mid y = \ln(x), x \in \mathrm{supp}(\ln(A_X))\},$$

$$\min(\ln(A_X{}^\alpha)) = \min\{y \mid y = e^x, x \in \ln(A_X{}^\alpha)\},$$

$$\max(\ln(A_X{}^\alpha)) = \max\{y \mid y = \ln(x), x \in \ln(A_X{}^\alpha)\}.$$

Thus, $\left[\ln(A_X)\right]^\alpha = \ln(A_X{}^\alpha)$. The membership function of $\ln(A_X)$ is defined as

$$\mu_{\ln(A_X)}(y) = \sup\{\alpha \in [0,1] \mid y \in \left[\ln(A_X)\right]^\alpha\}. \tag{2.82}$$

2.5. Continuous Z-numbers, Properties

Definition 2.31. A Continuous Z-number. A continuous Z-number is an ordered pair $Z = (A, B)$ where A is a continuous fuzzy number playing a role of a fuzzy constraint on values that a random variable X may take:

$$X \text{ is } A$$

and B is a continuous fuzzy number with a membership function $\mu_B : [0,1] \rightarrow [0,1]$, , playing a role of a fuzzy constraint on the probability measure of A :

$$P(A) \text{ is } B.$$

A concept of a continuous Z^+-number is closely related to the concept of a continuous Z-number. Given a continuous Z-number $Z = (A,B)$, Z^+-number Z^+ is a pair consisting of a continuous fuzzy number, A , and a random number R :

$$Z^+ = (A,R),$$

where A plays the same role as it does in a continuous Z-number $Z = (A,B)$ and R plays the role of the probability distribution p , such that $P(A) = \int_{\mathcal{R}} \mu_A(u) p_R(u)$, $P(A) \in \text{supp}(B)$.

In this section we discuss the algebraic properties of Z-numbers, under the four arithmetic operations, namely, $+, -, \cdot$ and $/$ which are defined by the extension principle [168]. The properties of continuous fuzzy numbers are given in [104]. These properties can be used for the first part of a Z-number (A part). Random variables have the properties: the sum of two random variables is a random variable, the product of two random variables is a random variable, addition and multiplication of random variables are both commutative; conjugation of random variables, satisfying $(XY)^* = X^* Y^*$ and $X^{**} = X$ for all random variables X, Y and coinciding with complex conjugation if X is a constant[126]. Consequently, random variables form complex commutative *-algebras. Therefore, we have got the following properties of Z-numbers under the union and the intersection combined with the four arithmetic operations. These properties are given below.

Let $Z_Y = (A_Y, B_Y)$ and $Z_X = (A_X, B_X)$ be Z-numbers and let $*$ be a binary operation defined in $\mathcal{R}$. Then the operation $*$ can be extended to the Z-numbers A and B by the extension principle.

Let $f(X,Y) = X * Y$ where the binary operation $*$ be replaced by the four basic arithmetic operations of $+, -, \cdot$ and $/$. Then the four arithmetic operations over Z-numbers are defined by the following.

Sum of Z-numbers (A_X, B_X) **and** (A_Y, B_Y) **.**

$$(A_Z, B_Z) = (A_X, B_X) + (A_Y, B_Y)$$

$$\mu_{A_Z = A_X + A_Y}(v) = \sup_u (\mu_{A_X}(u) \wedge \mu_{A_Y}(v-u)), \tag{2.83}$$

$$p_{R_X + R_Y}(v) = \int_{\mathcal{R}} p_{R_X}(u) p_{R_Y}(v-u) du, \tag{2.84}$$

$$\mu_{p_Z}(p_Z) = \sup_{p_X, p_Y} \left(\mu_{B_X} \left(\int_{\mathcal{R}} \mu_{A_X}(u) p_X(u) du \right) \wedge \mu_{B_Y} \left(\int_{\mathcal{R}} \mu_{A_Y}(u) p_Y(u) du \right) \right) \tag{2.85}$$

$$\mu_{B_Z}(w) = \sup_{p_Z} (\mu_{p_Z}(p_Z)), \tag{2.86}$$

$$\text{s.t. } w = \int_{\mathcal{R}} \mu_{A_Z}(u) p_Z(u) du. \tag{2.87}$$

Subtraction of Z-numbers (A_X, B_X) **and** (A_Y, B_Y) **.**

$$(A_Z, B_Z) = (A_X, B_X) - (A_Y, B_Y)$$

$$\mu_{A_Z = A_X - A_Y}(v) = \sup_u (\mu_{A_X}(u) \wedge \mu_{A_Y}(v+u)), \tag{2.88}$$

$$p_{R_X - R_Y}(v) = \int_{\mathcal{R}} p_{R_X}(u) p_{R_Y}(v+u) du, \tag{2.89}$$

$$\mu_{p_Z}(p_Z) = \sup_{p_X, p_Y} \left(\mu_{B_X} \left(\int_{\mathcal{R}} \mu_{A_X}(u) p_X(u) du \right) \wedge \mu_{B_Y} \left(\int_{\mathcal{R}} \mu_{A_Y}(u) p_Y(u) du \right) \right) \tag{2.90}$$

$$\mu_{B_Z}(w) = \sup_{p_Z}(\mu_{p_Z}(p_Z)) \,, \tag{2.91}$$

$$\text{s.t. } w = \int_{\mathcal{R}} \mu_{A_Z}(u) p_Z(u) du \,. \tag{2.92}$$

Multiplication of Z-numbers (A_X, B_X) and (A_Y, B_Y).

$$(A_Z, B_Z) = (A_X, B_X) \cdot (A_Y, B_Y)$$

$$\mu_{A_Z = A_X \cdot A_Y}(v) = \sup_u(\mu_{A_X}(u) \wedge \mu_{A_Y}(v/u)) \,, \tag{2.93}$$

$$p_{R_X \cdot R_Y}(v) = \int_{\mathcal{R}} p_{R_X}(u) p_{R_Y}(v/u) du \,, \tag{2.94}$$

$$\mu_{p_Z}(p_Z) = \sup_{p_X, p_Y}\left(\mu_{B_X}\left(\int_{\mathcal{R}} \mu_{A_X}(u) p_X(u) du\right) \wedge \mu_{B_Y}\left(\int_{\mathcal{R}} \mu_{A_Y}(u) p_Y(u) du\right)\right) \tag{2.95}$$

$$\mu_{B_Z}(w) = \sup_{p_Z}(\mu_{p_Z}(p_Z)) \,, \tag{2.96}$$

$$\text{s.t. } w = \int_{\mathcal{R}} \mu_{A_Z}(u) p_Z(u) du \,. \tag{2.97}$$

Division of Z-numbers (A_X, B_X) and (A_Y, B_Y).

$$(A_Z, B_Z) = (A_X, B_X) / (A_Y, B_Y)$$

$$\mu_{A_Z = A_X / A_Y}(v) = \sup_u(\mu_{A_X}(u) \wedge \mu_{A_Y}(v \cdot u)) \,, \tag{2.98}$$

$$p_{R_X/R_Y}(v) = \int_{\mathcal{R}} p_{R_X}(u) p_{R_Y}(v \cdot u) du \qquad (2.99)$$

$$\mu_{p_Z}(p_Z) = \sup_{p_X, p_Y} \left(\mu_{B_X}\left(\int_{\mathcal{R}} \mu_{A_X}(u) p_X(u) du \right) \wedge \mu_{B_Y}\left(\int_{\mathcal{R}} \mu_{A_Y}(u) p_Y(u) du \right) \right) \qquad (2.100)$$

$$\mu_{B_Z}(w) = \sup_{p_Z}(\mu_{p_Z}(p_Z)), \qquad (2.101)$$

$$\text{s.t. } w = \int_{\mathcal{R}} \mu_{A_Z}(u) p_Z(u) du. \qquad (2.102)$$

Positive Z-numbers. A Z-number (A_X, B_X) is said to be positive if $0 < a_1 \leq a_2$ holds for the support $[a_1, a_2]$ of A_X that is, A_X is in the positive real line. Similarly, A Z-number (A_X, B_X) is said to be negative if $a_1 \leq a_2 < 0$ and zero if $a_1 \leq 0 \leq a_2$ holds for the support $[a_1, a_2]$ of A_X.

Below we give the algebraic properties of Z-numbers under $+, -, \cdot$ and $/$ operations.

For any Z-numbers, $X, Y,$ and $Z,$ we have

$$((A_X, B_X) + (A_Y, B_Y)) + (A_Z, B_Z)$$
$$= (A_X, B_X) + ((A_Y, B_Y) + (A_Z, B_Z))$$

(associative law)

$$((A_X, B_X) \times (A_Y, B_Y)) \times (A_Z, B_Z)$$
$$= (A_X, B_X) \times ((A_Y, B_Y) \times (A_Z, B_Z))$$

(associative law)

$$(A_X, B_X) + (A_Y, B_Y) = (A_Y, B_Y) + (A_X, B_X)$$

(commutative law)

$$(A_X, B_X) \times (A_Y, B_Y) = (A_Y, B_Y) \times (A_X, B_X)$$

(commutative law)

$$(A_X, B_X) + 0 = (A_X, B_X)$$

(identity law)

$$(A_X, B_X) \times 1 = (A_X, B_X)$$

(identity law)
Here 0 and 1 are zero and unity of the real line, respectively.
In case of Hukuhara difference for any Z-number

$$(A_X, B_X) -_h (A_X, B_X) = 0$$

is satisfied.

In general, for any Z-number the following conditions do not hold

$$(A_X, B_X) + (A_X, B_X)' = 0_.$$

$$(A_X, B_X) \times (A_X, B_X)'' = 1_,$$

where $(A_X, B_X)'$ and $(A_X, B_X)''$ are inverse Z-numbers under $+$ and $\cdot$, respectively.

For Z-numbers (A_X, B_X), (A_Y, B_Y) and (A_Z, B_Z) with convex fuzzy constraints the following properties are satisfied

$$(A_X, B_X) + ((A_Y, B_Y) \cup (A_Z, B_Z))$$
$$= ((A_X, B_X) + (A_Y, B_Y)) \cup ((A_X, B_X) + (A_Z, B_Z)),$$

$$(A_X, B_X) + ((A_Y, B_Y) \cap (A_Z, B_Z))$$
$$= ((A_X, B_X) + (A_Y, B_Y)) \cap ((A_X, B_X) + (A_Z, B_Z)),$$

$$(A_X, B_X) - ((A_Y, B_Y) \cup (A_Z, B_Z))$$
$$= ((A_X, B_X) - (A_Y, B_Y)) \cap ((A_X, B_X) - (A_Z, B_Z)),$$

$$(A_X, B_X) - ((A_Y, B_Y) \cap (A_Z, B_Z))$$
$$= ((A_X, B_X) - (A_Y, B_Y)) \cup ((A_X, B_X) - (A_Z, B_Z)),$$

$$((A_Y, B_Y) \cup (A_Z, B_Z)) - (A_X, B_X)$$
$$= ((A_X, B_X) - (A_Y, B_Y)) \cup ((A_X, B_X) - (A_Z, B_Z)).$$

In general, distributive law for any Z-numbers does not hold, i.e.

$$(A_X, B_X) \times ((A_Y, B_Y) + (A_Z, B_Z))$$
$$\neq ((A_X, B_X) \times (A_Y, B_Y)) + ((A_X, B_X) \times (A_Z, B_Z)).$$

In particular case, when Z-numbers are positive convex the distributive law is satisfied.

Now we give union and intersection of Z-numbers and algebraic properties of Z-numbers under t-norm and t-conorm with the arithmetic operations $+, -, \cdot$ and $/$.

Union of Z-numbers (A_X, B_X) and (A_Y, B_Y), denoted (A_Z, B_Z), is determined using extension principle as

$$(A_Z, B_Z) = (A_X, B_X) \cup (A_Y, B_Y)$$
$$= (A_Z = A_X \bigcup A_Y, B_Z = B_X \oplus B_Y),$$

where $\oplus$ is an algebraic sum[4,23].

Intersection of (A_X, B_X) and (A_Y, B_Y) is determined as

$$(A_Z, B_Z) = (A_X, B_X) \cap (A_Y, B_Y)$$
$$= (A_Z = A_X \cap A_Y, B_Z = B_X \cdot B_Y),$$

$$((A_Y, B_Y) \cap (A_Z, B_Z)) - (A_X, B_X)$$
$$= ((A_Y, B_Y) - (A_X, B_X)) \cap ((A_Z, B_Z) - (A_X, B_X)).$$

Sign "=" is used in sense of equality of Z-numbers considered in section 4.3 of the book.

For a Z-number with positive convex constraints the following properties are satisfied.

$$(A_X, B_X) \times ((A_Y, B_Y) \cup (A_Z, B_Z))$$
$$= ((A_X, B_X) \times (A_Y, B_Y)) \cup ((A_X, B_X) \times (A_Z, B_Z)),$$

$$(A_X, B_X) \times ((A_Y, B_Y) \cap (A_Z, B_Z))$$
$$= ((A_X, B_X) \times (A_Y, B_Y)) \cap ((A_X, B_X) \times (A_Z, B_Z)),$$

$$(A_X, B_X) \div ((A_Y, B_Y) \cup (A_Z, B_Z))$$
$$= ((A_X, B_X) \div (A_Y, B_Y)) \cup ((A_X, B_X) \div (A_Z, B_Z)),$$

$$(A_X, B_X) \div ((A_Y, B_Y) \cap (A_Z, B_Z))$$
$$= ((A_X, B_X) \div (A_Y, B_Y)) \cap ((A_X, B_X) \div (A_Z, B_Z)),$$

$$((A_Y, B_Y) \cup (A_Z, B_Z)) \div (A_X, B_X)$$
$$= ((A_Y, B_Y) \div (A_X, B_X)) \cup ((A_Z, B_Z) \div (A_X, B_X)),$$

$$((A_Y, B_Y) \cap (A_Z, B_Z)) \div (A_X, B_X)$$
$$= ((A_Y, B_Y) \div (A_X, B_X)) \cap ((A_Z, B_Z) \div (A_X, B_X)).$$

2.6. Discrete Z-numbers, Properties

Definition 2.32. A discrete Z-number [5,9]. A discrete Z-number is an ordered pair $Z = (A, B)$ where A is a discrete fuzzy number playing a role of a fuzzy constraint on values that a random variable X may take:

$$X \ is \ A$$

and B is a discrete fuzzy number with a membership function $\mu_B : \{b_1, ..., b_n\} \rightarrow [0,1]$, $\{b_1, ..., b_n\} \subset [0,1]$, playing a role of a fuzzy constraint on the probability measure of A:

$$P(A) \ is \ B.$$

A concept of a discrete Z^+-number is closely related to the concept of a discrete Z-number. Given a discrete Z-number $Z = (A, B)$, Z^+-number Z^+ is a pair consisting of a fuzzy number, A, and a random number R:

$$Z^+ = (A, R),$$

where A plays the same role as it does in a discrete Z-number $Z = (A, B)$ and R plays the role of the probability distribution p, such that $P(A) = \sum_{i=1}^{n} \mu_A(x_i) p(x_i)$, $P(A) \in \text{supp}(B)$.

As it shown in [19] MIN (Z_1, Z_2) and MAX(Z_1, Z_2) are discrete Z-numbers. The triple (Z, MIN, MAX) is a distributive lattice, where Z denotes the set of discrete Z-numbers support of which is a sequence of consecutive natural numbers.

For any, $Z_1, Z_2, Z_3 \in \mathcal{Z}$, where $\mathcal{Z}$ is set of discrete Z-numbers the following properties hold:

1) $Z_1 + Z_2 = Z_2 + Z_1$ (commutativity)

2) $(Z_1 + Z_2) + Z_3 = Z_1 + (Z_2 + Z_3)$ (associativity)

3) $Z + O^Z = Z$ for all $Z \in Z$ (neutral element) where O^Z is the zero Z-number $O^Z = (0,1)$.

Chapter 3

Operations on Continuous Z-numbers

3.1. Addition of Continuous Z-numbers

Let $Z_1 = (A_1, B_1)$ and $Z_2 = (A_2, B_2)$ be continuous Z-numbers describing imperfect information about values of real-valued random variables X_1 and X_2. Consider the problem of computation of addition $Z_{12} = Z_1 + Z_2$. Computation with Z-numbers, as it was shown in Section 1.2 starts with the computation over the corresponding Z^+-numbers. The Z^+-number $Z_{12}^+ = Z_1^+ + Z_2^+$ is determined as follows:

$$Z_1^+ + Z_2^+ = (A_1 + A_2, R_1 + R_2)$$.

In general, we consider broad family of probability distributions R_1 and R_2. For simplicity, let's consider normal distributions:

$$p_1 = \frac{1}{\sqrt{2\pi}\sigma_1} e^{-\frac{(x-\mu_1^2)}{2\sigma_1^2}} \,, \tag{3.1}$$

$$p_2 = \frac{1}{\sqrt{2\pi}\sigma_2} e^{-\frac{(x-\mu_2^2)}{2\sigma_2^2}} \,. \tag{3.2}$$

The addition $A_1 + A_2$ of fuzzy numbers is defined in accordance with (2.59), (2.60), (2.62) and $R_1 + R_2$ is a convolution $p_{12} = p_1 \circ p_2$ of continuous probability distributions defined in accordance with (2.18). Accordingly, one has:

$$p_{12} = \frac{1}{\sqrt{2\pi(\sigma_1^2 + \sigma_2^2)}} \exp\left[-\frac{(x-(\mu_1+\mu_2))^2}{2(\sigma_1^2 + \sigma_2^2)}\right] \qquad (3.3)$$

So, we will have Z_{12}^+ as $Z_{12}^+ = (A_1 + A_2, p_{12})$, which is the result of computation with Z^+-numbers being the first step of computation with Z-numbers.

At the next stage we realize that in Z-numbers $Z_1 = (A_1, B_1)$ and $Z_2 = (A_2, B_2)$, the 'true' probability distributions p_1 and p_2 are not exactly known. In contrast, the information available is represented by the fuzzy restrictions:

$$\int_{\mathcal{R}} \mu_{A_1}(x_1) p_{R_1}(x_1) dx_1 \text{ is } B_1, \qquad (3.4)$$

$$\int_{\mathcal{R}} \mu_{A_2}(x_2) p_{R_2}(x_2) dx_2 \text{ is } B_2, \qquad (3.5)$$

which are represented in terms of the membership functions as

$$\mu_{B_1}\left(\int_{\mathcal{R}} \mu_{A_1}(x_1) p_{R_1}(x_1) dx_1\right), \qquad (3.6)$$

$$\mu_{B_2}\left(\int_{\mathcal{R}} \mu_{A_2}(x_2) p_{R_2}(x_2) dx_2\right). \qquad (3.7)$$

These restrictions imply that one has the fuzzy sets of probability distributions of p_1 and p_2 with the membership functions defined as

$$\mu_{p_{R_1}}(p_{R_1}) = \mu_{B_1}\left(\int_{\mathcal{R}} \mu_{A_1}(x_1) p_{R_1}(x_1) dx_1\right) \qquad (3.6a)$$

$$\mu_{p_{R_2}}(p_{R_2}) = \mu_{B_2}\left(\int_{\mathcal{R}} \mu_{A_2}(x_2) p_{R_2}(x_2) dx_2\right). \qquad (3.7a)$$

Thus, $B_j, j = 1, 2$ is a fuzzy number, which play the role of a soft constraint on a value of a probability measure of A_j. Here we will use discretized version of (3.6)-(3.7). In this case basic values $b_{jl} \in \operatorname{supp}(B_j)$, $j = 1, 2; l = 1, ..., m$ of a discretized fuzzy number $B_j, j = 1, 2$ are values of a probability measure of A_j, $b_{jl} = P(A_j)$. Thus, given b_{jl}, we have to find such probability distribution p_{jl} which satisfy:

$$b_{jl} = \mu_{A_j}(x_{j1}) p_{jl}(x_{j1}) + \mu_{A_j}(x_{j2}) p_{jl}(x_{j2}) + ... + \mu_{A_j}(x_{jn_j}) p_{jl}(x_{jn_j}) .$$

At the same time we know that p_{jl} has to satisfy:

$$\sum_{k=1}^{n_j} p_{jl}(x_{jk}) = 1, p_{jl}(x_{jk}) \geq 0.$$

Therefore, the following goal programming problem should be solved to find p_j:

$$\mu_{A_j}(x_{j1}) p_{jl}(x_{j1}) + \mu_{A_j}(x_{j1}) p_{jl}(x_{j1}) + ... + \mu_{A_j}(x_{jn_j}) p_{jl}(x_{jn_j}) \to b_{jl} \quad (3.8)$$

subject to

$$\left. \begin{array}{l} p_{jl}(x_{j1}) + p_{jl}(x_{j2}) + ... + p_{jl}(x_{jn}) = 1 \\ p_{jl}(x_{j1}), p_{jl}(x_{j2}), ..., p_{jl}(x_{jn}) \geq 0 \end{array} \right\} \quad (3.9)$$

Now, denote $c_k = \mu_{A_j}(x_{jk})$ and $v_k = p_j(x_{jk}), k = 1, .., n$. As c_k and b_{jl} are known numbers, and v_k are unknown decision variables, we see that the problem (3.8)-(3.9) is nothing but the following goal linear programming problem:

$$c_1 v_1 + c_2 v_2 + ... + c_n v_n \to b_{jl} \quad (3.8a)$$

subject to

$$\left.\begin{array}{l} v_1 + v_2 + ... + v_n = 1 \\ v_1, v_2, ..., v_n \geq 0 \end{array}\right\}$$ (3.9a)

Having obtained the solution $v_k, k=1,..,n$ of problem (3.8a)-(3.9a) for each $l=1,...,m$, we recall that $v_k = p_{jl}(x_{jk})$, $k=1,..,n$. Therefore, the probability distribution p_{jl} is obtained. Next, as p_{jl} is obtained given b_{jl}, the desired degree is $\mu_{p_{jl}}(p_{jl}) = \mu_{B_j}(b_{jl})$, $j=1,2$, that is

$$\mu_{p_{jl}}(p_{jl}) = = \mu_{B_j}\left(\sum_{k=1}^{n_j} \mu_{A_j}(x_{jk})p_{jl}(x_{jk})\right).$$ Thus, to construct a fuzzy set of

probability distributions p_{jl}, it is needed to solve n simple goal linear programming problems (3.8a)-(3.9a). For normal random variables, taking into account compatibility conditions (Section 1.2.2), this problem is reduced to optimization problem with one parameter σ. This problem may be solved by a simple optimization method.

The fuzzy sets of probability distributions p_1 and p_2 obtained from approximation of calculated $p_{jl}(x_{jk})$ by a normal distribution, induce the fuzzy set of convolutions p_{12s}, $s=1,...,m^2$, with the membership function defined as

$$\mu_{p_{12}}(p_{12}) = \max_{p_1,p_2}[\mu_{p_1}(p_1) \wedge \mu_{p_2}(p_2)]$$ (3.10)

subject to $p_{12} = p_1 \circ p_2$, (3.11)

where $\wedge$ is *min* operation.

At the next step we should compute probability measure of $A_{12} = A_1 + A_2$ given p_{12}, that is, to compute probability measure $P(A_{12})$ of the fuzzy event X *is* A_{12}:

$$P(A_{12}) = \int_{\mathcal{R}} \mu_{A_{12}}(u) p_{12}(u) du.$$ (3.12)

Thus, when p_{12} is known, $P(A_{12})$ is a number $P(A_{12}) = b_{12}$. However, what is only known is a fuzzy restriction on p_{12} described by the membership function $\mu_{p_{12}}$. Therefore, $P(A_{12})$ will be a fuzzy set B_{12} with the membership function $\mu_{B_{12}}$ defined as follows:

$$\mu_{B_{12}}(b_{12s}) = \sup(\mu_{p_{12s}}(p_{12s})) \tag{3.13}$$

subject to

$$b_{12s} = \int_{\mathcal{R}} \mu_{A_{12}}(x) p_{12s}(x_k) dx. \tag{3.14}$$

As a result, $Z_{12} = Z_1 + Z_2$ is obtained as $Z_{12} = (A_{12}, B_{12})$.

An example. Let the following continuous Z-numbers with components as TFNs be given: $Z_1 = ((1,2,3),(0.7,0.8,0.9))$, $Z_2 = ((7,8,9),(0.4,0.5,0.6))$. Consider computation of $Z_{12} = Z_1 + Z_2$. Let us consider the case when the pdfs underlying the considered Z-numbers are normal pdfs. First, the Z^+-number $Z_{12}^+ = (A_{12}, R_1 + R_2)$ should be determined:

$$Z_{12}^+ = (A_1 + A_2, R_1 + R_2).$$

where R_1 and R_2 are the following normal pdfs:

$$p_1 = N(2, 0.217),$$

$$p_2 = N(8, 0.77).$$

In accordance with (2.59), (2.60), (2.62), we computed $A_{12} = A_1 + A_2$:

$$A_{12} = (8, 10, 12).$$

In turn, according to (3.3), $R_1 + R_2$ will be described by the following pdf p_{12}:

$$p_{12} = (10, 0.8).$$

Thus, $Z_{12}^+ = (A_1 + A_2, R_1 + R_2) = (A_1 + A_2, p_{12})$ I s obtained.

At the *third step* we realize, that 'true' probability distributions p_1 and p_2 are not exactly known, but only fuzzy restrictions $\mu_{p_1}()$ and $\mu_{p_2}()$ for p_1 and p_2 are available which are induced by B_1 and B_2 respectively. Therefore, we should extract distributions $p_j, j = 1, 2$ underlying $B_j, j = 1, 2$ (let us mention that a fuzzy set of distributions p_j underlies B_j) and compute the membership degrees $\mu_{p_j}(p_j), j = 1, 2$. The determination of $p_j = (\mu_j, \sigma_j), j = 1, 2$, taking into account that μ_j are fixed due to compatibility conditions, is represented as the following simple nonlinear optimization problem with respect to σ_j:

$$\int_{supp(A_1)} \mu_{A_1}(x) \frac{1}{\sqrt{2\pi}\sigma_{jl}} e^{\frac{(x-\mu_1^2)}{2\sigma_{jl}^2}} dx \longrightarrow b_{jl} \tag{3.15}$$

subject to

$$\sigma_{jl} \geq \varepsilon > 0. \tag{3.16}$$

This problem can be easily solved by using the Newton method. We have solved this problem for discretized $B_j, j = 1, 2$ and obtained the following results (Table 3.1):

Table 3.1. The obtained solutions σ_{jl} to (3.15)-(3.16).

b_{1l}	0.7	0.76	0.8	0.84	0.9
σ_{1l}	0.39	0.31	0.26	0.22	0.15
b_{2l}	0.4	0.46	0.5	0.54	0.6
σ_{2l}	0.91	0.77	0.68	0.61	0.52

Let us now consider determination of the membership degrees $\mu_{p_1}(p_1)$ and $\mu_{p_2}(p_2)$ based on (3.6a) and (3.7a). For example, given distributions p_1 and p_2 considered above, one has

$$\int_{\mathcal{R}} \mu_{A_1}(x_1) \frac{1}{0.217\sqrt{2\pi}} e^{-\frac{(x-2^2)}{2(0.217)^2}} dx_1 \approx 0.84$$

$$\int_{\mathcal{R}} \mu_{A_2}(x_2) \frac{1}{0.77\sqrt{2\pi}} e^{-\frac{(x-8^2)}{2(0.77)^2}} dx_2 \approx 0.46.$$

Therefore, $\mu_{p_1}(p_1) = \mu_{B_1}(0.84) = 0.6$ and $\mu_{p_2}(p_2) = \mu_{B_2}(0.46) = 0.6$. Analogously, we computed the membership degrees of for all the considered p_1 and p_2.

At the *fourth step*, given $\mu_{p_1}()$ and $\mu_{p_2}()$, we should determine the fuzzy restriction $\mu_{p_{12}}()$ over all the convolutions p_{12} obtained on the base of (3.3) from all the considered p_1 and p_2. For example, the membership degree of this fuzzy restriction for the convolution p_{12} obtained above is

$$\mu_{p_{12}}(p_{12}) = \mu_{p_1}(p_1) \wedge \mu_{p_2}(p_2) = 0.6 \wedge 0.6 = 0.6.$$

Analogously, we computed the degrees for all the considered p_{12} (let us mention that a fuzzy set of distributions p_1 and a fuzzy set of distributions p_2 induce a fuzzy set of convolution p_{12}).

At the *fifth step*, we proceed to construction of B_{12} as a soft constraint on a probability measure $P(A_{12})$ based on (3.13)-(3.14). First we need to compute values of probability measure $P(A_{12})$ for the obtained convolutions p_{12}. For example, $P(A_{12})$ computed with respect to $p_{12} = (10, 0.8)$ considered above is

$$P(A_{12}) = \int_{\mathcal{R}} \mu_{A_{12}}(x_2) \frac{1}{0.8\sqrt{2\pi}} e^{-\frac{(x-10)^2}{2(0.8)^2}} dx_{12} \approx 0.69.$$

The computed $P(A_{12})$ is one possible value within the fuzzy restriction B_{12} to be constructed, and we can say that one basic value of B_{12} is found as $b_{12} = 0.69$. Recalling (3.13)-(3.14), we can write

$\mu_{B_{12}}\left(b_{12}=\int_{\mathcal{R}}\mu_{A_{12}}(x_{12})p_{12}(x_{12})dx_{12}\right)=\mu_{P_{12}}(p_{12})$. Next, taking into account

that $\mu_{P_{12}}(p_{12}=(10,0.8))=0.6$, we obtain $\mu_{B_{12}}(b_{12}=0.69)=0.6$ for

$b_{12}=\int_{\mathcal{R}}\mu_{A_2}(x_2)\dfrac{1}{0.8\sqrt{2\pi}}e^{-\frac{(x-10^2)}{2(0.8)^2}}dx_2$. By carrying out analogous

computations, we constructed B_{12}. The obtained result approximated as a triangular fuzzy number (TFN) is as follows:

$$B_{12}=(0.62,0.72,0.79).$$

Thus, the result of addition $Z_{12}=(A_{12},B_{12})$ is obtained, where A_{12},B_{12} are shown in Fig. 3.1.

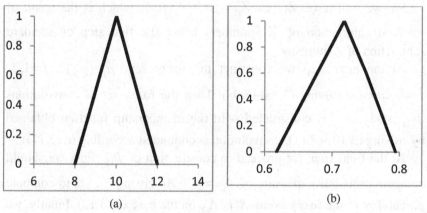

(a)   (b)

Fig. 3.1. The results of addition of the continuous Z-numbers: (a) A_{12}, (b) B_{12}.

3.2. Standard Subtraction of Continuous Z-numbers

Let us consider standard subtraction $Z_{12}=Z_1-Z_2$ of Z-numbers $Z_1=(A_1,B_1)$ and $Z_2=(A_2,B_2)$. First, a discrete Z^+-number $Z_{12}^+=Z_1^+-Z_2^+$ should be determined:

$$Z_1^+-Z_2^+=(A_1-A_2,R_1-R_2)$$

where R_1 and R_2 are represented by probability distributions (3.1) and (3.2).

The difference $A_1 - A_2$ of fuzzy numbers is defined in accordance with and $R_1 - R_2$ is a convolution $p_{12} = p_1 \circ p_2$ of normal probability distributions defined as

$$p_{12} = \frac{e^{-[x-(\mu_1 - \mu_2)]^2 / [2(\sigma_1^2 + \sigma_2^2)]}}{\sqrt{2\pi(\sigma_1^2 + \sigma_2^2)}}, \qquad (3.17)$$

here

$$\mu_{12} = \mu_1 - \mu_2, \quad \sigma_{12} = \sigma_1^2 + \sigma_2^2.$$

So, we will have Z_{12}^+ as $Z_{12}^+ = (A_1 - A_2, p_{12})$, which is the result of standard subtraction of Z^+-numbers being the first step of standard subtraction of Z-numbers.

At the next step we construct the fuzzy sets $\mu_{p_{jl}}(p_{jl})$, $j = 1, 2$, $l = 1, ..., m$ by solving (3.8a)-(3.9a). Then the fuzzy set of convolutions p_{12s}, $s = 1, ..., m^2$ is constructed with the membership function obtained by solving (3.10)-(3.11) (convolution is computed according to (3.17)).

At the final *step*, we proceed to construction of B_{12}. First we should compute probability measure of $A_{12} = A_1 - A_2$ given p_{12}, i.e. to compute probability of the fuzzy event X *is* A_{12} on the base of (3.12). Finally, we compute a fuzzy set B_{12} a according to (3.13)-(3.14). As a result, $Z_{12} = Z_1 - Z_2$ is obtained as $Z_{12} = (A_{12}, B_{12})$.

An example. Consider computation of $Z_{12} = Z_1 - Z_2$ for the Z-numbers given in the previous example.

First, the Z^+-number $Z_{12}^+ = (A_{12}, R_1 - R_2)$ should be determined. $A_{12} = A_1 - A_2$ is found on the base of (2.59), (2.60), (2.64):

$$A_{12} = (4, 6, 8).$$

$R_1 - R_2$ is convolution p_{12} computed based on (3.17) for normal pdfs considered in the previous example:

$$p_{12} = (6, 0.8).$$

Thus, $Z_{12}^+ = (A_1 - A_2, R_1 - R_2) = (A_1 - A_2, p_{12})$ is obtained.

Next we need to construct distributions p_1 and p_2 and compute membership degrees $\mu_{p_1}(p_1)$ and $\mu_{p_2}(p_2)$ for the fuzzy restrictions (3.6a)-(3.7a). These distributions and membership degrees were determined in the previous example.

At the *fourth step*, we compute the membership degrees $\mu_{p_{12}}(p_{12})$ of the convolutions p_{12}. Let us mention that $\mu_{p_{12}}(p_{12})$ depends only on the degrees $\mu_{p_1}(p_1)$ and $\mu_{p_2}(p_2)$ of distributions p_1 and p_2 from which p_{12} is obtained and does not depend on a type of arithmetic operation. Therefore, they will be obtained analogously to the case of addition. Indeed, the membership degree of p_{12} obtained above is

$$\mu_{p_{12}}(p_{12}) = 0.6.$$

At the *fifth step*, we proceed to construction of B_{12}. First, we compute values of probability measure $P(A_{12})$ with respect to the obtained convolutions p_{12}. For example, $P(A_{12})$ computed based on p_{12} considered above is

$$P(A_{12}) = \int_{\mathcal{R}} \mu_{A_2}(x_2) \frac{1}{0.8\sqrt{2\pi}} e^{-\frac{(x-6)^2}{2(0.8)^2}} dx_1 \approx 0.69.$$

Therefore, one basic value of B_{12} is found as $b_{12} = 0.69$ with $\mu_{\tilde{B}_{12}}(b_{12} = 0.69) = 0.8$.

At the final stage, we construct B_{12} based on (3.13)-(3.14).The constructed B_{12} is given below:

$$B_{12} = (0.62, 0.72, 0.79).$$

Thus, $Z_{12} = (A_{12}, B_{12})$ is obtained as the result of subtraction and A_{12}, B_{12}

are shown in Fig. 3.2.

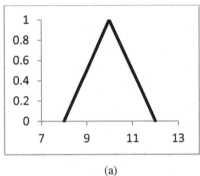
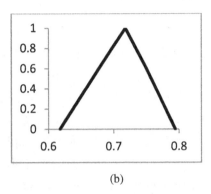

(a)   (b)

Fig. 3.2. The results of subtraction of the continuous Z-numbers: (a) A_{12}, (b) B_{12}.

3.3. Multiplication of Continuous Z-numbers

Let us consider multiplication $Z_{12} = Z_1 \cdot Z_2$ of $Z_1 = (A_1, B_1)$ and $Z_2 = (A_2, B_2)$. First, $Z_{12}^+ = Z_1^+ \cdot Z_2^+$ should be determined:

$$Z_1^+ \cdot Z_2^+ = (A_1 \cdot A_2, R_1 \cdot R_2),$$

where R_1 and R_2 are represented by normal probability distributions (3.1)-(3.2). The product $A_1 \cdot A_2$ of fuzzy numbers is defined in accordance with (2.59), (2.60), (2.66) and $R_1 \cdot R_2$ is a convolution $p_{12} = p_1 \circ p_2$ of probability distributions defined in accordance with (2.30)-(2.31).

Thus, we will have $Z_{12}^+ = (A_1 \cdot A_2, p_{12})$. Next, analogously to Section 3.1, we construct the fuzzy sets $\mu_{p_{jl}}(p_{jl})$, $l = 1, ..., m$, and the fuzzy set of convolutions p_{12s}, $s = 1, ..., m^2$, with the membership function defined by solving (3.10)-(3.11) (convolution is defined according to (2.30)-(2.31)).

Finally, a fuzzy set B_{12} is constructed according to (3.13)-(3.14). As a result, $Z_{12} = Z_1 \cdot Z_2$ is obtained as $Z_{12} = (A_{12}, B_{12})$.

An example. Consider computation of $Z_{12} = Z_1 \cdot Z_2$ for the Z-numbers given in the previous example. First, the Z^+-number $Z_{12}^+ = (A_{12}, R_1 \cdot R_2)$ should be determined. $A_{12} = A_1 \cdot A_2$ is found based on (2.59), (2.60), (2.66) and is shown in Fig. 3.3a. $R_1 \cdot R_2$ is convolution p_{12} of distributions considered in the previous example and is found on base of (2.30)-(2.31) as $p_{12} \approx (16, 5.5)$.

Next, it is needed to compute membership degrees $\mu_{p_1}(p_1)$ and $\mu_{p_2}(p_2)$ of distributions p_1 and p_2. These distributions and membership degrees were determined in the previous example.

Fourth, the membership degrees of the convolutions p_{12} are obtained on the basis of $\mu_{p_1}(p_1)$ and $\mu_{p_2}(p_2)$ analogously to the cases of addition and subtraction. Indeed $\mu_{p_{12}}(p_{12})$ for p_{12} obtained above is $\mu_{p_{12}}(p_{12}) = 0.6$.

Fifth, we compute $\tilde{B}_{12}$. For this, we compute values of probability measure $P(A_{12})$ with respect to the obtained convolutions p_{12} according to (3.12). For example, $P(A_{12})$ computed for p_{12} considered above is $P(A_{12}) = b_{12} = 0.67$.

At the final stage, we construct B_{12} based on (3.13)-(3.14). For example, $\mu_{B_{12}}(b_{12} = 0.67) = 0.8$. The constructed B_{12} is given in Fig. 3.3b.

Thus, $Z_{12} = (A_{12}, B_{12})$ as the result of multiplication is obtained and A_{12}, B_{12} are shown in Fig. 3.3.

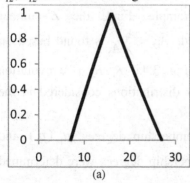 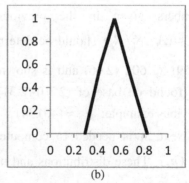

(a) (b)

Fig. 3.3. The results of multiplication of the continuous Z-numbers: (a) A_{12}, (b) B_{12}.

3.4. Standard Division of Continuous Z-numbers

Let us consider standard division $Z_{12} = Z_1 \big/ Z_2$ of $Z_1 = (A_1, B_1)$ and $Z_2 = (A_2, B_2)$, where $0 \notin \text{supp}(A_2)$. First, $Z_{12}^+ = (A_{12}, p_{12})$ is determined:

$$Z_{12}^+ = (A_{12}, p_{12}),$$

where the standard division $A_{12} = A_1 \big/ A_2$ of continuous fuzzy numbers is defined in accordance with (2.59), (2.60), (2.67). Convolution $p_{12} = p_1 \circ p_2$ of probability distributions p_1 and p_2 is defined by (2.32)-(2.33).

Next, analogously to Section 3.1, we construct the fuzzy sets $\mu_{p_{jl}}(p_{jl})$, $j = 1, 2$, $l = 1, \dots, m$ and the fuzzy set of convolutions p_{12s}, $s = 1, \dots, m^2$, with the membership function defined by solving (3.10)-(3.11), where convolution is defined according to (2.32)-(2.33).

At the next step probability measure of A_{12} is computed on the base of (3.12). Finally, a fuzzy set B_{12} is constructed according to (3.13)-(3.14). As a result, $Z_{12} = Z_1 \big/ Z_2$ is obtained as $Z_{12} = (A_{12}, B_{12})$.

An example. Consider computation of $Z_{12} = Z_1 \big/ Z_2$ for the Z-numbers given in the previous example. First, the Z^+-number $Z_{12}^+ = (A_{12}, R_1 / R_2)$ should be determined. $A_{12} = A_1 \big/ A_2$ is found based on (2.59), (2.60), (2.66) and is shown in Fig. 3.4a. $R_1 \cdot R_2$ is convolution p_{12} found on base of (2.30)-(2.31) for distributions considered in the previous example: $p_{12} \approx (4, 0.34)$.

Next, it is needed to compute membership degrees $\mu_{p_1}(p_1)$ and $\mu_{p_2}(p_2)$. These distributions and membership degrees were determined in the previous example.

Fourth, the membership degrees of the convolutions p_{12} are obtained on the basis of $\mu_{p_1}(p_1)$ and $\mu_{p_2}(p_2)$ analogously to the cases of addition and subtraction. Indeed $\mu_{p_{12}}(p_{12})$ for p_{12} obtained above is $\mu_{p_{12}}(p_{12}) = 0.6$.

Fifth, we compute B_{12}. For this we compute values of probability measure $P(A_{12})$ with respect to the obtained convolutions p_{12} according to (3.12). For example, $P(A_{12})$ computed for p_{12} considered above is $P(A_{12}) = b_{12} = 0.77$.

At the final stage, we construct B_{12} based on (3.13)-(3.14). For example, $\mu_{B_{12}}(b_{12} = 0.77) = 0.6$. The constructed B_{12} is given in Fig. 3.4b.

Thus, $Z_{12} = (A_{12}, B_{12})$ as the result of multiplication is obtained and A_{12}, B_{12} are shown in Fig. 3.4.

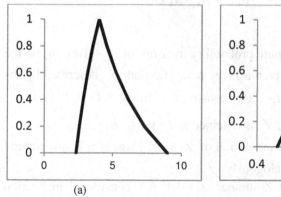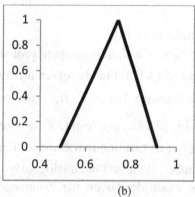

(a)   (b)

Fig. 3.4. The results of division of the continuous Z-numbers: (a) A_{12}, (b) B_{12}.

3.5. Square of a Continuous Z-number

Let us now consider computation of $Z_Y = Z_X^2$. Let $Z_X^+ = (A_X, R_X)$ where R_X is represented as (3.1). Then the continuous Z^+-number Z_Y^+ is determined as follows:

$$Z_Y^+ = (A_Y, R_Y),$$

where $A_Y = A_X^2$, A_X^2 is determined on the base of (2.69) and R_Y is determined by (2.15). Next we compute $\mu_{p_X}(p_X)$ by solving linear programming problem (3.8a)-(3.9a).

Now we realize that the fuzzy set of probability distributions p_X with membership function $\mu_{p_X}(p_{X,l})$ naturally induces the fuzzy set of probability distributions $p_{Y,l}$ with the membership function defined as

$$\mu_{p_Y}(p_{Y,l}) = \mu_{p_X}(p_{X,l}),$$

subject to (2.15).

Next, we should compute probability measure of A_Y given p_Y on the base of (3.12). Finally, given a fuzzy restriction on p_Y described by the membership function μ_{p_Y}, we construct a fuzzy set B_Y by solving (3.13)-(3.14). As a result, Z^2 is obtained as $Z^2 = (A_Y, B_Y)$.

Let us mention that computation of $Z_Y = Z_X^n$, where n is any natural number, is carried out analogously.

An example. Given the Z-number $Z_1 = (A_1, B_1)$ considered in Section 3.1, let us compute its square $Z = (A, B) = Z_1^2$. $A = A_1^2$ computed on the base of (2.69) and B computed as it is shown above are given in Fig. 3.5.

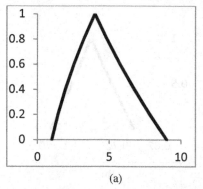 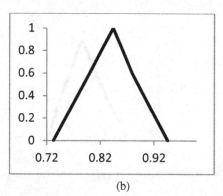

(a)   (b)

Fig. 3.5. The square of the continuous Z-number: (a) A, (b) B.

3.6. Square Root of a Continuous Z-number

In [168] Zadeh poses a question: "What is a square root of a Z-number?". In this section we will answer this question. Let us consider computation of $Z_Y = \sqrt{Z_X}$. Let Z_X^+ and Z_X be the same as those considered in Section 3.5. Then the continuous Z^+-number Z_Y^+ is determined as follows:

$$Z_Y^+ = (A_Y, R_Y),$$

where $A_Y = \sqrt{A_X}$, $\sqrt{A_X}$ is determined as it is shown in Section 2.4.2 and R_Y is determined by (2.17). Next we compute $\mu_{p_X}(p_X)$ by solving linear programming problem (3.8a)-(3.9a) and recall that

$$\mu_{p_Y}(p_{Y,l}) = \mu_{p_X}(p_{X,l}),$$

subject to (2.17). Next we compute probability measure of A_Y and, given the membership function μ_{p_Y}, we construct a fuzzy set B_Y analogously to what we did in Section 3.5.

An example. Given the Z-number $Z_1 = (A_1, B_1)$ considered in Section 3.1, let us compute its square root $Z = (A, B) = \sqrt{Z_1}$. $A = \sqrt{A_1}$ computed as it is shown in Section 2.4.2, and B computed as it is shown above, are given in Fig. 3.6.

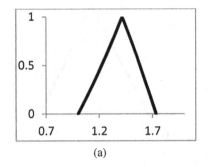 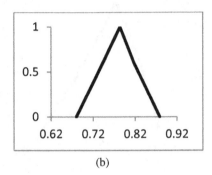

Fig. 3.6. The square root of the continuous Z-number: (a) *A* , (b) *B*.

Chapter 4

Operations on Discrete Z-numbers

4.1. Arithmetic Operations[5,9]

4.1.1. *Continuous and Discrete Z-numbers: Discussion*

The framework of computation with Z-numbers suggested by Zadeh [168] is considered in Section 1.2.2. In general, this involves handling two nonlinear variational problems. We suggest an alternative approach in order to reduce computational complexity of operations with continuous Z-numbers under a small loss of accuracy. This approach consists in consideration of discrete Z-numbers as discrete analogs of continuous Z-numbers. The main reason to use discrete Z-numbers is the fact that real-world problems are characterized by linguistic relevant information[9]. In turn, linguistic information is always described by a set of meaningful linguistic terms. For example, consider the following Z-number-based evaluation[168]:

(the price of oil in the near future is *medium, very likely*)

As one can see, linguistic terms are used in this evaluation. This means that Z-numbers are based on the use of sets of linguistic terms. Such sets can be represented by ordinal linguistic scales.In the considered case, one may consider the ordinal linguistic scales with, for example, eleven linguistic terms $\mathcal{M} = \{VL, L, ..., M, ..., H, VH\}$, where the letters denote terms *very low, low,...,medium,..., high, very high* and $\mathcal{N} = \{U, NVL, ..., L, ..., VL, EL\}$, where the letters denote term s*unlikely, not very likely,..., likely,..., very likely, extremely likely*. The linguistic terms of the considered scales are ordered in an increasing order: $VL \prec L \prec ... \prec M \prec ... \prec H \prec VH$ and $U \prec NVL \prec ... \prec L \prec ... \prec VL \prec EL$.

Therefore, one can consecutively number the linguistic terms in the considered scales and arrive at an ordered set $L = \{0,1,...,n\}$.

Consideration of discrete Z-numbers instead of their continuous counterparts also allows us to significantly improve tradeoff between adequacy and universality from the one side and computational complexity from the other side. Universality implies that one does not need to think about type of probability distributions and can consider a general case. Concerning loss of accuracy as a result of proceeding from continuous forms of membership functions and probability distributions to discrete forms, in many problems it may not be significant from qualitative point of view. At the same time, computational complexity of dealing with discrete Z-numbers is significantly lower than that with continuous Z-numbers.

4.1.2. A Z-number and a Z⁺-number

Definition 4.1[150]. Probability measure of a discrete fuzzy number. Let A be a discrete fuzzy number. A probability measure of A denoted $P(A)$ is defined as

$$P(A) = \sum_{i=1}^{n} \mu_A(x_i) p(x_i) = \mu_A(x_{j1}) p_j(x_{j1})$$
$$+ \mu_A(x_{j2}) p_j(x_{j2}) + ... + \mu_A(x_{jn_j}) p_j(x_{jn_j}).$$

In order to better understand the difference between the concepts of a discrete Z-number and a discrete Z+-number, let us consider an example: (*"oil price will be about* 50 *dollars/barrel"*, *very likely*).

This linguistic partially reliable information can be described by a Z-number $Z = (A,B)$ where A and B are shown in Fig. 4.1. For better illustration in this figure and the other figures in this chapter, we mainly use continuous representation for graphs of membership functions, where discrete points are connected by continuous curves.

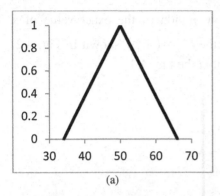 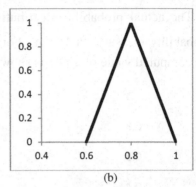

(a)   (b)

Fig. 4.1. Z-number $Z = (A, B)$ usedto describe linguistic partially reliable information on oil price: (a) a discrete fuzzy number A (b) a discrete fuzzy number B.

The fuzzy number B plays a role of a soft constraint on a value ofprobability measure $P(A)$ of A. As $P(A)$ is determined on the base of some probability distribution (see Definition 4.1), fuzziness of $P(A)$ implies that actual probability distribution is not known. In contrast, due to natural imprecision of the term *'very likely'*, one has to use soft constraint on possible probability distributions, or, in other words, a fuzzy set of probability distributions.

In the case when the actual probability distribution p is known, the concept of a discrete Z^+-number $Z^+ = (A, p)$ is used (Fig. 4.2). This is the case when information related to probability measure $P(A)$ is more complete, and that is why '+' is used in the upper index of Z.

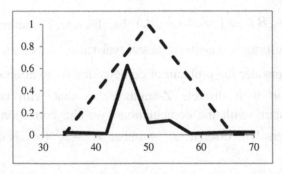

Fig. 4.2. Z^+-number $Z^+ = (A, p)$ with a discrete fuzzy number A (dashed curve) and a discrete probability distribution (solid curve)·

The actual probability distribution p induces the exact value of a probability measure $P(A)$ of A. For the $Z^+ = (A, p)$ shown in Fig. 4.2, the computed value of $P(A)$ is shown in the Fig. 4.3.

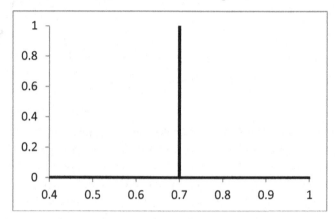

Fig. 4.3. The exact value of a probability measure $P(A)$.

Therefore, the considered $Z^+ = (A, p)$ encodes the following information:

("*oil price will be about* 50 *dollars/barrel*", the probability is 0.7).

Surely, this is more certain statement than the previous one, but it is not realistic.

4.1.3. *Addition of Discrete Z-numbers*

Let $Z_1 = (A_1, B_1)$ and $Z_2 = (A_2, B_2)$ be discrete Z-numbers describing imperfect information about values of real-valued uncertain variables X_1 and X_2. Consider the problem of computation of addition $Z_{12} = Z_1 + Z_2$. Computation with discrete Z-numbers, as that with continuous Z-numbers, starts with the computation over the corresponding discrete Z^+-numbers. The discrete Z^+-number $Z_{12}^+ = Z_1^+ + Z_2^+$ is determined as follows:

$$Z_1^+ + Z_2^+ = (A_1 + A_2, R_1 + R_2),$$

where R_1 and R_2 are represented by discrete probability distributions:

$$p_1 = p_1(x_{11}) \backslash x_{11} + p_1(x_{12}) \backslash x_{12} + \ldots + p_1(x_{1n}) \backslash x_{1n},$$

$$p_2 = p_2(x_{21}) \backslash x_{21} + p_2(x_{22}) \backslash x_{22} + \ldots + p_2(x_{2n}) \backslash x_{2n},$$

for which one necessarily has

$$\sum_{k=1}^{n} p_1(x_{1k}) = 1, \tag{4.1}$$

$$\sum_{k=1}^{n} p_2(x_{2k}) = 1. \tag{4.2}$$

As the operands in $A_1 + A_2$ and in $R_1 + R_2$ are represented by different types of restrictions, then the meanings of $*$ are also different [168]. The addition $A_1 + A_2$ of discrete fuzzy numbers is defined in accordance with Definition 2.20 (Chapter 2) and $R_1 + R_2$ is a convolution $p_{12} = p_1 \circ p_2$ of discrete probability distributions defined in accordance with (2.36):

$$p_{12}(x) = \sum_{x=x_1+x_2} p_1(x_1) p_2(x_2).$$

So, we will have Z_{12}^+ as $Z_{12}^+ = (A_1 + A_2, p_{12})$, which is the result of computation with discrete Z^+-numbers being the first step of computation with Z-numbers.

At the next stage we realize that in Z-numbers $Z_1 = (A_1, B_1)$ and $Z_2 = (A_2, B_2)$, the 'true' probability distributions p_1 and p_2 are not exactly known. In contrast, the information available is represented by the fuzzy restrictions:

$$\sum_{k=1}^{n_1} \mu_{A_1}(x_{1k}) p_1(x_{1k}) \text{ is } B_1,$$

$$\sum_{k=1}^{n_2} \mu_{A_2}(x_{2k}) p_2(x_{2k}) \; is \; B_2,$$

which are represented in terms of the membership functions as

$$\mu_{B_1}\left(\sum_{k=1}^{n_1} \mu_{A_1}(x_{1k}) p_1(x_{1k})\right),$$

$$\mu_{B_2}\left(\sum_{k=1}^{n_2} \mu_{A_2}(x_{2k}) p_2(x_{2k})\right).$$

These restrictions imply that one has the fuzzy sets of probability distributions of p_1 and p_2 with the membership functions defined as

$$\mu_{p_1}(p_1) = \mu_{B_1}\left(\sum_{k=1}^{n_1} \mu_{A_1}(x_{1k}) p_1(x_{1k})\right),$$

$$\mu_{p_2}(p_2) = \mu_{B_2}\left(\sum_{k=1}^{n_2} \mu_{A_2}(x_{2k}) p_2(x_{2k})\right).$$

Thus, B_j, $j = 1, 2$ is a discrete fuzzy number, which plays the role of a soft constraint on a value of a probability measure of A_j. Therefore, basic values $b_{jl} \in \text{supp}(B_j)$, $j = 1, 2$; $l = 1, ..., m$ of a discrete fuzzy number B_j, $j = 1, 2$ are values of a probability measure of A_j, $b_{jl} = P(A_j)$. Thus, according to Definition 4.1, given b_{jl}, we have to find such probability distribution p_{jl} which satisfies:

$$b_{jl} = \mu_{A_j}(x_{j1}) p_{jl}(x_{j1}) + \mu_{A_j}(x_{j2}) p_{jl}(x_{j2}) + ... + \mu_{A_j}(x_{jn_j}) p_{jl}(x_{jn_j}).$$

At the same time we know that p_{jl} has to satisfy:

$$\sum_{k=1}^{n_j} p_{jl}(x_{jk}) = 1, p_{jl}(x_{jk}) \ge 0.$$

Therefore, the following goal programming problem should be solved to find p_j:

$$\mu_{A_j}(x_{j1})p_{jl}(x_{j1})+\mu_{A_j}(x_{j1})p_{jl}(x_{j1})+...+\mu_{A_j}(x_{jn_j})p_{jl}(x_{jn_j})\to b_{jl} \quad (4.3)$$

subject to

$$\left.\begin{array}{l} p_{jl}(x_{j1})+p_{jl}(x_{j2})+...+p_{jl}(x_{jn})=1\\ p_{jl}(x_{j1}),p_{jl}(x_{j2}),...,p_{jl}(x_{jn})\geq 0 \end{array}\right\}. \quad (4.4)$$

Now, denote $c_k=\mu_{A_j}(x_{jk})$ and $v_k=p_j(x_{jk})$, $k=1,..,n$. As c_k and b_{jl} are known numbers and v_k are unknown decision variables, we see that problem (4.3)-(4.4) is nothing but the following goal linear programming problem:

$$c_1v_1+c_2v_2+...+c_nv_n\to b_{jl} \quad (4.3a)$$

subject to

$$\left.\begin{array}{l} v_1+v_2+...+v_n=1\\ v_1,v_2,...,v_n\geq 0 \end{array}\right\}. \quad (4.4a)$$

Having obtained the solution $v_k, k=1,..,n$ of problem (4.3a)-(4.4a) for each $l=1,...,m$, recall that $v_k=p_{jl}(x_{jk}), k=1,..,n$. As a result, $p_{jl}(x_{jk}), k=1,..,n$ is found and, therefore, the probability distribution p_{jl} is obtained. Next, as p_{jl} is obtained given b_{jl}, then the desired membership degree is $\mu_{p_{jl}}(p_{jl})=\mu_{B_j}(b_{jl})$, $j=1,2$, that is $\mu_{p_{jl}}(p_{jl})=\mu_{B_j}\left(\sum_{k=1}^{n_j}\mu_{A_j}(x_{jk})p_{jl}(x_{jk})\right)$. Thus, to construct a fuzzy set of probability distributions p_{jl}, we need to solve n simple goal linear programming problems (4.3a)-(4.4a).

The fuzzy sets of probability distributions p_{1l} and p_{2l} induce the fuzzy set of convolutions p_{12s}, $s=1,...,m^2$, with the membership function defined as

$$\mu_{p_{12}}(p_{12}) = \max_{p_1,p_2}[\mu_{p_1}(p_1) \wedge \mu_{p_2}(p_2)] \qquad (4.5)$$

subject to $p_{12} = p_1 \circ p_2$, $\qquad\qquad\qquad\qquad\qquad\qquad$ (4.6)

where $\wedge$ is *min* operation.

At the next step we should compute probability measure of $A_{12} = A_1 + A_2$ given p_{12}, that is, to compute probability of the fuzzy event X *is* A_{12} on the base of Definition 4.1.

Thus, when p_{12} is known, $P(A_{12})$ is a number $P(A_{12})=b_{12}$. However, what is only known is a fuzzy restriction on p_{12} described by the membership function $\mu_{p_{12}}$. Therefore, $P(A_{12})$ will be a fuzzy set B_{12} with the membership function $\mu_{B_{12}}$ defined as follows:

$$\mu_{B_{12}}(b_{12s}) = \sup(\mu_{p_{12s}}(p_{12s})) \qquad (4.7)$$

subject to

$$b_{12s} = \sum_k p_{12s}(x_k)\mu_{A_{12}}(x_k). \qquad (4.8)$$

As a result, $Z_{12} = Z_1 + Z_2$ is obtained as $Z_{12} = (A_{12}, B_{12})$.

An example. Let us consider computation of an addition $Z_{12} = Z_1 + Z_2$ of two discrete Z-numbers $Z_1 = (A_1, B_1)$ and $Z_2 = (A_2, B_2)$, given:

$$A_1 = 0/1 + 0.3/2 + 0.5/3 + 0.6/4 + 0.7/5 + 0.8/6 + 0.9/7 + 1/8$$
$$+ 0.8/9 + 0.6/10 + 0/11,$$
$$B_1 = 0/0 + 0.5/0.1 + 0.8/0.2 + 1/0.3 + 0.8/0.4 + 0.7/0.5 + 0.6/0.6$$
$$+ 0.4/0.7 + 0.2/0.8 + 0.1/0.6 + 0/1;$$

$$A_2 = 0/1 + 0.5/2 + 0.8/3 + 1/4 + 0.8/5 + 0.7/6 + 0.6/7 + 0.4/8$$
$$+ 0.2/9 + 0.1/10 + 0/11,$$

$$B_2 = 0/0 + 0.3/0.1 + 0.5/0.2 + 0.6/0.3 + 0.7/0.4 + 0.8/0.5$$
$$+ 0.9/0.6 + 1/0.7 + 0.9/0.8 + 0.8/0.6 + 0/1.$$

At the *first step* of computation of Z_{12} we proceed to the discrete Z^+-numbers. Let us consider $Z_1^+ = (A_1, R_1)$ and $Z_2^+ = (A_2, R_2)$ where R_1 and R_2 are the following discrete probability distributions R_1 and R_2:

$$p_1 = 0.27 \backslash 1 + 0 \backslash 2 + 0 \backslash 3 + 0.0027 \backslash 4 + 0.04 \backslash 5 + 0.075 \backslash 6$$
$$+ 0.11 \backslash 7 + 0.15 \backslash 8 + 0.075 \backslash 9 + 0.0027 \backslash 10 + 0.27 \backslash 11,$$
$$p_2 = 0.09 \backslash 1 + 0 \backslash 2 + 0.18 \backslash 3 + 0.32 \backslash 4 + 0.18 \backslash 5 + 0.1 \backslash 6$$
$$+ 0.036 \backslash 7 + 0 \backslash 8 + 0 \backslash 9 + 0 \backslash 10 + 0.09 \backslash 11.$$

As one can verify, the constraints (4.1)-(4.2) are satisfied.

At the *second step* we should determine the discrete Z^+-number $Z_{12}^+ = (A_1 + A_2, R_1 + R_2)$. Here we first compute $A_{12} = A_1 + A_2$. In accordance with Definition 2.20 we have:

$$A_{12} = \bigcup_{\alpha \in [0,1]} \alpha A_{12}^\alpha,$$

$$A_{12}^\alpha = \{x \in \{\text{supp}(A_1) + \text{supp}(A_2)\} \mid \min\{A_1^\alpha + A_2^\alpha\} \le x \le \max\{A_1^\alpha + A_2^\alpha\}\}.$$

We will use $\alpha = 0, 0.1, \ldots, 1$. The resulting A_{12} is found as follows.

$$A_{12} = 0/1 + 0/2 + 0.19/3 + 0.36/4 + 0.5/5 + 0.58/6 + 0.65/7 + 0.73/8$$
$$+ 0.8/9 + 0.87/10 + 0.93/11 + 1/12 + 0.9/13 + 0.8/14 + 0.73/15$$
$$+ 0.7/16 + 0.6/17 + 0.45/18 + 0.3/19 + 0.17/20 + 0.086/21.$$

Next we compute $R_1 + R_2$ as a convolution $p_{12} = p_1 \circ p_2$ of the considered p_1 and p_2 is obtained by using (2.36).

For example, compute $p_{12}(x)$ for $x = 4$. The latter can be $x = x_{11} + x_{23} = 1 + 3 = 4$, $x = x_{13} + x_{21} = 3 + 1 = 4$ or $x = x_{12} + x_{22} = 2 + 2 = 4$. Then

$$p_{12}(4) = p_1(1)p_2(3) + p_1(3)p_2(1) + p_1(2)p_2(2) = 0.27 \cdot 0.18 + 0 \cdot 0.09$$
$$+ 0 \cdot 0 = 0.0486.$$

The p_{12} obtained in accordance with (2.36) is given below:

$$p_{12} = 0\backslash 1 + 0.0243\backslash 2 + 0\backslash 3 + 0.0486\backslash 4 + \ldots + 0.007\backslash 19$$
$$+ 0.0002\backslash 20 + 0.0243\backslash 21.$$

Thus, $Z_{12}^+ = (A_1 + A_2, R_1 + R_2) = (A_1 + A_2, p_{12})$ is obtained.

At the *third step* we realize, that 'true' probability distributions p_1 and p_2 are not exactly known, but only fuzzy restrictions μ_{p_1} and μ_{p_2} for p_1 and p_2 are available which are induced by B_1 and B_2 respectively. We compute the membership degrees $\mu_{p_j}(p_j)$, $j = 1, 2$, of the fuzzy restrictions given the solutions of the goal linear programming problems (4.3a)-(4.4a). Let us consider determination of the membership degrees $\mu_{p_1}(p_1)$ and $\mu_{p_2}(p_2)$ for distributions p_1 and p_2 considered above. It is known that $\mu_{p_1}(p_1) = \mu_{B_1}\left(\sum_{k=1}^{n_1} \mu_{A_1}(x_{1k})p_1(x_{1k})\right)$, and as for p_1 considered above we have

$$\sum_{k=1}^{n_1} \mu_{A_1}(x_{1k})p_1(x_{1k}) = 0 \cdot 0.27 + 0.3 \cdot 0 + 0.5 \cdot 0 + 0.6 \cdot 0.003$$

$$+ 0.7 \cdot 0.04 + 0.8 \cdot 0.075 + 0.9 \cdot 0.11 + 1 \cdot 0.15 + 0.8 \cdot 0.075$$
$$+ 0.6 \cdot 0.002 + 0 \cdot 0.27 = 0.4,$$

then $\mu_{p_1}(p_1) = \mu_{B_1}(0.4) = 0.8$. Analogously, we find that $\mu_{p_2}(p_2) = 1$ for p_2 considered above. Finally, we compute the membership degrees for all the considered p_1 and p_2.

At the *fourth step*, we should determine the fuzzy restriction $\mu_{p_{12}}$ over all the convolutions p_{12} obtained on the base of (4.5)-(4.6) from all the considered p_1 and p_2. It is clear that the fuzzy restriction $\mu_{p_{12}}$ is induced by fuzzy restrictions μ_{p_1} and μ_{p_2}. For example, the membership degree of this fuzzy restriction for the convolution p_{12} obtained above is

$$\mu_{p_{12}}(p_{12}) = \mu_{p_1}(p_1) \wedge \mu_{p_2}(p_2) = 0.8 \wedge 1 = 0.8.$$

Analogously, we computed the degrees for all the considered p_{12}.

At the *fifth step*, we should proceed to construction of B_{12} as a soft constraint on aprobability measure $P(A_{12})$ based on (4.7)-(4.8). First we compute values of probability measure $P(A_{12})$ based on Definition 4.1 by using the obtained convolutions p_{12}. For example, $P(A_{12})$ computed with respect to p_{12} considered above is

$$P(A_{12}) = \sum_{k=1}^{n_1} \mu_{A_{12}}(x_{12k}) p_{12}(x_{12k}) = 0 \cdot 0 + 0 \cdot 0.243 + 0.19 \cdot 0$$
$$+ 0.36 \cdot 0.0486 + 0.087 \cdot 0.5 + \dots + 0.086 \cdot 0.243 = 0.63.$$

As the computed $P(A_{12})$ is one possible value of probability measure within the fuzzy restriction B_{12} to be constructed, we can say that one basic value of B_{12} is found as $b_{12} = 0.63$.Now we recall that

$$\mu_{B_{12}}\left(b_{12} = \sum_k \mu_{A_{12}}(x_{12k}) p_{12}(x_{12k})\right) = \mu_{p_{12}}(p_{12}).$$ Then, given $\mu_{p_{12}}(p_{12}) = 0.8,$

we obtain $\mu_{B_{12}}(b_{12} = 0.63) = 0.8$ for $b_{12} = \sum_k \mu_{A_{12}}(x_{12k}) p_{12}(x_{12k})$. By carrying out analogous computations, we constructed B_{12} as follows:

$$B_{12} = 0/0.56 + 0.5/0.60 + 0.8/0.63 + 1/0.66 + 0.8/0.69 + 0.7/0.72$$
$$+ 0.6/0.75 + 0.4/0.78 + 0.2/0.81 + 0.1/0.84 + 0/0.86 + 0/1.$$

Thus, the result of addition $Z_{12} = (A_{12}, B_{12})$ is obtained, where A_{12}, B_{12} are shown in Fig. 4.4.

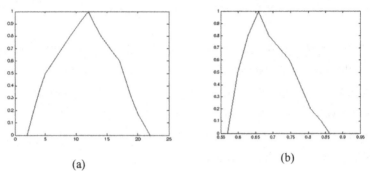

(a)   (b)

Fig. 4.4. The results of addition of the discrete Z-numbers: (a) A_{12}, (b) B_{12}.

4.1.4. *Standard Subtraction of Discrete Z-numbers*

Let us consider standard subtraction $Z_{12} = Z_1 - Z_2$ of discrete Z-numbers $Z_1 = (A_1, B_1)$ and $Z_2 = (A_2, B_2)$. First, a discrete Z^+-number $Z_{12}^+ = Z_1^+ - Z_2^+$ should be determined:

$$Z_1^+ - Z_2^+ = (A_1 - A_2, R_1 - R_2)$$

where R_1 and R_2 are represented by discrete probability distributions:

$$p_1 = p_1(x_{11}) \backslash x_{11} + p_1(x_{12}) \backslash x_{12} + \ldots + p_1(x_{1n}) \backslash x_{1n},$$

$$p_2 = p_2(x_{21}) \backslash x_{21} + p_2(x_{22}) \backslash x_{22} + \ldots + p_2(x_{2n}) \backslash x_{2n},$$

for which (4.1)-(4.2) are satisfied.

The standard subtraction $A_1 - A_2$ of discrete fuzzy numbers is defined in accordance with Definition 2.21 and $R_1 - R_2$ is a convolution $p_{12} = p_1 \circ p_2$ of discrete probability distributions defined in accordance with (2.37):

$$p_{12}(x) = \sum_{x = x_1 - x_2} p_1(x_1) p_2(x_2).$$

So, we will have Z_{12}^+ as $Z_{12}^+ = (A_1 - A_2, p_{12})$, which is the result of standard subtraction of discrete Z^+-numbers being the first step of standard subtraction of discrete Z-numbers.

At the *third step*, we should construct the fuzzy sets $\mu_{p_{jl}}(p_{jl}) =$

$\mu_{B_j}\left(\sum_{k=1}^{n_j} \mu_{A_j}(x_{jk}) p_{jl}(x_{jk})\right)$, $j = 1, 2$, $l = 1,...,m$ by solving (4.3a)-(4.4a).

Fourth, the fuzzy set of convolutions p_{12s}, $s = 1,...,m^2$, with the membership function constructed by solving (4.5)-(4.6), where convolution is computed according to (2.37).

At the *fifth step*, we proceed to construction of B_{12}. First we should compute probability measure of $A_{12} = A_1 - A_2$ given p_{12}, i.e. to compute probability of the fuzzy event X *is* A_{12} on the base of Definition 4.1. Finally, we compute a fuzzy set B_{12} according to (4.7)-(4.8). As a result, $Z_{12} = Z_1 - Z_2$ is obtained as $Z_{12} = (A_{12}, B_{12})$.

An example. Let us compute standard subtraction of the Z-numbers considered in the previous example. At the *first step* we proceed to the discrete Z^+ -numbers.

Second, we should calculate Z^+ -number $Z_{12}^+ = (A_{12}, R_{12}) = (A_1 - A_2, R_1 - R_2)$. First we compute $A_{12} = A_1 - A_2$. The resulting A_{12} is obtained by using α -cuts-based approach shown in Definition 2.21 as follows:

$$A_{12} = 0/-10 + 0.075/-9 + 0.15/-8 + 0.24/-7 + 0.35/-6 + 0.45/-5$$
$$+ 0.53/-4 + 0.6/-3 + 0.65/-2 + 0.7/-1 + 0/0.75 + 0.8/1 + 0.87/2$$
$$+ 0.93/3 + 1/4 + 0.9/5 + 0.8/6 + 0.68/7 + 0.53/8 + 0.27/9 + 0/10.$$

Next we compute $R_1 - R_2$ as a convolution $p_{12} = p_1 \circ p_1$ of distributions p_1 and p_2 which were considered in Section 4.1.3. p_{12} isobtained in accordance with (2.37). For example, let us compute $p_{12}(x)$ for $x = -5$. The latter can be $x = x_{1,5} - x_{2,10} = 5 - 10 = -5$, or $x = x_{1,6} - x_{2,11} = 6 - 11 = -5$. Then we have:

$$p_{12}(5) = p_1(5)p_2(10) + p_1(6)p_2(11) = 0.04 \cdot 0 + 0.075 \cdot 0.09 = 0.00675.$$

The computed p_{12} is given below:

$$p_{12} = 0.025 \backslash -10 + 0 \backslash -9 + 0 \backslash -8 + 0 \backslash -7 + 0.0135 \backslash -6$$
$$+ 0.00675 \backslash -5 + ... + 0.243 \backslash 10.$$

Thus, $Z_{12}^+ = (A_1 - A_2, p_{12})$ is obtained.

At the *third step* it is needed to compute membership degrees $\mu_{p_1}(p_1)$ and $\mu_{p_2}(p_2)$ for the fuzzy restrictions over distributions p_1 and p_2. These degrees were determined previously in Section 4.1.3.

At the *fourth step*, we compute the membership degrees $\mu_{p_{12}}(p_{12})$ of the convolutions p_{12}. Let us mention that these degrees depend only on the degrees $\mu_{p_1}(p_1)$ and $\mu_{p_2}(p_2)$ of distributions p_1 and p_2 from which p_{12} is obtained and does not depend on a type of arithmetic operation. Therefore, they will be obtained analogously to the case of addition. Indeed, the membership degree of p_{12} obtained above is $\mu_{p_{12}}(p_{12}) = 0.8$.

At the *fifth step*, we proceed to construction of B_{12}. First, by using Definition 4.1, we compute values of probability measure $P(A_{12})$ with respect to the obtained convolutions p_{12}. For example, $P(A_{12})$ computed based on p_{12} considered above is

$$P(A_{12}) = \sum_k \mu_{A_{12}}(x_k) p_{12}(x_k) = 0 \cdot 0 + 0 \cdot 0.243 + 0.19 \cdot 0$$
$$+ 0.36 \cdot 0.0486 + 0.087 \cdot 0.5 + ... + 0.086 \cdot 0.243 = 0.71.$$

Therefore, one basic value of B_{12} is found as $b_{12} = 0.63$ with $\mu_{B_{12}}(b_{12} = 0.71) = 0.8$.

At the *final stage*, we construct B_{12} based on (4.7)-(4.8). The constructed B_{12} is given below:

$$B_{12} = 0/0.59 + 0.5/0.62 + 0.8/0.65 + 1/0.68 + 0.8/0.71 + 0.7/0.74$$
$$+ 0.6/0.77 + 0.4/0.8 + 0.2/0.83 + 0.1/0.86 + 0/0.88.$$

Thus, $Z_{12} = (A_{12}, B_{12})$ is obtained as the result of subtraction and

A_{12}, B_{12} are shown in Fig. 4.5.

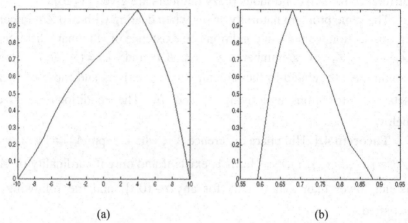

(a) (b)

Fig. 4.5. The result of standard subtraction of the discrete Z-numbers: (a) A_{12}, (b) B_{12}.

4.1.5. *Hukuhara Difference of Discrete Z-numbers*

As it is known, in general case, for three fuzzy numbers or intervals (continuous or discrete) C_1, C_2, C_3 satisfying

$$C_1 = C_2 + C_3,$$

one has

$$C_3 \neq C_1 - C_2,$$

where "–" denotes standard subtraction.

Therefore, it is needed to have a type of subtraction operation which removes this problem to represent pure concept of difference. This operation is necessary to define derivative of fuzzy set-valued mappings, dealing with difference equations and other purposes. For this aim, Hukuhara suggested the concept of Hukuhara difference [70]:

$$C_3 = C_1 -_h C_2 \Leftrightarrow C_1 = C_2 + C_3.$$

It is also well known that not for any two fuzzy numbers C_1, C_2 the

Hukuhara difference exists. The conditions for existence of the Hukuhara difference for two continuous fuzzy numbers are given in [26].

The same problem naturally arises when dealing with two Z-numbers. In this section we present conditions on existence of Hukuhara difference $Z_{12} = Z_1 -_h Z_2$ of Z-numbers $Z_1 = (A_1, B_1)$ and $Z_2 = (A_2, B_2)$. These conditions are related to the structures of A_1 and A_2 and those of fuzzy sets of distributions underlying B_1 and B_2. The conditions are given below.

Theorem 4.1. Hukuhara difference A_{12}, where $\operatorname{supp}(A_{12}) = \{x_1, \ldots, x_k\}$, $A_{12}^\alpha = \{x_{l_\alpha}, \ldots, x_{r_\alpha}\}$, $l_\alpha, r_\alpha \in \{1, \ldots, k\}$, exists if and only if cardinality of A_1^α is not lower than that of A_2^α for any $\alpha \in (0,1]$, and the following is satisfied:

$$A_1^\alpha = \bigcup_{i=1}^{r_\alpha - l_\alpha + 1} A_{1,i}^\alpha, \tag{4.9}$$

where $A_{1,i}^\alpha = \{x_{1\,i,1}^\alpha, \ldots, x_{1\,i,m}^\alpha\}$, $x_{1\,i,j+1}^\alpha - x_{1\,i,j}^\alpha = x_{2,j+1}^\alpha - x_{2,j}^\alpha$, $j = 1, \ldots, m$; $\alpha \in (0,1]$.

Proof. Denote $\operatorname{supp}(A_1) = \{x_{11}, \ldots, x_{1n}\}$, $A_1^\alpha = \{x_{1\,1_\alpha}^\alpha, \ldots, x_{1\,n_\alpha}^\alpha\}$, $1_\alpha, n_\alpha \in \{1, \ldots, n\}$ and $\operatorname{supp}(A_2) = \{x_{21}, \ldots, x_{2m}\}$, $A_2^\alpha = \{x_{2\,1_\alpha}^\alpha, \ldots, x_{2\,m_\alpha}^\alpha\}$, $1_\alpha, m_\alpha \in \{1, \ldots, m\}$. Let us show that from (4.9) it follows that Hukuhara difference A_{12} exists and vice versa. From $x_{1\,i,j+1}^\alpha - x_{1\,i,j}^\alpha = x_{2,j+1}^\alpha - x_{2,j}^\alpha$ it can be easily found that $x_{1\,i,j+1}^\alpha = x_{2,j+1}^\alpha + (x_{1\,i1}^\alpha - x_{2,1}^\alpha)$. Indeed, for $j = 1$ the following holds:

$$x_{1\,i,2}^\alpha = x_{1\,i,1}^\alpha + (x_{2,2}^\alpha - x_{2,1}^\alpha) = x_{2,2}^\alpha + (x_{1\,i,1}^\alpha - x_{2,1}^\alpha).$$

Then, for $j = 2$ we have:

$$x_{1\,i,3}^\alpha = x_{1\,i,2}^\alpha + (x_{2,3}^\alpha - x_{2,2}^\alpha) = x_{1\,i,1}^\alpha + (x_{2,2}^\alpha - x_{2,1}^\alpha) + (x_{2,3}^\alpha - x_{2,2}^\alpha)$$

$$= x_{2,3}^\alpha + (x_{1\,i,1}^\alpha - x_{2,1}^\alpha)$$

Therefore,

$$x^{\alpha}_{1\ i,j+1} = x^{\alpha}_{2,j+1} + (x^{\alpha}_{1\ i,1} - x^{\alpha}_{2,1}).$$

Taking into account that $x^{\alpha}_{1\ i,1} = x^{\alpha}_{2,1} + (x^{\alpha}_{1\ i,1} - x^{\alpha}_{2,1})$, we can write:

$$\{x^{\alpha}_{1\ i1},...,x^{\alpha}_{1\ im}\} = \{x^{\alpha}_{2\ 1_{\alpha}},...,x^{\alpha}_{2\ m_{\alpha}}\} + c^{\alpha}_i,$$

where $c^{\alpha}_i = (x^{\alpha}_{1\ i,1} - x^{\alpha}_{2,1})$. Thus ,

$$A^{\alpha}_{1,i} = A^{\alpha}_2 + c^{\alpha}_i.$$

Therefore,

$$A^{\alpha}_1 = \bigcup_{i=1}^{s} A^{\alpha}_{1,i} = \bigcup_{i=1}^{s}\left(A^{\alpha}_2 + c^{\alpha}_i\right)$$
$$= A^{\alpha}_2 + \{c^{\alpha}_1,...,c^{\alpha}_s\}.$$

Taking into account that as $A^{\alpha''}_1 \subseteq A^{\alpha'}_1$, one has $\{c^{\alpha''}_1,...,c^{\alpha''}_s\} \subseteq \{c^{\alpha'}_1,...,c^{\alpha'}_s\}$ for $\alpha'' \geq \alpha'$, $\alpha'',\alpha' \in (0,1]$. Thus, we can say that $\{c^{\alpha}_1,...,c^{\alpha}_s\}$ is an α -cut of some discrete fuzzy number c . Then $A_1 = A_2 + C$. Therefore, c is the Hukuhara difference $C = A_1 -_h A_2 = A_{12}$. The proof is complete. The proof of the opposite direction of Theorem 4.1 is obvious.

Now we need to uncover necessary conditions of existence of B_{12} .

Lemma. Hukuhara difference $Z_{12} = Z_1 -_h Z_2$ of Z-numbers $Z_1 = (A_1, B_1)$ and $Z_2 = (A_2, B_2)$ exists if the of cardinality of B^{α}_1 is not smaller to that of B^{α}_2 , $\forall \alpha \in (0,1]$.

Proof. Any element $b_j \in B^{\alpha}_j, j = 1,2$ is obtained as a probability measure of A_j , $P(A_j) = \sum_{i=1}^{n} \mu_{A_1}(x_{ji})p_j(x_{ji})$, based on at least one probability distribution p_j . In other words, any element $b_j \in B^{\alpha}_j, j = 1,2$ is induced by some probability distribution p_j .

According to $\mu_{p_j}(p_j) = \mu_{B_j}\left(\sum_{k=1}^{n_j} \mu_{A_j}(x_{jk})p_j(x_{jk})\right)$, for this p_1 we have

$\mu_{p_1}(p_1) \geq \alpha$. At the same time, we have $\mu_{p_2}(p_2) \geq \alpha$ and $\mu_{p_{12}}(p_{12}) \geq \alpha$. Therefore, any p_1 which induces $b_1 \in B_1^\alpha$ is obtained from p_2 which induces $b_2 \in B_2^\alpha$ and p_{12} which induces $b_{12} \in B_{12}^\alpha$: $p_1 = p_2 \circ p_{12}$. The number of convolutions p_1 is naturally not smaller than that of distributions p_2. Therefore, the cardinality of B_1^α is not smaller than that of B_2^α, $\forall \alpha \in (0,1]$. The proof is complete.

Let us now consider the procedures underlying computation of Hukuhara difference $Z_{12} = Z_1 -_h Z_2$ of Z-numbers $Z_1 = (A_1, B_1)$ and $Z_2 = (A_2, B_2)$. Hukuhara difference $Z_{12} = Z_1 -_h Z_2$ exists only if Hukuhara difference $A_{12} = A_1 -_h A_2$ (see Definition 2.22) exists. Suppose that $A_{12} = A_1 -_h A_2$ exists. Then, $A_{12}^\alpha, \alpha \in (0,1]$ will be computed as

$$A_{12}^\alpha = \bigcup_{i=1}^{r_\alpha - l_\alpha + 1} \left(A_{1,i}^\alpha -_h A_2^\alpha\right)$$

$$= \bigcup_{i=1}^{r_\alpha - l_\alpha + 1} \left(\{x_{1\,i1}^\alpha, \ldots, x_{1\,im}^\alpha\} -_h \{x_{2\,1_\alpha}^\alpha, \ldots, x_{2\,m_\alpha}^\alpha\}\right)$$

$$= \bigcup_{i=1}^{r_\alpha - l_\alpha + 1} \left(x_{1\,i1}^\alpha - x_{2\,1_\alpha}^\alpha\right)$$

$$= \bigcup_{i=1}^{r_\alpha - l_\alpha + 1} \left(x_{1\,im}^\alpha - x_{2\,m_\alpha}^\alpha\right)$$

A_{12} is then obtained as $A_{12} = \bigcup_\alpha \alpha A_{12}^\alpha$. Next it is needed to compute B_{12}. This requires to determine $\mu_{p_{12}}()$. The latter in turn requires determination of all the distributions p_{12}. The determination of p_{12} is implemented as follows. It is known that

$$p_1(x_1) = \sum_{x = x_{2i} + x_{12j}} p_2(x_{2i})p_{12}(x_{12j}).$$

Therefore, given $p_2(x_2)$ and $p_1(x_{1i})$ the problem of determination of $p_{12}(x_{12})$ can be formalized as follows:

$$
\begin{cases}
p_{12}(x_{12,1})a_{11} + p_{12}(x_{12,2})a_{12} + ... + p_{12}(x_{12,n})a_{1n} = p_1(x_{11}) \\
p_{12}(x_{12,1})a_{21} + p_{12}(x_{12,2})a_{22} + ... + p_{12}(x_{12,n})a_{2n} = p_1(x_{12}) \\
\cdot \\
\cdot \\
\cdot \\
p_{12}(x_{12,1})a_{i1} + p_{12}(x_{12,2})a_{i2} + ... + p_{12}(x_{12,n})a_{in} = p_1(x_{1i}) \quad , \\
\cdot \\
\cdot \\
\cdot \\
p_{12}(x_{12,1})a_{n1} + p_{12}(x_{12,2})a_{n2} + ... + p_{12}(x_{12,n})a_{nn} = p_1(x_{1n}) \\
p_{12}(x_{12,1}) + p_{12}(x_{12,2}) + ... + p_{12}(x_{12,n}) = 1
\end{cases}
\tag{4.10}
$$

where

$$
a_{ij} = \begin{cases} p_2(x_{2j}) \ if \ x_{1i} = x_{2j} + x_{12,j} \\ 0, otherwise \end{cases} ; i = 1,...,n; \ j = 1,...,n.
$$

Now, denote $u_1 = p_{12}(x_{12,1}),...,u_n = p_{12}(x_{12,n})$ and $w_i = p_1(x_{1i})$, $i = 1,..,n$. As $u_1,...,u_n$ are unknown variables and w_j are known values, we see that (4.10) is nothing but the following system of linear algebraic equations:

$$\begin{cases} u_1 a_{11} + u_2 a_{12} + \ldots + u_n a_{1n} = w_1 \\ u_1 a_{21} + u_2 a_{22} + \ldots + u_n a_{2n} = w_2 \\ \cdot \\ \cdot \\ \cdot \\ u_1 a_{i1} + u_2 a_{i2} + \ldots + u_n a_{in} = w_i \quad , \\ \cdot \\ \cdot \\ \cdot \\ u_1 a_{n1} + u_2 a_{n2} + \ldots + u_n a_{nn} = w_n \\ u_1 + u_2 + \ldots + u_n = 1 \end{cases} \qquad (4.11)$$

It is known that the system (4.11) has a unique solution when $Rg(A) = Rg(A^*)=n$, where

$$A = \left\| \begin{matrix} a_{11}, a_{12}, \ldots, a_{1n} \\ a_{21}, a_{22}, \ldots, a_{2n} \\ \cdot \\ \cdot \\ \cdot \\ a_{i1}, a_{i2}, \ldots, a_{in} \\ \cdot \\ \cdot \\ a_{n1}, a_{n2}, \ldots, a_{nn} \\ 1, 1, \ldots, 1 \end{matrix} \right\| ,$$

$$A^* = \begin{Vmatrix} a_{11}, a_{12}, ..., a_{1n}, w_1 \\ a_{21}, a_{22}, ..., a_{2n}, w_2 \\ \cdot \\ \cdot \\ a_{i1}, a_{i2}, ..., a_{in}, w_i \\ \cdot \\ \cdot \\ a_{n1}, a_{n2}, ..., a_{nn}, w_n \\ 1, 1, ..., 1, 1 \end{Vmatrix} .$$

The solution $u_1, u_2, ..., u_n$ of system (4.11) is nothing but p_{12}. If the number of distributions p_1 is N and the number of distributions p_2 is M then the number of problems (4.11) is equal to $N*M$. Let us mention that not all of them will have the exact solution p_{12}. The issue is that not for all pairs of p_1 and p_2, there exists p_{12} satisfying $p_1 = p_2 \circ p_{12}$. However, for any p_1 there is such p_2, that the exact solution p_{12} to (4.11) exists. The number of the exact solutions is naturally $K=N/M$. Indeed, the number of convolutions p_1, N, is $N= K*M$. As any p_{12} to be found convolves with the all distributions p_2, it will repeat as the exact solution to (4.11) M times. Thus, $\mu_{p_{12}}(p_{12})$ should be found as

$$\mu_{p_{12}}(p_{12}) = \max_{\{p_1, p_2 | p_1 = p_2 \circ p_{12}\}} \min\{\mu_{p_1}(p_1), \mu_{p_2}(p_2)\} .$$

That is, max is taken over all the M cases when the same exact solution p_{12} to (4.11) repeats.

Finally, given $\mu_{p_{12}}()$ one can construct B_{12} by solving the problem analogous to (4.7)-(4.8). Thus, $Z_{12} = (A_{12}, B_{12})$ will be obtained. Let us mention that under $\mu_{p_{12}}(p_{12}) = \mu_{p_2}(p_2)$ condition, the minimal fuzzy set B_{12} will be found.

An example. Let us consider the Z-numbers $Z_1 = (A_1, B_1)$ and $Z_2 = (A_2, B_2)$ (Figs. 4.6, 4.7):

$$A_1 = 0.1/2 + 0.1/4 + 0.1/5 + 0.1/6 + 0.1/7 + 0.8/9 + 0.8/10$$
$$+ 0.8/11 + 1/12 + 0.8/13 + 0.8/14 + 0.1/15 + 0.1/16$$
$$+ 0.1/17 + 0.1/19 + 0.1/20 + 0.1/22,$$

$$B_1 = 0.1/0.589 + 0.1/0.594 + 0.1/0.616 + 0.1/0.623 + 0.8/0.664$$
$$+ 0.8/0.686 + 0.8/0.703 + 0.8/0.706 + 0.8/0.734 + 0.8/0.783$$
$$+ 0.8/0.784 + 1/0.795 + 0.8/0.799 + 0.8/0.800 + 0.8/0.835$$
$$+ 0.8/0.850 + 0.8/0.862 + 0.8/0.875 + 0.1/0.900 + 0.1/0.950;$$

$$A_2 = 0/1 + 0.8/3 + 1/4 + 0.8/5 + 0.1/11,$$

$$B_2 = 0.1/0.8 + 0.8/0.85 + 1/0.9 + 0.8/0.9 + 0.8/0.95.$$

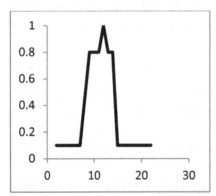 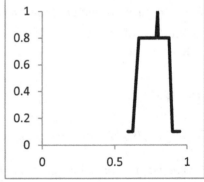

Fig. 4.6. Z-number $Z_1 = (A_1, B_1)$.

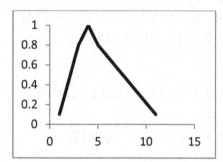 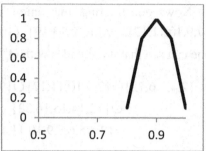

Fig. 4.7. Z-number $Z_2 = (A_2, B_2)$.

Let us verify whether the Hukuhara difference $Z_{12} = Z_1 -_h Z_2$ exists. First we should verify whether $A_{12} = A_1 -_h A_2$ exists. In accordance with Theorem 4.1, this is the case when for each $\alpha \in (0,1]$ cardinality of A_1^α is not lower than that of A_2^α and the A_1^α is the union of discrete sets which follow the same spacing pattern as A_2^α. Consider $\alpha = 0.1$:

$$A_1^{\alpha=0.1} = \{2,4,5,6,7,9,10,11,12,13,14,15,16,17,19,20,22\},$$

$$A_2^{\alpha=0.1} = \{1,3,4,5,11\}.$$

The spacing of $A_2^{\alpha=0.1}$ is: 3-1=**2**; 4-3=**1**; 5-4=**1**; 11-5=**6**. Let us verify whether there are sets in $A_1^{\alpha=0.1}$ which follow the same spacing pattern. We start with the first element of $A_1^{\alpha=0.1}$ which is 2. Adding to this element consequtively 2,1,1,6 and obtaining the results, we will check whether the obtained numbers are in $A_1^{\alpha=0.1}$. Thus, the first result is 2+2=4, the second is 4+1=5, the third is 5+1=6, the fourth is 6+6=12. Therefore, together with the first element 2 we have 4,5,6,12: $\{2,4,5,6,12\}$. As one can see, the resulting set is a subset of $A_1^{\alpha=0.1}$: $\{2,4,5,6,12\} \subset A_1^{\alpha=0.1}$. Analogously, we have found that there are other sets in $A_1^{\alpha=0.1}$ which follow the same spacing pattern as that of $A_2^{\alpha=0.1}$:

$$\{7,9,10,11,17\}, \{9,11,12,13,19\}, \{10,12,13,14,20\}, \{12,14,15,16,22\}.$$

Now, constructing the union of the discrete sets $\{2,4,5,6,12\}$, $\{7,9,10,11,17\}$, $\{9,11,12,13,19\}$, $\{10,12,13,14,20\}$, $\{12,14,15,16,22\}$, one can see that it coincides with $A_1^{\alpha=0.1}$:

$$\{2,4,5,6,12\} \cup \{7,9,10,11,17\} \cup \{9,11,12,13,19\} \cup \{10,12,13,14,20\}$$
$$\cup \{12,14,15,16,22\}$$
$$= \{2,4,5,6,7,9,10,11,12,13,14,15,16,17,19,20,22\}$$

Therefore, the Hukuhara difference $A_1^{\alpha=0.1} -_h A_2^{\alpha=0.1}$ between a-cuts $A_1^{\alpha=0.1}$ and $A_2^{\alpha=0.1}$ exists and is equal to $A_1^{\alpha=0.1} -_h A_2^{\alpha=0.1} = \{1,6,8,9,11\}$. Indeed, we have

$$\{2,4,5,6,12\} = A_2^{\alpha=0.1} + 1 = \{1,3,4,5,11\} + 1,$$

$$\{7,9,10,11,17\} = A_2^{\alpha=0.1} + 6 = \{1,3,4,5,11\} + 6,$$

$$\{9,11,12,13,19\} = A_2^{\alpha=0.1} + 8 = \{1,3,4,5,11\} + 8,$$

$$\{10,12,13,14,20\} = A_2^{\alpha=0.1} + 9 = \{1,3,4,5,11\} + 9,$$

$$\{12,14,15,16,22\} = A_2^{\alpha=0.1} + 11 = \{1,3,4,5,11\} + 11.$$

That is, $A_2^{\alpha=0.1} + \{1,6,8,9,11\} = A_1^{\alpha=0.1}$.

By using analogous procedures we found out that the Hukuhara difference exists for all $\alpha \in (0,1]$:

$$A_2^{\alpha=0.8} + \{6,8,9\} = A_1^{\alpha=0.8}, \quad A_1^{\alpha=0.8} -_h A_2^{\alpha=0.8} = \{6,8,9\},$$

$$A_2^{\alpha=1} + \{6,8,9\} = A_1^{\alpha=1}, \quad A_1^{\alpha=1} -_h A_2^{\alpha=1} = \{8\}.$$

Therefore, the Hukuhara difference $A_{12} = A_1 -_h A_2$ exists:

$$A_{12} = A_1 -_h A_2 = 0.1\big/1 + 0.8\big/6 + 1\big/8 + 0.8\big/9 + 0.1\big/11.$$

Now we should verify whether there exists such B_{12} that:

$$Z_{12} = Z_1 -_h Z_2 = (A_1,B_1) -_h (A_2,B_2) = (A_{12},B_{12}).$$

This requires to determine whether there exist such distributions p_{12} that (4.11) is satisfied. Therefore, let us consider all possible pairs of distributions p_1 and p_2 to determine for which pairs there exist distributions p_{12} satisfying (4.11). For example, let us consider the following distributions:

$$p_1 = 0\backslash 2 + 0.053292\backslash 4 + 0.056285\backslash 5 + 0.047351\backslash 6 + 0\backslash 7$$
$$+ 0.068214\backslash 9 + 0.072046\backslash 10 + +0.125626\backslash 11 + 0.152964\backslash 12$$
$$+ 0.129814\backslash 13 + 0.113902\backslash 14 + 0.056285\backslash 15 + 0.047351\backslash 16$$
$$+ 0.020584\backslash 17 + 0.019619\backslash 19 + 0.020584\backslash 20 + 0.016081\backslash 22,$$

$$p_2 = 0\backslash 1 + 0.30803\backslash 3 + 0.32533\backslash 4 + 0.27369\backslash 5 + 0.09295\backslash 11.$$

Then (4.11) will have the form:

$$\begin{cases} u_1 \cdot 0 = 0 \\ u_1 \cdot 0.3083 = 0,053292 \\ \cdot \\ \cdot \\ \cdot \\ u_2 \cdot 0.3083 + u_3 \cdot 0 = 0.068214, \\ \cdot \\ \cdot \\ \cdot \\ u_5 \cdot 0.09295 = 0.016081 \\ u_1 + u_2 + u_3 + u_4 + u_5 = 1 \end{cases}$$

where $u_1 = p_{12}(x_{12,1}), u_2 = p_{12}(x_{12,2}), ..., u_5 = p_{12}(x_{12,5})$.

For this system of equations, we have found p_{12} as its exact solution:

$$p_{12} = 0.17301\backslash 1 + 0.22145\backslash 6 + 0.21107\backslash 8 + 0.22145\backslash 9 + 0.17301\backslash 11.$$

Now we should verify whether p_{12} exactly satisfies (4.11).

Substituting values of p_{12} into the left part of (4.11) we found that the right part coincides with p_1 exactly. Thusm for the considered p_1 and p_2, there exists p_{12} such that $p_1 = p_2 \circ p_{12}$. We have found that for the considered p_1 and any other p_2, there does not exists p_{12} which exactly satisfies (4.11). In general, for any distribution p_1, there exists a unique p_2 such that an exact solution p_{12} to (4.11) exists. By using the same procedures for all the distributions p_1, we found the corresponding exact solutions p_{12} of (4.11).

As the numbers of distributions p_1 and p_2 are $N=25$ and $M=5$ respectively, the number of the obtained distributions p_{12} is 5. The obtained p_{12} and the membership degrees $\mu_{p_{12}}(p_{12})$ are given below:

$$p_{12} = 0.0817 \backslash 1 + 0.249 \backslash 6 + 0.28 \backslash 8 + 0.249 \backslash 9 + 0.14 \backslash 11,$$

$$\mu_{p_{12}}(p_{12}) = 0.1;$$

$$p_{12} = 0.17301 \backslash 1 + 0.221453 \backslash 6 + 0.211073 \backslash 8 + 0.221453 \backslash 9 + 0.17301 \backslash 11,$$
$$\mu_{p_{12}}(p_{12}) = 0.8 ;$$

$$p_{12} = 0 \backslash 1 + 0.30803 \backslash 6 + 0.32533 \backslash 8 + 0.27369 \backslash 9 + 0.09295 \backslash 11,$$
$$\mu_{p_{12}}(p_{12}) = 1 ;$$

$$p_{12} = 0 \backslash 1 + 0.22361 \backslash 6 + 0.5 \backslash 8 + 0.27369 \backslash 9 + 0 \backslash 11,$$

$$\mu_{p_{12}}(p_{12}) = 0.8;$$

$$p_{12} = 0 \backslash 1 + 0 \backslash 6 + 1 \backslash 8 + 0 \backslash 9 + 0 \backslash 11,$$

$$\mu_{p_{12}}(p_{12}) = 0.1.$$

Therefore, given A_{12} and the fuzzy set of distributions p_{12} described by membership function $\mu_{p_{12}}$ we can construct B_{12} by solving the problem analogous to (4.7)-(4.8) . The obtained B_{12} is shown below:

$$B_{12} = 0.1/0.6 + 0.8/0.7 + 1/0.8 + 0.8/0.9 + 0.1/1.$$

The obtained $Z_{12} = (A_{12}, B_{12})$ is shown in Fig. 4.8.

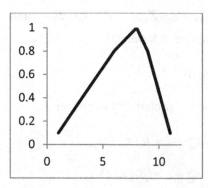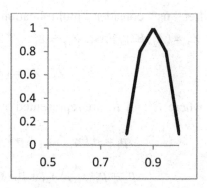

Fig. 4.8. Z-number $Z_{12} = (A_{12}, B_{12})$.

We have checked the obtained result by computing addition of Z_{12} and Z_2: $Z = Z_2 + Z_{12}$. The resulting Z-number $Z = (A, B)$ coincides with the Z-number Z_1:

$$A = 0.1/2 + 0.1/4 + 0.1/5 + 0.1/6 + 0.1/7 + 0.8/9 + 0.8/10$$
$$+ 0.8/11 + 1/12 + 0.8/13 + 0.8/14 + 0.1/15 + 0.1/16 + 0.1/17$$
$$+ 0.1/19 + 0.1/20 + 0.1/22,$$

$$B = 0.1/0.589 + 0.1/0.594 + 0.1/0.616 + 0.1/0.623 + 0.8/0.664$$
$$+ 0.8/0.686 + 0.8/0.703 + 0.8/0.706 + 0.8/0.734 + 0.8/0.783$$
$$+ 0.8/0.784 + 1/0.795 + 0.8/0.799 + 0.8/0.800 + 0.8/0.835$$
$$+ 0.8/0.850 + 0.8/0.862 + 0.8/0.875$$
$$+ 0.1/0.900 + 0.1/0.950.$$

Therefore, the result of computation of Hukuhara difference is valid.

4.1.6. *Multiplication of Discrete Z-numbers*

Let us consider multiplication $Z_{12} = Z_1 \cdot Z_2$ of $Z_1 = (A_1, B_1)$ and $Z_2 = (A_2, B_2)$. First, $Z_{12}^+ = Z_1^+ \cdot Z_2^+$ should be determined:

$$Z_1^+ \cdot Z_2^+ = (A_1 \cdot A_2, R_1 \cdot R_2),$$

where R_1 and R_2 are represented by discrete probability distributions:

$$p_1 = p_1(x_{11}) \setminus x_{11} + p_1(x_{12}) \setminus x_{12} + \ldots + p_1(x_{1n}) \setminus x_{1n},$$

$$p_2 = p_2(x_{21}) \setminus x_{21} + p_2(x_{22}) \setminus x_{22} + \ldots + p_2(x_{2n}) \setminus x_{2n},$$

for which (4.1)-(4.2) are satisfied. The product $A_1 \cdot A_2$ of discrete fuzzy numbers is defined in accordance with Definition 2.23 and $R_1 \cdot R_2$ is a convolution $p_{12} = p_1 \circ p_2$ of discrete probability distributions defined in accordance with (2.38):

$$p_{12}(x) = \sum_{x = x_1 \cdot x_2} p_1(x_1) p_2(x_{2j}).$$

Thus, we will have $Z_{12}^+ = (A_1 \cdot A_2, p_{12})$. Next, analogously to the procedure described in Section 4.1.3, we construct the fuzzy sets $\mu_{p_{jl}}(p_{jl})$, $l = 1, \ldots, m$, and the fuzzy set of convolutions p_{12s}, $s = 1, \ldots, m^2$, with the membership function defined by (4.5)-(4.6) and a convolution defined according to (2.38).

At the next step probability measure of $A_{12} = A_1 \cdot A_2$ is computed on the base of Definition 4.1. Finally, a fuzzy set B_{12} is constructed according to (4.7)-(4.8). As a result, $Z_{12} = Z_1 \cdot Z_2$ is obtained as $Z_{12} = (A_{12}, B_{12})$.

An example. Let us consider multiplication of the Z-numbers considered in Section 4.1.3. Again, *first* we proceed to the discrete Z^+ -numbers. *Second*, we should calculate $Z_{12}^+ = (A_{12}, R_{12}) = (A_1 \cdot A_2, R_1 \cdot R_2)$. In accordance with the approach described above, we compute $A_{12} = A_1 \cdot A_2$ on the base of Definition 2.23 and $R_1 \cdot R_2$ as a convolution of p_1 and p_2

(taken the same as in the case of addition) on the base of (2.38). The results (obtained analogously to the procedures used previously for addition and subtraction)are shown below:

$$A_{12} = 0/1 + 0.16/2 + ... + 1/32 + ... + 0.17/100 + 0/121.$$

$$p_{12} = 0.243 \backslash 1 + 0 \backslash 2 + ... + 0 \backslash 100 + 0.243 \backslash 121.$$

As a result, $Z_{12}^+ = (A_1 \cdot A_2, p_{12})$ is obtained.

Third, we compute membership degrees $\mu_{p_1}(p_1)$ and $\mu_{p_2}(p_2)$. *Fourth*, the membership degrees of the convolutions p_{12} are obtained on the basis of $\mu_{p_1}(p_1)$ and $\mu_{p_2}(p_2)$ analogously to the cases of addition.

Fifth, we compute B_{12}. For thispurpose, we compute values of probability measure $P(A_{12})$ with respect to the obtained convolutions p_{12} (Definition 4.1). For example, $P(A_{12})$ computed for p_{12} considered above is

$$P(A_{12}) = b_{12} = 0.67.$$

At the final stage, we construct B_{12} based on (4.7)-(4.8). For example, $\mu_{B_{12}}(b_{12} = 0.67) = 0.8$. The constructed B_{12} is given below:

$$B_{12} = 0/0.54 + 0.5/0.57 + 0.8/0.61 + 1/0.63 + 0.8/0.67 + 0.7/0.7 + 0.6/0.73$$
$$+ 0.4/0.76 + 0.2/0.79 + 0.1/0.819 + 0/0.82.$$

Thus, $Z_{12} = (A_{12}, B_{12})$ as the result of multiplication is obtained and A_{12}, B_{12} are shown in Fig. 4.9.

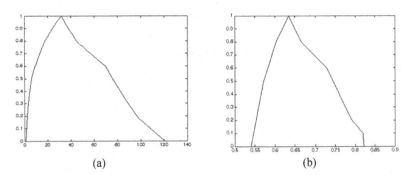

Fig. 4.9. The results of multiplication of the discrete Z-numbers: (a) A_{12}, (b) B_{12}.

4.1.7. *Standard Division of Discrete Z-numbers*

Let us consider standard division $Z_{12} = Z_1 / Z_2$ of discrete Z-numbers $Z_1 = (A_1, B_1)$ and $Z_2 = (A_2, B_2)$, $0 \notin \text{supp}(A_2)$. First, $Z_{12}^+ = (A_{12}, p_{12})$ is determined:

$$Z_{12}^+ = (A_{12}, p_{12}),$$

where the standard division $A_{12} = A_1 / A_2$ of discrete fuzzy numbers is defined in accordance with Definition 2.24 and a convolution $p_{12} = p_1 \circ p_2$ of discrete probability distributions is defined in accordance with (2.39):

$$p_{12}(x) = \sum_{\substack{x = x_1 / x_2, \\ x_2 \neq 0}} p_1(x_1) p_2(x_2).$$

Next, analogously to the procedure described in Section 4.1.3, we construct the fuzzy sets $\mu_{p_{jl}}(p_{jl})$, $j = 1, 2$, $l = 1, ..., m$ and the fuzzy set of convolutions p_{12s}, $s = 1, ..., m^2$, with the membership function defined by solving (4.5)-(4.6), where convolution is defined according to (2.39).

At the next step probability measure of A_{12} is computed on the base of Definition 4.1. Finally, a fuzzy set B_{12} is constructed according to (4.7)-(4.8) . As a result, $Z_{12} = Z_1 / Z_2$ is obtained as $Z_{12} = (A_{12}, B_{12})$.

An example. Let us consider standard division of the considered Z-numbers. Again, first we should calculate $Z_{12}^+ = (A_{12}, R_{12}) = \left(A_1 / A_2, R_1 / R_2 \right)$, where R_1 and R_2 are taken as in the case of addition. In accordance with the approach described above, we compute $A_{12} = A_1 / A_2$ on the base of Definition 2.24 and compute R_1 / R_2 as a convolution $p_{12} = p_1 \circ p_2$ on the base of (2.39). The obtained results are shown below:

$$A_{12} = 0.07/0.36 + 0.1/0.375 + ... + 1/1.6 + ... + 0.17/100 + 0/121,$$

$$p_{12} = 0.025 \backslash 1 + 0 \backslash 2 + ... + 0 \backslash 1.6 + ... + 0 \backslash 100 + 0.025 \backslash 121.$$

As a result, $Z_{12}^+ = \left(A_1 / A_2, p_{12} \right)$ is obtained.

Next we compute membership degrees $\mu_{p_1}(p_1)$ and $\mu_{p_2}(p_2)$ for distributions p_1 and p_2, and the membership degrees $\mu_{p_{12}}(p_{12})$ of the convolutions p_{12}.

Given the membership degrees $\mu_{p_{12}}(p_{12})$ of the convolutions p_{12}, we compute values of probability measure $P(A_{12})$ by using Definition 4.1. For example, $P(A_{12})$ computed on the base of p_{12} considered above is

$$P(A_{12}) = b_{12} = 0.44.$$

At the final stage, we construct B_{12} based on (4.7)-(4.8). For example, $\mu_{B_{12}}(0.44) = 0.8$. The constructed B_{12} is given below:

$$B_{12} = 0/0.24 + 0.5/0.29 + 0.8/0.34 + 1/0.38 + 0.8/0.44 + 0.7/0.49$$
$$+ 0.6/0.54 + 0.4/0.59 + 0.2/0.64 + 0.1/0.69 + 0/0.68.$$

The result $Z_{12} = (A_{12}, B_{12})$ of the standard division is obtained. A_{12}, B_{12}

are shown in Fig. 4.10.

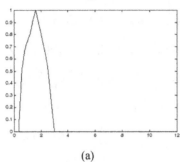 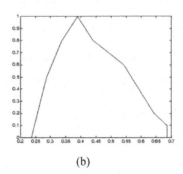

               (a)   (b)

Fig. 4.10. The results of division of the discrete Z-numbers: (a) A_{12}, (b) B_{12}.

4.2. Power of a Discrete Z-number[5,9]

4.2.1. *Square of a Discrete Z-number*

Let us now consider computation of $Z_Y = Z_X^2$. Let $Z_X^+ = (A_X, R_X)$ where R_X is represented as

$$p_X = p_X(x_1) \backslash x_1 + p_X(x_2) \backslash x_2 + ... + p_X(x_n) \backslash x_n.$$

Then the discrete Z^+-number Z_Y^+ is determined as follows:

$$Z_Y^+ = (A_Y, R_Y),$$

where $A_Y = A_X^2$ isdetermined on the base of Definition 2.25 and R_Y is a discrete probability distribution defined by (2.43) as follows:

$$p_Y = p_Y(y_1) \backslash y_1 + p_Y(y_2) \backslash y_2 + ... + p_Y(y_m) \backslash y_m, \qquad (4.12)$$

such that

$$y_r = x_k^2 \text{ and } p_Y(y_r) = \sum_{y_r = x^2} p_X(x), r = 1, ..., m. \qquad (4.13)$$

Next we compute $\mu_{p_X}(p_{X,l}) = \mu_{B_X}\left(\sum_{k=1}^{n}\mu_{A_X}(x_k)p_{X,l}(x_k)\right)$ by solving goal linear programming problem (4.3a)-(4.4a).

Nowwe realize that the fuzzy set of probability distributions p_X with membership function $\mu_{p_X}(p_{X,l})$ naturally induces the fuzzy set of probability distributions $p_{Y,l}$ with the membership function defined as

$$\mu_{p_Y}(p_{Y,l}) = \mu_{p_X}(p_{X,l}),$$

subject to (4.12)-(4.13).

Next, we should compute probability measure of A_Y given p_Y on the base of Definition 4.1. Finally, given a fuzzy restriction on p_Y described by the membership function μ_{p_Y}, we construct a fuzzy set B_Y with the membership function μ_{B_Y} defined as follows:

$$\mu_{B_Y}(b_{Y,l}) = \sup(\mu_{p_Y}(p_{Y,l}))$$

subject to

$$b_{Y,l} = \sum_{k} p_{Y,l}(x_k)\mu_{A_Y}(x_k).$$

As a result, Z^2 is obtained as $Z^2 = (A_Y, B_Y)$. Let us mention that for $x_i \geq 0, i = 1,...,n$, one has $p_{Y,l}(y_k) = p_{X,l}(x_k)$, $\mu_{p_Y}(p_{Y,l}) = \mu_{p_X}(p_{X,l})$, and $\mu_{A_Y}(y_k) = \mu_{A_X}(x_k)$ with $y_k = x_k^2$. Thus, one has

$$b_{Y,l} = b_{X,l} \text{ and } \mu_{B_Y}(b_{Y,l}) = \mu_{B_X}(b_{X,l}),$$

which means $B_Y = B_X$. Therefore, for the case $x_i \geq 0, i = 1,...,n$, it is not needed to carry out computation of B_Y because it is the same as B_X.

Let us mention that computation of $Z_Y = Z_X^n$, where n is any natural number, is carried out analogously.

An example. Given the Z-number $Z_2 = (A_2, B_2)$ considered in Section 4.1.3, let us compute its square $Z_3 = Z_2^2$. First we proceed to the Z^+-

number $Z_2^+ = (A_2, R_2)$ with R_2 represented as

$$p_2 = 0.09\backslash1 + 0\backslash2 + 0.18\backslash3 + 0.32\backslash4 + 0.18\backslash5 + 0.1\backslash6$$
$$+ 0.036\backslash7 + 0\backslash8 + 0\backslash9 + 0\backslash10 + 0.09\backslash11.$$

Then we compute the corresponding Z^+-number $Z^+ = (A, R)$, where $A_3 = A_2^2$ computed on the base of Definition 2.25 and R_3 computed on the base of (4.12)-(4.13) are given below:

$$A_3 = 0/1 + 0.5/4 + 0.8/9 + 1/16 + 0.8/25 + 0.7/36$$
$$+ 0.6/49 + 0.4/64 + 0.2/81 + 0.1/100 + 0/121,$$

$$p_3 = 0.09\backslash1 + 0\backslash4 + 0\backslash9 + 0.32\backslash16 + 0.18\backslash25 + 0.1\backslash36$$
$$+ 0.036\backslash49 + 0\backslash64 + 0\backslash81 + 0\backslash100 + 0.09\backslash121.$$

As it was shown above, $B_3 = B_2$. However, we computed B_3 given A_3, membership degrees $\mu_{p_2}(p_2) = \mu_{B_2}\left(\sum_{k=1}^{n} \mu_{A_2}(x_k)p_2(x_k)\right)$ and taking into account the fact that $\mu_{p_3}(p_3) = \mu_{p_2}(p_2)$. Thus, Z-number $Z_3 = (A_3, B_3)$ as the square of Z_2 is obtained. A_3, B_3 are shown in Fig. 4.11.

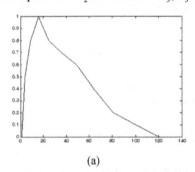 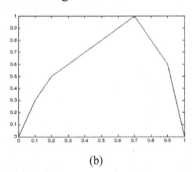

(a)   (b)

Fig. 4.11. The square of the discrete Z-number: (a) A_3, (b) B_3.

As one can see, $B_3 = B_2$.

4.2.2. *Square Root of a Discrete Z-number*

In [168] Zadeh poses a question: "What is a square root of a Z-number". In this section we will answer this question for a discrete Z-number.

Let us consider computation of $Z_Y = \sqrt{Z_X}$. Let Z_X^+ and Z_X be the same as those considered in Section 4.2.1. Then the discrete Z^+-number Z_Y^+ is determined as follows:

$$Z_Y^+ = (A_Y, R_Y),$$

where $A_Y = \sqrt{A_X}$, $\sqrt{A_X}$ is determined on the base of Definition 2.26 and R_Y is represented by a discrete probability distribution (see 2.44)

$$p_{R_Y} = p_{R_Y}(y_1) \backslash y_1 + p_{R_Y}(y_2) \backslash y_2 + \dots + p_{R_Y}(y_n) \backslash y_n, \tag{4.14}$$

such that

$$y_k = \sqrt{x_k} \text{ and } p_{R_Y}(y_k) = p_{R_X}(x_k), \tag{4.15}$$

Then we construct $\mu_{p_X}(p_{X,l}) = \mu_{B_X}\left(\sum_{k=1}^{n} \mu_{A_X}(x_k) p_{X,l}(x_k)\right)$ and recall that

$$\mu_{p_Y}(p_{Y,l}) = \mu_{p_X}(p_{X,l}),$$

subject to (4.14)-(4.15).

Next we compute probability measure of A_Y and, given the membership function μ_{p_Y}, we construct a fuzzy set B_Y analogously to that we did in Section 4.2.1. As a result, $\sqrt{Z}$ I s obtained as $\sqrt{Z} = (A_Y, B_Y)$. Let us mention that analogously to the case of the square of a discrete Z-number with non-negative first component, it is not needed to carry out computation of B_Y. One can easily verify that for the case of the square root of a discrete Z-number, $B_Y = B_X$ holds.

An example. Let us consider computation of the square root $Z_3 = \sqrt{Z_2}$ of $Z_2 = (A_2, B_2)$ considered in Section 4.1.3. Given the Z^+-number $Z_2^+ = (A_2, R_2)$ used in the example above, we computed the corresponding Z^+-number $Z_3^+ = (A_3, R_3)$, where $A_3 = \sqrt{A_2}$ computed on the base of Definition 2.26 and R_3 computed on the base of (4.14)-(4.15) are given below:

$$A_3 = 0/1 + 0.5/1.4 + 0.8/1.7 + 1/2 + 0.8/2.2 + 0.7/2.4 + 0.6/2.6$$
$$+ 0.4/2.8 + 0.2/3 + 0.1/3.2 + 0/3.3,$$

$$p_3 = 0.09\backslash1 + 0\backslash1.4 + 0\backslash1.7 + 0.32\backslash2 + 0.18\backslash2.2 + 0.1\backslash2.4$$
$$+ 0.036\backslash2.6 + 0\backslash2.8 + 0.2\backslash3 + 0.1\backslash3.2 + 0.09\backslash3.3.$$

As it was shown above, $B_3 = B_2$. However, we computed B_3 given A_3, the membership degrees $\mu_{p_2}(p_2) = \mu_{B_2}\left(\sum_{k=1}^{n}\mu_{A_2}(x_k)p_2(x_k)\right)$ and taking into account the fact that $\mu_{p_3}(p_3) = \mu_{p_2}(p_2)$. Thus, Z-number $Z_3 = (A_3, B_3)$ as the square root of Z_2 is obtained and A_3, B_3 are shown in Fig. 4.12.

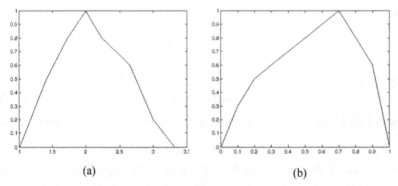

(a)   (b)

Fig. 4.12. The square root of the discrete Z-number: (a) A_3, (b) B_3.

As one can see, we have $B_3 = B_2$.

4.3. Ranking of Discrete Z-numbers[5,9]

Ranking of discrete Z-numbers is a necessary operation in arithmetic of Z-numbers and is a challenging practical issue. Zadeh addresses the problem of ranking Z-numbers as a very important problem and mentions a simple example: "*Is (approximately 100, likely) greater than (approximately 90, very likely)?*" [168]. Without doubt, this is a meaningful question and it is worth to mention that our everyday decisions are often characterized by imprecise and vague information both on future consequences and the related reliability. In this section we suggest an approach to ranking of discrete Z-numbers.

In contrast to real numbers, Z-numbers are ordered pairs, for ranking of which there can be no unique approach. For purpose of comparison, we suggest to consider a Z-number as a pair of values of two attributes – one attribute measures value of a variable, the other one measures the associated reliability. Then it will be adequate to compare Z-numbers as multiattribute alternatives. Basic principle of comparison of multiattribute alternatives is the Pareto optimality principle which is based on a counterintuitive assumption that all alternatives within a Pareto optimal set are considered equally optimal. The fuzzy Pareto optimality (FPO) concept[58] fits very well multi-attribute decision making problems. This concept is an implementation of the ideas of CW-based redefinitions of the existing scientific concepts[166]. In this approach, by directly comparing alternatives, one arrives at total degrees to which one alternative is better than, is equivalent to and is worse than another one. These degrees are determined as graded sums of differences between attribute values for considered alternatives[3,15,58]. Such comparison is closer to the way humans compare alternatives by confronting their attribute values.

We suggest to consider comparison of Z-numbers on the base of FPO principle[3,15,58] as follows. Let Z-numbers $Z_1 = (A_1, B_1)$ and $Z_2 = (A_2, B_2)$ be given. It is needed to compare the corresponding components of these Z-numbers. For this purpose it is needed to calculate the functions n_b, n_e, n_w which evaluate how much one of the Z-numbers is better, equivalent and worse than the other one with respect to the first and the second components A and B. The total degree n_b

measures the number of components with respect to which $Z_1 = (A_1, B_1)$ dominates $Z_2 = (A_2, B_2)$ (minimum is 0, maximum is 2). The total degree n_w measures the number of components with respect to which $Z_1 = (A_1, B_1)$ is dominated by $Z_2 = (A_2, B_2)$ (minimum is 0, maximum is 2). The total degree n_e measures the number of components with respect to which $Z_1 = (A_1, B_1)$ is equivalent to $Z_2 = (A_2, B_2)$ (minimum is 0, maximum is 2).

The functions n_b, n_e, n_w are defined as follows:

$$n_b(Z_i, Z_j) = P_b(\delta_A^{i,j}) + P_b(\delta_B^{i,j}), \tag{4.16}$$

$$n_e(Z_i, Z_j) = P_e(\delta_A^{i,j}) + P_e(\delta_B^{i,j}), \tag{4.17}$$

$$n_w(Z_i, Z_j) = P_w(\delta_A^{i,j}) + P_w(\delta_B^{i,j}), \tag{4.18}$$

where $\delta_A^{i,j} = A_i - A_j$, $\delta_B^{i,j} = B_i - B_j$, $i, j = 1, 2, i \neq j$. The meaning of these functions is as follows. As superiority, equivalence and inferiority of one Z-number with respect to the other is actually a matter of a degree for human intuition, $\delta_A^{i,j} = A_i - A_j$ and $\delta_B^{i,j} = B_i - B_j$ may be evaluated by using the function:

$$P_l(\delta_A^{i,j}) = \frac{Poss\left(\delta_A^{i,j} \big| n_l\right)}{\sum\limits_{t \in \{b,e,w\}} Poss\left(\delta_A^{i,j} \big| n_t\right)},$$

$$P_l(\delta_B^{i,j}) = \frac{Poss\left(\delta_B^{i,j} \big| n_l\right)}{\sum\limits_{t \in \{b,e,w\}} Poss\left(\delta_B^{i,j} \big| n_t\right)},$$

where $Poss$ is a possibility measure[3] to fuzzy terms of n_b, n_e, n_w shown in Fig. 4.13, $t \in \{b, e, w\}$, $i, j = 1, 2, i \neq j$.

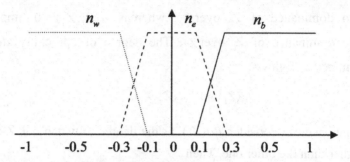

Fig. 4.13. The membership functions for n_b, n_e, n_w.

The function $P_l()$ is therefore used as a weighted possibility measure. As $\sum_{t \in \{b,e,w\}} P_l(\delta_k^{i,j}) = 1$ will always hold, one will always have $n_b(Z_i, Z_j) + n_e(Z_i, Z_j) + n_w(Z_i, Z_j) = N$, where N is the number of components of a Z-number, i.e. $N = 2$.

Next, on the base of n_b, n_e, n_w, the $(1-k)$-dominance [58] is determined as dominance in the terms of its degree. This concepts suggests that Z_1 $(1-k)$-dominates Z_2 iff [3,15,58]

$$n_e(Z_i, Z_j) < 2, \quad n_b(Z_i, Z_j) \geq \frac{2 - n_e(Z_i, Z_j)}{k+1}, \tag{4.19}$$

with $k \in [0,1]$.

Next it is needed to determine the greatest k such that Z_i Pareto dominates Z_j to the degree $(1-k)$. For this purpose, a function d is introduced[3,15,58]:

$$d(Z_i, Z_j) = \begin{cases} 0, & \text{if } n_b(Z_i, Z_j) \leq \dfrac{2 - n_e(Z_i, Z_j)}{2} \\ \dfrac{2 \cdot n_b(Z_i, Z_j) + n_e(Z_i, Z_j) - 2}{n_b(Z_i, Z_j)}, & \text{otherwise} \end{cases} \tag{4.20}$$

Given a value of d, the desired greatest k is found as $k = 1 - d(Z_i, Z_j)$, and then $(1-k) = d(Z_i, Z_j)$. $d(Z_i, Z_j) = 1$ implies

Pareto dominance of Z_i over Z_j, whereas $d(Z_i, Z_j) = 0$ implies no Pareto dominance of Z_i over Z_j. The degree of optimality $do(Z_i)$ is determined as follows:

$$do(Z_i) = 1 - d(Z_j, Z_i). \tag{4.21}$$

Thus, we can consider $do(Z_i)$ as the degree to which one Z-number is higher than the other one. Then

$$Z_i > Z_j \text{ iff } do(Z_i) > do(Z_j),$$

$$Z_i < Z_j \text{ iff } do(Z_i) < do(Z_j)$$

and $Z_i = Z_j$ otherwise.

Recall that comparison of fuzzy numbers is a matter of a degree due to related vagueness. For Z-numbers, which are more complex constructs characterized by possibilistic-probabilistic uncertainty, degree-based comparison is even more desirable.

The suggested approach may be considered as basis of a human-oriented ranking of Z-numbers. In this viewpoint, we suggest to take into account degree of pessimism $\beta \in [0,1]$ as a mental factor which influences a choice of a preferred Z-number. The degree of pessimism is submitted by a human observer who wishes to compare the considered Z-numbers but does not completely rely on the results obtained by the above mentioned FPO approach. In this viewpoint, given $do(Z_j) \leq do(Z_i)$, we define for two Z-numbers Z_1 and Z_2:

$$r(Z_i, Z_j) = \beta do(Z_j) + (1 - \beta) do(Z_i).$$

Then

$$\left. \begin{array}{l} Z_i > Z_j \text{ iff } r(Z_i, Z_j) > \dfrac{1}{2}(do(Z_i) + do(Z_j)) \\[4mm] Z_i < Z_j \text{ iff } r(Z_i, Z_j) < \dfrac{1}{2}(do(Z_i) + do(Z_j)) \\[4mm] \text{and} \\[2mm] Z_i = Z_j \text{ otherwise} \end{array} \right\}$$

The degree of pessimism β is submitted by a human being and adjust ranking of Z-numbers to reflect human attitude to the *do* degree-based comparison. This attitude may result from the different importance of A and B components for a human being and other issues.

An example. Consider the following problem. Manufacturing company must determine the mix of its commercial products B and C to be produced next year. The company produces two product lines, the B and the C. The average profit is (about \$400, very likely) for each B and (about \$800, likely) for each C. The resources limitations for production are fabrication and assembly capacities which are also described by Z-numbers to account for uncertainty of future. Assume that the solution of the considered problem (x_1^1, x_2^1) provides overall profit (about \$100 *mln*, likely) , and the solution (x_1^2, x_2^2) provides overall profit (about \$90 *mln*, very likely). The problem is to rank these solutions.

Let the information about imprecise random quantities mentioned in the example be described by Z-numbers $Z_1 = (A_1, B_1)$ and $Z_2 = (A_2, B_2)$ given (in \$ *mln*):

$$A_1 = 0/95 + 0.5/97.5 + 1/100 + 0.5/102.5 + 0/105,$$

$$B_1 = 0/0.75 + 0.5/0.775 + 1/0.8 + 0.5/0.825 + 0/0.85;$$

$$A_2 = 0/85 + 0.5/87.5 + 1/90 + 0.5/92.5 + 0/95,$$

$$B_2 = 0/0.85 + 0.5/0.875 + 1/0.9 + 0.5/0.925 + 0/0.95.$$

In order to solve the considered problem, let us compare these Z-numbers on the base of the FPO approach. In accordance with (4.16)-(4.18), first we calculated values of the functions n_b, n_e, n_w:

$$n_b(Z_1, Z_2) = 0.095, \ n_b(Z_2, Z_1) = 0.105,$$
$$n_e(Z_1, Z_2) = 1.8, \ n_e(Z_2, Z_1) = 1.8,$$
$$n_w(Z_1, Z_2) = 0.105, \ n_w(Z_2, Z_1) = 0.095.$$

At the second step, a function d is calculated according to (4.20):

$$d(Z_1, Z_2) = 0; \ d(Z_2, Z_1) = 0.095.$$

Next, $do(Z_1) = 0.905$ and $do(Z_2) = 1$ are obtained on the base of (4.21). Therefore, Z_2 is higher than $Z_1 : Z_2 > Z_1$. Let us now consider a human-oriented ranking of these Z-numbers with degree of pessimism $\beta = 0.6$. For this case we will have:

$$r(Z_1, Z_2) = 0.943 < \frac{1}{2}(0.905 + 1) = 0.953.$$

Therefore, $Z_1 > Z_2$.

4.4. Minimum and Maximum of Discrete Z-numbers

Let $Z_1 = (A_1, B_1)$ and $Z_2 = (A_2, B_2)$ be discrete Z-numbers describing imperfect information about values of real-valued random variables X_1 and X_2. Consider the problem of computation of minimum $Z_{12} = MIN(Z_1, Z_2)$. Computation of the maximum, $Z_{12} = MAX(Z_1, Z_2)$ is treated analogously.

Computation with discrete Z-numbers, as that with continuous Z-numbers, starts with the computation over the corresponding discrete Z^+-numbers. The discrete Z^+-number $Z_{12}^+ = \min(Z_1^+, Z_2^+)$ is determined as follows:

$$\min(Z_1^+, Z_2^+) = (MIN(A_1, A_2), \min(R_1, R_2)) \tag{4.22}$$

where R_1 and R_2 are represented by discrete probability distributions for which one necessarily has (4.1)-(4.2) satisfied. As the operands in $MIN(A_1, A_2)$ and in $\min(R_1, R_2)$ are represented by different types of restrictions, then the meanings of MIN and $\min$ are also different [168].

The minimum $MIN(A_1, A_2)$ of DFNs is defined in accordance with Definition 2.27. $\min(R_1, R_2)$ is a convolution $p_{12} = p_1 \circ p_2$ of discrete probability distributions and is defined by (2.40).

For the case of the maximum of Z_1, Z_2, $Z_{12} = MAX(Z_1, Z_2)$, instead of the *MIN* operation over discrete fuzzy numbers and *min* operation over probability distributions, *MAX* operation defined in Definition 2.27 and *max* operation defined by (2.41) are used respectively.

So, we will have Z_{12}^+ as $Z_{12}^+ = (MIN(A_1, A_2), p_{12})$, which is the result of computation with discrete Z^+-numbers, being the first step of computation with Z-numbers.

Next we realize that the 'true' probability distributions p_1 and p_2 are not exactly known, but the fuzzy restrictions which may be represented in terms of membership functions are only available:

$$\mu_{B_1}\left(\sum_{k=1}^{n}\mu_{A_1}(x_{1k})p_1(x_{1k})\right), \ \mu_{B_2}\left(\sum_{k=1}^{n}\mu_{A_2}(x_{2k})p_2(x_{2k})\right).$$

These restrictions induce fuzzy sets of probability distributions of p_1 and p_2:

$$\mu_{p_1}(p_1) = \mu_{B_1}\left(\sum_{k=1}^{n}\mu_{A_1}(x_{1k})p_1(x_{1k})\right),$$

$$\mu_{p_2}(p_2) = \mu_{B_2}\left(\sum_{k=1}^{n}\mu_{A_2}(x_{2k})p_2(x_{2k})\right).$$

Next, to construct B_1 and B_2, one needs to compute the values of $\mu_{B_j}(b_{jl})$, $b_{jl} \in \text{supp } B_j$, $j=1,2; l=1,...,n$, by solving a series of n goal linear programming problems (4.3a)-(4.4a).

The fuzzy sets of probability distributions p_{1l} and p_{2l} induce the fuzzy set of convolutions p_{12s}, $s=1,...,m^2$, with the membership function defined as

$$\mu_{P_{12}}(p_{12}) = \max_{p_1,p_2}[\mu_{p_1}(p_1) \wedge \mu_{p_2}(p_2)]$$

subject to $p_{12} = p_1 \circ p_2$,

where $\wedge$ is *min* operation.

At the next step, we should compute probability measure of $A_{12} = MIN(A_1, A_2)$:

$$P(A_{12}) = \sum_{x_k} p_{12}(x_k)\mu_{A_{12}}(x_k).$$

However, as a fuzzy restriction on p_{12} described by the membership function $\mu_{P_{12}}$ is only known, $P(A_{12})$ will be defined as a fuzzy set B_{12} with the membership function $\mu_{B_{12}}$ defined as follows:

$$\mu_{B_{12}}(b_{12s}) = \sup(\mu_{P_{12s}}(p_{12s}))$$

subject to

$$b_{12s} = \sum_k p_{12s}(x_k)\mu_{A_{12}}(x_k).$$

As a result, $Z_{12} = MIN(Z_1, Z_2)$ is obtained as $Z_{12} = (A_{12}, B_{12})$.

Examples. *Minimum of discrete Z-numbers.* Let us consider computation of a minimum $Z_{12} = \min(Z_1, Z_2)$ of the following two discrete Z-numbers $Z_1 = (A_1, B_1)$ and $Z_2 = (A_2, B_2)$ (see also Figs. 4.14, 4.15):

$$A_1 = 0/0.0 + 0/0.1 + 0.0/0.2 + 0.0/0.3 + 0.0003/0.4 + 0.01/0.5$$
$$+ 0.14/0.6 + 0.61/0.7 + 1.0/0.8 + 0.61/0.9 + 0.14/1.0,$$

$$B_1 = 0/0 + 0.0/0.1 + 0.0/0.2 + 0.0/0.3 + 0.0/0.4 + 0.0003/0.5$$
$$+ 0.01/0.6 + 0.14/0.7 + 0.61/0.8 + 1.0/0.9 + 0.61/1.0;$$

$$A_2 = 0/0.0 + 0.01/0.1 + 0.14/0.2 + 0.61/0.3 + 1.0/0.4 + 0.61/0.5$$
$$+ 0.14/0.6 + 0.01/0.7 + 0.0/0.8 + 0.0/0.9 + 0.0/1.0,$$

$$B_2 = 0/0 + 0.01/0.1 + 0.14/0.2 + 0.61/0.3 + 1.0/0.4 + 0.61/0.5$$
$$+ 0.14/0.6 + 0.01/0.7 + 0.0/0.8 + 0.0/0.9 + 0.0/1.0.$$

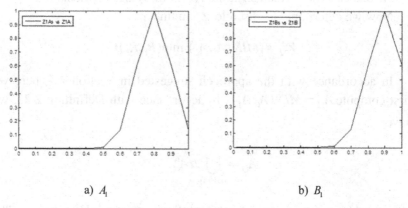

a) A_1 b) B_1

Fig. 4.14. The discrete Z-number $Z_1 = (A_1, B_1)$.

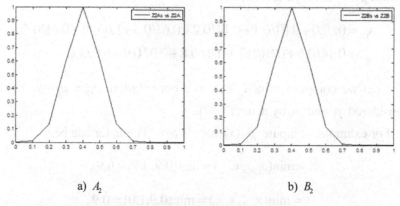

a) A_2 b) B_2

Fig. 4.15. The discrete Z-number $Z_2 = (A_2, B_2)$.

At the first step of computation of Z_{12} we proceed to the discrete Z^+-numbers. Let us consider $Z_1^+ = (A_1, R_1)$ and $Z_2^+ = (A_2, R_2)$ where R_1 and R_2 are the following discrete probability distributions R_1 and R_2:

$$p_1 = 0.0\backslash0.0 + 0.0\backslash0.1 + 0.0\backslash0.2 + 0.0\backslash0.3 + 0.0\backslash0.4 + 0.0\backslash0.5$$
$$+ 0.45\backslash0.6 + 0.03\backslash0.7 + 0.04\backslash0.8 + 0.03\backslash0.9 + 0.45\backslash1.0,$$

$$p_2 = 0.0\backslash0.0 + 0.0\backslash0.1 + 0.33\backslash0.2 + 0.04\backslash0.3 + 0.26\backslash0.4$$
$$+ 0.04\backslash0.5 + 0.33\backslash0.6 + 0.0\backslash0.7 + 0.0\backslash0.8 + 0.0\backslash0.9 + 0.0\backslash1.0.$$

As one can verify, the constraints (4.1)-(4.2) are satisfied.
Now we determine the discrete Z^+ -number

$$Z_{12}^+ = (MIN(A_1, A_2), \min(R_1, R_2)).$$

In accordance with the approach suggested in Section 4.4, here we first compute $A_{12} = MIN(A_1, A_2)$. In accordance with Definition 2.27, we have:

$$A_{12} = \bigcup_{\alpha \in [0,1]} \alpha A_{12}^\alpha,$$

$A_{12}^\alpha = \{x \in \{\text{supp}(A_1) \wedge \text{supp}(A_2)\} \mid \min\{x_1^\alpha, y_1^\alpha\} \le z \le \min\{x_p^\alpha, y_k^\alpha\}\}$. The resulting A_{12} is found as follows:

$$A_{12} = 0 / 0.0 + 0.01/0.1 + 0.14/0.2 + 0.61/0.3 + 1.0/0.4 + 0.61/0.5$$
$$+ 0.14/0.6 + 0.01/0.7 + 0.0/0.8 + 0.0/0.9 + 0.0/1.0.$$

Next we compute $\min(R_1, R_2)$ as a convolution $p_{12} = p_1 \circ p_2$ of the considered p_1 and p_2 by using (2.40).

For example, compute $p_{12}(x)$ for $x = 0.9$. The latter can be

$$x = \min(x_{1,10}, x_{2,10}) = \min(0.9, 0.9) = 0.9,$$

$$x = \min(x_{1,10}, x_{2,11}) = \min(0.9, 1.0) = 0.9,$$

or

$$x = \min(x_{1,11}, x_{2,10}) = \min(1.0, 0.9) = 0.9.$$

Then

$$p_{12}(0.9) = p_1(0.9)p_2(0.9) + p_1(0.9)p_2(1.0) + p_1(1.0)p_2(0.9)$$
$$= 0.03 \cdot 0.0 + 0.03 \cdot 0.0 + 0.0 \cdot 0.45 = 0.0.$$

The p_{12} obtained in accordance with (2.40) is given below:

$$p_{12} = 0.0 \backslash 0.0 + 0.0 \backslash 0.1 + 0.33 \backslash 0.2 + 0.04 \backslash 0.3 + 0.26 \backslash 0.4$$
$$+ 0.04 \backslash 0.5 + 0.33 \backslash 0.6 + 0.0 \backslash 0.7 + 0.0 \backslash 0.8 + 0.0 \backslash 0.9 + 0.0 \backslash 1.0.$$

Thus, $Z_{12}^+ = (MIN(A_1, A_2), \min(R_1, R_2)) = (MIN(A_1, A_2), p_{12})$ is obtained.

At the next step we realize, that 'true' probability distributions p_1 and p_2 are not exactly known, but only fuzzy restrictions μ_{p_1} and μ_{p_2} for p_1 and p_2 are available which are induced by B_1 and B_2 respectively. We compute the membership degrees $\mu_{p_j}(p_j)$, $j = 1, 2$, of the fuzzy restrictions given the solutions of the goal linear programming problems (4.3a)-(4.4a). Let us consider determination of the membership degrees $\mu_{p_1}(p_1)$ and $\mu_{p_2}(p_2)$ for distributions p_1 and p_2 considered above. It is known that $\mu_{p_1}(p_1) = \mu_{B_1}\left(\sum_{k=1}^{n_1} \mu_{A_1}(x_{1k})p_1(x_{1k})\right)$, and as for p_1 considered above we have

$$\sum_{k=1}^{n_1} \mu_{A_1}(x_{1k})p_1(x_{1k}) = 0.0 \cdot 0.0 + 0.0 \cdot 0.0 + 0.0 \cdot 0.0 + 0.0 \cdot 0.0$$
$$+ 0.0003 \cdot 0.0 + 0.01 \cdot 0.0 + 0.14 \cdot 0.45 + 0.61 \cdot 0.03$$
$$+ 1.0 \cdot 0.04 + 0.61 \cdot 0.003 + 0.14 \cdot 0.45 = 0.2,$$

then $\mu_{p_1}(p_1) = \mu_{B_1}(0.2) = 0.0$. For p_2 considered above:

$$\sum_{k=1}^{n_1} \mu_{A_2}(x_{2k})p_2(x_{2k}) = 0.0 \cdot 0.0 + 0.01 \cdot 0.0 + 0.14 \cdot 0.33 + 0.61 \cdot 0.04$$
$$+ 1.0 \cdot 0.26 + 0.61 \cdot 0.04 + 0.14 \cdot 0.33 + 0.01 \cdot 0.0$$
$$+ 0.0 \cdot 0.0 + 0.0 \cdot 0.0 + 0.0 \cdot 0.0 = 0.4.$$

Thus, $\mu_{p_2}(p_2) = \mu_{B_2}(0.4) = 1.0$.

Finally, we compute the membership degrees of for all the considered p_1 and p_2. The latter are constructed by solving linear programming problems (4.3a)-(4.4a). Consider construction of p_1, construction of p_2 is analogous. For example, to fined p_1 which satisfy $P(A_1) = \sum_{k=1}^{n_1} \mu_{A_1}(x_{1k}) p_1(x_{1k}) = 0.3$, one needs to solve the following problem:

$$0.0v_1 + 0.0v_2 + 0.0v_3 + 0.0v_4 + 0.0003v_5 + 0.01v_6 + 0.14v_7 + 0.61v_8$$
$$+1.0v_9 + 0.61v_{10} + 0.14v_{11} \rightarrow 0.3$$

subject to

$$\left. \begin{array}{l} v_1 + v_2 + ... + v_n = 1 \\ v_1, v_2, ..., v_n \geq 0 \end{array} \right\}.$$

Coefficients of the objective function in this problem are values of membership function μ_{A_1} (see above), the goal 0.3 is a basic value of B_1, and decision variables $v_1, v_2, ..., v_n$ are the values $p_1(x_{11})$, $p_1(x_{12}), ..., p_1(x_{1n})$ of probability distribution p_1 to be found. Therefore, it is needed to find such a distribution p_1 which induces $b \in B_1, b = 0.3$. The obtained result is as follows:

$$p_1 = 0.0 \backslash 0.0 + 0.0 \backslash 0.1 + 0.0 \backslash 0.2 + 0.0 \backslash 0.3 + 0.0 \backslash 0.4 + 0.0 \backslash 0.5$$
$$+ 0.449 \backslash 0.6 + 0.0 \backslash 0.7 + 0.19 \backslash 0.8 + 0.0 \backslash 0.9 + 0.405 \backslash 1.0.$$

Analogously, we obtained probability distributions for the rest values of $b \in B_1$. The results are as follows.
For $b = 0$:

$$p_1 = 0.176 \backslash 0.0 + 0.176 \backslash 0.1 + 0.176 \backslash 0.2 + 0.176 \backslash 0.3 + 0.174 \backslash 0.4$$
$$+ 0.12 \backslash 0.5 + 0.0 \backslash 0.6 + 0.0 \backslash 0.7 + 0.0 \backslash 0.8 + 0.0 \backslash 0.9 + 0.0 \backslash 1.0,$$

for $b = 0.1$:

$$p_1 = 0.0795 \backslash 0.0 + 0.0795 \backslash 0.1 + 0.0795 \backslash 0.2 + 0.0794 \backslash 0.3$$
$$+ 0.078 \backslash 0.4 + 0.035 \backslash 0.5 + 0.26 \backslash 0.6 + 0.024 \backslash 0.7 + 0.0 \backslash 0.8$$
$$+ 0.024 \backslash 0.9 + 0.26 \backslash 1.0,$$

for $b = 0.2$:

$$p_1 = 0.0 \backslash 0.0 + 0.0 \backslash 0.1 + 0.0 \backslash 0.2 + 0.0 \backslash 0.3 + 0.0 \backslash 0.4 + 0.0 \backslash 0.5$$
$$+ 0.449 \backslash 0.6 + 0.0304 \backslash 0.7 + 0.042 \backslash 0.8 + 0.0304 \backslash 0.9 + 0.449 \backslash 1.0,$$

for $b = 0.4$:

$$p_1 = 0.0 \backslash 0.0 + 0.0 \backslash 0.1 + 0.0 \backslash 0.2 + 0.0 \backslash 0.3 + 0.0 \backslash 0.4 + 0.0 \backslash 0.5$$
$$+ 0.347 \backslash 0.6 + 0.0 \backslash 0.7 + 0.306 \backslash 0.8 + 0.0 \backslash 0.9 + 0.347 \backslash 1.0,$$

for $b = 0.5$:

$$p_1 = 0.0 \backslash 0.0 + 0.0 \backslash 0.1 + 0.0 \backslash 0.2 + 0.0 \backslash 0.3 + 0.0 \backslash 0.4 + 0.0 \backslash 0.5$$
$$+ 0.289 \backslash 0.6 + 0.0 \backslash 0.7 + 0.422 \backslash 0.8 + 0.0 \backslash 0.9 + 0.289 \backslash 1.0,$$

for $b = 0.6$:

$$p_1 = 0.0 \backslash 0.0 + 0.0 \backslash 0.1 + 0.0 \backslash 0.2 + 0.0 \backslash 0.3 + 0.0 \backslash 0.4 + 0.0 \backslash 0.5$$
$$+ 0.23 \backslash 0.6 + 0.0 \backslash 0.7 + 0.537 \backslash 0.8 + 0.0 \backslash 0.9 + 0.231 \backslash 1.0,$$

for $b = 0.7$:

$$p_1 = 0.0 \backslash 0.0 + 0.0 \backslash 0.1 + 0.0 \backslash 0.2 + 0.0 \backslash 0.3 + 0.0 \backslash 0.4 + 0.0 \backslash 0.5$$
$$+ 0.173 \backslash 0.6 + 0.0 \backslash 0.7 + 0.65 \backslash 0.8 + 0.0 \backslash 0.9 + 0.173 \backslash 1.0,$$

for $b = 0.8$:

$$p_1 = 0.0 \backslash 0.0 + 0.0 \backslash 0.1 + 0.0 \backslash 0.2 + 0.0 \backslash 0.3 + 0.0 \backslash 0.4 + 0.0 \backslash 0.5$$
$$+ 0.116 \backslash 0.6 + 0.0 \backslash 0.7 + 0.769 \backslash 0.8 + 0.0 \backslash 0.9 + 0.116 \backslash 1.0,$$

for $b = 0.9$:

$$p_1 = 0.0\backslash 0.0 + 0.0\backslash 0.1 + 0.0\backslash 0.2 + 0.0\backslash 0.3 + 0.0\backslash 0.4 + 0.0\backslash 0.5$$
$$+ 0.058\backslash 0.6 + 0.0\backslash 0.7 + 0.884\backslash 0.8 + 0.0\backslash 0.9 + 0.058\backslash 1.0,$$

for $b = 1.0$:

$$p_1 = 0.0\backslash 0.0 + 0.0\backslash 0.1 + 0.0\backslash 0.2 + 0.0\backslash 0.3 + 0.0\backslash 0.4 + 0.0\backslash 0.5$$
$$+ 0.0\backslash 0.6 + 0.0\backslash 0.7 + 0.0\backslash 0.8 + 0.0\backslash 0.9 + 1.0\backslash 1.0.$$

Then, according to (4.5)-(4.6),we determine the fuzzy restriction $\mu_{p_{12}}$ over all the convolutions p_{12} obtained on the base of (2.40) from all the considered p_1 and p_2. It is clear that the fuzzy restriction $\mu_{p_{12}}$ is induced by μ_{p_1} and μ_{p_2}.

Next we should proceed to construction of B_{12} as a soft constraint on a probability measure $P(A_{12})$. First we need to compute values of probability measure $P(A_{12})$ by using the obtained convolutions.

The computed $P(A_{12})$ is one possible value of probability measure within the fuzzy restriction B_{12} to be constructed. Now we recall that $\mu_{B_{12}}\left(b_{12} = \sum_{k=1}^{n} \mu_{A_{12}}(x_{12k}) p_{12}(x_{12k})\right) = \mu_{p_{12}}(p_{12})$. By carrying these computations, we constructed B_{12} as follows:

$$B_{12} = 0.0/0.253 + 0.1/0.259 + 0.14/0.26 + 0.61/0.3 + 1.0/0.4$$
$$+ 0.61/0.5 + 0.14/0.6 + 0.01/0.7 + 0.0/0.8 + 0.0/0.9 + 0.0/1.0.$$

Thus, the result of minimum $Z_{12} = (A_{12}, B_{12})$ is obtained, where A_{12}, B_{12} are shown in Fig. 4.16.

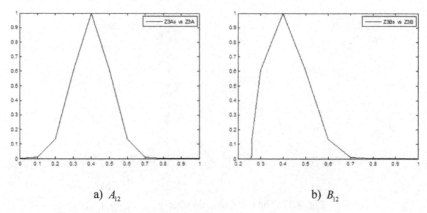

a) A_{12} b) B_{12}

Fig. 4.16. The discrete Z-number $Z_{12} = (A_{12}, B_{12})$.

Maximum of discrete Z-numbers. Let us consider computation of a maximum $Z_{12} = MAX(Z_1, Z_2)$ of two discrete Z-numbers $Z_1 = (A_1, B_1)$ and $Z_2 = (A_2, B_2)$ given (Figs. 4.17, 4.18):

$$A_1 = 0.0/0.0 + 0/0.1 + 0.0/0.2 + 0.0/0.3 + 0.0003/0.4 + 0.01/0.5$$
$$+ 0.14/0.6 + 0.61/0.7 + 1.0/0.8 + 0.61/0.9 + 0.14/1.0,$$

$$B_1 = 0/0 + 0.0/0.1 + 0.0/0.2 + 0.0/0.3 + 0.0/0.4 + 0.0003/0.5$$
$$+ 0.01/0.6 + 0.14/0.7 + 0.61/0.8 + 1.0/0.9 + 0.61/1.0;$$

$$A_2 = 0/0.0 + 0.01/0.1 + 0.14/0.2 + 0.61/0.3 + 1.0/0.4 + 0.61/0.5$$
$$+ 0.14/0.6 + 0.01/0.7 + 0.0/0.8 + 0.0/0.9 + 0.0/1.0,$$

$$B_2 = 0/0 + 0.01/0.1 + 0.14/0.2 + 0.61/0.3 + 1.0/0.4 + 0.61/0.5$$
$$+ 0.14/0.6 + 0.01/0.7 + 0.0/0.8 + 0.0/0.9 + 0.0/1.0.$$

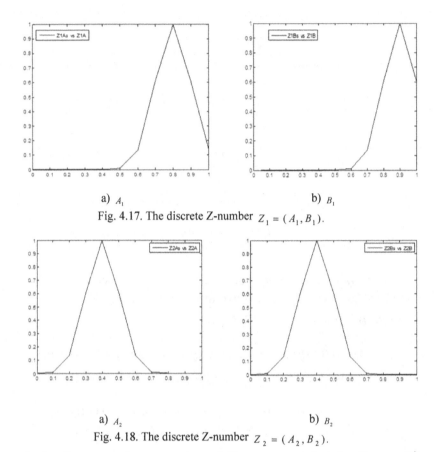

a) A_1 b) B_1

Fig. 4.17. The discrete Z-number $Z_1 = (A_1, B_1)$.

a) A_2 b) B_2

Fig. 4.18. The discrete Z-number $Z_2 = (A_2, B_2)$.

At the first step of computation of Z_{12} we proceed to the discrete Z^+-numbers $Z_1^+ = (A_1, R_1)$ and $Z_2^+ = (A_2, R_2)$ where R_1 and R_2 are the following discrete probability distributions:

$$p_1 = 0.0 \setminus 0.0 + 0.0 \setminus 0.1 + 0.0 \setminus 0.2 + 0.0 \setminus 0.3 + 0.0 \setminus 0.4 + 0.0 \setminus 0.5$$
$$+ 0.45 \setminus 0.6 + 0.03 \setminus 0.7 + 0.04 \setminus 0.8 + 0.03 \setminus 0.9 + 0.45 \setminus 1.0,$$

$$p_2 = 0.0 \setminus 0.0 + 0.0 \setminus 0.1 + 0.33 \setminus 0.2 + 0.04 \setminus 0.3 + 0.26 \setminus 0.4 + 0.04 \setminus 0.5$$
$$+ 0.33 \setminus 0.6 + 0.0 \setminus 0.7 + 0.0 \setminus 0.8 + 0.0 \setminus 0.9 + 0.0 \setminus 1.0.$$

As one can verify, the constraints (4.1)-(4.2) are satisfied.
Next we determine the discrete Z^+-number

$$Z_{12}^+ = (MAX(A_1, A_2), \max(R_1, R_2)).$$

In accordance with the approach suggested in Section 4.4, we first compute $A_{12} = MAX(A_1, A_2)$. In accordance with Definition 2.27 we have:

$$A_{12} = \bigcup_{\alpha \in [0,1]} \alpha A_{12}^{\alpha},$$

where

$$A_{12}^{\alpha} = \{x \in \{\operatorname{supp}(A_1) \vee \operatorname{supp}(A_2)\} \mid \max\{x_1^{\alpha}, y_1^{\alpha}\} \leq z \leq \max\{x_p^{\alpha}, y_k^{\alpha}\}\}.$$

The resulting A_{12} is found as follows:

$$A_{12} = 0.0/0.0 + 0/0.1 + 0.0/0.2 + 0.0/0.3 + 0.0003/0.4 + 0.01/0.5$$
$$+ 0.14/0.6 + 0.61/0.7 + 1.0/0.8 + 0.61/0.9 + 0.14/1.0.$$

Next we compute $\max(R_1, R_2)$ as a convolution $p_{12} = p_1 \circ p_2$ of the considered p_1 and p_2 by using (2.41).

For example, compute $p_{12}(x)$ for $x = 0.6$. The latter can be

$$x = \max(x_{1,7}, x_{2,7}) = \max(0.6, 0.6) = 0.6,$$

$$x = \max(x_{1,7}, x_{2,6}) = \max(0.6, 0.5) = 0.6,$$

$$x = \max(x_{1,6}, x_{2,7}) = \max(0.5, 0.6) = 0.6,$$

$$x = \max(x_{1,7}, x_{2,5}) = \max(0.6, 0.4) = 0.6,$$

$$x = \max(x_{1,5}, x_{2,7}) = \max(0.4, 0.6) = 0.6,$$

$$x = \max(x_{1,7}, x_{2,4}) = \max(0.6, 0.3) = 0.6,$$

$$x = \max(x_{1,4}, x_{2,7}) = \max(0.3, 0.6) = 0.6,$$

$$x = \max(x_{1,7}, x_{2,3}) = \max(0.6, 0.2) = 0.6,$$

$$x = \max(x_{1,3}, x_{2,7}) = \max(0.2, 0.6) = 0.6,$$

$$x = \max(x_{1,7}, x_{2,2}) = \max(0.6, 0.1) = 0.6,$$

$$x = \max(x_{1,2}, x_{2,7}) = \max(0.1, 0.6) = 0.6,$$

$$x = \max(x_{1,7}, x_{2,1}) = \max(0.6, 0.0) = 0.6,$$

$$x = \max(x_{1,1}, x_{2,7}) = \max(0.0, 0.6) = 0.6.$$

Then we have for $p_{12}(0.6)$:

$$
\begin{aligned}
p_{12}(0.6) =\ & p_1(0.6)p_2(0.6) + p_1(0.6)p_2(0.5) + p_1(0.5)p_2(0.6) \\
& + p_1(0.6)p_2(0.4) + p_1(0.4)p_2(0.6) + p_1(0.6)p_2(0.3) \\
& + p_1(0.3)p_2(0.6) + p_1(0.6)p_2(0.2) + p_1(0.2)p_2(0.6) \\
& + p_1(0.6)p_2(0.1) + p_1(0.1)p_2(0.6) + p_1(0.6)p_2(0.0) \\
& + p_1(0.0)p_2(0.6) = 0.45 \cdot 0.33 + 0.45 \cdot 0.04 + 0.0 \cdot 0.33 + 0.45 \cdot 0.26 \\
& + 0.0 \cdot 0.33 + 0.45 \cdot 0.04 + 0.0 \cdot 0.33 + 0.45 \cdot 0.33 + 0.0 \cdot 0.33 \\
& + 0.45 \cdot 0.0 + 0.0 \cdot 0.33 + 0.45 \cdot 0.0 + 0.0 \cdot 0.33 = 0.45.
\end{aligned}
$$

The obtained p_{12} is given below:

$$
\begin{aligned}
p_{12} =\ & 0.0\backslash 0.0 + 0.0\backslash 0.1 + 0.0\backslash 0.2 + 0.0\backslash 0.3 + 0.0\backslash 0.4 + 0.0\backslash 0.5 \\
& + 0.45\backslash 0.6 + 0.0\backslash 0.7 + 0.2\backslash 0.8 + 0.0\backslash 0.9 + 0.4\backslash 1.0.
\end{aligned}
$$

Thus, $Z_{12}^{+} = (MAX(A_1, A_2), p_{12})$ is obtained.

Next we realize, that 'true' probability distributions p_1 and p_2 are not exactly known, but only fuzzy restrictions μ_{p_1} and μ_{p_2} for p_1 and p_2 are available which are induced by B_1 and B_2 respectively. We compute the degrees $\mu_{p_j}(p_j)$, $j = 1, 2$, of the fuzzy restrictions given the solutions of the goal linear programming problems (4.3a)-(4.4a). Let us consider determination of the degrees $\mu_{p_1}(p_1)$ and $\mu_{p_2}(p_2)$ for distributions p_1

and p_2 considered above. It is known that $\mu_{p_1}(p_1) = \mu_{B_1}\left(\sum_{k=1}^{n_1}\mu_{A_1}(x_{1k})p_1(x_{1k})\right)$, and as for p_1 considered above we have

$$\sum_{k=1}^{n_1}\mu_{A_1}(x_{1k})p_1(x_{1k}) = 0.0 \cdot 0.0 + 0.0 \cdot 0.0 + 0.0 \cdot 0.0 + 0.0 \cdot 0.0$$

$$+ 0.0003 \cdot 0.0 + 0.01 \cdot 0.0 + 0.14 \cdot 0.45 + 0.61 \cdot 0.03$$
$$+ 1.0 \cdot 0.04 + 0.61 \cdot 0.003 + 0.14 \cdot 0.45 = 0.2,$$

then $\mu_{p_1}(p_1) = \mu_{B_1}(0.2) = 0.0$.

For p_2 considered above:

$$\sum_{k=1}^{n_2}\mu_{A_2}(x_{2k})p_2(x_{2k}) = 0.0 \cdot 0.0 + 0.01 \cdot 0.0 + 0.14 \cdot 0.33 + 0.61 \cdot 0.04$$

$$+ 1.0 \cdot 0.26 + 0.61 \cdot 0.04 + 0.14 \cdot 0.33 + 0.01 \cdot 0.0$$
$$+ 0.0 \cdot 0.0 + 0.0 \cdot 0.0 + 0.0 \cdot 0.0 = 0.4.$$

Thus, $\mu_{p_2}(p_2) = \mu_{B_2}(0.4) = 1.0$ for p_2 considered above. Finally, we compute the membership degrees of for all the considered p_1 and p_2.

Then according to (4.5)-(4.6), we should determine the fuzzy restriction $\mu_{p_{12}}$ over all the convolutions p_{12} obtained on the base of (2.41) from all the considered p_1 and p_2. It is clear that the fuzzy restriction $\mu_{p_{12}}$ is induced by fuzzy restrictions μ_{p_1} and μ_{p_2}. Next we should proceed to construction of B_{12} as a soft constraint on a probability measure $P(A_{12})$. At the constructed B_{12} is as follows:

$$B_{12} = 0.0/0.253 + 0.1/0.259 + 0.14/0.26 + 0.61/0.3 + 1.0/0.4$$
$$+ 0.61/0.5 + 0.14/0.6 + 0.01/0.7 + 0.0/0.8 + 0.0/0.9 + 0.0/1.0.$$

Thus, the result of maximum $Z_{12} = (A_{12}, B_{12})$ is obtained, where A_{12}, B_{12} are shown in Fig. 4.19.

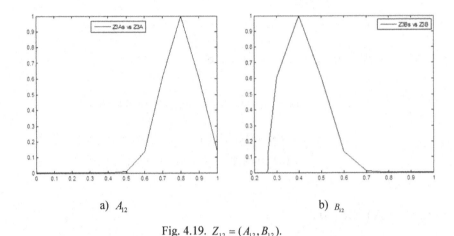

a) A_{12} b) B_{12}

Fig. 4.19. $Z_{12} = (A_{12}, B_{12})$.

4.5. Comparison of Processing Pure Fuzzy and Z-information

Let us emphasize the benefit of the use of fuzzy information with partial reliability as compared to the use of pure fuzzy information. We consider two examples:

1) compare multiplication of fuzzy numbers $A_1 \cdot A_2$ with their Z-valued analogs which are Z-numbers $Z_1 = (A_1, B_1)$ and $Z_2 = (A_2, B_2)$ with $B_1 = 1$ and $B_2 = 1$. Indeed, a fuzzy number A is nothing but a Z-number $Z_1 = (A, 1)$, that is, a fully reliable A. Thus, in this case we consider an imprecise (fuzzy) but a fully reliable (certain) information. We computed $A_1 \cdot A_2$ where

$$A_1 = 0/1 + 0.3/2 + 0.5/3 + 0.6/4 + 0.7/5 + 0.8/6 + 0.9/7 + 1/8$$
$$+ 0.8/9 + 0.6/10 + 0/11,$$

$$A_2 = 0/1 + 0.5/2 + 0.8/3 + 1/4 + 0.8/5 + 0.7/6 + 0.6/7 + 0.4/8$$
$$+ 0.2/9 + 0.1/10 + 0/11,$$

and obtained

$$A_1 \cdot A_2 = 0/1 + 0.16/2 + ... + 1/32 + ... + 0.17/100 + 0/121.$$

Next we computed $Z_1 \cdot Z_2 = (A_1, 1) \cdot (A_2, 1)$ and obtained $Z_1 \cdot Z_2 = (A_{12}, B_{12})$, with the following results:

$$A_1 \cdot A_2 = 0/1 + 0.16/2 + \ldots + 1/32 + \ldots + 0.17/100 + 0/121,$$

$$B_{12} = 0/0.47 + 0/0.52 + 0/0.57 + \ldots + 0/0.88 + 0/0.94 + 1/1.$$

This means that B_{12} is singleton 1. Therefore, the obtained $Z_1 \cdot Z_2 = (A_{12}, B_{12})$ where $B_{12} = 1$ coincides with A_{12}.

2) Let us now consider multiplication of $Z_1^+ = (A_1, p_1)$ and $Z_2^+ = (A_2, p_2)$, where A_1 and A_2 are the same as in the previous example, and p_1 and p_2 are probability distributions which reflect randomness of A_1 and A_2. In other words, we deal with an imprecise (fuzzy) and partially reliable (random) information. The considered p_1 and p_2 are as follows:

$$p_1 = 0.39 \backslash 1 + 0 \backslash 2 + 0 \backslash 3 + 0.001 \backslash 4 + 0.0195 \backslash 5 + 0.0377 \backslash 6$$
$$+ 0.0559 \backslash 7 + 0.074 \backslash 8 + 0.0377 \backslash 9 + 0.0013 \backslash 10 + 0.3862 \backslash 11,$$

$$p_2 = 0.266 \backslash 1 + 0 \backslash 2 + 0.102 \backslash 3 + 0.1822 \backslash 4 + 0.1015 \backslash 5$$
$$+ 0.0612 \backslash 6 + 0.021 \backslash 7 + 0 \backslash 8 + 0 \backslash 9 + 0 \backslash 10 + 0.2664 \backslash 11.$$

The computed Z^+-number $Z_{12}^+ = Z_1^+ \cdot Z_2^+$ is $Z_{12}^+ = (A_{12}, p_{12})$, where A_{12} is the same as in the previous example, and convolution p_{12} is as follows:

$$p_{12} = 0.104 \backslash 1 + 0 \backslash 2 + 0.398 \backslash 3 + 0.07132 \backslash 4 + \ldots + 0 \backslash 100$$
$$+ 0.000346 \backslash 110 + 0.1028 \backslash 121$$

So, in case of partial reliability of an available information, the result of processing of this information is only of some partial reliability too. This is quite intuitive and is the effect of the use of Z^+-information (partially reliable information). In a more realistic setting, an available information is characterized by imprecisely known p, i.e. there is a fuzzy restriction on p as a result of linguistic uncertainty of reliability of A. In such cases it is needed to compute with Z-numbers.

Let us mention that the effect of a partial reliability is like an effect of a footprint of uncertainty in type-2 fuzzy sets. Processing of Z-information offers better capabilities to deal with linguistic uncertainties by modeling imprecise and partially reliable information.

Chapter 5

Algebraic System of Z-numbers

5.1. Absolute Value of a Z-number

Let us consider a discrete case for computation of $Z_Y = abs(Z_X)$. Let $Z_X^+ = (A_X, R_X)$ where R_X is represented as

$$p_X = p_X(x_1) \backslash x_1 + p_X(x_2) \backslash x_2 + ... + p_X(x_n) \backslash x_n .$$

Then the discrete Z^+-number Z_Y^+ is determined as follows:

$$Z_Y^+ = (A_Y, R_Y),$$

where $A_Y = abs(A_X)$, $abs(A_X)$ is determined on the base of Definition 2.28 and R_Y is represented based on (2.45) as

$$p_Y = p_Y(y_1) \backslash y_1 + p_Y(y_2) \backslash y_2 + ... + p_Y(y_m) \backslash y_m, \quad m \le n \qquad (5.1)$$

such that

$$p_Y(y_r) = \sum_{abs(x)=y_r} p_X(x), r = 1,...,m. \qquad (5.2)$$

Next we compute $\mu_{p_X}(p_{X,l}) = \mu_{B_X}\left(\sum_{k=1}^{n} \mu_{A_X}(x_k) p_{X,l}(x_k)\right)$ by solving a goal linear programming problem (4.3a)-(4.4a).

Now, recalling (5.1)-(5.2), we realize that the fuzzy set of probability distributions p_X with membership function $\mu_{p_X}(p_{X,l})$ naturally induces the fuzzy set of probability distributions $p_{Y,l}$ with the membership function defined as

$$\mu_{p_Y}(p_{Y,l}) = \mu_{p_X}(p_{X,l}),$$

subject to (5.1)-(5.2).

Next, we should compute probability measure of A_Y given p_Y on the base of Definition 4.1. Finally, given a fuzzy restriction on p_Y described by the membership function μ_{p_Y}, we construct a fuzzy set B_Y with the membership function μ_{B_Y} defined as follows:

$$\mu_{B_Y}(b_{Y,l}) = \sup(\mu_{p_Y}(p_{Y,l}))$$

subject to

$$b_{Y,l} = \sum_k p_{Y,l}(x_k)\mu_{A_Y}(x_k).$$

An Example. Consider the following discrete Z-number $Z_X = (A_X, B_X)$:

$$A_X = 0/-3 + 0.2/-2 + 0.4/-1 + 0.6/0 + 0.8/1 + 1/2$$
$$+ 0.8/3 + 0.6/4 + 0.4/5 + 0.2/6 + 0/7,$$
$$B_X = 0/0.675 + 0.2/0.7 + 0.4/0.725 + 0.6/0.75 + 0.8/0.775$$
$$+ 1/0.8 + 0.8/0.825 + 0.6/0.85 + 0.4/0.875 + 0.2/0.9 + 0/0.925.$$

Let us compute its absolute value $Z_Y = abs(Z_X)$. First we proceed to the Z^+-number $Z_X^+ = (A_X, R_X)$ with R_X represented as

$$p_X = 0/-3 + 0/-2 + 0/-1 + 0.14/0 + 0.173/1 + 0.21/2 + 0.173/3$$
$$+ 0.134/4 + 0.0957/5 + 0.057/6 + 0.019/7.$$

We compute the corresponding Z^+-number $Z_Y^+ = (A_Y, R_Y)$ as follows. $A_Y = abs(A_X)$ is computed on the base of Definition 2.28. The obtained result is shown below:

$$A_Y = 0.6/0 + 0.8/1 + 1/2 + 0.8/3 + 0.6/4 + 0.4/5 + 0.2/6 + 0/7,$$

R_Y is computed on the base of (5.1)-(5.2) as follows. As

$$abs(-3) = abs(3) = 3, abs(-2) = abs(2) = 2, abs(-1) = abs(1) = 1,$$

given (5.1)-(5.2) one has

$$p_Y(3) = p_X(-3) + p_X(3), \ p_Y(2) = p_X(-2) + p_X(2), \ p_Y(1)$$
$$= p_X(-1) + p_X(1).$$

At the same time, one has $p_Y(0) = p_X(0)$, $p_Y(1) = p_X(1)$, $p_Y(4) = p_X(4),..., p_Y(7) = p_X(7)$. Therefore, R_Y is as it is shown below:

$$p_Y = 0.14/0 + 0.173/1 + 0.21/2 + 0.173/3 + 0.134/4$$
$$+ 0.0957/5 + 0.057/6 + 0.019/7.$$

As the 'true' distribution p_X is unknown, we compute $\mu_{p_X}(p_{X,l}) = \mu_{B_X}\left(\sum_{k=1}^{n}\mu_{A_X}(x_k)p_{X,l}(x_k)\right)$. For p_X considered above, the obtained result is $\mu_{p_X}(p_{X,l}) \approx \mu_{B_X}(0.7) = 0.2$. By solving goal linear programming problems (4.3a)-(4.4a) we construct the membership function μ_{p_X}.

Next we construct μ_{p_Y} induced by μ_{p_X}:

$$\mu_{p_Y}(p_{Y,l}) = \mu_{p_X}(p_{X,l}),$$

subject to (5.1)-(5.2).

For example, given p_Y considered above, the obtained result is

$$\mu_{p_Y}(p_{Y,l}) = \mu_{p_X}(p_{X,l}) = 0.2.$$

Finally, we compute probability measure of A_Y given p_Y on the base of Definition 4.1 and, given fuzzy restriction on p_Y described by the membership function μ_{p_Y}, we construct a fuzzy set B_Y. The obtained result is as follows:

$$B_Y = 0/0.68 + 0.2/0.7 + 0.4/0.725 + 0.6/0.75 + 0.8/0.775$$
$$+ 1/0.8 + 0.8/0.825 + 0.6/0.85 + 0.4/0.875 + 0.2/0.9 + 0/0.925.$$

Thus, Z-number $Z_Y = (A_X, B_X)$ as the absolute value of Z_X is obtained. A_X, B_X are shown in Fig. 5.1.

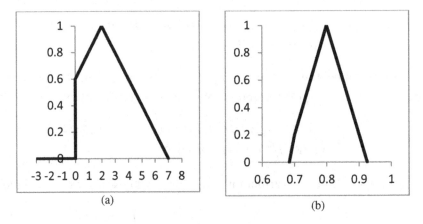

(a)   (b)

Fig. 5.1. The absolute value of the discrete Z-number: (a) A_Y, (b) B_Y.

Let us mention that in the considered example, the obtained B_Y slightly differs from the given B_X (see Fig. 5.2).

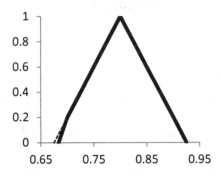

Fig. 5.2. The obtained B_Y (thick solid curve) and the given B_X (thin dotted curve).

5.2. Distance Between Two Z-numbers

Denote by $\mathcal{D}$ the space of discrete fuzzy sets of $\mathcal{R}$. Denote by $\mathcal{D}_{[a,b]}$ the space of discrete fuzzy sets of $[a,b] \subset \mathcal{R}$.

Definition 5.1. The supremum metric on $\mathcal{D}$ [55,92]. The supremum metric d on $\mathcal{D}$ is defined as

$$d(A_1, A_2) = \sup\{d_H(A_1^{\alpha}, A_2^{\alpha}) | 0 < \alpha \leq 1\}, \ A_1, A_2 \in \mathcal{D}$$

where d_H is the Hausdorff distance.

$(\mathcal{D}, d)$ is a complete metric space[55,92].

Definition 5.2. Fuzzy Hausdorff distance [6,16]. The fuzzy Hausdorff distance d_{fH} between $A_1, A_2 \in \mathcal{D}$ is defined as

$$d_{fH}(A_1, A_2) = \bigcup_{\alpha \in [0,1]} \alpha d_{fH}^{\alpha}(A_1, A_2),$$

where

$$d_{fH}^{\alpha}(A_1, A_2) = \left\{ \sup_{\alpha \leq \bar{\alpha} \leq 1} d_H(A_1^{\bar{\alpha}}, A_2^{\bar{\alpha}}) \right\},$$

where $\bar{\alpha}$ is the value which is within α-cut and 1-cut. $(\mathcal{D}, d_{fH})$ is a complete metric space.

Denote $\mathcal{Z}$ the space of discrete Z-numbers:

$$\mathcal{Z} = \left\{ Z = (A,B) | A \in \mathcal{D}^1, B \in \mathcal{D}^1_{[0,1]} \right\}.$$

Definition 5.3. Supremum metrics on $\mathcal{Z}$. The supremum metrics on $\mathcal{Z}$ is defined as

$$D(Z_1, Z_2) = d(A_1, A_2) + d(B_1, B_2) \tag{5.3}$$

$(\mathcal{Z}, D)$ is a complete metric space. This follows from the fact that $(\mathcal{D}^1, d)$ is a complete metric space.

$D(Z_1,Z_2)$ has the following properties:

$$D(Z_1 + Z, \ Z_2 + Z) = D(Z_1, \ Z_2),$$

$$D(Z_2,Z_1) = D(Z_1, \ Z_2),$$

$$D(\lambda Z_1, \lambda Z_2) = |\lambda| D(Z_1,Z_2), \ \lambda \in \mathcal{R},$$

$$D(Z_1,Z_2) \le D(Z_1,Z) + D(Z,Z_2).$$

Example. Let us consider computation of the supremum metrics $D(Z_1,Z_2)$ of two discrete Z-numbers $Z_1 = (A_1,B_1)$ and $Z_2 = (A_2,B_2)$ given:

$$A_1 = 0/2 + 0.2/3 + 0.4/4 + 0.6/5 + 0.8/6 + 1/7 + 0.8/8 + 0.6/9$$
$$+ 0.4/10 + 0.2/11 + 0/12,$$

$$B_1 = 0/0.675 + 0.2/0.7 + 0.4/0.725 + 0.6/0.75 + 0.8/0.775$$
$$+ 1/0.8 + 0.8/0.825 + 0.6/0.85 + 0.4/0.875 + 0.2/0.9 + 0/0.925;$$

$$A_2 = 0/10 + 0.5/15 + 0.8/20 + 1/25 + 0.8/30 + 0.7/35 + 0.6/40$$
$$+ 0.4/45 + 0.2/50 + 0.1/55 + 0/60,$$

$$B_2 = 0/0.575 + 0.2/0.6 + 0.4/0.625 + 0.6/0.65 + 0.8/0.675 + 1/0.7$$
$$+ 0.8/0.725 + 0.6/0.75 + 0.4/0.775 + 0.2/0.8 + 0/0.825.$$

At first we need to calculate $d(A_1,A_2)$. This requires to calculate the Hausdorff distance d_H between α-cuts $A_1{}^\alpha, A_2{}^\alpha$, where $\alpha = 0, 0.2, 0.4, 0.6, 0.8, 1$. For example, for $\alpha = 0.2$ one has:

$$d_H(A_1{}^{\alpha=0.2}, \ A_2{}^{\alpha=0.2}) = d_H(\{3,4,5,6,7,8,9,10,11\},$$
$$\{15,20,25,30,35,40,45,50,55\}) = \max(|3-15|,|11-55|) = 44.$$

The Hausdorff distances computed for the other α-cuts are as follows.

$$d_H(A_1^{\alpha=0}, A_2^{\alpha=0}) = \max(|2-10|, |12-60|) = 48;$$

$$d_H(A_1^{\alpha=0.4}, A_2^{\alpha=0.4}) = \max(|4-20|, |10-50|) = 40;$$

$$d_H(A_1^{\alpha=0.6}, A_2^{\alpha=0.6}) = \max(|5-25|, |9-45|) = 36;$$

$$d_H(A_1^{\alpha=0.8}, A_2^{\alpha=0.8}) = \max(|6-30|, |8-40|) = 32;$$

$$d_H(A_1^{\alpha=1}, A_2^{\alpha=1}) = |7-35| = 28.$$

$$d(A_1, A_2) = \sup\{d_H(A_1^{\alpha}, A_2^{\alpha}) | \alpha = 0, 0.2, 0.4, 0.6, 0.8, 1\} = 48.$$

Analogously, we computed the supremum metric between B_1, B_2 and obtained $d(B_1, B_2) = 0.1$. Therefore, the supremum metric $D(Z_1, Z_2)$ between the considered discrete Z-numbers is equal to

$$D(Z_1, Z_2) = d(A_1, A_2) + d(B_1, B_2) = 0.1 + 48 = 48.1.$$

Definition 5.4. Fuzzy Hausdorff distance between Z-numbers. The fuzzy Hausdorff distance d_{fHZ} between Z-numbers $Z_1 = (A_1, B_1)$, $Z_2 = (A_2, B_2) \in \mathcal{Z}$ is defined as

$$d_{fHZ}(Z_1, Z_2) = d_{fH}(A_1, A_2) + d_{fH}(B_1, B_2). \tag{5.4}$$

An example. Let us consider computation of the Fuzzy Hausdorff distance $d_{fHZ}(Z_1, Z_2)$ between two discrete Z-numbers $Z_1 = (A_1, B_1)$ and $Z_2 = (A_2, B_2)$ considered in the example above.

At first we calculate $d_{fH}(A_1, A_2)$ in accordance with Definition 5.2. This requires to determine $d(A_1^{\alpha=1}, A_2^{\alpha=1})$ and $\sup\limits_{\alpha \leq \bar{\alpha} \leq 1} d(A_1^{\bar{\alpha}}, A_2^{\bar{\alpha}})$. In order to determine the latter, we need to have $d(A_1^{\bar{\alpha}}, A_2^{\bar{\alpha}})$, $\bar{\alpha} = 0, 0.2, 0.4, 0.6, 0.8, 1$ which were computed above. Then the results for $\sup\limits_{\alpha \leq \bar{\alpha} \leq 1} d(A_1^{\bar{\alpha}}, A_2^{\bar{\alpha}})$, $\alpha = 0, 0.2, 0.4, 0.6, 0.8, 1$ will be found as follows. For $\alpha = 0$, we have

$$\sup_{\alpha \leq \bar{\alpha} \leq 1} d(A_1^{\bar{\alpha}}, A_2^{\bar{\alpha}}) = \sup_{0 \leq \bar{\alpha} \leq 1} d(A_1^{\bar{\alpha}}, A_2^{\bar{\alpha}}) = \sup_{\bar{\alpha} \in \{0,0.2,0.4,0.6,0.8,1\}} d(A_1^{\bar{\alpha}}, A_2^{\bar{\alpha}})$$

$$= \max\{48, 44, 40, 36, 32, 28\} = 48.$$

The results for the other $\bar{\alpha}$-cuts are shown below:

for $\alpha = 0.2$, $\sup_{\alpha \leq \bar{\alpha} \leq 1} d(A_1^{\bar{\alpha}}, A_2^{\bar{\alpha}}) = \max\{44, 40, 36, 32, 28\} = 44$;

for $\alpha = 0.4$, $\sup_{\alpha \leq \bar{\alpha} \leq 1} d(A_1^{\bar{\alpha}}, A_2^{\bar{\alpha}}) = \max\{40, 36, 32, 28\} = 40$;

for $\alpha = 0.6$, $\sup_{\alpha \leq \bar{\alpha} \leq 1} d(A_1^{\bar{\alpha}}, A_2^{\bar{\alpha}}) = \max\{36, 32, 28\} = 36$;

for $\alpha = 0.8$, $\sup_{\alpha \leq \bar{\alpha} \leq 1} d(A_1^{\bar{\alpha}}, A_2^{\bar{\alpha}}) = \max\{32, 28\} = 32$;

for $\alpha = 1$, $\sup_{\alpha \leq \bar{\alpha} \leq 1} d(A_1^{\bar{\alpha}}, A_2^{\bar{\alpha}}) = 28$.

Thus, we will have:

$$d_{fH}^{\alpha=0}(A_1, A_2) = \{48, 44, 40, 36, 32, 28\} ;$$

$$d_{fH}^{\alpha=0.2}(A_1, A_2) = \{44, 40, 36, 32, 28\} ;$$

$$d_{fH}^{\alpha=0.4}(A_1, A_2) = \{40, 36, 32, 28\} ;$$

$$d_{fH}^{\alpha=0.6}(A_1, A_2) = \{36, 32, 28\} ;$$

$$d_{fH}^{\alpha=0.8}(A_1, A_2) = \{32, 28\} ;$$

$$d_{fH}^{\alpha=1}(A_1, A_2) = \{28\} .$$

Thus, the fuzzy Hausdorff distance $d_{fH}(A_1, A_2)$ is

$$d_{fH}(A_1, A_2) = 1/28 + 0.8/32 + 0.6/36 + 0.4/40 + 0.2/44 + 0/48.$$

Analogously we have determined the fuzzy Hausdorff distance $d_{fH}(B_1, B_2)$ which is obtained as a singleton:

$$d_{fH}(B_1, B_2) = 0.1.$$

Now, based on (5.4) we compute the Fuzzy Hausdorff distance between Z-numbers $d_{fHZ}(Z_1, Z_2)$ by adding the obtained discrete fuzzy numbers according to Definition 2.20:

$$d_{fHZ}(Z_1, Z_2) = d_{fH}(A_1, A_2) + d_{fH}(B_1, B_2)$$
$$= 1/28.1 + 0.8/32.1 + 0.6/36.1 + 0.4/40.1 + 0.2/44.1 + 0/48.1.$$

Definition 5.5. Z-valued Euclidean distance between discrete Z-numbers. Given two discrete Z-numbers $Z_1 = (A_1, B_1)$, $Z_2 = (A_2, B_2) \in \mathcal{Z}$, Z-valued Euclidean distance $d_E(Z_1, Z_2)$ between Z_1 and Z_2 is defined as

$$d_E(Z_1, Z_2) = \sqrt{(Z_1 - Z_2)^2} \qquad (5.5)$$

An example. Consider the discrete Z-numbers $Z_1 = (A_1, B_1)$ and $Z_2 = (A_2, B_2)$:

$$A_1 = 0/1 + 0.3/2 + 0.5/3 + 0.6/4 + 0.7/5 + 0.8/6 + 0.9/7$$
$$+ 1/8 + 0.8/9 + 0.6/10 + 0/11,$$

$$B_1 = 0/0 + 0.5/0.1 + 0.8/0.2 + 1/0.3 + 0.8/0.4 + 0.7/0.5 + 0.6/0.6$$
$$+ 0.4/0.7 + 0.2/0.8 + 0.1/0.6 + 0/1;$$

$$A_2 = 0/15 + 0.5/25 + 0.8/35 + 1/45 + 0.8/55 + 0.7/65 + 0.6/75$$
$$+ 0.4/85 + 0.2/95 + 0.1/105 + 0/115,$$

$$B_2 = 0/0 + 0.3/0.1 + 0.5/0.2 + 0.6/0.3 + 0.7/0.4 + 0.8/0.5$$
$$+ 0.9/0.6 + 1/0.7 + 0.9/0.8 + 0.8/0.6 + 0/1.$$

In order to compute $d_E(Z_1, Z_2)$ we need first to compute the standard subtraction $Z_{12} = Z_1 - Z_2$ as it is shown in Section 4.1.4. Determination of $Z_{12} = Z_1 - Z_2$ requires construction of probability distributions p_1 and p_2 underlying discrete Z-numbers $Z_1 = (A_1, B_1)$ and $Z_2 = (A_2, B_2)$. These problems are goal linear programming problems (4.3a)-(4.4a) which should be solved for $Z_1 = (A_1, B_1)$ and $Z_2 = (A_2, B_2)$. Consider construction of p_1, construction of p_2 is analogous. For example, to find p_1 for which $P(A_1) = \sum_{k=1}^{n_1} \mu_{A_1}(x_{1k}) p_1(x_{1k}) = 0.2$, one needs to solve:

$$0v_1 + 0.3v_2 + 0.5v_3 + 0.6v_4 + 0.7v_5 + 0.8v_6 + 0.9v_7 + 1v_8$$
$$+ 0.8v_9 + 0.6v_{10} + 0v_{11} \to 0.2 \tag{5.6}$$

subject to

$$\left. \begin{array}{l} v_1 + v_2 + \ldots + v_n = 1 \\ v_1, v_2, \ldots, v_n \geq 0 \end{array} \right\} . \tag{5.7}$$

Coefficients of the objective function (5.6) are values of membership function μ_{A_1} (see above), the goal 0.2 is a basic value of B_1, and decision variables $v_1, v_2, \ldots, v_n$ are the values $p_1(x_{11}), p_1(x_{12}), \ldots, p_1(x_{1n})$ of probability distribution p_1 to be found. Therefore, it is needed to find such a distribution p_1 which induces $b \in B_1$, $b = 0.2$. The obtained result is as follows:

$$p_1 = 0.3862 \backslash 1 + 0 \backslash 2 + 0 \backslash 3 + 0.0013 \backslash 4 + 0.0195 \backslash 5 + 0.0377 \backslash 6$$
$$+ 0.0559 \backslash 7 + 0.0741 \backslash 8 + 0.0377 \backslash 9 + 0.0013 \backslash 10 + 0.3862 \backslash 11.$$

Analogously we obtained probability distributions for the rest values of $b \in B_1$. The results are as follows.

For $b = 0$:

$$p_1 = 0.5 \backslash 1 + 0 \backslash 2 + 0 \backslash 3 + 0 \backslash 4 + 0 \backslash 5 + 0 \backslash 6 + 0 \backslash 7 + 0 \backslash 8$$
$$+ 0 \backslash 9 + 0 \backslash 10 + 0.5 \backslash 11;$$

for $b = 0.1$:

$$p_1 = 0.4431 \backslash 1 + 0 \backslash 2 + 0 \backslash 3 + 0 \backslash 4 + 0.0098 \backslash 5 + 0.0189 \backslash 6 + 0.028 \backslash 7$$
$$+ 0.037 \backslash 8 + 0.0189 \backslash 9 + 0 \backslash 10 + 0.4431 \backslash 11;$$

for $b = 0.3$:

$$p_1 = 0.3293 \backslash 1 + 0 \backslash 2 + 0 \backslash 3 + 0 \backslash 4 + 0.0098 \backslash 5 + 0.0189 \backslash 6$$
$$+ 0.028 \backslash 7 + 0.037 \backslash 8 + 0.0189 \backslash 9 + 0 \backslash 10 + 0.4431 \backslash 11;$$

for $b = 0.4$:

$$p_1 = 0.2724 \backslash 1 + 0 \backslash 2 + 0 \backslash 3 + 0.0027 \backslash 4 + 0.039 \backslash 5 + 0.0754 \backslash 6$$
$$+ 0.1118 \backslash 7 + 0.1482 \backslash 8 + 0.0189 \backslash 9 + 0 \backslash 10 + 0.4431 \backslash 11;$$

for $b = 0.5$:

$$p_1 = 0.2155 \backslash 1 + 0 \backslash 2 + 0 \backslash 3 + 0.0033 \backslash 4 + 0.0488 \backslash 5 + 0.0943 \backslash 6$$
$$+ 0.1398 \backslash 7 + 0.1852 \backslash 8 + 0.943 \backslash 9 + 0.0033 \backslash 10 + 0.2155 \backslash 11;$$

for $b = 0.6$:

$$p_1 = 0.1586 \backslash 1 + 0 \backslash 2 + 0 \backslash 3 + 0.0040 \backslash 4 + 0.0586 \backslash 5 + 0.1131 \backslash 6$$
$$+ 0.1677 \backslash 7 + 0.2223 \backslash 8 + 0.1131 \backslash 9 + 0.0040 \backslash 10 + 0.1586 \backslash 11;$$

for $b = 0.7$:

$$p_1 = 0.1017 \backslash 1 + 0 \backslash 2 + 0 \backslash 3 + 0.0047 \backslash 4 + 0.0683 \backslash 5 + 0.132 \backslash 6$$
$$+ 0.1957 \backslash 7 + 0.2593 \backslash 8 + 0.132 \backslash 9 + 0.0047 \backslash 10 + 0.1017 \backslash 11;$$

for $b = 0.8$:

$$p_1 = 0.0448 \backslash 1 + 0 \backslash 2 + 0 \backslash 3 + 0.0053 \backslash 4 + 0.0781 \backslash 5 + 0.1508 \backslash 6$$
$$+ 0.2236 \backslash 7 + 0.2964 \backslash 8 + 0.1508 \backslash 9 + 0.0053 \backslash 10 + 0.0448 \backslash 11;$$

for $b = 0.9$:

$$p_1 = 0 \backslash 1 + 0 \backslash 2 + 0 \backslash 3 + 0 \backslash 4 + 0.0385 \backslash 5 + 0.1538 \backslash 6 + 0.2692 \backslash 7$$
$$+ 0.3846 \backslash 8 + 0.1538 \backslash 9 + 0 \backslash 10 + 0 \backslash 11;$$

for $b = 1$:

$$p_1 = 0 \backslash 1 + 0 \backslash 2 + 0 \backslash 3 + 0 \backslash 4 + 0 \backslash 5 + 0 \backslash 6 + 1 \backslash 7 + 0 \backslash 8$$
$$+ 0 \backslash 9 + 0 \backslash 10 + 0 \backslash 11.$$

The resulting Z_{12} is shown below (Fig. 5.3):

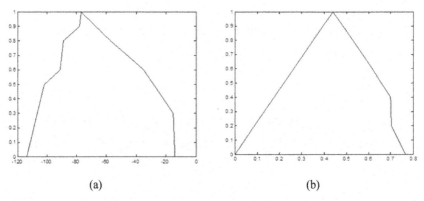

(a)   (b)

Fig. 5.3. The standard subtraction Z_{12} : (a) A_{12} , (b) B_{12}.

Next, the square $Z_3 = Z_{12}^2$ should be found in accordance with Section 4.2.1. The result is shown below:

$$A_3 = 0/16 + 0.5/196 + 0.6/225 + 0.8/1225 + 0.9/2116 + 1/3249 + 0.8/5929$$
$$+ 0.7/6084 + 0.6/7921 + 0.3/8281 + 0/12996,$$

$$B_3 = 0/0 + 0.2/0.088 + 0.4/0.18 + 0.6/0.26 + 0.8/0.35 + 1/0.44 + 0.8/0.53$$
$$+ 0.6/0.62 + 0.4/0.7 + 0.2/0.704 + 0/0.77$$

The graphs of A_3 and B_3 are shown in Fig. 5.4.

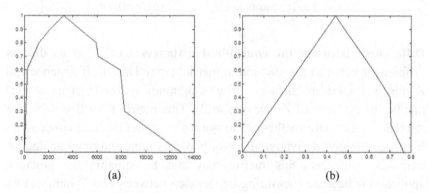

(a) (b)

Fig. 5.4. The square of discrete Z-number $Z_3 = Z_{12}^2$: (a) A_3, (b) B_3.

At the final stage, the square root $Z_4 = \sqrt{Z_3}$ is found as it is shown in Section 4.2.2. The result is shown below:

$$A_4 = 0/4 + 0.5/14 + 0.6/15 + 0.8/35 + 0.9/46 + 1/57 + 0.8/77 + 0.7/78$$
$$+ 0.6/89 + 0.3/91 + 0/114,$$
$$B_4 = 0/0 + 0.2/0.088 + 0.4/0.18 + 0.6/0.26 + 0.8/0.35 + 1/0.44$$
$$+ 0.8/0.53 + 0.6/0.62 + 0.4/0.7 + 0.2/0.704 + 0/0.77.$$

Therefore, $d_E(Z_1, Z_2)$ is found as $d_E(Z_1, Z_2) = \sqrt{(Z_1 - Z_2)^2} = (A_4, B_4)$. The graphs of A_4 and B_4 are shown in Fig. 5.5.

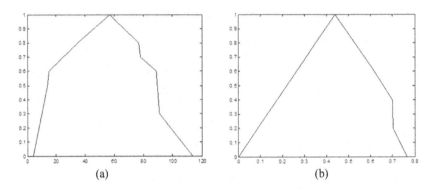

(a)   (b)

Fig. 5.5. The square root $Z_4 = \sqrt{Z_3}$: (a) A_4, (b) B_4.

Differences between the considered distances on $\mathcal{Z}$. Let us discuss differences between the supremum metric, fuzzy Hausdorff distance and Z-valued Euclidean distance. The supremum metric assigns a real number to any pair of Z-numbers in $\mathcal{Z}$. This metric is well suitable for 'technical', i.e. pure mathematical purposes, to define such concepts as limits, continuity, derivative, for proofs of theorems and other analogous purposes. However, this metric may not be suitable for practical applications because measuring of distance between two Z-numbers by using numerical value leads to a significant loss of information.

Fuzzy Hausdorff distance is also suitable for 'technical' purposes like the supremum metric, but is more complex to deal with in mathematical operations. From the other side, Fuzzy Hausdorff distance as opposed to the supremum metrics, preserves imprecise information contained in Z-numbers better. However, it losses reliability information because the resulting distance here is a discrete fuzzy number.

Z-valued Euclidean distance is not well suitable for 'technical' purposes as it is significantly complex to be used in mathematical operations over spaces of Z-numbers. However, this metric is well suitable for practical purposes, it preserves both fuzziness and partial reliability of initial information in $\mathcal{Z}$, and provides intuitive results. Conceptually, Z-valued Euclidean distance is intended to measure distance under Z-number based information.

5.3. Functions of Discrete Z-numbers

5.3.1. *Main Definitions*

Denote $\mathcal{Z}$ the space of discrete Z-numbers:

$$\mathcal{Z} = \left\{ Z = (A,B) \mid A \in \mathcal{D}, B \in \mathcal{D}_{[0,1]} \right\}.$$

Then denote $\mathcal{Z}^n$ the space elements of which are n-vectors of discrete Z-numbers $\mathbf{Z} = (Z_1, Z_2, ..., Z_n) = ((A_1, B_1), (A_2, B_2), ..., (A_n, B_n))$. Also, we denote $\mathcal{Z}^{\{B\}} = \left\{ (A,B) \in \mathcal{Z} \mid B = const \right\}$ as a set of discrete Z-numbers with fixed B. Denote $\mathcal{Z}_{[c,d]} = \left\{ (A,B) \mid A \in \mathcal{D}_{[c,d]}, B \in \mathcal{D}_{[0,1]} \right\}$, $[c,d] \subset \mathcal{R}$, and $\mathcal{Z}_+ = \left\{ (A,B) \in \mathcal{Z} \mid A \in \mathcal{D}_{[0,\infty)} \right\}$, $\mathcal{Z}_- = \mathcal{Z} \setminus \mathcal{Z}_+$.

A new fundamental theory of discrete sets and discrete functions was suggested in [38,39]. This theory is a systematic approach to dealing with discrete structures which result from the fact that our intelligent, technological, technical and other possibilities often lead to 'discrete' nature of processing of real-world continuous information. In this section we suggest foundations of discrete Z-number valued functions.

Let us consider a discrete subset $A \subset \mathcal{Z}$. The following definitions apply as adopted from [40].

Definition 5.6. A discrete ordered set. A discrete ordered set $\mathcal{A} = \{Z_1, Z_2, ..., Z_n\} \subseteq \mathcal{Z}$ is called:

1) *uniform* if $d(Z_i, Z_{i+1}) = const$ for any $Z_i, Z_{i+1} \in \mathcal{A}$, that is, all distances between any two consecutive points in $\mathcal{A}$ are equal;

2) *bounded down* if for some $k > 0$ one has $d(Z_i, Z_{i+1}) > k$ for any $Z_i, Z_{i+1} \in \mathcal{A}$, that is, all distances between any two consecutive points in $\mathcal{A}$ are larger than some $k > 0$;

3) *bounded up* if for some $k > 0$ one has $d(Z_i, Z_{i+1}) < k$ for any $Z_i, Z_{i+1} \in \mathcal{A}$, that is, all distances between any two consecutive points in $\mathcal{A}$ are less than some $k > 0$.

Definition 5.7. Spacing of a uniform discrete set. 1) In a uniform discrete set $\mathcal{A}$, the distances between any two consecutive points is called the *spacing* of $\mathcal{A}$.

2) In a bounded down discrete set $\mathcal{A}$, the lower bound of distances between consecutive points in $\mathcal{A}$ is called the *lower inner bound* of $\mathcal{A}$; it is denoted by $lib\mathcal{A}$.

3) In a bounded up discrete set $\mathcal{A}$, the lower bound of distances between consecutive points in $\mathcal{A}$ is called the *upper inner bound* of $\mathcal{A}$; it is denoted by $uib\mathcal{A}$.

Lemma 5.1. If $\mathcal{A}$ and $\mathcal{A}'$ are discrete sets and $\mathcal{A} \subseteq \mathcal{A}'$, then $lib\mathcal{A}' \leq lib\mathcal{A}$ and $uib\mathcal{A}' \leq uib\mathcal{A}$.

The proof is obvious.

Definition 5.8. A discrete Z-number valued infinity. Let $Z = (A,B)$ be a discrete Z-number. If for every positive real number M, there exists $\alpha_0 \in (0,1]$ such that $M < A_2^{\alpha_0}$ or $A_1^{\alpha_0} < -M$, then $Z = (A,B)$ is called discrete Z-number valued infinity, denoted by Z_∞.

Denote $\mathcal{F}$ a σ-algebra of $\mathcal{A}^n$. Let us define for two Z-numbers $Z_1 = (A_1,B_1)$ and $Z_2 = (A_2,B_2)$ that $Z_1 = Z_2$ iff $A_1 = A_2$ and $B_1 = B_2$, where equality of fuzzy numbers is defined in terms of Definition 2.9.

Let $\mathcal{A} \subseteq \mathcal{Z}$ be a metric space with a metric d, and r be a non-negative real number, and $l = \{Z_i | Z_i \in \mathcal{A}, i = 1,2,...,n,...\}$ be a sequence in $\mathcal{A}$.

Definition 5.9. An r-limit. An element $Z \in \mathcal{A}$ is called an r-limit of l (denoted $Z = r\text{-}\lim l$) if for any $k \in R^+ \setminus \{0\}$ the inequality $\rho(Z,Z_i) \leq r + k$ I s valid for almost all Z_i.

Definition 5.10. A discrete Z-number valued function of discrete Z-numbers. A discrete Z-number valued function of discrete Z-numbers is a mapping $f : \mathcal{A} \to \mathcal{A}$.

Consider a general case $f : \Omega \to \mathcal{A}$, where Ω is a universe of discourse. Given a Z-number valued function $f : \Omega \to \mathcal{Z}$, a fuzzy number valued function $\varphi : \Omega \to \mathcal{D}$ is called its A-valued function whenever for any $\omega \in \Omega$ one has $\varphi(\omega) = A \in \mathcal{D}$ iff $f(\omega) = (A,B) \in \mathcal{Z}$. A fuzzy number valued function $\gamma : \Omega \to \mathcal{D}_{[0,1]}$ is called B-valued function for

$f : \Omega \to \mathcal{Z}$ whenever for any $\omega \in \Omega$ one has $\gamma(\omega) = B \in \mathcal{D}_{[0,1]}$ iff $f(\omega) = (A, B) \in \mathcal{Z}$.

Definition 5.11. An r-limit of Z-valued function. An element $Z_b \in f(l)$ is called an r-limit of f at a point $Z_{a,i} \in l$ and denoted $Z_b = r\text{-}\lim_{Z_x \to Z_a} f(Z_x)$ if for any sequence l satisfying the condition $Z_a = \lim l$, the equality $Z_b = r\text{-}\lim f(l)$ is valid.

Definition 5.12. (q, r)-continuous Z-valued function. A function $f : \mathcal{A} \to \mathcal{A}$ is called (q, r)-*continuous* at a point $Z_a \in \mathcal{A}$ if for any $\varepsilon > 0$ there is $\delta > 0$ such that the inequality $d(Z_a, Z_x) < q + \delta$ implies the inequality $d(f(Z_a), f(Z_x)) < r + \varepsilon$, or in other words, for any Z_x with $d(Z_a, Z_x) < q + \delta$, we have $d(f(Z_a), f(Z_x)) < r + \varepsilon$.

Let us consider the concept of measurability of a discrete fuzzy number valued function which is based on the concept of measurability of an interval valued function[144].

Definition 5.13. Measurability of a discrete fuzzy number valued function [144]. A discrete fuzzy number-valued function $\varphi : \Omega \to \mathcal{D}^1$ is called a measurable if its α-cut $\varphi^\alpha(\omega) = \left\{ y \middle| \mu_{f(\omega)}(y) \geq \alpha \right\}$ is a measurable set function for every $\alpha \in (0,1]$, where $\mu_{\varphi(\omega)}$ is the membership function of the value of φ at ω.

We suggest the following definition of measurability of a Z-number valued function on the base of a concept of measurability of a discrete fuzzy function [144]:

Definition 5.14. Measurability of a discrete Z-number valued function. A Z-valued function $f : \Omega \to \mathcal{Z}$ is called a measurable Z-valued function if its A-valued function $\varphi : \Omega \to \mathcal{D}$ and B-valued function $\gamma : \Omega \to \mathcal{D}_{[0,1]}$ are measurable fuzzy mappings.

Now we proceed to investigation of typical functions shown in Fig. 5.6.

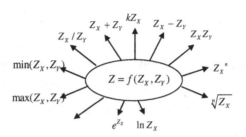

Fig. 5.6. Typical Z-number valued functions.

Fig. 5.6 shows several widely-used typical forms of Z-number valued functions of Z-numbers. Functions $Z_X + Z_Y$, kZ_X, $Z_X - Z_Y$, $Z_X Z_Y$, Z_X / Z_Y, Z_X^n, $\sqrt[n]{Z_X}$, $\min(Z_X, Z_Y)$, $\max(Z_X, Z_Y)$ are described in details in Chapter 4. In the following sections we will consider e^{Z_X}, $\ln Z_X$, $P_n(Z_X) = Z_{a_0} Z_X^n + Z_{a_1} Z_X^{n-1} + \ldots + Z_{a_n}$, and Z-rules.

5.3.2. Typical Functions

5.3.2.1. A Discrete Z-number Valued Exponential Function

Let us consider determination of $Z_Y = e^{Z_X}$. Let $Z_X^+ = (A_X, R_X)$ where R_X is represented as

$$p_X = p_X(x_1) \backslash x_1 + p_X(x_2) \backslash x_2 + \ldots + p_X(x_n) \backslash x_n.$$

Then the discrete Z^+-number Z_Y^+ is determined as follows:

$$Z_Y^+ = (A_Y, R_Y),$$

where $A_Y = e^{A_X}$, e^{A_X} is determined on the base of Definition 2.29 and R_Y is represented on the base of (2.46) as a discrete probability distribution

$$p_Y = p_Y(y_1) \backslash y_1 + p_Y(y_2) \backslash y_2 + \ldots + p_Y(y_m) \backslash y_m, \tag{5.8}$$

such that

$$y_k = e^{x_k} \text{ and } p_Y(y_k) = p_X(x_k), \, k = 1, \ldots, n. \tag{5.9}$$

Next we compute $\mu_{p_X}(p_{X,l}) = \mu_{B_X}\left(\sum_{k=1}^{n} \mu_{A_X}(x_k)p_{X,l}(x_k)\right)$ by solving a goal linear programming problem (4.3a)-(4.4a). The fuzzy set of probability distributions p_X with membership function $\mu_{p_X}(p_{X,l})$ naturally induces the fuzzy set of probability distributions $p_{Y,l}$ with the membership function defined as

$$\mu_{p_Y}(p_{Y,l}) = \mu_{p_X}(p_{X,l}),$$

subject to (5.8)-(5.9).

Next, we compute probability measure of A_Y given p_Y on the base of Definition 4.1. Finally, given a fuzzy restriction described by μ_{p_Y}, we construct a fuzzy set B_Y as follows:

$$\mu_{B_Y}(b_{Y,l}) = \sup(\mu_{p_Y}(p_{Y,l}))$$

subject to

$$b_{Y,l} = \sum_{k} p_{Y,l}(x_k)\mu_{A_Y}(x_k).$$

As a result, $Z_Y = e^{Z_X}$ is obtained as $e^{Z_X} = (A_Y, B_Y) = (e^{A_X}, B_Y)$. Let us mention that as $p_{Y,l}(y_k) = p_{X,l}(x_k)$, $\mu_{p_Y}(p_{Y,l}) = \mu_{p_X}(p_{X,l})$, and $\mu_{A_Y}(y_k) = \mu_{A_X}(x_k)$ with $y_k = e^{x_k}$ hold, one has

$$b_{Y,l} = b_{X,l} \text{ and } \mu_{B_Y}(b_{Y,l}) = \mu_{B_X}(b_{X,l}),$$

which means $B_Y = B_X$.

An example. Let us compute value of the exponential function $Z_Y = e^{Z_X}$ at $Z_X = (A_X, B_X)$:

$$A_X = 0/1 + 0.3/2 + 0.5/3 + 0.6/4 + 0.7/5 + 0.8/6 + 0.9/7$$
$$+ 1/8 + 0.8/9 + 0.6/10 + 0/11,$$

$$B_X = 0/0 + 0.5/0.1 + 0.8/0.2 + 1/0.3 + 0.8/0.4 + 0.7/0.5 + 0.6/0.6$$
$$+ 0.4/0.7 + 0.2/0.8 + 0.1/0.6 + 0/1.$$

First we proceed to the Z^+-number $Z_X^+ = (A_X, R_X)$ with R_X represented as

$$p_X = 0.27 \backslash 1 + 0 \backslash 2 + 0 \backslash 3 + 0.0027 \backslash 4 + 0.04 \backslash 5 + 0.075 \backslash 6$$
$$+ 0.11 \backslash 7 + 0.15 \backslash 8 + 0.075 \backslash 9 + 0.0027 \backslash 10 + 0.27 \backslash 11.$$

Then we determine the corresponding Z^+-number $Z_Y^+ = (A_Y, R_Y)$, where $A_Y = e^{A_X}$ computed on the base of Definition 2.29 and R_Y computed on the base of (5.8)-(5.9) are given below:

$$A_Y = 0.1/2.72 + 0.3/7.39 + 0.5/20.1 + 0.6/55 + 0.7/148 + 0.8/403$$
$$+ 0.9/1096 + 1/2980 + 0.8/8103 + 0.6/22026 + 0/59874,$$

$$p_Y = 0.27 \backslash 2.72 + 0 \backslash 7.39 + 0 \backslash 20.1 + 0.0027 \backslash 55 + 0.04 \backslash 148$$
$$+ 0.075 \backslash 403 + 0.11 \backslash 1096 + 0.15 \backslash 2980 + 0.075 \backslash 8103$$
$$+ 0.0027 \backslash 22026 + 0.27 \backslash 59874.$$

As it was shown above, $B_Y = B_X$. However, we computed B_Y given A_Y, $\mu_{p_X}(p_X) = \mu_{B_X}\left(\sum_{k=1}^{n} \mu_{A_X}(x_k) p_X(x_k)\right)$ and taking into account the fact that $\mu_{p_Y}(p_Y) = \mu_{p_X}(p_{R_X})$. Thus, Z-number $Z_Y = (A_Y, B_Y)$ as the value of the exponential function at $Z_X = (A_X, B_X) = (A_1, B_1)$ is obtained. A_Y, B_Y are shown in Fig. 5.7.

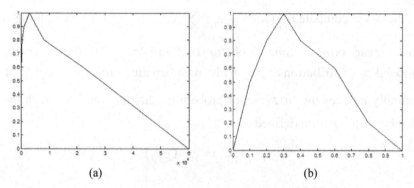

(a)   (b)

Fig. 5.7. The exponential of the discrete Z-number: (a) A_Y, (b) B_Y.

As one can see, $B_Y = B_X$.

5.3.2.2. A Discrete Z-number Valued Natural Logarithm

Let us consider determination of $Z_Y = \ln(Z_X)$. Let $Z_X^+ = (A_X, R_X)$ where R_X is represented as

$$p_X = p_X(x_1) \backslash x_1 + p_X(x_2) \backslash x_2 + \ldots + p_X(x_n) \backslash x_n.$$

Then the discrete Z^+-number Z_Y^+ is determined as follows:

$$Z_Y^+ = (A_Y, R_Y),$$

where $A_Y = \ln(A_X)$, $\ln(A_X)$ is determined on the base of Definition 2.30 and R_Y is represented on base of (2.47) as a discrete probability distribution

$$p_Y = p_Y(y_1) \backslash y_1 + p_Y(y_2) \backslash y_2 + \ldots + p_Y(y_m) \backslash y_m, \tag{5.10}$$

such that

$$y_k = \ln(x_k) \text{ and } p_Y(y_k) = p_X(x_k), \, k = 1, \ldots, n. \tag{5.11}$$

Next we compute $\mu_{p_X}(p_{X,l}) = \mu_{B_X}\left(\sum_{k=1}^{n}\mu_{A_X}(x_k)p_{X,l}(x_k)\right)$ by solving a goal linear programming problem (4.3a)-(4.4a). The fuzzy set of probability distributions p_X with membership function $\mu_{p_X}(p_{X,l})$ naturally induces the fuzzy set of probability distributions $p_{Y,l}$ with the membership function defined as

$$\mu_{p_Y}(p_{Y,l}) = \mu_{p_X}(p_{X,l}),$$

subject to (5.10)-(5.11).

Next, we compute probability measure of A_Y given p_Y on the base of Definition 4.1. Finally, given a fuzzy restriction described by μ_{p_Y}, we construct a fuzzy set B_Y as follows:

$$\mu_{B_Y}(b_{Y,l}) = \sup(\mu_{p_Y}(p_{Y,l}))$$

subject to

$$b_{Y,l} = \sum_{k}p_{Y,l}(x_k)\mu_{A_Y}(x_k).$$

As a result, $Z_Y = \ln(Z_X)$ is obtained as $\ln(Z_X) = (A_Y, B_Y) = (\ln(A_X), B_Y)$. Let us mention that analogously to the exponential of a discrete Z-number, one has $B_Y = B_X$.

An example. Let us compute value of the natural logarithm $Z_Y = \ln(Z_X)$ at $Z_X = (A_X, B_X)$ considered in the previous example. First we proceed to the Z^+-number $Z_X^+ = (A_X, R_X)$ with R_X represented as

$$p_X = 0.09\backslash 1 + 0\backslash 2 + 0.18\backslash 3 + 0.32\backslash 4 + 0.18\backslash 5 + 0.1\backslash 6 + 0.036\backslash 7$$
$$+ 0\backslash 8 + 0\backslash 9 + 0\backslash 10 + 0.09\backslash 11.$$

Then we compute the corresponding Z^+-number $Z_Y^+ = (A_Y, R_Y)$, where $A_Y = \ln(A_X)$ computed on the base of Definition 2.30 and R_Y computed on the base of (5.10)-(5.11) are given below:

$$A_Y = 0.1/0 + 0.3/0.69 + 0.5/1.1 + 0.6/1.39 + 0.7/1.61 + 0.8/1.79$$
$$+ 0.9/1.95 + 1/2.08 + 0.8/2.2 + 0.6/2.3 + 0/2.4,$$

$$p_Y = 0.09 \backslash 0 + 0 \backslash 0.69 + 0.18 \backslash 1.1 + 0.32 \backslash 1.39 + 0.18 \backslash 1.61$$
$$+ 0.1 \backslash 1.79 + 0.036 \backslash 1.95 + 0 \backslash 2.08 + 0 \backslash 2.19 + 0 \backslash 2.3 + 0.09 \backslash 2.4.$$

As it was shown above, $B_Y = B_X$. However, we computed B_Y given $A_Y, \mu_{p_X}(p_X) = \mu_{B_X}\left(\sum_{k=1}^{n} \mu_{A_X}(x_k)p_X(x_k)\right)$ and taking into account the fact that $\mu_{p_Y}(p_Y) = \mu_{p_X}(p_{R_X})$. Thus, Z-number $Z_Y = (A_Y, B_Y)$ as the value of the natural logarithm of $Z_X = (A_X, B_X)$ is obtained. A_Y, B_Y are shown in Fig. 5.8.

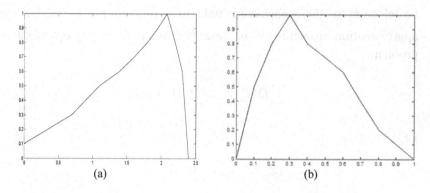

(a) (b)

Fig. 5.8. The natural logarithm of the discrete Z-number: (a) A_Y, (b) B_Y.

As one can see, $B_Y = B_X$.

Definition 5.15. A discrete Z-number valued polynomial. A discrete Z-number valued polynomial of an order n is a function $P_n : \mathcal{Z} \to \mathcal{Z}$ defined

$$P_n(Z_X) = Z_{a_0} Z_X{}^{n} + Z_{a_1} Z_X{}^{n-1} + ... + Z_{a_n} = \sum_{j=0}^{n} Z_{a_j} Z_X{}^{n-j}, \qquad (5.12)$$

where $Z_{a_j} = (A_j, B_j), \ Z_X{}^{n-j} = (A_X{}^{n-j}, B_{X^{n-j}}), \ j = 0,...,n.$

5.3.3. *Approximation of an Unknown Discrete Z-number Valued Mappings*

5.3.3.1. *Approximation by Using a Discrete Z-number Valued Polynomial*

Let $\mathcal{X} = \{Z_i | i = 1,...,m\}$ be a set of m distinct points of $\mathcal{Z}$, that is, $Z_i \neq Z_l$ whenever $i \neq l$, and $f(Z_i)$ be the corresponding values of an unknown Z-number valued function $f : \mathcal{Z} \rightarrow \mathcal{Z}$ at these points. It may be necessary to have a convenient analytical approximation of f for theoretical and practical purposes. Let us consider a problem of an approximation of f by P_n. The problem consists in determination of such coefficients $a_j = (A_j, B_j)$, $j = 0,...,n$, which provide the polynomial function (5.12) to be closest to the considered unknown function f. Formally, the approximation problem may be described as the following optimization problem:

$$\sum_{i=1}^{m} D\left(P_n(Z_i), f(Z_i)\right) \rightarrow \min$$

s.t.

$$(Z_{a_0}, Z_{a_1}, ..., Z_{a_n}) \in \mathcal{A} \subset \mathcal{Z}^n.$$

Here D is the supremum metric of discrete Z-numbers.

5.3.3.2. *Z-interpolation*

Z-rule base concept plays pivotal role in economics, decision making, forecasting and other human centric systems functioning in Z-information environment. The Z-rule base is complete when for all the possible observations there exists at least one rule whose Z-antecedent part overlaps the current antecedent Z-valuation, at least partially. Otherwise, the Z-rule base is incomplete. In case if there is incomplete (sparse) Z-rule base, the classical reasoning methods based on compositional rule of inference (Zadeh [149,152,155,165,167], Mamdani

[100], Aliev [7,13,14]) or Takagi-Sugeno reasoning approach are not so effective to adapt generating an output for the observation covered by none of the rules. Consequently, we will use inference techniques which can perform an approximate reasoning in the lack of matching rules, namely Z-interpolation methods.

A problem of Z-interpolation, an interpolation of Z-rules, was suggested by Zadeh[as a challenging problem168]. This problem is the generalization of interpolation of fuzzy rules. The problem of Z-interpolation is given below.

Given the following Z-rules:

$$If \ X \ is \ (A_{X,1}, B_{X,1}) \ then \ Y \ is \ (A_{Y,1}, B_{Y,1})$$
$$If \ X \ is \ (A_{X,2}, B_{X,2}) \ then \ Y \ is \ (A_{Y,2}, B_{Y,2})$$
$$...$$
$$If \ X \ is \ (A_{X,n}, B_{X,n}) \ then \ Y \ is \ (A_{Y,n}, B_{Y,n})$$

and a current observation

$$X \ is \ (A_X, B_X),$$

find the Z-value of Y.

The idea underlying the suggested interpolation approach is that the ratio of distances between the conclusion and the consequent parts is identical to ones between the observation and the antecedent parts[85]. For Z-rules interpolation we have:

$$Z_Y = \frac{\displaystyle\sum_{i=1}^{n} \frac{1}{dist(Z_X, Z_{X,i})} Z_{Y,i}}{\displaystyle\sum_{k=1}^{n} \frac{1}{dist(Z_X, Z_{X,i})}}, \tag{5.13}$$

where *dist* is the distance between Z-numbers. As *dist*, one of the distances suggested in Section 5.2 can be used.

Let us consider the special case of the considered problem of Z-rules interpolation, suggested in [173,176].

Given the Z-rules

$$If\ X\ is\ A_{X,1}\ then\ Y\ is\ (A_{Y,1}, B)$$

$$If\ X\ is\ A_{X,2}\ then\ Y\ is\ (A_{Y,2}, B)$$

$$...$$

$$If\ X\ is\ A_{X,n}\ then\ Y\ is\ (A_{Y,n}, B)$$

and a current observation $X\ is(A_X, B_X)$, find the Z-value of Y.

For this case, formula (5.13) is reduced to

$$Z_Y = \frac{\sum_{i=1}^{n} \frac{1}{dist(Z_X, Z_{X,i})} Z_{Y,i}}{\sum_{k=1}^{n} \frac{1}{dist(Z_X, Z_{X,i})}} = \frac{\sum_{i=1}^{n} \frac{1}{dist(A_X, A_{X,i})}(A_{Y,i}, B)}{\sum_{k=1}^{n} \frac{1}{dist(A_X, A_{X,i})}}.$$

For example, using the supremum metric d of fuzzy numbers considered in Section 5.2, one will have:

$$Z_Y = \frac{\sum_{i=1}^{n} \frac{1}{dist(A_X, A_{X,i})}(A_{Y,i}, B)}{\sum_{k=1}^{n} \frac{1}{dist(A_X, A_{X,i})}} = \frac{\sum_{i=1}^{n} \frac{1}{d(A_X, A_{X,i})}(A_{Y,i}, B)}{\sum_{k=1}^{n} \frac{1}{d(A_X, A_{X,i})}}.$$

Taking into account that $\dfrac{1}{d(A_X, A_{X,i})}$ is a scalar and applying the approach to scalar multiplication of a Z-number described in Section 4.1.6, we will have:

$$Z_Y = (A_Y, B),\ with\ A_Y = \frac{\sum_{i=1}^{n} \frac{1}{d(A_X, A_{X,i})} A_{Y,i}}{\sum_{k=1}^{n} \frac{1}{d(A_X, A_{X,i})}}.$$

Example. Let us consider modeling of a fragment of a relationship between the student motivation, attention, anxiety and educational achievement. The information on the considered characteristics is naturally imprecise and partially reliable. For this reason, the use of Z-rules, as rules with Z-number valued inputs and outputs based on linguistic terms from a predefined codebook is adequate way for modeling of this relationship. This rules will help to evaluate a student with a given Z-number based evaluations of the characteristics. Consider the following Z-rules:

The 1st rule:
If Motivation is (M,U) and Attention is (H,U) and Anxiety is (L,U) Then Achivement is (E,U)

The 2nd rule:
If Motivation is (M,U) and Attention is (M,U) and Anxiety is (M,U) Then Achivement is (G,U)

Here the pairs (,) are Z-numbers where uppercase letters denote the following linguistic terms: H-High; L-Low; M- Medium; G-Good; E-Excellence; U-Usually. The considered Z-numbers are given below.
The 1st rule inputs:

$$Z_{A_M} = 0.1/_{0.1} + 0.5/_{0.3} + 1/_{0.5} + 0.5/_{0.65} + 0.1/_{0.8},$$

$$Z_{B_U} = 0.1/_{0.7} + 0.5/_{0.75} + 1/_{0.8} + 0.5/_{0.85} + 0.1/_{0.9};$$

$$Z_{A_H} = 0.1/_{0.5} + 0.25/_{0.57} + 0.5/_{0.65} + 0.75/_{0.72} + 1/_{0.8},$$

$$Z_{B_U} = 0.1/_{0.7} + 0.5/_{0.75} + 1/_{0.8} + 0.5/_{0.85} + 0.1/_{0.9};$$

$$Z_{A_L} = 1/_{0.1} + 0.75/_{0.2} + 0.5/_{0.3} + 0.25/_{0.4} + 0.1/_{0.5},$$

$$Z_{B_U} = 0.1/_{0.7} + 0.5/_{0.75} + 1/_{0.8} + 0.5/_{0.85} + 0.1/_{0.9}.$$

The 1st rule output:

$$Z_{A_E} = 0.1/_{0.75} + 0.25/_{0.8} + 0.5/_{0.85} + 0.75/_{0.9} + 1/_{0.95},$$

$$Z_{B_U} = 0.1/_{0.7} + 0.5/_{0.75} + 1/_{0.8} + 0.5/_{0.85} + 0.1/_{0.9}.$$

The 2nd rule inputs:

$$Z_{A_M} = {}^{0.1}\!/_{0.1} + {}^{0.5}\!/_{0.3} + {}^{1}\!/_{0.5} + {}^{0.5}\!/_{0.65} + {}^{0.1}\!/_{0.8},$$

$$Z_{B_U} = {}^{0.1}\!/_{0.7} + {}^{0.5}\!/_{0.75} + {}^{1}\!/_{0.8} + {}^{0.5}\!/_{0.85} + {}^{0.1}\!/_{0.9};$$

$$Z_{A_M} = {}^{0.1}\!/_{0.1} + {}^{0.5}\!/_{0.3} + {}^{1}\!/_{0.5} + {}^{0.5}\!/_{0.65} + {}^{0.1}\!/_{0.8},$$

$$Z_{B_U} = {}^{0.1}\!/_{0.7} + {}^{0.5}\!/_{0.75} + {}^{1}\!/_{0.8} + {}^{0.5}\!/_{0.85} + {}^{0.1}\!/_{0.9};$$

$$Z_{A_M} = {}^{0.1}\!/_{0.1} + {}^{0.5}\!/_{0.3} + {}^{1}\!/_{0.5} + {}^{0.5}\!/_{0.65} + {}^{0.1}\!/_{0.8},$$

$$Z_{B_U} = {}^{0.1}\!/_{0.7} + {}^{0.5}\!/_{0.75} + {}^{1}\!/_{0.8} + {}^{0.5}\!/_{0.85} + {}^{0.1}\!/_{0.9}.$$

The 2nd rule output:

$$Z_{A_G} = {}^{0.1}\!/_{0.5} + {}^{0.5}\!/_{0.62} + {}^{1}\!/_{0.75} + {}^{0.5}\!/_{0.85} + {}^{0.1}\!/_{0.95},$$

$$Z_{B_U} = {}^{0.1}\!/_{0.7} + {}^{0.5}\!/_{0.75} + {}^{1}\!/_{0.8} + {}^{0.5}\!/_{0.85} + {}^{0.1}\!/_{0.9}.$$

Consider a problem of reasoning within the given Z-rules by using the suggested Z-interpolation approach. Let the current input information for motivation, attention and anxiety is described by the following Z-numbers $Z_1 = (Z_{A_1}, Z_{B_1})$, $Z_2 = (Z_{A_2}, Z_{B_2})$, $Z_3 = (Z_{A_3}, Z_{B_3})$ respectively:

$$Z_{A_1} = {}^{0.1}\!/_{0.3} + {}^{0.5}\!/_{0.35} + {}^{1}\!/_{0.4} + {}^{0.5}\!/_{0.45} + {}^{0.1}\!/_{0.5},$$

$$Z_{B_1} = {}^{0.1}\!/_{0.6} + {}^{0.5}\!/_{0.65} + {}^{1}\!/_{0.7} + {}^{0.5}\!/_{0.75} + {}^{0.1}\!/_{0.8};$$

$$Z_{A_2} = {}^{0.1}\!/_{0.2} + {}^{0.5}\!/_{0.25} + {}^{1}\!/_{0.3} + {}^{0.5}\!/_{0.35} + {}^{0.1}\!/_{0.4},$$

$$Z_{B_2} = {}^{0.1}\!/_{0.6} + {}^{0.5}\!/_{0.65} + {}^{1}\!/_{0.7} + {}^{0.5}\!/_{0.75} + {}^{0.1}\!/_{0.8};$$

$$Z_{A_3} = {}^{0.1}\!/_{0.62} + {}^{0.5}\!/_{0.67} + {}^{1}\!/_{0.7} + {}^{0.5}\!/_{0.73} + {}^{0.1}\!/_{0.8},$$

$$Z_{B_3} = 0.1\big/0.6 + 0.5\big/0.65 + 1\big/0.7 + 0.5\big/0.75 + 0.1\big/0.8 .$$

Z-interpolation approach based reasoning consists of two main stages.

1) For each rule compute *dist* as distance D_i between the current input Z-information $Z_1 = (Z_{A_1}, Z_{B_1})$, $Z_2 = (Z_{A_2}, Z_{B_2})$, $Z_3 = (Z_{A_3}, Z_{B_3})$ and Z-antecedents of Z-rules base $Z_{i1} = (A_{i1}, B_{i1})$, $Z_{i2} = (A_{i2}, B_{i2})$, $Z_{i3} = (A_{i3}, B_{i3})$, $i = 1,2$:

$$D_i = \sum_{j=1}^{3} D(Z_j, Z_{ij}),$$

were $D(Z_j, Z_{ij})$ is the supremum metric (5.3).

Consider computation of D_i for the 1st and 2nd rules. Thus, we need to determine $D_1 = \sum_{j=1}^{3} D(Z_j, Z_{1j})$ where values $D(Z_1, Z_{11})$, $D(Z_2, Z_{12})$, $D(Z_3, Z_{13})$ are computed on the base of (5.3). We have obtained the results:

$$D(Z_1, Z_{11}) = d_H(A_1, A_{11}) + d_H(B_1, B_{11}) = 0.3 + 0.1 = 0.4,$$

$$D(Z_2, Z_{12}) = 0.5,$$

$$D(Z_3, Z_{13}) = 0.62 .$$

Thus, the distance for the 1st rule is

$$D_1 = 1.52$$

Analogously, we computed the distance for the 2nd rule as
$$D(Z_1, Z_{2,1}) = 0.4, \quad D(Z_2, Z_{2,2}) = 0.5, D(Z_3, Z_{2,3}) = 0.62 ; D_2 = 1.52 .$$

2) Computation of the aggregated output Z_Y for Z-rules base by using linear Z-interpolation:

$$Z_Y = \sum_{i=1}^{n} w_i Z_{Y,i} \ , \ w_i = \dfrac{1}{D_i \sum\limits_{k=1}^{n} \dfrac{1}{D_k}} .$$

Thus, we need to compute convex combination of outputs $Z_{Y_i}, i=1,2$ of the rules. The aggregated output Z_Y is defined as

$$Z_Y = 0.5 Z_{Y_1} + 0.5 Z_{Y_2} = (A_Y, B_Y) .$$

We have obtained the following result:

$$Z_{A_Y} = {0.1}\big/{0.625} + {0.5}\big/{0.71} + {1}\big/{0.8} + {0.5}\big/{0.875} + {0.1}\big/{0.95},$$

$$Z_{B_Y} = {0.1}\big/{0.7} + {0.5}\big/{0.75} + {1}\big/{0.8} + {0.5}\big/{0.85} + {0.1}\big/{0.9}.$$

In accordance with the codebook we have: Achievement is "medium" with the reliability "usually".

5.4 Equations with Z-numbers

One of the typical problems in algebra is solving linear equations. Linear equations have a very wide spectrum of real-life applications in ecology, economics, production, everyday life etc. Let us mention that as real-world problems are characterized by a combination of possibilistic and probabilistic uncertainties, dealing with real-world linear equations may require the use of Z-numbers. In this section we will consider solving of the following linear equations whose parameters and variables are described by Z-numbers:

$$Z_1 + Z_X = Z_2 \tag{5.14}$$

$$Z_1 \cdot Z_X = Z_2 \tag{5.15}$$

In contrast to the real-valued equations, the solutions to the considered Z-number valued equations don't always exist (one may recall the same problem related to the fuzzy equations[34,35]). The solution of equation (5.14) exists if the Hukuhara difference

$$Z_{21} = Z_2 -_h Z_1 = (A_{21}, B_{21})$$

exists, and then

$$Z_X = Z_{21}.$$

The conditions of existence of Hukuhara difference of two Z-numbers are given in Section 4.1.5. An approximate solution $Z_X' = (A_{21}', B_{21}')$ to this equation can be found as a result of standard subtraction

$$Z_X' = Z_2 - Z_1.$$

Let us mention that $A_{21} \subseteq A_{21}'$, $B_{21} \subseteq B_{21}'$. In other words, the approximate solution Z_X' includes an exact solution Z_X, just the former contains redundant uncertainty.

Analogously, the solution of the second equation exists if the Hukuhara division

$$Z_{21} = Z_2 /_h Z_1 = (A_{21}, B_{21})$$

exists and then

$$Z_X = Z_{21}.$$

We would like to mention that the conditions of existence of Hukuhara division are analogous to those of Hukuhara difference. Analogously to the first equation, we can also use an approximate solution as a result of standard division $Z_X' = Z_2 / Z_1 = (A_{21}', B_{21}')$, because $A_{21} \subseteq A_{21}'$, $B_{21} \subseteq B_{21}'$.

The considered linear equations (5.14) and (5.15) are special case of the following equation:

$$Z_1 Z_X + Z_2 = Z_3. \tag{5.16}$$

The exact solution of this equation is

$$Z_X = (Z_3 -_h Z_2) /_h Z_1.$$

As an approximate solution, the following can be used:

$$Z_X = (Z_3 - Z_2) / Z_1.$$

An example. Let us consider linear equation of type (5.14) where Z-numbers $Z_1 = (A_1, B_1)$ and $Z_2 = (A_2, B_2)$ are as follows (Figs. 5.9, 5.10):

$$A_1 = 0/4.5 + 0.8/13.5 + 1/18 + 0.8/22.5 + 0.1/49.5 \,,$$

$$B_1 = 0.1/0.8 + 0.8/0.85 + 1/0.9 + 0.8/0.9 + 0.8/0.95 \,;$$

$$A_2 = 0.1/9 + 0.1/18 + 0.1/22.5 + 0.1/27 + 0.1/31.5 + 0.8/40.5$$
$$+ 0.8/45 + 0.8/49.5 + 1/54 + 0.8/58.5 + 0.8/63 + 0.1/67.5 + 0.1/72$$
$$+ 0.1/76.5 + 0.1/85.5 + 0.1/90 + 0.1/99,$$

$$B_2 = 0.1/0.589 + 0.1/0.594 + 0.1/0.616 + 0.1/0.623 + 0.8/0.664 + 0.8/0.686$$
$$+ 0.8/0.703 + 0.8/0.706 + 0.8/0.734 + 0.8/0.783 + 0.8/0.784 + 1/0.795$$
$$+ 0.8/0.799 + 0.8/0.800 + 0.8/0.835 + 0.8/0.850 + 0.8/0.862 + 0.8/0.875$$
$$+ 0.1/0.900 + 0.1/0.950.$$

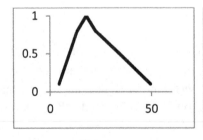

a) A_1

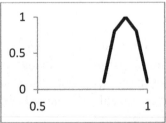

b) B_1

Fig. 5.9. Z-number $Z_1 = (A_1, B_1)$.

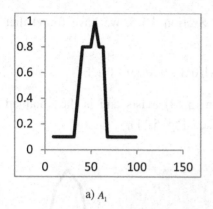

a) A_1

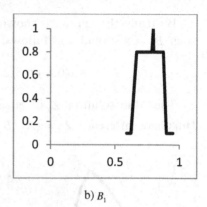

b) B_1

Fig. 5.10. Z-number $Z_2 = (A_2, B_2)$.

Let us verify whether the solution of (5.14) exists. This implies to verify whether Hukuhara difference $Z_{21} = Z_2 -_h Z_1$ exists. For this purpose we use the approach shown in Section 4.1.5. Thus, first we should verify whether $A_{21} = A_2 -_h A_1$ exists. We have found that the following hold:

$$A_1^{\alpha=0.1} + \{4.5, 27, 36, 40.5, 49.5\} = A_2^{\alpha=0.1},$$

$$A_1^{\alpha=0.8} + \{27, 36, 40.5\} = A_2^{\alpha=0.8},$$

$$A_1^{\alpha=1} + \{36\} = A_2^{\alpha=1}.$$

Therefore, the Hukuhara difference $A_{21} = A_2 -_h A_1$ exists:

$$A_{21} = A_1 -_h A_2 = {}^{0.1}\!/_{4.5} + {}^{0.8}\!/_{27} + {}^{1}\!/_{36} + {}^{0.8}\!/_{40.5} + {}^{0.1}\!/_{49.5}.$$

Now we need to verify whether there exists such B_{12} that:

$$Z_1 = Z_2 + Z_{21} = (A_2, B_2) + (A_{21}, B_{21}) = (A_1, B_1),$$

that is

$$Z_{21} = Z_2 -_h Z_1 = (A_2, B_2) -_h (A_1, B_1) = (A_{21}, B_{21}).$$

By using the approach shown in Section 4.1.5, we have found that such B_{21} exists and is as follows:

$$B_{21} = 0.1/0.6 + 0.8/0.7 + 1/0.8 + 0.8/0.9 + 0.1/1.$$

Thus, the solution Z_X of equation (5.14) exists and is the obtained Hukuhara difference $Z_X = (A_{12}, B_{12})$ (see, Fig. 5.11).

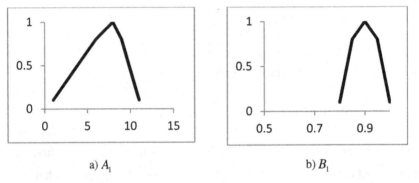

a) A_1 b) B_1

Fig. 5.11. Z-number $Z_{21} = (A_{21}, B_{21})$.

An example. Let us consider linear equation of type (5.14) with the following Z-numbers $Z_1 = (A_1, B_1)$ and $Z_2 = (A_2, B_2)$:

$$A_1 = 0/0 + 0/0.1 + 0.1/0.2 + 0.5/0.3 + 1/0.4 + 0.5/0.5 + 0.1/0.6$$
$$+ 0/0.7 + 0/0.8 + 0/0.9 + 0/1,$$

$$B_1 = 0/0 + 0.1/0.1 + 0.5/0.2 + 1/0.3 + 0.5/0.4 + 0.1/0.5 + 0/0.6$$
$$+ 0/0.7 + 0/0.8 + 0/0.9 + 0/1;$$

$$A_2 = 0/0 + 0.1/0.2 + 0.5/0.4 + 1/0.6 + 0.5/0.7 + 0.1/0.9 + 0/1$$
$$+ 0/1.1 + 0/1.2 + 0/1.3 + 0/1.4,$$

$$B_2 = 0/0 + 0/0.1 + 0.1/0.2 + 0.5/0.3 + 1/0.4 + 0.5/0.5 + 0.1/0.6$$
$$+ 0/0.7 + 0/0.8 + 0/0.9 + 0/1.$$

Let us compute an approximate solution to (5.14)as a result of a standard subtraction $Z'_X = Z_2 - Z_1$. By applying the approach described in Section 4.1.4, we obtained the following result $Z'_X = (A'_X, B'_X)$:

$A'_X = 0.1/-0.4 + 0.5/-0.1 + 1/0.2 + 0.5/0.3 + 0.1/0.5 + 0/0.6 + 0/0.7$
$+ 0/0.8 + 0/0.9 + 0/1 + 0/1,$

$B'_X = 0/0 + 0.1/0.1 + 0.5/0.2 + 1/0.3 + 0.5/0.4 + 0.1/0.5 + 0/0.6$
$+ 0/0.7 + 0/0.8 + 0/0.9 + 0/1.$

An example. Let us consider computation of an approximate solution of equation (5.15) where Z-numbers $Z_1 = (A_1, B_1)$ and $Z_2 = (A_2, B_2)$ are as follows:

$A_1 = 0/1 + 0.5/2 + 0.8/3 + 1/4 + 0.8/5 + 0.7/6 + 0.6/7 + 0.4/8 + 0.2/9$
$+ 0.1/10 + 0/11,$
$B_1 = 0/0 + 0.3/0.1 + 0.5/0.2 + 0.6/0.3 + 0.7/0.4 + 0.8/0.5 + 0.9/0.6 + 1/0.7$
$+ 0.9/0.8 + 0.8/0.6 + 0/1;$
$A_2 = 0/1 + 0.3/2 + 0.5/3 + 0.6/4 + 0.7/5 + 0.8/6 + 0.9/7 + 1/8 + 0.8/9$
$+ 0.6/10 + 0/11,$
$B_2 = 0/0 + 0.5/0.1 + 0.8/0.2 + 1/0.3 + 0.8/0.4 + 0.7/0.5 + 0.6/0.6$
$+ 0.4/0.7 + 0.2/0.8 + 0.1/0.6 + 0/1.$

We compute an approximate solution to (5.15) as a standard division $Z'_X = Z_2/Z_1$. By applying the approach described in Section 4.1.7, we obtained the following result $Z'_X = (A'_X, B'_X)$ (see Fig. 5.12):

$A'_X = 0/0.33 + 0.07/0.36 + 0.1/0.38 + 0.14/0.40 + 0.19/0.43$
$+ 0.22/0.44 + ... + 0.96/1.50 + 0.99/1.57 + 1/1.60 + 0.96/1.67 + 0.92/1.75$
$+ 0.89/1.80 + ... + 0.35/2.67 + 0.26/2.75 + 0/3.00,$

$B'_X = 0/0.24 + 0.5/0.29 + 0.8/0.34 + 1/0.38 + 0.8/0.44 + 0.7/0.49$
$+ 0.6/0.54 + 0.4/0.59 + 0.2/0.64 + 0.1/0.69 + 0/0.68.$

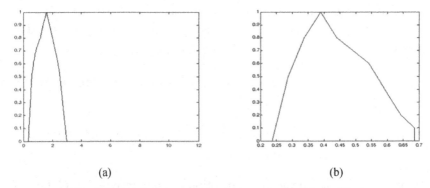

(a)   (b)

Fig. 5.12. Approximate solution $Z'_X = (A'_X, B'_X)$: (a) A'_X , (b) B'_X.

5.5. Derivative of a Function of Z-numbers

In classical calculus the concept of derivative is one of the main concepts. In discrete calculus, the discrete derivative as a finite difference of a function is used. In this section we will consider discrete derivative of a discrete Z-number valued function. Let us mention that there is a series of works on systematic development of the theory of differentiability of fuzzy mappings [26,27,57,127,128], and the one of the most general concepts referred to as generalized Hukuhara differentiability was suggested by Bede and colleagues in [26,27].

In the research area of differentiability of fuzzy mappings there are two main directions: an investigation of derivatives of a fuzzy mapping of a real-valued variable and an investigation of derivatives of a fuzzy mapping at a fuzzy point. We also will deal with the analogous two types of derivatives of a Z-number valued function. The first type is based on a finite difference Δf of a discrete Z-number valued function at a numerical point, defined as Hukuhara difference of values of f at two neighbor numerical points. This type is useful for modeling dynamical systems or processes characterized by combination of probabilistic and possibilistic uncertainties. The second type is a discrete derivative of a discrete Z-number valued function at a Z-point. This type is useful for estimation of a behavior of a function under uncertain information on the value of its argument.

5.5.1. *Discrete Derivative of a Discrete Z-number Valued Function at a Numerical Point*

Let us consider the first type of derivative of a discrete Z-number valued function $f : \Omega \rightarrow \mathcal{Z}$. Let $\Omega \subseteq N$, where N is the set of natural numbers. We suggest the following definition.

Definition 5.16. Discrete derivative of a discrete Z-valued function at a crisp point. $f : \Omega \rightarrow \mathcal{Z}$ may have the following discrete derivatives $\Delta f(n)$ at n:

    1) the forward right hand discrete derivative
$$\Delta_r f(n) = f(n+1) -_h f(n)$$

    2) the backward right hand discrete derivative
$$\Delta_{r^-} f(n) = \frac{f(n) -_h f(n+1)}{-1}$$

    3) the forward left hand discrete derivative
$$\Delta_l f(n) = f(n) -_h f(n-1).$$

    4) the backward left hand discrete derivative
$$\Delta_{l^-} f(n) = \frac{f(n-1) -_h f(n)}{-1}.$$

An existence of $\Delta_r f(n)$ or $\Delta_l f(n)$ implies that the length of support of the first component A_n of a Z-number $f(n) = (A_n, B_n)$ is non-decreasing. Existence of the other two derivatives implies non-increasing support of the first component of a Z-number $f(n) = (A_n, B_n)$.

Based on definition 5.16, we define the concept of a generalized Hukuhara differentiability as follows.

Definition 5.17. Generalized Hukuhara differentiability. Let $f : \Omega \rightarrow \mathcal{Z}$ and $n \in \Omega$. We say that f is differentiable at $n \in \Omega$ if

    a) $\Delta_r f(n)$ and $\Delta_l f(n)$ exist

    or

    b) $\Delta_{r^-} f(n)$ and $\Delta_{l^-} f(n)$ exist

    or

    c) $\Delta_r f(n)$ and $\Delta_{l^-} f(n)$ exist

      or

d) $\Delta_{r^-} f(n)$ and $\Delta_l f(n)$ exist.

Let us mention that discrete derivative Δf has the following properties:

Linearity: $\Delta_r (f + g)(n) = \Delta_r f(n) + \Delta_r g(n)$, $\Delta_r (cf)(n) = c\Delta_r f(n)$

Product rule: $\Delta_r (f \cdot g)(n) = f(n+1)\Delta_r g(n) + \Delta_r f(n)g(n)$.

The important special case of the generalized Hukuhara differentiability is the strongly generalized differentiability. For a discrete Z-number valued function this case implies the same rate (the same increment) of a function both in forward and backward directions. The following definition applies.

Definition 5.18. Strongly generalized differentiability of a discrete Z-number valued function. Let $f : \Omega \to \mathcal{Z}$ and $n \in \Omega$. We say that f is strongly generalized differentiable at $n \in \Omega$ if

a) $\Delta_r f(n)$ and $\Delta_l f(n)$ exist and $\Delta_r f(n) = \Delta_l f(n)$

   or

b) $\Delta_{r^-} f(n)$ and $\Delta_{l^-} f(n)$ exist and $\Delta_{r^-} f(n) = \Delta_{l^-} f(n)$

   or

c) $\Delta_r f(n)$ and $\Delta_{l^-} f(n)$ exist and $\Delta_r f(n) = \Delta_{l^-} f(n)$

   or

d) $\Delta_{r^-} f(n)$ and $\Delta_l f(n)$ exist and $\Delta_{r^-} f(n) = \Delta_l f(n)$.

Let us consider examples for computation of discrete derivative Δf.

Example 1. Let us consider a Z-valued function of a crisp variable f which takes the following $f(n) = (A_n, B_n)$ values for $n = 1, 2, 3$ (see Figs. 5.13, 5.14 and 5.15):

$A_1 = 0.1/4 + 0.1/8 + 0.1/10 + 0.1/12 + 0.1/14 + 0.8/18 + 0.8/20 + 0.8/22$
$\quad + 1/24 + 0.8/26 + 0.8/28 + 0.1/30 + 0.1/32 + 0.1/34 + 0.1/38 + 0.1/40$
$\quad + 0.1/44,$

$$B_1 = 0.1/0.589 + 0.1/0.594 + 0.1/0.616 + 0.1/0.623 + 0.8/0.664 + 0.8/0.686$$
$$+ 0.8/0.703 + 0.8/0.706 + 0.8/0.734 + 0.8/0.783 + 0.8/0.784 + 1/0.795$$
$$+ 0.8/0.799 + 0.8/0.800 + 0.8/0.835 + 0.8/0.850 + 0.8/0.862 + 0.8/0.875$$
$$+ 0.1/0.900 + 0.1/0.950;$$

$$A_2 = 0/2 + 0.8/6 + 1/8 + 0.8/10 + 0.1/22,$$
$$B_2 = 0.1/0.8 + 0.5/0.85 + 1/0.9 + 0.5/0.9 + 0.1/0.95;$$
$$A_3 = 0/-8 + 0.8/-4 + 1/-2 + 0.8/0 + 0.1/12,$$
$$B_2 = 0.1/0.8 + 0.8/0.85 + 1/0.9 + 0.8/0.9 + 0.1/0.95.$$

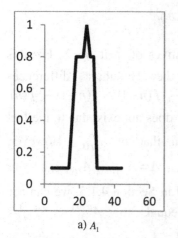

a) A_1

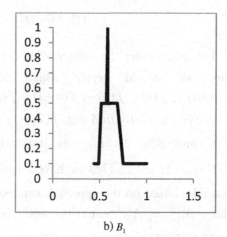

b) B_1

Fig. 5.13. $f(1) = (A_1, B_1)$.

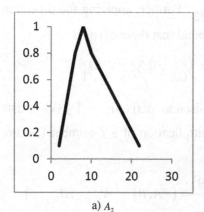

a) A_2

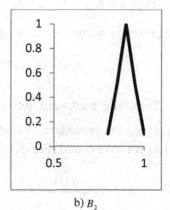

b) B_2

Fig. 5.14. $f(2) = (A_2, B_2)$.

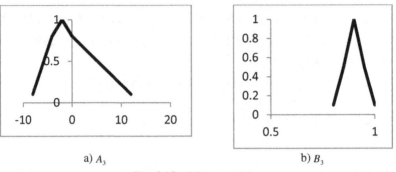

a) A_3 b) B_3

Fig. 5.15. $f(3) = (A_3, B_3)$.

Let us consider the existence of derivatives of f at $n = 2$. For this aim, we should verify which of the Hukuhara differences $f(n+1) -_h f(n)$, $f(n) -_h f(n+1)$, $f(n) -_h f(n-1)$, $f(n-1) -_h f(n)$ exist. We can easily find that $f(2) -_h f(1)$ does not exist due to the fact that cardinality of $A_{f(2)}^{\alpha}$ is lower than that of $A_{f(1)}^{\alpha}$. However, $f(1) -_h f(2)$ exists. First we have found that $A = A_{f(1)} -_h A_{f(2)}$ exist. For example, based on the approach suggested in Section 4.1.5, we can see that $A_{f(1)}^{\alpha=0.1} -_h A_{(2)}^{\alpha=0.1}$ exists and is equal to $A_{f(1)}^{\alpha=0.1} -_h A_{f(2)}^{\alpha=0.1} = \{2, 12, 16, 18, 22\}$. Hukuhara difference $A = A_{f(1)} -_h A_{f(2)}$ is found as $A = {0.1}/{2} + {0.8}/{12} + {1}/{16} + {0.8}/{18} + {0.1}/{22}$. Further, applying the procedure suggested in Section 4.1.5, we have found that there exists B :

$$B = {0.1}/{0.6} + {0.5}/{0.7} + {1}/{0.8} + {0.5}/{0.9} + {0.1}/{1} .$$

Thus, the backward left hand discrete derivative $\bigtriangleup_{\!\!r} f(2)$ exists. Applying the procedure of scalar multiplication of a Z-number (Section 4.1.6) we have found (Fig. 5.16):

$$\bigtriangleup_{\!\!r} f(2) = \frac{f(1) -_h f(2)}{-1} = \frac{(A, B)}{-1} = (-A, B) = \left(A_{\bigtriangleup_{\!\!r} f(2)}, B_{\bigtriangleup_{\!\!r} f(2)} \right),$$

where

$$A_{4_r f(2)} = 0.1\!\!\Big/\!\!{-22} + 0.8\!\!\Big/\!\!{-18} + 1\!\!\Big/\!\!{-16} + 0.8\!\!\Big/\!\!{-16} + 0.1\!\!\Big/\!\!{-2},$$

$$B_{4_r f(2)} = 0.1\!\!\Big/\!\!{0.6} + 0.5\!\!\Big/\!\!{0.7} + 1\!\!\Big/\!\!{0.8} + 0.5\!\!\Big/\!\!{0.9} + 0.1\!\!\Big/\!\!{1}.$$

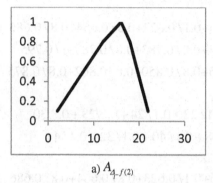　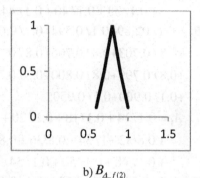

a) $A_{4_r f(2)}$　　　　　　　　　b) $B_{4_r f(2)}$

Fig. 5.16. $4_r f(2) = \left(A_{4_r f(2)}, B_{4_r f(2)} \right)$.

Analogously, we have found that both Hukuhara differences $f(3) -_h f(2)$ and $f(2) -_h f(3)$ exist and are equal to Z-numbers whose components are the following singletons:

$$A_{32} = 1/{-10}, \; B_{32} = 1/1; \; A_{23} = 1/10, \; B_{32} = 1/1.$$

Therefore, both the forward right hand discrete derivative $4 f(2) = (A_{4 f(2)}, B_{4 f(2)})$ and the backward right hand discrete derivative $4_r f(2) = (A_{4_r f(2)}, B_{4_r f(2)})$ exist and are as follows:

$$A_{4 f(2)} = 1/{-10}, B_{4 f(2)} = 1/1; A_{4_r f(2)} = 1/{-10}, B_{4_r f(2)} = 1/1.$$

Thus, $4 f(2) = 4_r f(2)$ and, according to Definition 5.18, f is strongly generalized differentiable at $n = 2$.

An example. Let us consider a Z-valued function f of a crisp variable which takes the following $f(n) = (A_n, B_n)$ values for $n = 1, 2, 3$ (Figs. 5.17, 5.18 and 5.19):

$$A_1 = 0/3 + 0.8/9 + 1/12 + 0.8/15 + 0.1/33,$$

$$B_1 = 0.1/0.8 + 0.8/0.85 + 1/0.9 + 0.8/0.9 + 0.1/0.95 ;$$

$$A_2 = 0.1/4 + 0.1/8 + 0.1/10 + 0.1/12 + 0.1/14 + 0.8/18 + 0.8/20$$
$$+ 0.8/22 + 1/24 + 0.8/26 + 0.8/28 + 0.1/30 + 0.1/32 + 0.1/34$$
$$+ 0.1/38 + 0.1/40 + 0.1/44,$$

$$B_2 = 0.1/0.589 + 0.1/0.594 + 0.1/0.616 + 0.1/0.623 + 0.8/0.664 + 0.8/0.686$$
$$+ 0.8/0.703 + 0.8/0.706 + 0.8/0.734 + 0.8/0.783 + 0.8/0.784 + 1/0.795$$
$$+ 0.8/0.799 + 0.8/0.800 + 0.8/0.835 + 0.8/0.850 + 0.8/0.862 + 0.8/0.875$$
$$+ 0.1/0.900 + 0.1/0.950;$$

$$A_3 = 0.1/14 + 0.1/18 + 0.1/20 + 0.1/22 + 0.1/24 + 0.8/28 + 0.8/30$$
$$+ 0.8/32 + 1/34 + 0.8/36 + 0.8/38 + 0.1/40 + 0.1/32 + 0.1/44$$
$$+ 0.1/48 + 0.1/50 + 0.1/54,$$

$$B_3 = 0.1/0.589 + 0.1/0.594 + 0.1/0.616 + 0.1/0.623 + 0.8/0.664 + 0.8/0.686$$
$$+ 0.8/0.703 + 0.8/0.706 + 0.8/0.734 + 0.8/0.783 + 0.8/0.784 + 1/0.795$$
$$+ 0.8/0.799 + 0.8/0.800 + 0.8/0.835 + 0.8/0.850 + 0.8/0.862 + 0.8/0.875$$
$$+ 0.1/0.900 + 0.1/0.950.$$

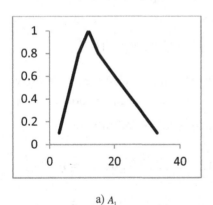

a) A_1

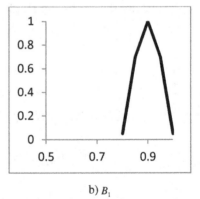

b) B_1

Fig. 5.17. $f(1) = (A_1, B_1)$.

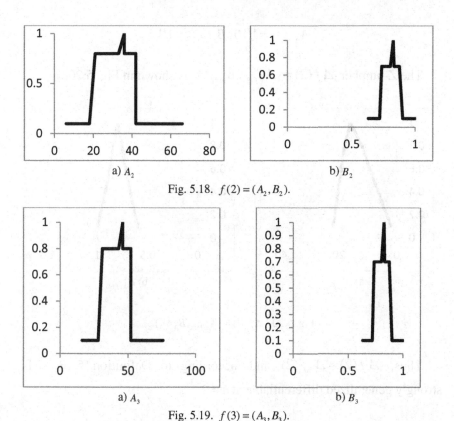

a) A_2

b) B_2

Fig. 5.18. $f(2) = (A_2, B_2)$.

a) A_3

b) B_3

Fig. 5.19. $f(3) = (A_3, B_3)$.

Let us consider the existence of derivatives of f at $n = 2$. By conducting an investigation analogously to the previous example, we have found that only the forward left hand discrete derivative $\Delta_l f(2) = (A_{\Delta_l f(1)}, B_{\Delta_l f(1)})$, the forward right hand discrete derivative $\Delta_r f(2) = (A_{\Delta_r f(2)}, B_{\Delta_r f(2)})$ and the backward right hand discrete derivative $\Delta_{r^-} f(2) = (A_{\Delta_{r^-} f(2)}, B_{\Delta_{r^-} f(2)})$ exist and are as follows:

$$A_{\Delta f(2)} = {0.1}\big/{2} + {0.8}\big/{10} + {1}\big/{24} + {0.8}\big/{32} + {0.1}\big/{34},$$
$$B_{\Delta f(2)} = {0.1}\big/{0.6} + {0.8}\big/{0.7} + {1}\big/{0.8} + {0.8}\big/{0.9} + {0.1}\big/{1};$$

$$A_{\Delta_r f(2)} = 1/10, \, B_{\Delta_r f(2)} = 1/1;$$

$$A_{\Delta_r f(2)} = 1/10, B_{\Delta_r f(2)} = 1/1.$$

The Z-number $\Delta_r f(2) = (A_{\Delta_r f(1)}, B_{\Delta_r f(1)})$ is shown in Fig. 5.20.

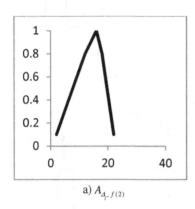

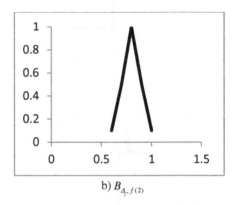

a) $A_{\Delta_r f(2)}$ b) $B_{\Delta_r f(2)}$

Fig. 5.20. $\Delta_r f(2) = (A_{\Delta_r f(1)}, B_{\Delta_r f(1)})$.

Thus, $\Delta_r f(2) = \Delta_r f(2)$ and, according to Definition 5.18, f is strongly generalized differentiable at $n = 2$.

5.5.2. Discrete Derivative of a Discrete Z-number Valued Function at a Z-point

Let us consider a Z-number valued function of a Z-number, $f : Z \to Z$. The important issue is to investigate the increment of $\Delta f = f(Z_2) - f(Z_1)$ with respect to increment $\Delta Z = Z_2 -_h Z_1$. This requires to determine such Z-number Z that $\Delta f = Z \cdot \Delta Z$, and which is referred to as a Hukuhara division $Z = \Delta f /_h \Delta Z = (A_{\Delta f /_h \Delta Z}, B_{\Delta f /_h \Delta Z})$. Let us mention, that analogously to Hukuhara difference, verification of existence of Hukuhara division and its computation is rather complex. To escape these difficulties, but to do have the possibility to estimate the rate Δf with respect to ΔZ, one can use the standard division

$\dfrac{\Delta f}{\Delta Z} = (A_{\frac{\Delta f}{\Delta Z}}, B_{\frac{\Delta f}{\Delta Z}})$. The motivation is that despite the fact $\Delta f /_h \Delta Z \neq \dfrac{\Delta f}{\Delta Z}$,

one has $A_{\Delta f /_h \Delta Z} \subseteq A_{\frac{\Delta f}{\Delta Z}}, B_{\Delta f /_h \Delta Z} \subseteq B_{\frac{\Delta f}{\Delta Z}}$ whenever $\Delta f /_h \Delta Z$ exists. The

latter fact can help to linguistically estimate Δf with respect to ΔZ.
Indeed, suppose we have two codebooks, to assign appropriate linguistic labels to the first component and the second component of a given Z-number. If this assignment is based on intersection of Z-numbers, then the same linguistic label will be assigned to $A_{\Delta f /_h \Delta Z}$ and $A_{\frac{\Delta f}{\Delta Z}}$ due to the

fact $A_{\Delta f /_h \Delta Z} \subseteq A_{\frac{\Delta f}{\Delta Z}}$. The same is true for $B_{\Delta f /_h \Delta Z}$ and $B_{\frac{\Delta f}{\Delta Z}}$. As a result, the

linguistic estimation of $\dfrac{\Delta f}{\Delta Z}$ and $\Delta f /_h \Delta Z$ will be the same. Then we

can write $\Delta f /_h \Delta Z \approx \dfrac{\Delta f}{\Delta Z}$. Based on this fact, we suggest the following

definition.

Definition 5.19. An approximate discrete derivative of a discrete Z-number valued function at a Z-point. Given a function $f : \mathcal{Z} \to \mathcal{Z}$, its
approximate right hand discrete derivative denoted $d_r f$ and approximate
left hand discrete derivative denoted $d_l f$ are defined as

$$d_r f = \frac{\Delta_r f}{\Delta_r Z} = \frac{f(Z_{n+1}) -_h f(Z_n)}{Z_{n+1} -_h Z_n}, \quad \text{provided that} \quad Z_{n+1} -_h Z_n \quad \text{and}$$

$f(Z_{n+1}) -_h f(Z_n)$ exist,

$$d_l f = \frac{\Delta_l f}{\Delta_l Z} = \frac{f(Z_n) -_h f(Z_{n-1})}{Z_n -_h Z_{n-1}}, \quad \text{provided that} \quad Z_n -_h Z_{n-1} \quad \text{and}$$

$f(Z_n) -_h f(Z_{n-1})$ exist.

An example. Let us consider a Z-valued function:

$$f(Z) = 5Z.$$

Consider the following values of Z: Z_1, Z_2, Z_3:

$$A_1 = 0/1 + 0.8/2 + 1/3 + 0.8/4 + 0.1/5 \,,$$

$$B_1 = 0.1/0.8 + 0.5/0.85 + 1/0.9 + 0.5/0.9 + 0.8/0.95 \,;$$

$$A_2 = 0/3 + 0.8/4 + 1/5 + 0.8/6 + 0.1/7 \,,$$

$$B_2 = 0.1/0.8 + 0.5/0.85 + 1/0.9 + 0.5/0.9 + 0.8/0.95 \,;$$

$$A_3 = 0/4 + 0.8/5 + 1/6 + 0.8/7 + 0.1/8 \,,$$

$$B_3 = 0.1/0.8 + 0.5/0.85 + 1/0.9 + 0.5/0.9 + 0.8/0.95 \,.$$

and compute approximate discrete derivatives of $d_r f$ and $d_l f$ of f at point Z_2.

According to the procedure of scalar multiplication of a Z-number (Section 4.1.6), we have $f(Z_1), f(Z_2), f(Z_3)$:

$$A_{f(Z_1)} = 0/5 + 0.8/10 + 1/5 + 0.8/20 + 0.1/25 \,,$$

$$B_{f(Z_1)} = 0.1/0.8 + 0.5/0.85 + 1/0.9 + 0.5/0.9 + 0.8/0.95 \,;$$

$$A_{f(Z_2)} = 0/15 + 0.8/20 + 1/25 + 0.8/30 + 0.1/35 \,,$$

$$B_{f(Z_2)} = 0.1/0.8 + 0.5/0.85 + 1/0.9 + 0.5/0.9 + 0.8/0.95 \,;$$

$$A_{f(Z_3)} = 0/20 + 0.8/25 + 1/30 + 0.8/35 + 0.1/40 \,,$$

$$B_{f(Z_3)} = 0.1/0.8 + 0.5/0.85 + 1/0.9 + 0.5/0.9 + 0.8/0.95 \,.$$

We have easily found:

$$d_r f = \frac{\varDelta_r f}{\varDelta_r Z} = \frac{f(Z_2) -_h f(Z_1)}{Z_2 -_h Z_1} = \frac{(10,1)}{(2,1)} = (5,1) \,,$$

$$d_r f = \frac{\varDelta_r f}{\varDelta_r Z} = \frac{f(Z_3) -_h f(Z_2)}{Z_3 -_h Z_2} = \frac{(5,1)}{(1,1)} = (5,1) \,.$$

In general, given $f(Z) = kZ, k \in \mathcal{R}$, one has $d_r f = d_l f = (k,1)$.

5.6. T-norm and T-conorm of Z-numbers

In this section we consider discrete T-norm and T-conorm on the partially ordered set of discrete Z-numbers whose constituents' supports are subsets of natural numbers.

Let $(P;\leq)$ be a non-trivial bounded partially ordered set with min and max elements.

Definition 5.20. A triangular norm, T-norm [23,47,57,125,180]. A triangular norm T-norm on P is a binary operation $T : P \times P \rightarrow P$ such that for all $x, y, z \in P$ the following axioms are satisfied:

1. $T(x, y) = T(y, x)$ (commutativity).
2. $T(T(x, y), z) = T(x, T(y, z))$ (associativity).
3. $T(x, y) \leq T(x', y')$ whenever $x \leq x'$, $y \leq y'$ (monotonicity).
4. $T(x, m) = x$ (boundary condition).

Definition 5.21. A triangular conorm, T-conorm [23,47,57,125,180]. A triangular conorm T-conorm on P is a binary operation $S : P \times P \rightarrow P$ which, for all $x, y, z \in P$ satisfies (1), (2), (3) and $(4') : S(x, e) = x$, as boundary condition.

Let as consider a discrete T-norm (T-conorm) on the finite chain $\{0, 1, ..., n\}$. Assume that $Z_1(A_1, B_1), Z_2(A_2, B_2)$ are from a subset of discrete Z-numbers and X, Y are subsets of a finite chain.

First we consider $T(A_1^\alpha, A_2^\alpha)$ and $S(A_1^\alpha, A_2^\alpha)$ for the α-cut sets $A_1^\alpha = \{X_1^\alpha, ..., X_p^\alpha\}$, $A_2^\alpha = \{Y_1^\alpha, ..., Y_K^\alpha\}$:

$$T(A_1^\alpha, A_2^\alpha) = \{T(x, y) \mid x \in A_1^\alpha, y \in A_2^\alpha\} \qquad (5.17)$$

and

$$S(A_1^\alpha, A_2^\alpha) = \{S(x, y) \mid x \in A_1^\alpha, y \in A_2^\alpha\} \qquad (5.18)$$

for each $\alpha \in [0, 1]$.

As it is shown in [125,180] for each $\alpha \in [0,1]$ we can write

$$C^{\alpha} = \left\{ z \in T(\text{supp}(A), \text{supp}(B)) \mid T(x_1^{\alpha}, y_1^{\alpha}) \leq z \leq T(x_p^{\alpha}, y_k^{\alpha}) \right\} \qquad (5.19)$$

$$D^{\alpha} = \left\{ z \in S(\text{supp}(A), \text{supp}(B)) \mid S(x_1^{\alpha}, y_1^{\alpha}) \leq z \leq S(x_p^{\alpha}, y_k^{\alpha}) \right\} \qquad (5.20)$$

for $\alpha = 0$: $C^0 = T(\text{supp}(A), \text{supp}(B))$ *and* $\mid D^0 = S(\text{supp}(A), \text{supp}(B))$.
There exist unique discrete fuzzy numbers

$$T(A_1, A_2)(z) = \sup\left\{ \alpha \in [0,1]: z \in C^{\alpha} \right\} \qquad (5.21)$$

and

$$S(A_1, A_2)(z) = \sup\left\{ \alpha \in [0,1]: z \in D^{\alpha} \right\}. \qquad (5.22)$$

$T(B_1, B_2)$ is obtained based on the procedure analogous to that shown in Section 4.1.3.

Let T is discrete T-norm on subset of Z-numbers. For any Z_1, Z_2 and Z_3 the following properties hold

1) $T(Z_1, Z_2) = T(Z_2, Z_1)$ (commutativity)
2) $T(T(Z_1, Z_2), Z_3) = T(Z_1, T(Z_2, Z_3))$ (associativity)

An example. T-norm. Let us compute the result of T-norm operation $T(Z_1, Z_2) = (A_{12}, B_{12})$ for the following Z-numbers $Z_1 = (A_1, B_1)$, $Z_2 = (A_2, B_2)$:

$$A_1 = \frac{0}{0} + \frac{0}{1} + \frac{0.5}{2} + \frac{0.6}{3} + \frac{0.7}{4} + \frac{1}{5} + \frac{0.7}{6} + \frac{0}{7} + \frac{0}{8} + \frac{0}{9},$$

$$B_1 = \frac{0}{0} + \frac{0}{0.1} + \frac{0}{0.2} + \frac{0}{0.3} + \frac{0}{0.4} + \frac{0.01}{0.5} + \frac{0.14}{0.6} + \frac{0.6}{0.7}$$
$$+ \frac{1}{0.8} + \frac{0.6}{0.9};$$

$$A_2 = \frac{0}{0} + \frac{0}{1} + \frac{0}{2} + \frac{0.4}{3} + \frac{0.6}{4} + \frac{1}{5} + \frac{0.8}{6} + \frac{0}{7} + \frac{0}{8} + \frac{0}{9},$$

$$B_2 = \frac{0}{0} + \frac{0}{0.1} + \frac{0}{0.2} + \frac{0}{0.3} + \frac{0}{0.4} + \frac{0.01}{0.5} + \frac{0.14}{0.6} + \frac{0.6}{0.7}$$
$$+ \frac{1}{0.8} + \frac{0.6}{0.9}.$$

Consider the case when the *min* function $T(Z_1, Z_2) = \min(Z_1, Z_2)$ is used. The first component $A_{12} = T(A_1, A_2)$ is determined on the base of (5.19)-(5.21). The obtained result is as follows:

$$A_{12} = \frac{0}{1} + \frac{0.5}{2} + \frac{0.6}{3} + \frac{0.7}{4} + \frac{1}{5} + \frac{0.7}{6} + \frac{0}{1} + \frac{0}{1} + \frac{0}{1} + \frac{0}{1}.$$

Next the second component B_{12} is computed as follows. For each pair of probability distributions p_1 and p_2 corresponding to the second components B_1 and B_2, the resulting convolution p_{12} is computed. For example, consider the following distributions:

$$p_1 = \frac{0.06}{1} + \frac{0.28}{2} + \frac{0.4}{3} + \frac{0.23}{4} + \frac{0}{5} + \frac{0}{6} + \frac{0}{7} + \frac{0}{8} + \frac{0}{9} + \frac{0}{10},$$

$$p_2 = \frac{0}{1} + \frac{0}{2} + \frac{0}{3} + \frac{0.1}{4} + \frac{0.8}{5} + \frac{0.1}{6} + \frac{0}{7} + \frac{0}{8} + \frac{0}{9} + \frac{0}{10}.$$

By using T-norm operation, a convolution $p_{12} = T(p_1, p_2) = \min(p_1, p_2)$ is determined as follows. For example, compute $p_{12}(x)$ for $x = 5$ taking into account that the latter is induced as:

$$x = \min(x_{1,5}, x_{2,5}) = \min(5,5) = 5;$$

$$x = \min(x_{1,5}, x_{2,6}) = \min(5,6) = 5;$$

$$x = \min(x_{1,5}, x_{2,7}) = \min(5,7) = 5;$$

$$\vdots$$

$$x = \min(x_{1,10}, x_{2,5}) = \min(10,5) = 5.$$

Therefore, one has for $p_{12}(5)$:

$$p_{12}(5) = p_1(5)p_2(5) + p_1(5)p_2(6) + \ldots + p_1(10)p_2(5) = 0.02 \, .$$

By conducting the analogous computations of $p_{12}(x)$ for all x, we obtain:

$$p_{12} = {0.06}/{1} + {0.28}/{2} + {0.4}/{3} + {0.23}/{4} + {0.02}/{5} + {0}/{6} + {0}/{7}$$
$$+ {0}/{8} + {0}/{9} + {0}/{10} .$$

Analogously, all the convolutions p_{12} are determined for all the remaining pairs p_1 and p_2.

Next, on the base of fuzzy sets of distributions p_1 and p_2 described by membership functions μ_{p_1}, μ_{p_2}, the induced fuzzy set of the convolutions p_{12} with the membership function $\mu_{p_{12}} = \min(\mu_{p_1}, \mu_{p_2})$ is constructed. For example, compute $\mu_{p_{12}}(p_{12})$ for p_{12} obtained above. First, to determine the values of membership functions μ_{p_1}, μ_{p_2} for the distributions considered above we compute:

$$\sum_{k=1}^{10} \mu_{A_1}(x_{1,k}) \cdot p_{A_1}(x_{1,k}) = 0 \cdot 0.06 + 0.5 \cdot 0.28 + 0.6 \cdot 0.4 + 0.7 \cdot 0.23$$
$$+ 1 \cdot 0 + 0.7 \cdot 0 + 0 \cdot 0 + 0 \cdot 0 + 0 \cdot 0 + 0 \cdot 0 = 0.14 \cdot 0.24 \cdot 0.161 = 0.541,$$

$$\sum_{k=1}^{10} \mu_{A_2}(x_{2,k}) \cdot p_{A_2}(x_{2,k}) = 0 \cdot 0 + 0 \cdot 0 + 0.4 \cdot 0 + 0.6 \cdot 0.1 + 1 \cdot 0.8$$
$$+ 0.8 \cdot 0.1 + 0 \cdot 0 + 0 \cdot 0 + 0 \cdot 0 + 0 \cdot 0 = 0.06 \cdot 0.8 \cdot 0.08 = 0.94.$$

Thus,

$$\mu_{p_1}(p_1) = \mu_{B_1}(0.5) = 0.01,$$

$$\mu_{p_2}(p_2) = \mu_{B_2}(0.9) = 0.6 \, .$$

Therefore, the degree of membership for the considered convolution p_{12} is

$$\mu_{p_{12}}(p_{12}) = \min(\mu_{p_1}, \mu_{p_2}) = \min(0.01, 0.6) = 0.01.$$

Finally, the fuzzy reliability B_{12} is computed as follows.

$$b_{12} = P(A_{12}) = \sum_{i=1}^{n} \mu_{A_{12}}(y_i) \cdot p_{12}(y_i),$$

$$\mu_{B_{12}}(b_{12}) = \mu_{p_{12}}(p_{12}).$$

Thus, for the considered convolution p_{12} we have:

$$b_{12} = P(A_{12}) = \sum_{i=1}^{10} \mu_{A_{12}}(y_i) \cdot p_{12}(y_i) = 0 \cdot 0.06 + 0.5 \cdot 0.28$$

$$+ 0.6 \cdot 0.4 + 0.7 \cdot 0.23 + 1 \cdot 0.02 + 0.7 \cdot 0 + 0 \cdot 0 + 0 \cdot 0$$

$$+ 0 \cdot 0 + 0 \cdot 0 = 0.14 + 0.161 + 0.02 = 0.561,$$

and, therefore,

$$\mu_{B_{12}}(b_{12} = 0.56) = \mu_{p_{12}}(p_{12}) = 0.01.$$

By conducting analogous computations, we obtain B_{12} as follows:

$$B_{12} = \frac{0}{0.68} + \frac{0}{0.71} + \frac{0}{0.73} + \frac{0}{0.75} + \frac{0}{0.77} + \frac{0.01}{0.79}$$

$$+ \frac{0.14}{0.81} + \frac{0.6}{0.84} + \frac{1}{0.86} + \frac{0.6}{0.9}.$$

Therefore, the result of T-norm operation is obtained: $Z_{12} = (A_{12}, B_{12})$.

An example. T-co-norm. Consider computation of the result of T-conorm operation $T(Z_1, Z_2) = (A_{12}, B_{12})$ for the following Z-numbers $Z_1 = (A_1, B_1)$, $Z_2 = (A_2, B_2)$:

$$A_1 = \frac{0.2}{0} + \frac{0.4}{1} + \frac{1}{2} + \frac{0.4}{3} + \frac{0.2}{4} + \frac{0}{0} + \frac{0}{0} + \frac{0}{0} + \frac{0}{0} + \frac{0}{0},$$

$$B_1 = \frac{0}{0.7} + \frac{0}{0.72} + \frac{0}{0.75} + \frac{0}{0.77} + \frac{0}{0.80} + \frac{0.01}{0.82} + \frac{0.14}{0.85}$$

$$+ \frac{0.6}{0.87} + \frac{1}{0.89} + \frac{0.6}{0.9}.$$

$$A_2 = \frac{0}{0} + \frac{0.6}{1} + \frac{0.8}{2} + \frac{1}{3} + \frac{0.7}{4} + \frac{0}{1} + \frac{0}{1} + \frac{0}{1} + \frac{0}{1} + \frac{0}{1},$$

$$B_2 = \frac{0}{0.45} + \frac{0}{0.50} + \frac{0}{0.54} + \frac{0}{0.59} + \frac{0}{0.64} + \frac{0.01}{0.68} + \frac{0.14}{0.73}$$
$$+ \frac{0.6}{0.77} + \frac{1}{0.82} + \frac{0.6}{0.90}.$$

Consider the case when the *max* function $S(Z_1, Z_2) = \max(Z_1, Z_2)$ is used as a T-conorm. At first, $A_{12} = S(A_1, A_2)$ component is computed on the base of (5.20)-(5.22):

$$A_{12} = \frac{0}{1} + \frac{0.5}{2} + \frac{0.6}{3} + \frac{0.7}{4} + \frac{1}{5} + \frac{0.7}{6} + \frac{0}{1} + \frac{0}{1} + \frac{0}{1} + \frac{0}{1}.$$

Next, the second component B_{12} is computed as follows. For each pair of probability distributions p_1 and p_2 corresponding to the second components B_1 and B_2, the resulting convolution p_{12} is computed. For example, consider the following distributions:

$$p_1 = \frac{0}{1} + \frac{0.4}{2} + \frac{0.05}{3} + \frac{0.03}{4} + \frac{0.15}{5} + \frac{0.15}{6} + \frac{0.15}{7}$$
$$+ \frac{0.15}{8} + \frac{0.15}{9} + \frac{0.15}{10},$$

$$p_2 = \frac{0.17}{1} + \frac{0.01}{2} + \frac{0.02}{3} + \frac{0.03}{4} + \frac{0.05}{5} + \frac{0.03}{6} + \frac{0.17}{7}$$
$$+ \frac{0.17}{8} + \frac{0.17}{9} + \frac{0.17}{10}.$$

Convolution p_{12}, $p_{12} = S(Z_{p_1}, Z_{p_2}) = \max(p_1, p_2)$ will be computed as follows. For example, compute $p_1(x)$ for $x = 5$. $x = 5$ is induced as follows:

$$x = \max(x_{1,5}, x_{2,1}) = \max(5,1) = 5;$$

$$x = \max(x_{1,5}, x_{2,2}) = \max(5,2) = 5;$$

$$x = \max(x_{1,5}, x_{2,3}) = \max(5,3) = 5;$$

$$\vdots$$

$$x = \max(x_{1,5}, x_{2,5}) = \max(5,5) = 5.$$

Thus, we will have

$$p_{12}(5) = p_1(5)p_2(5) + p_1(5)p_2(6) + \ldots + p_1(10)p_2(5) = 0.23.$$

Consequently, p_{12} is obtained:

$$p_{12} = \frac{0}{1} + \frac{0}{2} + \frac{0}{3} + \frac{0.11}{4} + \frac{0.23}{5} + \frac{0.32}{6} + \frac{0.15}{7} + \frac{0.15}{8} + \frac{0.15}{9} + \frac{0.15}{10}.$$

Analogously, all the convolutions p_{12} are determined for all the remaining pairs p_1 and p_2.

Next, on the base of the fuzzy sets of distributions p_1 and p_2 described by membership functions μ_{p_1} and μ_{p_2}, the induced fuzzy set of the convolutions p_{12} with membership functions $\mu_{p_{12}} = \min(\mu_{p_1}, \mu_{p_2})$ is constructed. For example, compute $\mu_{p_{12}}(p_{12})$ for p_{12} obtained above. First, to determine the values of membership functions μ_{p_1}, μ_{p_2} for the distributions considered above, we compute:

$$\sum_{k=1}^{10} \mu_{A_1}(x_{1,k}) \cdot p_1(x_{1,k}) = 0.4 \cdot 0 + 0.8 \cdot 0.4 + 1 \cdot 0.05 + 0.7 \cdot 0.03$$

$$+ 0 \cdot 0.15 + 0 \cdot 0.15 + 0 \cdot 0.15 + 0 \cdot 0.15 + 0 \cdot 0.15 + 0 \cdot 0.15$$

$$= 0.32 \cdot 0.05 \cdot 0.021 = 0.391,$$

$$\sum_{k=1}^{10} \mu_{A_2}(x_{2,k}) \cdot p_2(x_{2,k}) = 0 \cdot 0.17 + 0 \cdot 0.01 + 0 \cdot 0.02 + 0 \cdot 0.03$$

$$+ 0 \cdot 0.05 + 0.01 \cdot 0.03 + 0.14 \cdot 0.17 + 0.6 \cdot 0.17 + 1 \cdot 0.17 + 0.6 \cdot 0.17$$

$$= 0.001 \cdot 0.238 \cdot 0.102 + 0.17 + 0.102 = 0.613.$$

Thus, we obtain

$$\mu_{p_1}(p_1) = \mu_{B_1}(0.4) = 0,$$

$$\mu_{P_2}(p_2) = \mu_{B_2}(0.6) = 0.14.$$

Then we have

$$\mu_{P_{12}} = \min(\mu_{P_1}, \mu_{P_2}) = \min(0, 0.14) = 0.$$

Finally, the fuzzy reliability B_{12} is computed as follows:

$$b_{12} = P(A_{12}) = \sum_{i=1}^{n} \mu_{A_{12}}(y_i) \cdot p_{12}(y_i)$$

$$\mu_{B_{12}}(\dot{b}_{12}) = \mu_{P_{12}}(p_{12}).$$

For example, for the convolution p_{12} considered above we have:

$$b_{12} = P(A_{12}) = \sum_{i=1}^{10} \mu_{A_{12}}(y_i) \cdot p_{12}(y_i) = 0 \cdot 0 + 0.5 \cdot 0 + 0.6 \cdot 0 + 0.7 \cdot 0.01$$

$$+ 1 \cdot 0.2 + 0.7 \cdot 0.3 + 0 \cdot 0.1 + +0 \cdot 0.1 + 0 \cdot 0.1 + 0 \cdot 0.1 = 0.007 + 0.2 + 0.21$$

$$= 0.417,$$

and, therefore,

$$\mu_{B_{12}}(b_{12} \approx 0.4) = \mu_{P_{12}}(p_{12}) = 0.$$

By conducting analogous computations, we obtain B_{12} as follows:

$$B_{12} = \frac{0}{0.12} + \frac{0}{0.20} + \frac{0}{0.29} + \frac{0}{0.38} + \frac{0}{0.46} + \frac{0.01}{0.55} + \frac{0.14}{0.63}$$
$$+ \frac{0.61}{0.72} + \frac{1}{0.81} + \frac{0.6}{0.9}.$$

Therefore, the result of T-conorm operation is obtained: $Z_{12} = (A_{12}, B_{12})$.

5.7. Aggregation of Z-numbers

Aggregation refers to the process of combining numerical or non numerical quantities into an overall one so that the final result of aggregation takes into account all the individual contributions in a given fashion.

In the case of complex quantities such as linguistic quantities, aggregation can be provided in the framework of fuzzy sets [154]. In the probability theory aggregation problem occurs in calculus of functions of random variables.

We will consider four classes of aggregation operators each has distinct semantic. Conjunctive operators combine quantities by a logical "and" operator. Triangular norms are the suitable operators for doing conjunctive aggregation. Disjunctive operators combine quantities by "or" operator. The most common disjunctive operators are triangular conorms. Between conjunctive and disjunctive operators there is averaging operators. They are located between minimum and maximum, which are the bounds of the T-norm and T-conorm families. Main mathematical properties which can be requested for aggregation are the following [67]: idempotence; continuity; monotonicity with respect to each argument; nentrality; compensativeness; associativity; possibility of expressing the behavior of a decision maker.

Conjunctive operator. As it was mentioned above, conjunctive operators perform an aggregation where quantitives are connected by a logical "and".

Assume that a set of Z-numbers $Z = \{Z_1, Z_2, ..., Z_n\}$ is given. There exists a unique Z-number that will be denoted by Z^{agr} built using discrete T-norm. For simplicity, assume that $n=2$. Then

$$Z^{agg}(A^{agg}, B^{agg}) = T(Z(A_1, B_1), Z(A_2, B_2))$$

$$Z^{+agg}(A^{agg}, B^{agg}) = T(Z(A_1, R_1), Z^+(A_2, R_2)) = (T(A_1, A_2), T(R_1, R_2))$$

where

$$T(A_1^\alpha, A_2^\alpha) = \left\{ T(x, y) \middle| x \in A_1^\alpha, y \in A_2^\alpha \right\},$$

$$T(R_1, R_2) = R_1 \wedge R_2.$$

Calculation of B^{agg} is performed in accordance with Section 5.7.

Disjunctive operators. Maximum operators is the smallest T-conorm.

Let

$$Z^{agg}(A^{agg}, B^{agg}) = S(Z(A_1, B_1), Z(A_2, B_2)),$$

$$Z^{+agg}(A^{agg}, B^{agg}) = S(Z^+(A_1, R_1), Z^+(A_2, R_2)),$$

where

$$S(A_1^{\alpha}, A_2^{\alpha}) = \left\{ S(x, y) \middle| x \in A_1^{\alpha}, y \in A_2^{\alpha} \right\},$$

$$S(R_1, R_2) = R_1 \vee R_2.$$

Calculation of B^{agg} is performed by the methodology described in Section 5.7. Here T and S are discrete T-norm and discrete T-co-norm described in [47].

Weighted arithmetic mean. Let as consider real-valued weighting vector $W = (W_1, W_2, ..., W_n)$ and Z-valued vector $Z = (Z_1, Z_2, ..., Z_n)$. A weighted arithmetic mean operator $WA()$ assigns to any two vectors W and Z a unique Z-number Z_W:

$$WA(Z_1, Z_2, ..., Z_n) = Z_W = (A_W, B_W)$$

Components A_W, B_W are determined as follows.

$$A_W^{\alpha} = [W_1 A_1 + W_2 A_2 + ... + W_n A_n]^{\alpha} \text{ for each } \alpha \in [0,1],$$

$$R_W = W_1 R_1 + W_2 R_2 + ... + W_n R_n.$$

B_W is computed in accordance with methodology given in Section 5.7. Weighted arithmetic mean operator is a particular case of weighted averaging operator.

It is well known that an integral in the discrete case, with suitable normalization, is a particular case of weighted averaging operator. One of these operators is Choquet integral.

Choquet integral. Let g be a fuzzy measure on X. The discrete Choquet integral of $a_1,...,a_n$ with respect to g is defined by [67,124]

$$C_g(a_1,...,a_n) = \sum_{i=1}^{n} (a_{(i)} - a_{(i+1)}) g(\mathcal{S}_{(i)}),$$

where $(\cdot)$ implies indices are permuted such that $a_{(i)} \geq a_{(i+1)}$, $\mathcal{S}_{(i)} = \{(1),(2),...,(i)\}$. Choquet integral is based on usual linear operators and compute distorted average of $a_1,...,a_n$. Choquet integral is idempotent, continuous, monotonic, and compensative operators [67]. Similarly for aggregation of Z-numbers the discrete Choquet integral may be written as

$$C_g(Z_1,Z_2,...,Z_n) = \sum (Z_{(i)} - Z_{(i+1)}) g(\mathcal{S}_{(i)}), \qquad (5.23)$$

where g is fuzzy measure.

An example. Suppose that two experts suggest linguistic evaluations of the same uncertain value of interest and assign the reliabilities of the suggested evaluations. This information is formalized by using Z-numbers Z_1 and Z_2 respectively. At the same time, expert have various degrees of knowledge which are described by Z-numbers Z_{P_1} and Z_{P_2}. The problem is to aggregate expert's evaluations to arrive at a one average estimation of a considered value of interest. As the considered degrees of knowledge are of a second order uncertainty, human-like determination of an average value of expert's evaluations would involve ambiguity aversion[63,64]. Therefore, consider a discrete Choquet integral (5.23) based determination of a distorted average to account for non-additive aggregation under ambiguity aversion. In this case fuzzy measure g will be considered as a Z-valued lower probability.

Let Z_1, Z_2 and Z_{P_1}, Z_{P_2} be as follows:

$$A_1 = 0.1/8 + 0.1/16 + 0.1/20 + 0.1/24 + 0.1/28 + 0.8/36 + 0.8/40$$
$$+ 0.8/44 + 1/48 + 0.8/52 + 0.8/56 + 0.1/60 + 0.1/64 + 0.1/68$$
$$+ 0.1/72 + 0.1/80 + 0.1/88,$$

$$B_1 = 0.1/0.589 + 0.1/0.594 + 0.1/0.616 + 0.1/0.623 + 0.8/0.664$$
$$+ 0.8/0.686 + 0.8/0.703 + 0.8/0.706 + 0.8/0.734 + 0.8/0.783$$
$$+ 0.8/0.784 + 1/0.795 + 0.8/0.799 + 0.8/0.800 + 0.8/0.835$$
$$+ 0.8/0.850 + 0.8/0.862 + 0.8/0.875 + 0.1/0.900 + 0.1/0.950;$$

$$A_2 = 0.1/1 + 0.8/3 + 1/4 + 0.8/5 + 0.1/11,$$

$$B_2 = 0.1/0.8 + 0.8/0.85 + 1/0.9 + 0.8/0.9 + 0.8/0.95;$$

$$A_{P_1} = 0.1/0.5 + 0.8/0.6 + 1/0.7 + 0.8/0.8 + 0.1/0.9,$$

$$B_{P_1} = 0.1/0.8 + 0.8/0.85 + 1/0.9 + 0.8/0.9 + 0.8/0.95;$$

$$A_{P_2} = 0.1/0.1 + 0.8/0.2 + 1/0.3 + 0.8/0.4 + 0.1/0.5,$$

$$B_{P_2} = 0.1/0.8 + 0.8/0.85 + 1/0.9 + 0.8/0.9 + 0.8/0.95.$$

First, we need to rank Z-numbers Z_1, Z_2. As $Z_1 \geq Z_2$, we have $Z_{(1)} = Z_1$ and $Z_{(2)} = Z_2$. Then the considered Choquet integral will be

$$C_g(Z_1, Z_2) = (Z_{(1)} -_h Z_{(2)})g(Z_{(1)}) + Z_{(2)}g(Z_{(1)}, Z_{(2)})$$
$$= (Z_1 -_h Z_2)g(Z_1) + Z_2 g(Z_1, Z_2),$$

where

$$g(Z_{(1)}) = (A_{g(Z_{(1)})}, B_P), \ B_P = B_{P_1} = B_{P_2},$$

$$A_{g(Z_{(1)})} = \bigcup_{\alpha \in (0,1]} \alpha \left[A_{g(Z_{(1)})_1}{}^\alpha, A_{g(Z_{(1)})_2}{}^\alpha \right],$$

$$A_{g(Z_{(1)})_1}{}^\alpha = \min\{p_1 | (p_1, p_2) \in \mathcal{A}_P{}^\alpha\}, \ A_{g(Z_{(1)})_2}{}^\alpha = \min\{p_1 | (p_1, p_2) \in \mathcal{A}_P{}^{\alpha=1}\}$$

$$\mathcal{A}_P{}^\alpha = \{(p_1, p_2) \in A_{P_1}{}^\alpha \times A_{P_2}{}^\alpha | p_1 + p_2 = 1\}.$$

First we calculate Hukuhara difference $Z_{12} = Z_1 -_h Z_2$ on the base of the approach considered in Section 4.1.5. The obtained result $Z_{12} = (A_{12}, B_{12})$ is

$$A_{12} = 0.1/4 + 0.8/24 + 1/32 + 0.8/36 + 0.1/44,$$

$$B_{12} = 0.1/0.8 + 0.8/0.85 + 1/0.9 + 0.8/0.9 + 0.1/0.95.$$

Second, we compute $g(Z_{(1)}) = (A_{g(Z_{(1)})}, B_P)$ and $g(Z_{(1)}, Z_{(2)}) = (A_{g(Z_{(1)}, Z_{(2)})}, B_P)$. It is clear that $g(Z_{(1)}, Z_{(2)}) = (1, B_P)$ as $\{Z_{(1)}, Z_{(2)}\}$ is all the possible values of Z. Therefore, it is needed to only compute $g(Z_{(1)}) = (A_{g(Z_{(1)})}, B_P)$. This requires to determine $A_{g(Z_{(1)})_1}^{\alpha}$ and $A_{g(Z_{(1)})_2}^{\alpha}$. For example, for $\alpha = 0.1$ we have

$$A_{g(Z_{(1)})_1}^{\alpha=0.1} = \min\left\{ p_1 \big| (p_1, p_2) \in A_P^{\alpha=0.1} \right\} = \min\{0.5, 0.6, 0.7, 0.8, 0.9\} = 0.5,$$

$$A_{g(Z_{(1)})_2}^{\alpha} = \min\left\{ p_1 \big| (p_1, p_2) \in A_P^{\alpha=1} \right\} = \min\{0.7\} = 0.7.$$

As one can see, $A_{g(Z_{(1)})_2}^{\alpha} = 0.7$ for all $\alpha \in [0,1]$ as the $A_{P_1}^{\alpha=1} = \{0.7\}$. Analogously, we have found:

$$A_{g(Z_{(1)})_1}^{\alpha=0.8} = \min\left\{ p_1 \big| (p_1, p_2) \in A_P^{\alpha=0.8} \right\} = \min\{0.6, 0.7, 0.8\} = 0.6,$$

$$A_{g(Z_{(1)})_1}^{\alpha=1} = \min\left\{ p_1 \big| (p_1, p_2) \in A_P^{\alpha=1} \right\} = \min\{0.7\} = 0.7.$$

Therefore, we will have $g(Z_{(1)}) = (A_{g(Z_{(1)})}, B_P)$ as

$$A_{g(Z_{(1)})} = 0.1/0.5 + 0.8/0.6 + 1/0.7,$$

$$B_{g(Z_{(1)})} = 0.1/0.8 + 0.8/0.85 + 1/0.9 + 0.8/0.9 + 0.1/0.95.$$

Next we compute results of multiplication $(Z_1 -_h Z_2)g(\{Z_1\})$, $Z_2 g(\{Z_1, Z_2\})$ (Section 4.1.6), and then compute the sum of the results of multiplication (Section 4.1.3). The obtained sum yields the considered Choquet integral, which is the distorted average of Z_1, Z_2. The latter is shown below (see Fig. 5.21):

$$A_{12} = 0.1/6 + 1/38.4 + 0.8/41.2 + 0.1/46,$$

$$B_{12} = 0.1/0.45 + 0.8/0.5 + 1/0.52 + 0.8/0.62 + 0.1/0.63.$$

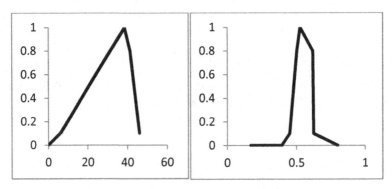

Fig. 5.21. The Choquet integral-based average of Z_1, Z_2.

Example. T-norm and T-co-norm based aggregation of Z-number based information. An expert group of 3 experts needs to generate group evaluation of a variable of interest Q. Each expert assigns his Z-number based evaluation of a value of Q, $Z_{Q_i} = (A_{Q_i}, B_{Q_i}), i = 1, ..., 3$:

$$A_{Q_1} = 0/1 + 0.3/1 + 0.4/2 + 0.7/3 + 1/4 + 0.8/5 + 0.6/6 + 0/7 + 0/8 + 0/9,$$

$$B_{Q_1} = 0/0 + 0/0.1 + 0/0.2 + 0/0.3 + 0/0.4 + 0.01/0.5 + 0.14/0.6 + 0.6/0.7$$
$$+ 1/0.8 + 0.6/0.9;$$

$$A_{Q_2} = 0.2/0 + 0.4/1 + 1/2 + 0.4/3 + 0.2/4 + 0/5 + 0/6 + 0/7 + 0/8 + 0/9,$$

$$B_{Q_2} = 0/0 + 0/0.1 + 0/0.2 + 0/0.3 + 0/0.4 + 0.01/0.5 + 0.14/0.6 + 0.6/0.7$$
$$+ 1/0.8 + 0.6/0.9;$$

$$A_{Q_3} = \frac{0}{0} + \frac{0}{1} + \frac{0.5}{2} + \frac{0.6}{3} + \frac{0.7}{4} + \frac{1}{5} + \frac{0.7}{6} + \frac{0}{7} + \frac{0}{8} + \frac{0}{9},$$

$$B_{Q_3} = \frac{0}{0} + \frac{0}{0.1} + \frac{0}{0.2} + \frac{0}{0.3} + \frac{0}{0.4} + \frac{0.01}{0.5} + \frac{0.14}{0.6} + \frac{0.6}{0.7} + \frac{1}{0.8} + \frac{0.6}{0.9}.$$

The degrees of knowledge of experts are also described by discrete Z-numbers $Z_{w_1} = (A_{w_1}, B_{w_1})$:

$$A_{w_1} = \frac{0}{0} + \frac{0.6}{1} + \frac{0.8}{2} + \frac{1}{3} + \frac{0.7}{4} + \frac{0}{5} + \frac{0}{6} + \frac{0}{7} + \frac{0}{8} + \frac{0}{9},$$

$$B_{w_1} = \frac{0}{0} + \frac{0}{0.1} + \frac{0}{0.2} + \frac{0}{0.3} + \frac{0}{0.4} + \frac{0.01}{0.5} + \frac{0.14}{0.6} + \frac{0.6}{0.7} + \frac{1}{0.8} + \frac{0.6}{0.9};$$

$$A_{w_2} = \frac{0}{0} + \frac{0}{1} + \frac{0.4}{2} + \frac{0.6}{3} + \frac{1}{4} + \frac{0.8}{5} + \frac{0}{6} + \frac{0}{7} + \frac{0}{8} + \frac{0}{9},$$

$$B_{w_2} = \frac{0}{0} + \frac{0}{0.1} + \frac{0}{0.2} + \frac{0}{0.3} + \frac{0}{0.4} + \frac{0.01}{0.5} + \frac{0.14}{0.6} + \frac{0.6}{0.7} + \frac{1}{0.8} + \frac{0.6}{0.9};$$

$$A_{w_3} = \frac{0}{0} + \frac{0}{1} + \frac{0}{2} + \frac{0.4}{3} + \frac{0.6}{4} + \frac{1}{5} + \frac{0.8}{6} + \frac{0}{7} + \frac{0}{8} + \frac{0}{9},$$

$$B_{w_3} = \frac{0}{0} + \frac{0}{0.1} + \frac{0}{0.2} + \frac{0}{0.3} + \frac{0}{0.4} + \frac{0.01}{0.5} + \frac{0.14}{0.6} + \frac{0.6}{0.7} + \frac{1}{0.8} + \frac{0.6}{0.9}.$$

The problem is to determine a final expert group evaluation as an aggregation:

$$Z_{agg} = S(S(T(Z_{Q_1}, Z_{w_1}), T(Z_{Q_2}, Z_{w_2})), T(Z_{Q_3}, Z_{w_3})).$$

The problem is solved as follows.

At the first step, an expert's weighted evaluation of Q denoted $Z_{Qw_i} = (A_{Qw_i}, B_{Qw_i})$ is determined on the base of T-norm operation described by (5.19)-(5.21). Let us consider computation of weighted evaluation for the third expert. As a T-norm, the *min* function $T(Z_Q, Z_w) = \min(Z_Q, Z_w)$ will be used. The results obtained according to (5.19)-(5.21) are as follows:

$$A_{Q_{W_1}} = \frac{0.2}{0} + \frac{0.4}{1} + \frac{1}{2} + \frac{0.4}{3} + \frac{0.2}{4} + \frac{0}{0} + \frac{0}{0} + \frac{0}{0} + \frac{0}{0} + \frac{0}{0},$$

$$B_{Q_{W_1}} = \frac{0}{0.7} + \frac{0}{0.72} + \frac{0}{0.75} + \frac{0}{0.77} + \frac{0}{0.80} + \frac{0.01}{0.82} + \frac{0.14}{0.85} + \frac{0.6}{0.87} + \frac{1}{0.89} + \frac{0.6}{0.9};$$

$$A_{Q_{W_2}} = \frac{0}{0} + \frac{0.6}{1} + \frac{0.8}{2} + \frac{1}{3} + \frac{0.7}{4} + \frac{0}{1} + \frac{0}{1} + \frac{0}{1} + \frac{0}{1} + \frac{0}{1},$$

$$B_{Q_{W_2}} = \frac{0}{0.45} + \frac{0}{0.50} + \frac{0}{0.54} + \frac{0}{0.59} + \frac{0}{0.64} + \frac{0.01}{0.68} + \frac{0.14}{0.73} + \frac{0.6}{0.77} + \frac{1}{0.82} + \frac{0.6}{0.90};$$

$$A_{Q_{W_3}} = \frac{0}{1} + \frac{0.5}{2} + \frac{0.6}{3} + \frac{0.7}{4} + \frac{1}{5} + \frac{0.7}{6} + \frac{0}{1} + \frac{0}{1} + \frac{0}{1} + \frac{0}{1},$$

$$B_{Q_{W_3}} = \frac{0}{0.68} + \frac{0}{0.71} + \frac{0}{0.73} + \frac{0}{0.75} + \frac{0}{0.77} + \frac{0.01}{0.79} + \frac{0.14}{0.81} + \frac{0.6}{0.84} + \frac{1}{0.86} + \frac{0.6}{0.9}.$$

At the second step, an aggregation of weighted evaluations is conducted on the base of T-conorm described by formula (5.20)-(5.22). At first, we need to compute the result $(Z_{A_{12}}, Z_{B_{12}})$ of T-conorm operation over weighted evaluations $Z_{Q_{W_1}} = (A_{Q_{W_1}}, B_{Q_{W_1}})$ and $Z_{Q_{W_2}} = (A_{Q_{W_2}}, B_{Q_{W_2}})$ of the first and the second experts. As a T-conorm, the *max* function $S(Z_{Q_{W_1}}, Z_{Q_{W_2}}) = \max(Z_{Q_{W_1}}, Z_{Q_{W_2}})$ will be used. The results obtained according to (5.20)-(5.22) are as follows:

$$A_{12} = \frac{0}{1} + \frac{0.5}{2} + \frac{0.6}{3} + \frac{0.7}{4} + \frac{1}{5} + \frac{0.7}{6} + \frac{0}{1} + \frac{0}{1} + \frac{0}{1} + \frac{0}{1},$$

$$B_{12} = \frac{0}{0.12} + \frac{0}{0.20} + \frac{0}{0.29} + \frac{0}{0.38} + \frac{0}{0.46} + \frac{0.01}{0.55}$$
$$+ \frac{0.14}{0.63} + \frac{0.61}{0.72} + \frac{1}{0.81} + \frac{0.6}{0.9}.$$

Therefore, the result of the aggregation of the considered experts' weighted evaluations yielded the Z-number $Z_{12} = (A_{12}, B_{12})$. Finally, we computed the result of T-conorm operation $S(Z_{12}, Z_{Q_{w_3}}) = (A, B)$ to obtain the final group evaluation based on (5.20)-(5.22):

$$A = \frac{0}{0} + \frac{0}{0} + \frac{0.5}{2} + \frac{0.6}{3} + \frac{0.7}{4} + \frac{1}{5} + \frac{0.7}{6} + \frac{0}{0} + \frac{0}{0} + \frac{0}{0},$$

$$B = \frac{0}{0.61} + \frac{0}{0.64} + \frac{0}{0.67} + \frac{0}{0.70} + \frac{0}{0.73} + \frac{0.01}{0.76} + \frac{0.14}{0.78}$$
$$+ \frac{0.61}{0.82} + \frac{1}{0.85} + \frac{0.6}{0.91}.$$

Therefore, the final expert group evaluation as an aggregation of individual expert opinions on the base of T-norm and T-conorm operations is obtained: $Z^{agg} = (A, B)$.

Chapter 6

Z-number Based Operation Research Problems

6.1. Z-number Valued Linear Programming[10]

Linear Programming (LP) is the operations research technique frequently used in the fields of Science, Economics, Business, Management Science and Engineering. Although it is investigated and applied for more than six decades, and LP models with different level of generalization of information about parameters including models with interval, fuzzy, generalized fuzzy, and random numbers are considered, till now there is no general approach to account for reliability of information within the framework of LP.

In this section we suggest a research on fully Z-number based LP (Z-LP) model in order to better fit real-world problems within the framework of LP. We propose the method to solve Z-LP problems which utilizes differential evolution optimization and Z-number arithmetic developed by the authors.

LP models representing real-world situations usually include a lot of parameters which are assigned by experts. In classical LP models values of these parameters required to be fixed, precisely known. But in real-world problems in many cases it becomes impossible to determine the precise values of parameters due to uncertainty and imprecision of relevant information. Interval analysis, Type-1 and Type-2 fuzzy set theories have been applied in formulation of LP models, and the corresponding methods to better capture uncertainty of an investigated real-world problem were developed[62,76].

An interval arithmetic-based LP approach is considered in [20,59]. The first research on taking into account real-world soft constraints in LP problem by using fuzzy sets was suggested in the famous work by Zadeh and Bellman[28]. The concept of fuzzy LP was first suggested by Zimmerman[181]. Nowadays there is a wide spectrum of works within application of the fuzzy set theory to modeling of imperfect information within LP problems. A lot of works are devoted to LP with parameters considered as fuzzy numbers[41,54,77,98,99,130]. In [114] a new concept of duality in fuzzy LP, weak and strong duality theorems are suggested. A series of works is devoted to comparison of fuzzy and stochastic LP problems[72,118]. Some works are devoted to LP problems with fuzzy parameters described by typical forms of membership functions[61,73].

In [33] an evolutionary algorithm-based solution to the fully fuzzified linear programming problem is proposed. In [2] they propose fuzzy chaos-based approach to solution of fuzzy linear programming problem and provide its application to product mix problem. In [56] solving of the Type-2 fuzzy linear programming problems by using two phases method is proposed. In [87] the authors propose generalized simplex algorithm to solve fuzzy LP problems with parameters described by generalized fuzzy numbers (GFNs). To our knowledge, this work is the first research on fuzzy LP with GFNs, which is close to an implementation of an idea to account for reliability of decision-relevant information. In this paper, on the base of the proposed new approach to ranking of GFNs, the authors develop generalized fuzzy simplex algorithm to solve real-world LP problems.

We can conclude that there is a large progress in taking into account uncertainty, imprecision, partial truth and soft constraints in real LP problems. However, the main drawback of the works mentioned above is that in these works the reliability of the decision relevant information is not taken into consideration to a considerable extent. Moreover, in the majority of works they only take into account imperfect information on parameters of LP models, whereas decision variables are considered accurate.

There are several papers in the literature, in which Z-numbers are used for solving problems related to decision making.

Studies [142,143] are devoted to new representations, approaches and applications of Z-numbers in various important fields. It is suggested to consider a Z-valuation (X, A, B) in terms of a $G(p)$ possibility distribution over probability distributions p which underlie the corresponding Z-number $Z = (A, B)$. Based on such representation, the author suggests manipulations over Z-valuations and their applications to reasoning, decision making and answering questions. Several detailed examples on computation with Z-information are provided to illustrate usefulness of the suggested approach which is based on the use of a possibility distribution $G(p)$. Another important potential impact of Z-numbers considered in [142,143] is their application to formalization of linguistic summaries. The author also suggests an alternative formulation of Z-information in terms of a Dempster-Shafer belief structure which involves type-2 fuzzy sets. In the paper, it is also suggested to rank Z-numbers by proceeding to the corresponding fuzzy numbers. Each fuzzy number is obtained from a Z-valuation (X, A, B) as a fuzzy expected value of X calculated by using a fuzzy set of probability distributions induced by A and B. The resulting fuzzy numbers are then compared on the base of their defuzzified values.

[17,18] are devoted to decision making based on hierarchical model with second order interval probabilities. The authors apply the suggested approach to a benchmark decision problem and a real-world decision problem (investment problem). The structure of second order interval probabilities can be considered as a special reduced case of a Z-number, components of which are intervals and not fuzzy numbers. The disadvantage of this work is that the approach is able to deal with imperfect information related to probabilities only. Moreover, for this purpose sharp constraints (intervals) are used which don't correspond to real-world information described in NL.

In [79] they consider an approach to multi-criteria decision making with criteria weights and criteria values described by informational constructs analogous to Z-numbers. The considered informational construct is a pair of fuzzy numbers, where the second component is intended to describe the reliability of the first component. Let us note, that it is not clearly mentioned whether the second component is a probability measure of the first, as it is assumed in the concept of Z-number[168]. In the considered approach, a pair of fuzzy numbers is reduced to one fuzzy number. Moreover, the overall performance of an alternative is computed as a crisp number. This leads to significant loss of information contained in the original informational constructs and, therefore, the comparison of alternatives may not be adequate or trustful.

[174] is devoted to the issues of computation over continuous Z-numbers and several important practical problems in control, decision making and other areas. The suggested investigation is based on the use of normal density functions for modeling random variables. A special emphasis in some of the examples is made on calculus of Z-rules. A series of detailed illustrative examples is provided on solving problems with Z-information in the realm of economics, social sphere, engineering, everyday activity and other fields. The examples are supported by a lot of conceptual schemes of processing Z-information.

[8] is devoted to decisions under uncertainty when decision-relevant information is described by Z-numbers. The authors formulate a problem of decision making when probabilities of states of nature and outcomes of alternatives are described by Z-numbers. The suggested decision analysis is based on two main stages. At the first stage, analogously to [79], Z-numbers are reduced to fuzzy numbers. At the second stage, values of fuzzy utility function for alternatives are computed and an alternative with the highest fuzzy utility value is chosen as the best one. The main disadvantage of the suggested approach is related to the loss of information resulting from converting Z-numbers to fuzzy numbers.

In [129] they suggest several approaches of approximate evaluation of a Z-number in order to reduce computational complexity. One of the suggested approaches is based on approximation of a fuzzy set of probability densities by means of fuzzy IF-THEN rules.

In [22] they consider an application of the AHP approach under Z-information. The suggested procedure is based on the approach used in [79]. However, despite that in the suggested procedure alternatives are described in the realm of Z-information, they are compared on the base of numeric overall utilities. Unfortunately, this significantly reduces benefits of using Z-information.

We can conclude that in the existing literature, a Z-number is almost always converted into a subnormal Type-1 fuzzy number. The latter is then converted into a normal Type-1 fuzzy number through normalization process[79]. We consider that this approach has a serious disadvantage. The double transformation of objective Z-information to fuzzy ordinary information results in significant loss of information, and, at the same time, to distinction from the idea of Z-information concept. Nowadays there is no approach to decision analysis with Z-information in existence, which would be based on a general and computationally effective framework of computation with Z-numbers. A new approach is needed that can be relatively easily applied for solving a wide spectrum of real-world decision problems.

In this section we propose a new LP model, namely Z-number based LP (Z-LP) model[10] which is based on Z-numbers arithmetic. This approach utilizes LP model with both the parameters and decision variables described by Z-numbers in order to better fit the real-world problems to LP with imprecise and partially reliable information. For solving the suggested Z-LP problem, a method based on Differential Evolution Optimization (DEO) is suggested.

As other stochastic and population-based methods, DEO algorithm uses an initial population of randomly generated individuals and applies to them operations of differential mutation, crossover, and selection. DEO considers individuals as vectors in n-dimensional Euclidean space. The population of $PopSize(PopSize \geq 4)$ individuals is maintained through consecutive generations. A new vector is generated by mutation, which, in this case is completed by adding a weighted difference vector of two individuals to a third individual as follows: $u_{new} = (u_{r1} - u_{r2})f + u_{r3}$, where u_{r1}, u_{r2}, u_{r3} ($r_1 \neq r_2 \neq r_3$) are 3 different individuals randomly picked from the population and f (>0) is the mutation parameter. The mutated vector then undergoes crossover with another vector thus generating a new offspring.

The selection process is realized as follows. If the resulting vector is better (e.g. yields a lower value of the cost function) than the member of the population with an index changing consequently, the newly generated vector will replace the vector with which it was compared in the following generation. Another approach, which we adopted in this research, is to randomly pick an existing vector for realizing crossover.

Fig. 6.1 illustrates a process of generation of a new trial solution (vector) u_{new} from three randomly selected members of the population

u_{r1}, u_{r2}, u_{r3}. Vector u_i, $i = 1,...,PopSize$, $i \neq r_1 \neq r_2 \neq r_3$ becomes the candidate for replacement by the new vector, if the former is better in terms of the DEO cost function. Here, for illustrative purposes, we assume that the solution vectors are of dimension $n=2$ (i.e., 2 parameters are to be optimized).

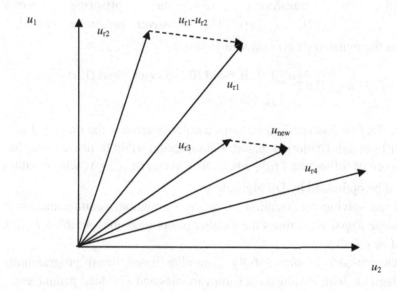

Fig. 6.1. Realization of DEO: a two-dimensional case.

The computation process of the algorithm denoted DEO(*PopSize, F, CR, MaxGen, MinimumCost*) can be described as follows. In step 1, randomly generate *PopSize* parameter vectors (from respective parameter spaces (e.g. in the range [-1, 1]) and form a population $P=\{u_1, u_2, ..., u_{ps}\}$. In Step 2, while the termination condition (maximum iterations MaxGenreached or minimum cost MinimumCost attained) is not met generate new parameter sets: Choose a next vector u_i ($i=1,...,PopSize$); Choose randomly different 3 vectors from P: u_{r1}, u_{r2}, u_{r3} each of which is different from current u_i. Generate trial vector $u_t=u_{r1}+f(u_{r2}-u_{r3})$. Generate a new vector from trial vector u_t. Individual vector parameters of u_t are inherited with probability cr into the new vector u_{new}. If u_{new} evaluates asbeing a better solution than u_i, then the current u_i is replaced in population P by u_{new}. In step 3, select from population P the parameter vector u_{best}, which is evaluated as the best solution. Usually the mutation rate f is chosen $f \in [0,2]$. After the crossover of the trial vector and the vector $u_i = (u_i[1], u_i[2], ..., u_i[n])$ from the population, at least one of the elements (dimensions) of the trial vector $u_t = (u_t[1], u_t[2], ..., u_t[n])$ should be transferred to the offspring vector $u_{new} = (u_{new}[1], u_{new}[2], ..., u_{new}[n])$. The crossover parameter $cr \in [0,1]$ affects the mutated (trial) vector as follows:

$$u_{new}[j] = \begin{cases} u_{new}[j], & \text{if } r \text{ and } (0,1) \le cr \text{ or } r \text{ and } (1,n) = j, \\ u_i[j], & \text{otherwise,} \end{cases}$$

where the function $rand(a,b)$ returns a random value in the range [a,b].

Differential Evolution based Optimization (DEO) usually implies existence of a function $f(u)$, where u is vector $(u_1, ..., u_n)$, whose values should be optimized by DE algorithm.

When solving optimization problems a common recommendation is to choose *PopSize* ten times the number of optimization variables, $F=0.9$, $CR=1$ or $CR=0.5$.

We consider solving a fully Z-number based linear programming problem, i.e. with Z-valued decision variables and Z-valued parameters. The general formulation of a Z-LP problem may be described as follows[10]:

$$Z_f(Z_{x_1}, Z_{x_2}, ..., Z_{x_n}) = Z_{c_1} Z_{x_1} + Z_{c_2} Z_{x_2} + ... + Z_{c_n} Z_{x_n} \to \max \qquad (6.1)$$

subject to

$$Z_{a_{11}} Z_{x_1} + Z_{a_{12}} Z_{x_2} + ... + Z_{a_{1n}} Z_{x_n} \preceq Z_{b_1},$$
$$Z_{a_{21}} Z_{x_1} + Z_{a_{22}} Z_{x_2} + ... + Z_{a_{2n}} Z_{x_n} \preceq Z_{b_2},$$
$$...$$
$$Z_{a_{m1}} Z_{x_1} + Z_{a_{m2}} Z_{x_2} + ... + Z_{a_{mn}} Z_{x_n} \preceq Z_{b_m}, \qquad (6.2)$$

$$Z_{x_1}, Z_{x_2}, ..., Z_{x_n} \succeq Z_0. \tag{6.3}$$

Here decision variables and parameters are described by Z-numbers

$$Z_{x_i} = (A_{x_i}, B_{x_i}),$$

$$Z_{c_i} = (A_{c_i}, B_{c_i}),\ Z_{a_{ij}} = (A_{a_{ij}}, B_{a_{ij}}),\ Z_{b_j} = (A_{b_j}, B_{b_j}), i = 1, ..., n, j = 1, ..., m,$$

$$Z_0 = (0,1).$$

To properly define the Z-LP problem we have to clarify what is $\max Z_f$ and what is Z-inequality. In this work $\max Z_f$ and Z-inequality are defined on the base of the approach to ranking of Z-numbers suggested in Section 4.3. Then, in accordance with the approach described in Section 4.3, the problem (6.1)-(6.3) may be transformed into the problem described below[10]:

$$Z_f(Z_{x_1}, Z_{x_2}, ..., Z_{x_n}) = Z_{c_1} Z_{x_1} + Z_{c_2} Z_{x_2} + ... + Z_{c_n} Z_{x_n} \rightarrow \max \tag{6.4}$$

subject to

$$Z_{a_{11}} Z_{x_1} + Z_{a_{12}} Z_{x_2} + ... + Z_{a_{1n}} Z_{x_n} \leq^Z Z_{b_1},$$

$$Z_{a_{21}} Z_{x_1} + Z_{a_{22}} Z_{x_2} + ... + Z_{a_{2n}} Z_{x_n} \leq^Z Z_{b_2}, \tag{6.5}$$

$$...$$

$$Z_{a_{m1}} Z_{x_1} + Z_{a_{m2}} Z_{x_2} + ... + Z_{a_{mn}} Z_{x_n} \leq^Z Z_{b_m},$$

$$Z_{x_1}, Z_{x_2}, ..., Z_{x_n} \geq^Z Z_0. \tag{6.6}$$

Let us consider solving of this problem. To our knowledge, there is no method for solving the Z-LP problem (6.4)-(6.6), that is to obtain optimal (max or min) value of Z_f. We will use a directed search method, namely DEO method, to find an optimal solution to the considered problem.

Definition 6.1. A Z-valued slack variable. Suppose that an *i*-th constraint of a Z-LP problem is

$$\sum_{j=1}^{n} Z_{a_{ij}} Z_{x_j} \leq^Z Z_{b_i}.$$

A Z-valued variable $Z_{x_{n+i}}$ such that

$$\sum_{j=1}^{n} Z_{a_{ij}} Z_{x_j} + Z_{x_{n+i}} = Z_{b_i}, \quad Z_{x_{n+i}} \geq^Z Z_0$$

is called a Z-valued slack variable.

Definition 6.2. A Z-valued surplus variable. Suppose that an i-th constraint of a Z-LP problem is

$$\sum_{j=1}^{n} Z_{a_{ij}} Z_{x_j} \geq^Z Z_{b_i}.$$

A Z-valued variable $Z_{x_{n+i}}$ such that

$$\sum_{j=1}^{n} Z_{a_{ij}} Z_{x_j} - Z_{x_{n+i}} = Z_{b_i}, \quad Z_{x_{n+i}} \geq^Z Z_0$$

is called a Z-valued surplus variable.

Definition 6.3. A Z-valued feasible solution. Any Z_x in (6.4) which satisfies constraints (6.5)-(6.6) is called a Z-valued feasible solution of (6.4)-(6.6).

Definition 6.4. A Z-valued optimal solution. Suppose that $\mathbf{Z}_s$ is set of all Z-valued feasible solutions of (6.4)-(6.6). A Z-valued feasible solution $Z_{x_0} \in \mathbf{Z}_s$ is called a Z-valued optimal solution of (6.4)-(6.6) if $Z_f(Z_{x_0}) \leq^Z Z_f(Z_x)$.

Let us proceed to solving of the problem (6.4)-(6.6).

At first we add the Z-valued slack variables[10]:

$$Z_f(Z_{x_1}, Z_{x_2}, ..., Z_{x_n}) = Z_{c_1} Z_{x_1} + Z_{c_2} Z_{x_2} + ... + Z_{c_n} Z_{x_n} \rightarrow \max$$

subject to

$$Z_{a_{11}} Z_{x_1} + Z_{a_{12}} Z_{x_2} + \ldots + Z_{a_{1n}} Z_{x_n} + Z_{x_{n+1}} = Z_{b_1},$$

$$Z_{a_{21}} Z_{x_1} + Z_{a_{22}} Z_{x_2} + \ldots + Z_{a_{2n}} Z_{x_n} + Z_{x_{n+2}} = Z_{b_2},$$

$$\ldots$$

$$Z_{a_{m1}} Z_{x_1} + Z_{a_{m2}} Z_{x_2} + \ldots + Z_{a_{mn}} Z_{x_n} + Z_{x_{n+m}} = Z_{b_m},$$

$$Z_{x_1}, Z_{x_2}, \ldots, Z_{x_n}, Z_{x_{n+1}}, Z_{x_{n+2}}, \ldots, Z_{x_{n+m}} \geq^Z Z_0.$$

Next we rewrite the considered problem in the following equivalent form:

$$Z_g(Z_{x_1}, Z_{x_2}, \ldots, Z_{x_n}, Z_{x_{n+1}}, Z_{x_{n+2}}, \ldots, Z_{x_{n+m}})$$

$$= -(Z_{c_1} Z_{x_1} + Z_{c_2} Z_{x_2} + \ldots + Z_{c_n} Z_{x_n})$$

$$+ (Z_{b_1} - (Z_{a_{11}} Z_{x_1} + Z_{a_{12}} Z_{x_2} + \ldots + Z_{a_{1n}} Z_{x_n} + Z_{x_{n+1}}))$$

$$+ (Z_{b_2} - (Z_{a_{21}} Z_{x_1} + Z_{a_{22}} Z_{x_2} + \ldots + Z_{a_{2n}} Z_{x_n} + Z_{x_{n+2}}))$$

$$\ldots$$

$$+ (Z_{b_m} - (Z_{a_{m1}} Z_{x_1} + Z_{a_{m2}} Z_{x_2} + \ldots + Z_{a_{mn}} Z_{x_n} + Z_{x_{n+m}})) \to \max \quad (6.7)$$

subject to

$$Z_{x_1}, Z_{x_2}, \ldots, Z_{x_n}, Z_{x_{n+1}}, Z_{x_{n+2}}, \ldots, Z_{x_{n+m}} \geq^Z Z_0. \quad (6.8)$$

The suggested solution method for solving of optimization problem (6.7)-(6.8) is described below.

At the first stage we set the parameters of the DEO algorithm, define the DEO cost function as the objective function Z_f (6.7), and choose the population size *PopSize*. As a rule of thumb, the population size is set at least ten times the number of optimization variables. Thus, as a Z-number has two components, the population size is $PopSize = 2 \cdot 10 N_{\text{var}}$, where N_{var} is the number of optimization variables. Then the DEO algorithm is started.

First we construct template parameter vector u of dimension $2N_{var}$ for holding data of all decision variables Z_x. Then we set algorithm parameters: F (mutation rate) and CR (crossover rate).

Next *PopSize* parameter vectors are randomly generated and a population $P = \{u_1, u_2, \ldots, u_{PN}\}$ is formed.

While the termination condition (a number of predefined generations is reached or a required error level is obtained) is not met, new parameter sets are generated. For a next vector u_i ($i=1, \ldots, PopSize$) 3 different vectors u_{r1}, u_{r2}, u_{r3} are chosen randomly from P each of which is different from the current u_i. A new trial vector $u_{new} = u_{r1} + F \cdot (u_{r2} - u_{r3})$ is used to generate a new vector in the population. Individual vector parameters of u_i are inherited with probability CR into the new vector u_{new}. If the cost function for u_{new} is better (lower) than the cost function for u_i then the current u_i is replaced in population P by u_{new}. Next the parameter vector u_{best} is selected with the best value of cost function (objective function) from population P.

The above process is continued until the termination condition is met. When the condition is met, we select the parameter vector u_{best} (best decision variables) with the lower cost function Z_f from population P. Finally, we extract from u_{best} all the decision variables.

6.2. Z-number Based Regression Analysis[74]

Regression models with different levels of generalization of information including interval, fuzzy and random information were considered in the existing literature. However, there is no general approach to account for imprecision and reliability of information in regression analysis.

In this section we consider Z-number based regression model. We formulate a problem and a solution method for construction of a Z-valued regression model. The suggested formalism is based on arithmetic of discrete Z-numbers.

Suppose that K data expressed as Z-numbers are given for multi input-single output process. The problem is to define regression model for fitting this type of data. The following Z-valued regression model is considered:

$$Z_{y^M}(Z_{x_1}, Z_{x_2}, ..., Z_{x_N}) = Z_{a_0} + \sum_{i=1}^{N} Z_{a_i} Z_{x_i} + \sum_{i=1}^{N} Z_{b_i} Z_{x_i}^2$$

$$+ \sum_{\substack{i=1 \\ i<j}}^{N} \sum_{j=1}^{N} Z_{c_{ij}} Z_{x_i} Z_{x_j}. \tag{6.9}$$

It is required to determine Z-valued coefficients (Z-numbers) Z_{a_i}, Z_{b_i}, $Z_{c_{ij}}$ $i = 0, ..., N$, $j = 1, ..., N$ given Z-valued input data $Z_{x_{ik}}$ and output data Z_{y_k}, $k = 1, ..., K$ so that

$$d(Z_y^M, Z_y) = \sum_{k=1}^{K} \left(Z_{y,i}^M - Z_{y,i} \right)^2 \to \min, \tag{6.10}$$

where $d(Z^M, Z_y)$ measures a distance in an n-dimensional Z-valued vector space between a vector of Z-valued output data Z_{y_k}, $k = 1, ..., K$ and a vector of the corresponding Z-numbers Z_y^M computed by (6.9). Use of gradient based methods for solving problem (6.9)-(6.10) is not suitable due to complexity of representation of derivative of a Z-valued function and a general form of the considered regression model. Thus, we suggest to use DEO approach described in Section 6.1 to solve problem (6.9)-(6.10).

An example. Production of gasoline at catalytic cracking unit is implemented in a fractionator column. The operation mode of the gasoline production is characterized by temperatures at the top and the bottom of column. Let us consider modeling of dependence of an amount of produced gasoline on the temperatures at the top and the bottom of column. Catalytic cracking is a very complex process characterized by uncertainty. Some indicators of this process cannot be directly measured. Due to these objective reasons, the data on the values of temperature at the top and the bottom of the column(input data of a model) and amount of produced gasoline (output data) are represented by means of Z-numbers. The Z-valued input and output data described with the use of discrete triangular fuzzy numbers are given in Table 6.1.

Table 6.1. Z-valued input and output data for gasoline production.

Temperature at top of a column, °C		Temperature at bottom of a column, °C		Amount of gasoline production,tons	
A_{x_1}	B_{x_1}	A_{x_2}	B_{x_2}	A_y	B_y
(125,4;132;138,6)	(0,76;0,8;0,84)	(237,5;250;262,5)	(0,76;0,8;0,84)	(107,35;113;118,65)	(0,76;0,8;0,84)
(123,5;130;136,5)	(0,76;0,8;0,84)	(234,65;247;259,35)	(0,76;0,8;0,84)	(109,25;115;120,75)	(0,76;0,8;0,84)
(126,35;133;139,65)	(0,76;0,8;0,84)	(237,5;250;262,5)	(0,76;0,8;0,84)	(103,55;109;114,45)	(0,76;0,8;0,84)
9125,4;132;138,6)	(0,76;0,8;0,84)	(237,5;250;262,5)	(0,76;0,8;0,84)	(115,9;122;128,1)	(0,76;0,8;0,84)
(125,4;132;138,6)	(0,76;0,8;0,84)	(237,5;250;262,5)	(0,76;0,8;0,84)	(91,2;96;100,8)	(0,76;0,8;0,84)
(125,4;132;138,6)	(0,76;0,8;0,84)	(237,5;250;262,5)	(0,76;0,8;0,84)	(127,3;134;140,7)	(0,76;0,8;0,84)
(128,25;135;141,75)	(0,76;0,8;0,84)	(237,5;250;262,5)	(0,76;0,8;0,84)	(112,1;118;123,9)	(0,76;0,8;0,84)
(130,15;137;143,85)	(0,76;0,8;0,84)	(237,5;250;262,5)	(0,76;0,8;0,84)	(105,45;111;116,55)	(0,76;0,8;0,84)
(131,1;138;144,9)	(0,76;0,8;0,84)	(238,45;251;263,55)	(0,76;0,8;0,84)	(105,45;111;116,55)	(0,76;0,8;0,84)
(128,25;135;141,75)	(0,76;0,8;0,84)	(234,65;247;259,35)	(0,76;0,8;0,84)	(134,9;142;149,1)	(0,76;0,8;0,84)
(130,15;137;143,85)	(0,76;0,8;0,84)	(235,6;248;260,4)	(0,76;0,8;0,84)	(112,1;118;123,9)	(0,76;0,8;0,84)
(130,15;137;143,85)	(0,76;0,8;0,84)	(237,5;250;262,5)	(0,76;0,8;0,84)	(104,5;110;115,5)	(0,76;0,8;0,84)
(128,25;135;141,75)	(0,76;0,8;0,84)	(237,5;250;262,5)	(0,76;0,8;0,84)	(100,7;106;111,3)	(0,76;0,8;0,84)
(128,25;135;141,75)	(0,76;0,8;0,84)	(237,5;250;262,5)	(0,76;0,8;0,84)	(108,3;114;119,7)	(0,76;0,8;0,84)
(128,25;135;141,75)	(0,76;0,8;0,84)	(237,5;250;262,5)	(0,76;0,8;0,84)	(109,25;115;120,75)	(0,76;0,8;0,84)
(127,3;134;140,7)	(0,76;0,8;0,84)	(237,5;250;262,5)	(0,76;0,8;0,84)	(114;120;126)	(0,76;0,8;0,84)
(127,3;134;140,7)	(0,76;0,8;0,84)	(240,35;253;265,65)	(0,76;0,8;0,84)	(114,95;121;127,05)	(0,76;0,8;0,84)
(124,45;131;137,55)	(0,76;0,8;0,84)	(231,8;244;256,2)	(0,76;0,8;0,84)	(100,7;106;111,3)	(0,76;0,8;0,84)
(131,1;138;144,9)	(0,76;0,8;0,84)	(239,4;252;264,6)	(0,76;0,8;0,84)	(115,9;122;128,1)	(0,76;0,8;0,84)
(130,15;137;143,85)	(0,76;0,8;0,84)	(237,5;250;262,5)	(0,76;0,8;0,84)	(95;100;105)	(0,76;0,8;0,84)

For simplicity, let us consider approximation of this dependence by means of a Z-valued linear regression model adopted from (6.9). The model will be of the following form:

$$Z_{y^M}(Z_{x_1}, Z_{x_2}) = Z_{a_1} Z_{x_1} + Z_{a_2} Z_{x_2} \qquad (6.11)$$

where Z_{x_1} and Z_{x_2} denote Z-valued variables handling the values of temperature at the top and the bottom of the column, Z_{a_1}, Z_{a_2} are Z-valued coefficients of the model, Z_{y^M} denotes Z-valued variable handling the values of the produced gasoline.

We have constructed the model (6.11) by solving the problem (6.9)-(6.10) on the base of the presented solution methodology. The Z-values of real gasoline production Z_y and the gasoline production Z_{y^M} computed by the constructed Z-valued linear regression modelare shown in Table 6.2. The corresponding minimized value of $d(Z^M, Z_y)$ and the resulting Z-valued coefficients Z_{a_1}, Z_{a_2} are shown in Figs. 6.2, 6.3 respectively.

Table 6.2. The real and the computed values of gasoline production.

Z_y		Z_{y^M}	
A	B	A	B
(07,35;113;118,65)	(0,76;0,8;0,84)	(0;114,74;304,06)	(0,01;0,47;0,53)
(109,25;115;120,75)	(0,76;0,8;0,84)	(0;113,23;304,06)	(0,02;0,62;0,88)
(103,55;109;114,45)	(0,76;0,8;0,84)	(0;115,06;304,06)	(0,01;0,55;0,61)
(115,9;122;128,1)	(0,76;0,8;0,84)	(0;114,74;304,06)	(0,01;0,47;0,53)
(91,2;96;100,8)	(0,76;0,8;0,84)	(0;114,74;304,06)	(0,01;0,47;0,53)
(127,3;134;140,7)	(0,76;0,8;0,84)	(0;114,74;304,06)	(0,01;0,47;0,83)
(112,1;118;123,9)	(0,76;0,8;0,84)	(0;115,7;304,06)	(0,01;0,55;0,62)
(105,45;111;116,55)	(0,76;0,8;0,84)	(0;116,34;304,06)	(0,01;0,47;0,53)
(105,45;111;116,55)	(0,76;0,8;0,84)	(0;116,95;304,06)	(0,01;0,45;0,64)
(134,9;142;149,1)	(0,76;0,8;0,84)	(0;114,83;304,06)	(0.01;0,61;0,70)
(112,1;118;123,9)	(0,76;0,8;0,84)	(0;115,76;304,06)	(0,02;0,60;0,88)
(104,5;110;115,5)	(0,76;0,8;0,84)	(0;116,34;304,06)	(0,01;0,47;0,53)
(100,7;106;111,3)	(0,76;0,8;0,84)	(0;115,7;304,06)	(0,01;0,55;0,62)
(108,3;114;119,7)	(0,76;0,8;0,84)	(0;115,7;304,06)	(0,01;0,55;0,62)
(109,25;115;120,75)	(0,76;0,8;0,84)	(0;115,7;304,06)	(0,01;0,55;0,62)
(114;120;126)	(0,76;0,8;0,84)	(0;15,38;304,06)	(0,01;0,55;0,62)
(114,95;121;127,05)	(0,76;0,8;0,84)	(0;116,25;304,06)	(0,02;0,09;0,10)
(100,7;106;111,3)	(0,76;0,8;0,84)	(0;112,68;328,67)	(0,01;0,46;0,54)
(115,9;122;128,1)	(0,76;0,8;0,84)	(0;117,24;304,06)	(0,02;0,22;0,25)
(95;100;105)	(0,76;0,8;0,84)	(0;116,34;304,06)	(0,01;0,47;0,53)

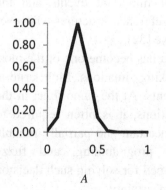 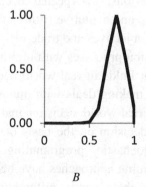

Fig. 6.2. The value of Z_{a_1}.

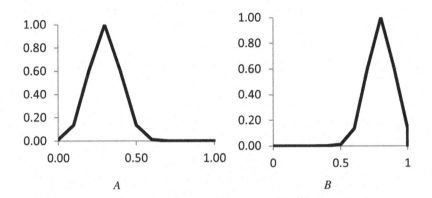

Fig. 6.3. The value of Z_{a_2}.

6.3. Z-resrtiction Based Multicriteria Choice

The most of realistic decision-making problems, essentially those stemming from complex and ill-structured situations, are characterized by the existence of multiple, conflicting and incommensurate objectives and are subject to the unavoidable influence of distinct sources of uncertainty. Therefore, models must take into account vague information, imprecise requirements, modifications of the original input data, imprecision stemming from the modeling phase, needed simplifications, unexpected occurrence of important events and the subjective and evolutive nature of human preference structures whenever multiple objectives and trade-offs are at stake [32].

Decision processes with multiple criteria has become one of the most important fields in real-world decision making situations. Multi-criteria decision making deals with human judgments. At the same time, in the most of real-world decision making situations, it is often required to make a decision on the basis of vague, uncertain and partially reliable data. Stochastic programming, interval programming, and fuzzy programming approaches have been developed for solving such decision making problems under different types of uncertainty.

First attempts to model decision processes with multiple criteria lead to concepts of goal programming [71]. In this approach, a decision maker

(DM) underpins each objective with a number of goals that should be satisfied [95]. Satisfying requires finding a solution to a multi-criteria problem, which is preferred, understood and implemented with confidence. The confidence that the best solution has been found is estimated through the "ideal solution" which is the solution optimizing all criteria simultaneously. Since this is practically unattainable, a DM considers feasible solutions closest to the ideal solution [179].

In order to eliminate time consuming component, the improvement was suggested to applying the weighted Chebyshev norm in a decision process [29,86,145,178]. It is suggested to minimize the distance between the objective-function values and so-called ideal values. In [111] authors propose new method for solving multi-criteria linear programming problems called moving optimal method.

Since Bellman and Zadeh's paper in 1970, the maxmin and simple additive weighting method using membership function of a fuzzy set is used in explanation of business decision making problems [28]. Lai and Hwang consider the application of the fuzzy set theory in multi-criteria decision problems to depart from oversimplified (numerical) models such as goal programming and ideal nadir vector models [90].

Let us mention that the use of the fuzzy set theory makes multi-criteria models robust and flexible. Fuzzy multicriteria models allow DMs not only to consider the existing alternatives under given constraints, "but also develop new alternatives by considering all possible situations" [90].

The transitional step towards fuzzy multi-criteria models is models that consider some fuzzy values. Some of these models are linear mathematical formulation of multiple objective decision making presented by mainly crisp and some fuzzy values. Many authors studied such models [50,51,89,90,181]. Zimmermann offered the solution for the fuzzy linear programming problem[181]. Lai's interactive multiple objective system technique contributed to the improvement of flexibility and robustness of multiple objective decision making methodology [113].

The majority of multi-criteria decision models in the existing literature is based on linear programming (LP). LP models representing real-world situations usually include a lot of parameters which are assigned by experts. In classical LP models values of these parameters required to be fixed, precisely known. But in real-world in many cases it becomes impossible to determine the precise values of parameters due to uncertainty and imprecision of relevant information. Interval analysis, Type-1 and Type-2 fuzzy set theories have been applied in development of LP models and provided methods to better capture uncertainty of an investigated real-world problem.

Interval arithmetic-based LP approach is considered in [20,59].

In a fuzzy environment, the main purpose is to find the "most satisfactory" solution under incomplete, subjective, imprecise and/or vague information. In the symmetric model proposed by Bellman and Zadeh [28], there is no difference between objectives and constraints. A fuzzy decision can be viewed as a fuzzy set resulting from the intersection of fuzzy goals and fuzzy constraints. An optimal decision is an element with maximum degree of membership to this set [32].

The concept of a fuzzy LP first was suggested in [181]. In [28,33, 41,54,61,72,77,98,99,114,118,130,181] different fuzzy models are considered and several methods for solving LP based decision models are proposed.

In [33] an evolutionary algorithm-based solution to the fully fuzzified linear programming problem is proposed. In [2] authors propose fuzzy chaos-based approach to solution of a fuzzy LP problem and its application to a product mix problem. In [56] authors propose solving the Type-2 fuzzy linear programming problems by using two phases method. In [87] authors propose Generalized Simplex algorithm to solve fuzzy LP problems which are based on generalized fuzzy numbers (GFNs). In our opinion, this work is the first research on fuzzy LP with GFNs, which is close to capture reliability of decision-relevant information. On the base of the proposed new ranking approach of GFNs, authors develop a generalized fuzzy simplex algorithm to solve real-world LP problems.

In [12] multiple criteria decision method based on an hierarchical fuzzy LP model is developed. The book [90] is devoted to the fuzzy set theory and optimization methods which are used to solve multi-objective group decision making problems in an uncertain environment.

In the most of practical situations, however, it is natural to consider that the uncertainty in real-world decision making problems is often expressed by a fusion of fuzziness and randomness rather than either fuzziness or randomness. For handling not only a DM's vague judgments in multiobjective problems, but also the randomness of the parameters involved in the objectives and/or constraints, Sakawa and his colleagues incorporated their interactive fuzzy satisficing methods for deterministic problems [120,121] into multiobjective stochastic programming problems.

A recently published book of Sakawa et al. [123] is devoted to introducing the latest advances in the field of multiobjective optimization under both fuzziness and randomness on the basis of authors' continuing research works. A special stress is placed on interactive decision making aspects of fuzzy stochastic multiobjective programming for realistic situations in human-centered systems under uncertainty when dealing with both fuzziness and randomness [122].

The main drawback of the above-mentioned works on multi-criteria decision making is that in these works the reliability of decision-relevant information is not taken into consideration.

There are several papers in the literature, in which Z-numbers are used for solving different decisions problems.

There are a lot of problems that need multi-criteria Z-LP approach. Let us consider one simple example. A manufacturing company produces n products X_i, $i = 1,2, ..., n$. Each product requires m processes P_j, $j = 1,2, ..., m$. Product X_i, through P_j, requires a_{ij} hours. Each process P_j provides b_j hours. The manufacturing company must determine the mix of its commercial products X_i, $i = 1,2, ..., n$ to be produced next year. The company manager formulates production planning decision as how many of each product should be produced each month in order to maximize simultaneously q objectives (for example, profit, quality, etc.). When formulating the decision problem, it is needed to take into account that different uncertain factors of the real-world decision situation which influence evaluation of the parameters of objective functions and constraints assigned by experts. Practically, the parameters of objective functions and the existing constraints assigned with some uncertainty and partial reliability are expressed by Z-numbers.

For example, total available labor hours may be assigned with some tolerance and reliability, because the company manager can ask workers to work overtime. So, the Z-information appears in the specification of resources. Since the market changes constantly, it may not be certain to describe the per unit profit of produced products X_i, $i = 1, 2, \ldots, n$ by using precise numbers, they could only be viewed as the possible values with some degree of reliability. Therefore, it is reasonable to represent the objective coefficients as Z-numbers.

Because of the inconsistence of human workers, a value of labor hours a_{ij} could only be viewed as a fuzzy number with given reliability. Therefore, it is reasonable to represent these coefficients as Z-numbers.

Under these circumstances let us formulate a problem of multi-criteria decision making on production of a mix of products. Let the quality produced for X_i be Z_{x_i}, $i = 1, 2, \ldots, n$. Let us now formulate a multi-criteria LP problem under Z-information for a general case.

$$Z_{f_1}(Z_{x_1}, Z_{x_2}, \ldots, Z_{x_n}) = Z_{C_1^1} \cdot Z_{x_1} + Z_{C_2^1} \cdot Z_{x_2} + \ldots + Z_{C_n^1} \cdot Z_{x_n} \to \max$$

$$Z_{f_2}(Z_{x_1}, Z_{x_2}, \ldots, Z_{x_n}) = Z_{C_1^2} \cdot Z_{x_1} + Z_{C_2^2} \cdot Z_{x_2} + \ldots + Z_{C_n^2} \cdot Z_{x_n} \to \max$$

$$\cdot$$
$$\cdot \qquad\qquad (6.12)$$
$$\cdot$$

$$Z_{f_q}(Z_{x_1}, Z_{x_2}, \ldots, Z_{x_n}) = Z_{C_1^q} \cdot Z_{x_1} + Z_{C_2^q} \cdot Z_{x_2} + \ldots + Z_{C_n^q} \cdot Z_{x_n} \to \max$$

subject to

$$Z_{a_{11}} Z_{x_1} + Z_{a_{12}} Z_{x_2} + \ldots + Z_{a_{1n}} Z_{x_n} \preceq Z_{b_1},$$

$$Z_{a_{21}} Z_{x_1} + Z_{a_{22}} Z_{x_2} + \ldots + Z_{a_{2n}} Z_{x_n} \preceq Z_{b_2},$$

$$\ldots \qquad\qquad (6.13)$$

$$Z_{a_{m1}} Z_{x_1} + Z_{a_{m2}} Z_{x_2} + \ldots + Z_{a_{mn}} Z_{x_n} \preceq Z_{b_m},$$

$$Z_{x_1}, Z_{x_2}, \ldots, Z_{x_n} \succeq Z_0.$$

Here decision variables and parameters are described by Z-numbers

$$Z_{x_i} = (A_{x_i}, B_{x_i})$$
$$Z_{c_i} = (A_{c_i}, B_{c_i}), \ Z_{a_{ij}} = (A_{a_{ij}}, B_{a_{ij}}), \ Z_{b_j} = (A_{b_j}, B_{b_j}), i = 1,...,n, \ j = 1,...,m,$$
$$Z_0 = (0,1).$$

To properly define the Z-LP problem we have to clarify what is $\max Z_f$ and what is Z-inequality. In this work $\max Z_f$ and Z-inequality on the base of the approach to ranking of Z-numbers suggested in Section 4.3. Then, in accordance with the approach suggested described in Section 4.3, the problem (6.12)-(6.13) may be transformed into the problem described below:

$$Z_{f_1}(Z_{x_1}, Z_{x_2},...,Z_{x_n}) = Z_{C_1^1} \cdot Z_{x_1} + Z_{C_2^1} \cdot Z_{x_2} + ... + Z_{C_n^1} \cdot Z_{x_n} \to \max$$
$$Z_{f_2}(Z_{x_1}, Z_{x_2},...,Z_{x_n}) = Z_{C_1^2} \cdot Z_{x_1} + Z_{C_2^2} \cdot Z_{x_2} + ... + Z_{C_n^2} \cdot Z_{x_n} \to \max$$
$$\vdots \qquad (6.14)$$
$$Z_{f_q}(Z_{x_1}, Z_{x_2},...,Z_{x_n}) = Z_{C_1^q} \cdot Z_{x_1} + Z_{C_2^q} \cdot Z_{x_2} + ... + Z_{C_n^q} \cdot Z_{x_n} \to \max$$

subject to

$$\left. \begin{aligned} Z_{a_{11}} Z_{x_1} + Z_{a_{12}} Z_{x_2} + ... + Z_{a_{1n}} Z_{x_n} &\leq^Z Z_{b_1}, \\ Z_{a_{21}} Z_{x_1} + Z_{a_{22}} Z_{x_2} + ... + Z_{a_{2n}} Z_{x_n} &\leq^Z Z_{b_2}, \\ &... \\ Z_{a_{m1}} Z_{x_1} + Z_{a_{m2}} Z_{x_2} + ... + Z_{a_{mn}} Z_{x_n} &\leq^Z Z_{b_m}, \\ Z_{x_1}, Z_{x_2}, ..., Z_{x_n} &\geq^Z Z_0. \end{aligned} \right\} \qquad (6.15)$$

Let us proceed to solving of the problem (6.14)-(6.15). At first we add the Z-valued slack variables:

$$Z_{a_{11}}Z_{x_1} + Z_{a_{12}}Z_{x_2} + ... + Z_{a_{1n}}Z_{x_n} + Z_{x_{n+1}} = Z_{b_1},$$

$$Z_{a_{21}}Z_{x_1} + Z_{a_{22}}Z_{x_2} + ... + Z_{a_{2n}}Z_{x_n} + Z_{x_{n+2}} = Z_{b_2},$$

...

$$Z_{a_{m1}}Z_{x_1} + Z_{a_{m2}}Z_{x_2} + ... + Z_{a_{mn}}Z_{x_n} + Z_{x_{n+m}} = Z_{b_m},$$

$$Z_{x_1}, Z_{x_2}, ..., Z_{x_n}, Z_{x_{n+1}}, Z_{x_{n+2}}, ..., Z_{x_{n+m}} \geq^Z Z_0.$$

Next we rewrite the considered problem in the following equivalent form:

$$Z_{g,1}(Z_{x_1}, Z_{x_2}, ..., Z_{x_n}, Z_{x_{n+1}}, Z_{x_{n+2}}, ..., Z_{x_{n+m}})$$
$$= -(Z_{c_1}Z_{x_1} + Z_{c_2}Z_{x_2} + ... + Z_{c_n}Z_{x_n})$$
$$+ (Z_{b_1} - (Z_{a_{11}}Z_{x_1} + Z_{a_{12}}Z_{x_2} + ... + Z_{a_{1n}}Z_{x_n} + Z_{x_{n+1}}))$$
$$+ (Z_{b_2} - (Z_{a_{21}}Z_{x_1} + Z_{a_{22}}Z_{x_2} + ... + Z_{a_{2n}}Z_{x_n} + Z_{x_{n+2}}))$$
$$+ ... + (Z_{b_m} - (Z_{a_{m1}}Z_{x_1} + Z_{a_{m2}}Z_{x_2} + ... + Z_{a_{mn}}Z_{x_n} + Z_{x_{n+m}})) \rightarrow \min$$

$$Z_{g,2}(Z_{x_1}, Z_{x_2}, ..., Z_{x_n}, Z_{x_{n+1}}, Z_{x_{n+2}}, ..., Z_{x_{n+m}}) = -(Z_{c_1}Z_{x_1} + Z_{c_2}Z_{x_2}$$
$$+ ... + Z_{c_n}Z_{x_n}) + (Z_{b_1} - (Z_{a_{11}}Z_{x_1} + Z_{a_{12}}Z_{x_2} + ... + Z_{a_{1n}}Z_{x_n} + Z_{x_{n+1}})) \quad (6.16)$$
$$+ (Z_{b_2} - (Z_{a_{21}}Z_{x_1} + Z_{a_{22}}Z_{x_2} + ... + Z_{a_{2n}}Z_{x_n} + Z_{x_{n+2}}))$$
$$+ ... + (Z_{b_m} - (Z_{a_{m1}}Z_{x_1} + Z_{a_{m2}}Z_{x_2} + ... + Z_{a_{mn}}Z_{x_n} + Z_{x_{n+m}})) \rightarrow \min$$

...

$$Z_{g,q}(Z_{x_1}, Z_{x_2}, ..., Z_{x_n}, Z_{x_{n+1}}, Z_{x_{n+2}}, ..., Z_{x_{n+m}}) = -(Z_{c_1}Z_{x_1} + Z_{c_2}Z_{x_2}$$
$$+ ... + Z_{c_n}Z_{x_n}) + (Z_{b_1} - (Z_{a_{11}}Z_{x_1} + Z_{a_{12}}Z_{x_2} + ... + Z_{a_{1n}}Z_{x_n} + Z_{x_{n+1}}))$$
$$+ (Z_{b_2} - (Z_{a_{21}}Z_{x_1} + Z_{a_{22}}Z_{x_2} + ... + Z_{a_{2n}}Z_{x_n} + Z_{x_{n+2}}))$$
$$+ ... + (Z_{b_m} - (Z_{a_{m1}}Z_{x_1} + Z_{a_{m2}}Z_{x_2} + ... + Z_{a_{mn}}Z_{x_n} + Z_{x_{n+m}})) \rightarrow \min$$

subject to

$$Z_{x_1}, Z_{x_2}, ..., Z_{x_n}, Z_{x_{n+1}}, Z_{x_{n+2}}, ..., Z_{x_{n+m}} \geq^Z Z_0. \tag{6.17}$$

The suggested solution method for solving of optimization problem (6.16)-(6.17) is described below.

At the first stage we construct q number of single objective Z-LP problems as follows:

$$\begin{aligned}
Z_{g,l}(Z_{x_1}, Z_{x_2}, ..., Z_{x_n}, Z_{x_{n+1}}, Z_{x_{n+2}}, ..., Z_{x_{n+m}}) &= -(Z_{c_1} Z_{x_1} + Z_{c_2} Z_{x_2} \\
+ ... + Z_{c_n} Z_{x_n}) + (Z_{b_1} - (Z_{a_{11}} Z_{x_1} + Z_{a_{12}} Z_{x_2} + ... + Z_{a_{1n}} Z_{x_n} + Z_{x_{n+1}})) \\
+ (Z_{b_2} - (Z_{a_{21}} Z_{x_1} + Z_{a_{22}} Z_{x_2} + ... + Z_{a_{2n}} Z_{x_n} + Z_{x_{n+2}})) \\
+ ... + (Z_{b_m} - (Z_{a_{m1}} Z_{x_1} + Z_{a_{m2}} Z_{x_2} + ... + Z_{a_{mn}} Z_{x_n} + Z_{x_{n+m}})) &\rightarrow \min
\end{aligned} \tag{6.18}$$

subject to

$$Z_{x_1}, Z_{x_2}, ..., Z_{x_n}, Z_{x_{n+1}}, Z_{x_{n+2}}, ..., Z_{x_{n+m}} \geq^Z Z_0, \tag{6.19}$$

$l = 1, 2, ..., q$. At the second stage we compute the optimal solution to the problem (6.18)-(6.19) using the DEO method.

We set the parameters of the DEO algorithm, define the DEO cost function as the objective functions $Z_{f,l}$, $l = 1, 2, ..., q$ (6.14), and choose the population size *PopSize*. As a rule of thumb, the population size is set at least ten times the number of optimization variables. Thus, as a Z-number has two components, the population size is $PopSize = 2 \cdot 10 N_{var}$, where N_{var} is the number of optimization variables. Then the DEO is started.

First we construct template parameter vector u of dimension $2N_{var}$ for holding data of all decision variables Z_x. Then we set algorithm parameters: mutation rate F, crossover rate CR.

Next *PN* parameter vectors are randomly generated and a population $P = \{u_1, u_2, ..., u_{PopSize}\}$ is formed.

While the termination condition (a number of predefined generations is reached or a required error level is obtained) is not met, new parameter sets are generated. For a next vector u_i ($i=1,...,PopSize$) 3 different vectors u_{r1}, u_{r2}, u_{r3} are chosen randomly from P, each of which is different from the current u_i. A new trial vector $u_{new} = u_{r1} + F \cdot (u_{r2} - u_{r3})$ is used to generate a new vector in the population. Individual vector parameters of u_i are inherited with probability CR into the new vector u_{new}. If the cost function for u_{new} is better (lower) than the cost function for u_i then the current u_i is replaced in population P by u_{new}. Next the parameter vector u_{best} is selected with the best value of cost function (objective function) from population P.

The above process is continued until the termination condition is met. When the condition is met, we select the parameter vector u_{best} (best decision variables) with the lower cost function Z_f^l, $l=1,2,...,q$ from population P. Finally, we extract from u_{best} all the decision variables.

At next step taking $l \in \{1,2,...,q\}$ we compute all feasible solutions for v LP problems, $v = 1,2,...,q$, $l \neq v$. For v-th single criterion Z-LP problem we find its optimal solution by using DEO algorithm considering the optimal solution to the l-th single criterion Z-LP problem as initial basic feasible solution. Repeating this procedure for $l \in \{1,2,...,q\}$ we construct all the efficient solutions to the multi-criteria problem (6.14)-(6.15).

At next step we find best compromise solution to problem (6.14)-(6.15). We can use two approaches. The first approach utilizes the fuzzy optimality principle-based ranking of Z-numbers described in Section 4.3. The second approach is to compute the distance between the ideal solution of the multi-criteria problem and each of the efficient solutions [179].

6.4. Decision Making under Z-information

The majority of the existing decision theories suffers from missing partial reliability of real decision-relevant information other factors[5]. Thus, it becomes needed to develop a theory of decisions that would be free of the limitations outlined in [5]. In this section, we propose the fundamentals of the new theory of decisions which is based on complex consideration of imperfect Z-restricted decision-relevant information issues and behavioral aspects.

Below we present the necessary preliminary material needed in the sequel.

Denote $\mathcal{Z}_{[a,b]} = \{Z = (A_{[a,b]}, B) \,|\, \text{supp}(A) \subseteq [a,b]\}$, $[a,b] \subseteq \mathcal{R}$ a set of Z-numbers whose first components are defined over an interval $[a,b]$ of the real line.

Definition 6.5. A Z-number valued capacity [5]. A Z-number valued capacity on $\mathcal{F}$ is a Z-number valued set function $\eta: \mathcal{F} \to \mathcal{Z}_{[0,1]}$ with the properties:

(1) $\eta(\varnothing) = (0,1)$;

(2) if $\mathcal{V} \subset \mathcal{W}$ then $\eta(\mathcal{V}) \leq \eta(\mathcal{W})$;

(3) if $\mathcal{V}_1 \subset \mathcal{V}_2 \subset ..., \mathcal{V}_n \subset ... \in \mathcal{F}$, then $\eta(\bigcup_{n=1}^{\infty} \mathcal{V}_n) = \lim_{n \to \infty} \eta(\mathcal{V}_n)$;

(4) if $\mathcal{V}_1 \supset \mathcal{V}_2 \supset ..., \mathcal{V}_n \in \mathcal{F}$, and there exists n_0 such that if $\eta(\mathcal{V}_{n_0}) \neq \infty$, then $\eta(\bigcap_{n=1}^{\infty} \mathcal{V}_n) = \lim_{n \to \infty} \eta(\mathcal{V}_n)$.

Definition 6.6. A Z-number valued bi-capacity [5]. A Z-number valued bi-capacity on $\mathcal{F}^2 = \mathcal{F} \times \mathcal{F}$ is a Z-number valued set function $\eta: \mathcal{F}^2 \to \mathcal{Z}_{[-1,1]}$ with the properties:

(1) $\eta(\varnothing, \varnothing) = (0,1)$;

(2) if $\mathcal{V} \subset \mathcal{V}'$ then $\eta(\mathcal{V}, \mathcal{W}) \leq \eta(\mathcal{V}', \mathcal{W})$;

(3) if $\mathcal{W} \subset \mathcal{W}'$ then $\eta(\mathcal{V}, \mathcal{W}) \geq \eta(\mathcal{V}, \mathcal{W}')$;

(4) $\eta(\Omega, \varnothing) = (1,1)$ and $\eta(\varnothing, \Omega) = (-1,1)$.

In the majority of the existing theories, a formal decision framework includes the following elements: a set of states of nature $\mathcal{S}$ that describes external environment conditions, a set of outcomes $\mathcal{X}$, a set of alternatives $\mathcal{A}$ as a set of actions $\mathcal{A} = \{f \,|\, f: \mathcal{S} \to \mathcal{X}\}$ generating outcomes $\mathcal{X}$ subject to external environment conditions $\mathcal{S}$, and preferences of a decision maker (DM) $\succsim$ representing choice over a set $\mathcal{A}$. In the suggested formal framework, we introduce a set of states of a

DM $\mathcal{H}$ in order to model subjective conditions of a choice in line with the objective conditions in an evident manner[5].

The suggested framework is a framework of processing of discrete information. Taking into account the fact that real problems are characterized by linguistic information which is, as a rule, described by a discrete set of meaningful linguistic terms, in our study we consider discrete Z-numbers.

Let $\mathcal{S} = \left\{ S \middle| S \in \mathcal{S} \right\}$ be a discrete space of vector-valued states of nature and $\mathcal{H} = \left\{ h \middle| h \in \mathcal{H} \right\}$ a discrete space of vector-valued states of a DM, such that

$$S = (S_1,...,S_m), \ h = (h_1,...,h_n),$$

where components $S_i, i = 1,...,m$ are important factors of decision environment (for economic problems the factors like *GDP*, *interest rates* etc) and components $h_j = (A_{h_j}, B_{h_j}) \ j = 1,...,n,$ are behavioral determinants (for example, *risk attitude, ambiguity attitude, reciprocity, trust* etc). Denote $S^{(i)} = \{S_1^{(i)},...,S_{m_i}^{(i)}\}$ a discrete set of values of S_i and denote $H^{(j)} = \{h_1^{(j)},...,h_{n_j}^{(j)}\}$ a discrete set of values of h_j.

Let us denote $\mathcal{X} = \{X_1,...,X_l\}$, $X_k \in \mathcal{Z}, k = 1,...,l$, a space of Z-valued vector outcomes. We call $\Omega = \mathcal{S} \times \mathcal{H}$ a space "nature-DM", elements of which are combined states $\omega = (S, h)$ where $S \in \mathcal{S}, h \in \mathcal{H}$. Consider $\mathcal{A} = \{f \mid f : \Omega \to \mathcal{X}\}$ the set of Z-valued actions as the set of Z-valued functions from Ω to $\mathcal{X}$. Let us denote $X_i = \{f(\omega_i) \mid f \in \mathcal{A}, \omega_i \in \Omega\}$. It is obvious that $\mathcal{X} = \bigcup_{i=1}^{nm} X_i$.

In the suggested framework, linguistic preference relation (LPR) [49] is used to account for vagueness of real-world preferences. The LPR used in our general model is composed by intra-combined state information and inter-combined states information. Intra-combined state information is used to form utilities representing preferences over outcomes $f(\omega_i) = X_i$, where $\omega_i = (S_{i_1}, h_{i_2})$, of an act $f \in \mathcal{A}$ with understanding that these are preferences at state of nature S_{i_1} conditioned by a state h_{i_2} of a DM.

Inter-combined states information is used to represent preferences inspired by dependence between combined states as human behaviors under imperfect information.

To model LPR, let's introduce a linguistic variable *"degree of preference"* with term-set $T = (T_1,...,T_n)$. The fact that preference of f against g is described by some $T_i \in T$ is expressed as $f T_i g$. We denote LPR as $\succsim_l$ and below we sometimes, for simplicity, write $f \succsim_l^j g$ or $f \succ_l^i g$ instead of $f T_i g$. Denote $0_i \in \mathcal{X}_i$ neutral, $-1_i \in \mathcal{X}_i$ the worst and $1_i \in \mathcal{X}_i$ the best outcomes from $\mathcal{X}_i$.

Intra-combined state information. Z-valued utilities of outcomes $u_i^\varsigma : \mathcal{X}_i \to \mathcal{Z}_\varsigma, \varsigma \in \{+,-\}$, satisfy

$$Monotonicity$$

$$\forall X_i, Y_i, (X_i, 0_i) \succsim_l (Y_i, 0_i) \Leftrightarrow u_i(X_i) \geq u_i(Y_i)$$

Interval scale condition

$\forall X_i, Y_i, Z_i, W_i$ such that $u_i(X_i) > u_i(Y_i)$ and $u_i(W_i) > u_i(Z_i)$ one has

$$\frac{u_i(X_i) - u_i(Y_i)}{u_i(Z_i) - u_i(W_i)} = k(X_i, Y_i, Z_i, W_i) \in \mathcal{D}_{[0,\infty)} \times \{1\}$$

iff the difference of satisfaction degree that the DM feels between $(X_i, 0_i)$ and $(Y_i, 0_i)$ is $k(X_i, Y_i, Z_i, W_i)$ as large as the difference of satisfaction between $(W_i, 0_i)$ and $(Z_i, 0_i)$.

Normalization

$$u_i^+(0_i) = (0,1), u_i^+(1_i) = (1,1), u_i^-(0_i) = (0,1) \text{ and } u_i^-(-1_i) = (-1,0).$$

Multiplicative transitivity

$\forall X_i, Y_i, Z_i, W_i, R_i, V_i$ such that $u_i(X_i) > u_i(Y_i)$, $u_i(W_i) > u_i(Z_i)$ and $u_i(R_i) > u_i(V_i)$ we have

$$k(X_i, Y_i, Z_i, W_i) \times k(Z_i, W_i, R_i, V_{ii}) = k(X_i, Y_i, R_i, V_i)$$

u_i^ς is stable under positive linear transformation

The ratio $\dfrac{u_i(X_i) - u_i(Y_i)}{u_i(Z_i) - u_i(W_i)}$ does not change if u_i is changed to $\alpha u_i + \beta$, $\alpha > 0, \beta \geq 0$.

Inter-combined states information. Z-valued bi-capacity η satisfies:

Monotonicity

$$\eta(\mathcal{V}, \mathcal{V}') \geq \eta(\mathcal{W}, \mathcal{W}') \Leftrightarrow (1_\mathcal{V}, -1_{\mathcal{V}'}, 0_{\neg(\mathcal{V} \cup \mathcal{V}')}) \succsim_l (1_\mathcal{W}, -1_{\mathcal{W}'}, 0_{\neg(\mathcal{W} \cup \mathcal{W}')})$$

Interval scale condition

$$\frac{\eta(\mathcal{V}, \mathcal{V}') - \eta(\mathcal{W}, \mathcal{W}')}{\eta(\overline{\mathcal{V}}, \overline{\mathcal{V}}') - \eta(\overline{\mathcal{W}}, \overline{\mathcal{W}}')} = k(\mathcal{V}, \mathcal{V}', \mathcal{W}, \mathcal{W}', \overline{\mathcal{V}}, \overline{\mathcal{V}}', \overline{\mathcal{W}}, \overline{\mathcal{W}}')$$

if the difference of satisfaction degrees that the DM feels between $(1_\mathcal{V}, -1_{\mathcal{V}'}, 0_{\neg(\mathcal{V} \cup \mathcal{V}')})$ and $(1_\mathcal{W}, -1_{\mathcal{W}'}, 0_{\neg(\mathcal{W} \cup \mathcal{W}')})$ is as large as the difference of satisfaction between $(1_{\overline{\mathcal{V}}}, -1_{\overline{\mathcal{V}}'}, 0_{\neg(\overline{\mathcal{V}} \cup \overline{\mathcal{V}}')})$ and $(1_{\overline{\mathcal{W}}}, -1_{\overline{\mathcal{W}}'}, 0_{\neg(\overline{\mathcal{W}} \cup \overline{\mathcal{W}}')})$.

Normalization

$$\eta(\varnothing, \varnothing) = (0,1), \eta(N, \varnothing) = (1,1) \text{ and } \forall(\mathcal{V}, \mathcal{V}') \in \mathfrak{A}^*(N),$$
$$\eta(\mathcal{V}, \mathcal{V}') \in \mathcal{Z}^1_{[-1,1]}.$$

Multiplicative transitivity

$\forall \mathcal{V}, \mathcal{V}', \mathcal{W}, \mathcal{W}', \overline{\mathcal{V}}, \overline{\mathcal{V}}', \overline{\mathcal{W}}, \overline{\mathcal{W}}', \mathcal{K}, \mathcal{K}', \mathcal{L}, \mathcal{L}' \subset N$ such that $\eta(\mathcal{V}, \mathcal{V}') > \eta(\mathcal{W}, \mathcal{W}')$, $\eta(\overline{\mathcal{V}}, \overline{\mathcal{V}}') > \eta(\overline{\mathcal{W}}, \overline{\mathcal{W}}')$ and $\eta(\mathcal{K}, \mathcal{K}') > \eta(\mathcal{L}, \mathcal{L}')$
one has

$$k(\mathcal{V}, \mathcal{V}', \mathcal{W}, \mathcal{W}', \overline{\mathcal{V}}, \overline{\mathcal{V}}', \overline{\mathcal{W}}, \overline{\mathcal{W}}') \times k(\overline{\mathcal{V}}, \overline{\mathcal{V}}', \overline{\mathcal{W}}, \overline{\mathcal{W}}', \mathcal{K}, \mathcal{K}', \mathcal{L}, \mathcal{L}')$$
$$= k(\mathcal{V}, \mathcal{V}', \mathcal{W}, \mathcal{W}', \mathcal{K}, \mathcal{K}', \mathcal{L}, \mathcal{L}')$$

Homogeneity

The ratio $\dfrac{u_i(X_i) - u_i(Y_i)}{u_i(Z_i) - u_i(W_i)}$ does not change if η changes to $\gamma\eta$, $\gamma \in R$.

If the preferences $\succsim_l$ of a DM over $\mathcal{A}$ satisfies the above mentioned assumptions then they can be described by a Z-valued overall utility $U(f)$ of $f \in \mathcal{A}$ expressed as a Z-valued Choquet-like aggregation of $u(f(S,h))$ w.r.t. Z-number-valued bi-capacity:

$$U(f) = \sum_{l=1}^{L}(u(f(\omega_{(l)})) -_h u(f(\omega_{(l+1)})))\eta(\mathcal{V},\mathcal{W})$$

$$= \sum_{l=1}^{n}((A_{u(f(\omega_{(l)}))}, B_{u(f(\omega_{(l)}))}) -_h (A_{u(f(\omega_{(l+1)}))}, B_{u(f(\omega_{(l+1)}))}))(A_{\eta(\mathcal{V},\mathcal{W})}, B_{\eta(\mathcal{V},\mathcal{W})}),$$

$$(6.20)$$

where indices (l) implies $u(f(\omega_{(l)})) \geq u(f(\omega_{(l+1)}))$; $u(f(\omega_{(L+1)})) = (0,1)$ by convention; $\mathcal{V} = \{\omega_{(1)},...,\omega_{(l)}\} \cap N^+$, $\mathcal{W} = \{\omega_{(1)},...,\omega_{(l)}\} \cap N^-$, $N^+ = \{\omega \in \Omega : u(f(\omega)) \geq (0,1)\}$, $N^- = \Omega \setminus N^+$. $\eta : \Omega \times \Omega \to \mathcal{Z}_{[-1,1]}$ is a Z-number-valued bi-capacity.

An optimal $f^* \in \mathcal{A}$, that is, such $f^* \in \mathcal{A}$ that $U(f^*) = \max\limits_{f \in \mathcal{A}}\left\{ \int_{\Omega} u(f(S,h))d\eta \right\}$, is determined by using the method of ranking of Z-numbers (Section 4.3).

An application of the suggested theory requires solving several related problems. As the basis of decision analysis in the suggested theory is the space of combined states, the adequate determination of the structure of a state of nature and a state of a DM is important. This begins with determination of influential factors m $S_1,...,S_m$ of objective conditions which are influential for the considered alternatives. On the base of analysis of the considered alternatives and factors $S_1,...,S_m$, a vector of behavioral determinants $h = (h_1,...,h_n)$ which are important for a considered choice, should be determined. In turn, for each component $S_i, i = 1,...,m$ and $h_j, j = 1,...,n$ it is needed to determine discrete sets $S^{(i)}$ and $H^{(j)}$ of their possible values. For example, if $\hat{h}_j$ is *risk attitude* then the set $H^{(j)}$ may be [5]

$$H^{(j)} = \{h_1^{(j)} = (risk\ averse, high), h_2^{(j)}$$
$$= (risk\ neutral, high), h_3^{(j)} = (risk\ seeking, high)\}.$$

If S_i is *GDP* then the set $S^{(i)}$ may be

$$S^{(i)} = \{S_1^{(i)} = low, S_2^{(i)} = medium, S_3^{(i)} = high\}.$$

A space of combined states as a space of multidimensional vectors $(S, h) = (S_{i_1}^{(1)}, ..., S_{i_m}^{(m)}, h_{j_1}^{(1)}, ..., h_{j_n}^{(n)}) = (S_{k_1}^{(1)}, ..., S_{k_m}^{(m)}, h_{k_{m+1}}^{(m+1)}, ..., h_{k_{m+n}}^{(m+n)})$ can then be used for comparison of alternatives. For this purpose, for each alternative it is necessary to determine Z-valued utilities $u(f(S, h))$ of its Z-valued outcomes at all the combined states. These utilities measure attractiveness or repulsiveness of each outcome from a DM's condition point of view. This can be done by using experience based-evaluation or by applying well-known techniques. The other necessary information for comparison of alternatives is measuring degrees of dependence of a DM's condition on objective conditions. These degrees will be represented by means of Z-valued joint probabilities. For determination of Z-valued joint probabilities, it is needed to estimate Z-valued marginal probabilities of $(S_1, ..., S_m), (h_1, ..., h_n)$. In turn, this requires the use of information on Z-valued probability distributions over $S^{(i)}$ and $H^{(j)}$:

$$P(S_i) = P_1^{(i)} / S_1^{(i)} + ... + P_{m_i}^{(i)} / S_{m_i}^{(i)}, i = 1, ..., m,$$

$$P(h_j) = P_1^{(j)} / h_1^{(j)} + ... + P_{n_j}^{(j)} / h_{n_j}^{(j)}, j = 1, ..., n,$$

where $P_1^{(i)} = (A_{P_1^{(i)}}, B_{P_1^{(i)}}), ..., P_{m_i}^{(i)} = (A_{P_{m_i}^{(i)}}, B_{P_{m_i}^{(i)}}), P_1^{(j)} = (A_{P_1^{(j)}}, B_{P_1^{(j)}}), ...,$ $P_{n_j}^{(j)} = (A_{P_{n_j}^{(j)}}, B_{P_{n_j}^{(j)}})$. Note that the condition $B_{P_1^{(i)}} = ... = B_{P_{m_i}^{(i)}} = B_{P^{(i)}},$ $B_{P_1^{(j)}} = ... = B_{P_{n_j}^{(j)}} = B_{P^{(j)}}$ should be satisfied for the purpose of consistency of Z-valued probability distributions. Given $P(S_i)$ and $P(h_j)$, the Z-valued marginal probability distributions $P(S)$ and $P(h)$ will be represented as follows:

$$P(S) = P(S_1)/S_1 + ... + P(S_m)/S_m,$$

$$P(h) = P(h_1)/h_1 ... + P(h_n)/h_n.$$

Given marginal $P(S)$ and $P(h)$, and information about signs of dependences between components of S and h, it is needed to determine the Z-valued joint probabilities over combined states

$$P(S,h) = P(S_{i_1}^{(1)},...,S_{i_m}^{(m)}, h_{j_1}^{(1)},...,h_{j_n}^{(n)}) = P(S_{k_1}^{(1)},...,S_{k_m}^{(m)}, h_{k_{m+1}}^{(m+1)},...,h_{k_{m+n}}^{(m+n)}):$$

$$P(S_{k_1}^{(1)},...,S_{k_m}^{(m)}, h_{k_{m+1}}^{(m+1)},...,h_{k_{m+n}}^{(m+n)}) = \phi(P(S_{k_1}^{(1)}),...,P(S_{k_m}^{(m)}), P(h_{k_{m+1}}^{(m+1)}),...,P(h_{k_{m+n}}^{(m+n)})).$$

The main problem in determination of $P(S,h)$ is to obtain information about interdependencies of $S_{k_1}^{(1)},...,S_{k_m}^{(m)}, h_{k_{m+1}}^{(m+1)},...,h_{k_{m+n}}^{(m+n)}$. Taking into account the complexity of relations between $S_{k_1}^{(1)},...,S_{k_m}^{(m)}, h_{k_{m+1}}^{(m+1)},...,h_{k_{m+n}}^{(m+n)}$, an adequate approach to obtain such information is the use of some intelligent procedure based on expert evaluations [25,30,31,60,93,109,117].

On the base of the Z-valued joint probabilities $P(\omega) = P(S,h) = (A_{P(\omega)}, B_P)$ a Z-valued bi-capacity η is then constructed to model relation between combined states under imprecise and partially reliable information, especially taking into account interaction between attractive and repulsive outcomes. A Z-valued bi-capacity η is to be constructed as the difference between two Z-valued capacities:

$$\eta(V, W) = v_1(V) - v_2(W).$$

Z-valued capacities $v_1(V), v_2(W)$ can be constructed as lower or upper probabilities or their convex combinations. As lower and upper probabilities, one can use lower and upper envelops of the set of priors which is defined by Z-valued restrictions $P(\omega) = P(S,h) = (A_{P(\omega)}, B_P)$. The lower envelope $v(V)$ can be found as [5]

$$\upsilon(\mathcal{V}) = (A_\upsilon(\mathcal{V}), B_\upsilon), \quad B_\upsilon = B_P$$

$$A_\upsilon(\mathcal{V}) = \bigcup_{\alpha \in (0,1]} \alpha\left[A_{\upsilon 1}^{\alpha}(\mathcal{V}), A_{\upsilon 2}^{\alpha}(\mathcal{V}) \right], \quad \mathcal{V} \subset \Omega = \{\omega_1,...,\omega_L\}, \qquad (6.21)$$

where

$$A_{\upsilon 1}^{\alpha}(\mathcal{V}) = \inf\left\{ \sum_{\omega_i \in V} p(\omega_i) \middle| (p(\omega_1),...,p(\omega_L)) \in A_P^{\alpha} \right\},$$

$$A_P^{\alpha} = \left\{ (p(\omega_1),...,p(\omega_L)) \in A_{P(\omega_1)}^{\alpha} \times ... \times A_{P(\omega_L)}^{\alpha} \middle| \sum_{l=1}^{L} p(\omega_l) = 1 \right\}. \qquad (6.22)$$

Here $A_{P(\omega_1)}^{\alpha},...,A_{P(\omega_L)}^{\alpha}$ are α-cuts of fuzzy probabilities $A_{P(\omega_1)},...,A_{P(\omega_L)}$ respectively, $p(\omega_1),...,p(\omega_L)$ are basic probabilities for $A_{P(\omega_1)},...,A_{P(\omega_L)}$ respectively, $\times$ denotes the Cartesian product. The upper prevision can be obtained by substituting inf by sup in (6.22).

For each alternative f, given its utilities for all the combined states and the Z-valued bi-capacity modeling dependence between combined states, the overall utility $U(f)$ can be determined according to (6.20). The best alternative is further found by determining the highest value of the Z-valued utility $U : \mathcal{A} \to \mathcal{Z}$. The determination of the highest value of U can be done by the fuzzy optimality principle-based ranking of Z-numbers described in Section 4.3.

6.5. Computing with Words and Z-numbers

The human brain, has decision-making ability, using perceptions transformedto words and phrases in natural language. Foundation of computation with information described in natural language is paradigm of computing with words (CWW) suggested by Prof. L. Zadeh [147,172]. As Zadeh mentions "CWW is a methodology in which the object of computation are words and propositions drawn from a natural language". CWW, mainly aims at providing the computer to 'compute' as do human beings, modeling human-responses to word-perceptions. This paradigm gives ability to the computer to 'learn', 'think' and 'respond' to 'words'. The concepts of CWW are essentially rooted in [147,148, 152,159,163,164], where Zadeh put foundation of CWW.Then others [53,78,82,94,102,103,116] investigated CWW concepts from different point of view.

We have to distinguish two levels of CWW. First level deals with words and phrases, second level with natural language statements.

CWW systems as input use a set of natural language sentences that describes an event, and presents as output the corresponding response.The output described in natural language is expected to be derived from a collection of propositions, I, $I=(p_1,...,p_n)$. Y is ans (q/I). Ans (q/I) identifies those values of Y which are consistent with I.

The basic structure for CWW is shown in Fig. 6.4.

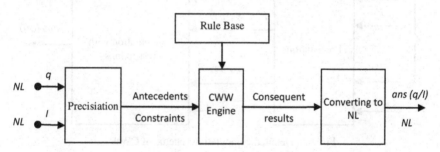

Fig. 6.4. The basic structure for CWW.

The components of the structure are: the precisiation module which translates input sentences to the corresponding antecedent constraints; the Rule Base which includes the antecedent-consequent event relationships, typical to the context of discourse; the CWW Engine, with processes the antecedent constraints to arrive at the consequent results; the converting module which translates consequent results into natural language sentences.

Computation model of CWW is shown in Fig. 6.5.

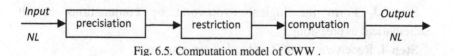

Fig. 6.5. Computation model of CWW .

First model (precisiation) performs precisiation of objects of computations. Here propositions given in NL represented in canonical form.

$$P{:}X\ isrR$$

where X, R, r variables which are implicit in P.

Usually we deal with different types of restrictions [166]. Restrictions may be possibilistic, probabilitistic or bimodal, i.e. possibilistic-probabilistic. The variable r is assigned depending on the context for disambiguation. Computation module in conjunction with rule base processes restrictions to perform reasoning and to get output results.

Detailed computation scheme of CWW is described Fig. 6.6.

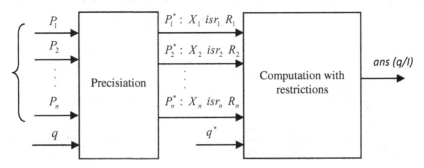

Fig. 6.6. Detailed computation scheme of CWW .

As it is shown in [110] Z-number is a formidable tool in the construction discourse-oriented CWW based systems and is a base of second level CWW.

If a considered environment is characterized by Z-information, i.e. collection of Z-valuations computation algorithm in CWW may be described as follows.

Step 1. Define the values X, A, and B in I, q to evaluate the Z-valuations.

Step 2. Transform Z-valuations into equivalent mathematical expressions.

Step 3. Form the logical expression by conjunctions of all mathematical expressions.

Step 4. Receive a set of Z-valuations in response.

More detailed description of an algorithm for CWW using Z-number is given in [171].

As example of application Z-number based CWW we consider here simulation process of differential diagnosis by acquiring patient symptoms given in [171]. Let consider sample discourse between a doctor (D) and patient (P).

D asks patient what is your problem (in NL)? Z-valuation equivalent is Z=(Problem, exists, expectedly). P-answer: I have high fever during last 2 days. Z-valuations are: Z_1=(Problem, high fever, certainly); Z_2=(Duration, 2 days, probably). D asks: dose the fever fluctuate, dos it come at fixed time? Z-valuation.

$$Z_{31}=(\text{fever occurrence, fixed time, certainly});$$

$$Z_{32}=(\text{fever, morning, certainly});$$

$$Z_{33}=(\text{fever, evening, certainly});$$

$$Z_4=(\text{fever temperature, 102-104 °F, certainly}).$$

P-answer: Fixed times in the morning and evening. Changes in interval 102-104°F. This time fill intense shivering, headache and mussel-ache, nauseous. The temperature falls after I have a bout of sweating. Z-valuation:

Z51=(fever presence symptom, intense chivering, certainly);

Z52=(fever presence symptom, intense chivering, headache);

Z53=(fever presence symptom, muscle-ache, headache);

Z54=(fever presence symptom, nausea, occasionally);

Z55=(fever fall symptom, sweating, certainly).

On the basic of Z-information given above, assuming the fuzzy numbers described the symptoms with respect to the patient and the level of certainty are available, the system on base of CWW evaluates the Z-valuation of the probable diseases using expression

$$(Z_1 \wedge Z_2 \wedge Z_{31} \wedge Z_{32} \wedge Z_{33} \wedge Z_4 \wedge Z_{51} \wedge Z_{52} \wedge Z_{53} \wedge Z_{54} \wedge Z_{55})$$

as Z-valuation: Z=(Disease, malaria, most likely).

Chapter 7

Application of Z-numbers

7.1. Business Behavioral Decision under Z-information

In this section we consider application of the suggested methods to solving of a real-world decision problem, which is characterized by Z-valued decision information and vector-valued states of nature and DM. The problem is described below.

An economic agent considers a problem of decision making on choosing one of the three alternatives for a short-term investment of up to 1 year: common bonds, stocks of enterprise, fixed-term deposit. These alternatives are evaluated under the three assumed economic conditions characterized by various values of GDP level and inflation rate: high GDP and low inflation rate, medium GDP and medium inflation rate, low GDP and high inflation rate. Having examined the relationships between the yields on the alternative investments and the economic conditions on the base of the past experience, the economic agent *is very sure* that the following trends will take place:

the first action will yield high income under the first economic condition, medium income under the second economic condition, less than medium income under the third economic condition;

the second action will yield very high income in the first economic condition, medium income in the second economic condition, small income in the third economic condition;

the third action will yield approximately the same medium income in all the considered states of economy.

At the same time, an economic agent is *sure* that the likelihoods of the assumed values of the considered economic indicators are as follows:

probability of high GDP is higher than medium, probability of medium GDP is about thirty percent, probability of low GDP is the smallest;
probability of low inflation rate is about seventy percent, probability of medium inflation rate is about twenty percent, probability of high inflation rate is the smallest.

Let us suppose that in the considered problem a DM will always think about uncertainty of future and various risks always related to investment problems. In other words, the choice of an economic agent (DM) will be depend on his risk and ambiguity attitudes. Consequently, we will consider a DM's state as vector of two behavioral determinants: risk attitude and ambiguity attitude. Further, we will consider that the following states of the DM (subjective conditions) may take place: risk and ambiguity aversion, risk aversion and ambiguity seeking, risk seeking and ambiguity aversion, risk and ambiguity seeking. The DM is sure that the likelihoods of the assumed intensities of the considered behavioral determinants are as follows:

probability of risk aversion is about sixty five percent and probability of ambiguity aversion is about sixty percent.

What option for investment to choose?
Formal description of the problem. The considered problem is formally described as follows. The set of alternatives is

$$\mathcal{A} = \{ f_1, f_2, f_3 \}$$

where f_1 is common bonds, f_2 is stocks of enterprise, f_3 is time deposit.
The set of states of nature is

$$\mathcal{S} = \{ S_1, S_2, S_3 \}$$

where $S_1 = (S_1^{(3)}, S_2^{(1)})$ is *high* GDP and *low* inflation rate, $S_2 = (S_1^{(2)}, S_2^{(2)})$ is *medium* GDP and *medium* inflation rate, $S_3 = (S_1^{(1)}, S_2^{(3)})$ *low* GDP and *high* inflation rate.

Now let us formalize the states of a DM. The set of states of the DM is

$$\mathcal{H} = \{h_1, h_2, h_3, h_4\},$$

where $h_1 = (h_1^{(1)}, h_2^{(1)})$ is risk and ambiguity aversion, $h_2 = (h_1^{(1)}, h_2^{(2)})$ is risk aversion and ambiguity seeking, $h_3 = (h_1^{(2)}, h_2^{(1)})$ is risk seeking and ambiguity aversion, $h_4 = (h_1^{(2)}, h_2^{(2)})$ is risk and ambiguity seeking.

Given imprecise and partially reliable information about possible outcomes of the considered alternatives let us assign the Z-valued utilities of these outcomes over the set of combined states as it is shown in Tables 7.1, 7.2, 7.3:

Table 7.1. Z-valued utilities for f_1.

	$S_1 = (S_1^{(3)}, S_2^{(1)})$	$S_2 = (S_1^{(2)}, S_2^{(2)})$	$S_3 = (S_1^{(1)}, S_2^{(3)})$
$h_1 = (h_1^{(1)}, h_2^{(1)})$	About 8, very sure	About 4, very sure	About 3, verysure
$h_2 = (h_1^{(1)}, h_2^{(2)})$	About 12, very sure	About 7, very sure	About 4, very sure
$h_3 = (h_1^{(2)}, h_2^{(1)})$	About 9, very sure	About 5, very sure	About 3, very sure
$h_4 = (h_1^{(2)}, h_2^{(2)})$	About 14, very sure	About 8, very sure	About 5, very sure

Table 7.2. Z-valued utilities for f_2.

	$S_1 = (S_1^{(3)}, S_2^{(1)})$	$S_2 = (S_1^{(2)}, S_2^{(2)})$	$S_3 = (S_1^{(1)}, S_2^{(3)})$
$h_1 = (h_1^{(1)}, h_2^{(1)})$	About 11.5, very sure	About 3.5, very sure	About -3.3, very sure
$h_2 = (h_1^{(1)}, h_2^{(2)})$	About 16.5, very sure	About 6.5, very sure	About -1.5, very sure
$h_3 = (h_1^{(2)}, h_2^{(1)})$	About 12.5, very sure	About 4.5, very sure	About -2.5, very sure
$h_4 = (h_1^{(2)}, h_2^{(2)})$	About 23, very sure	About 7.5, very sure	About -1, very sure

Table 7.3. Z-valued utilities for $\hat{f}_3$.

	$S_1 = (S_1^{(3)}, S_2^{(1)})$	$S_2 = (S_1^{(2)}, S_2^{(2)})$	$S_3 = (S_1^{(1)}, S_2^{(3)})$
$h_1 = (h_1^{(1)}, h_2^{(1)})$	About 3.5, very sure	About 4, very sure	About 6.5, very sure
$h_2 = (h_1^{(1)}, h_2^{(2)})$	About 8.5, very sure	About 6.5, very sure	About 8.5, very sure
$h_3 = (h_1^{(2)}, h_2^{(1)})$	About 4.25, very sure	About 4.25, very sure	About 7.5, very sure
$h_4 = (h_1^{(2)}, h_2^{(2)})$	About 11, very sure	About 7.5, very sure	About 9.5, very sure

In order to determine the DM's preferences over the considered alternatives we need to adequately model relation between his behavioral determinants and the considered economic indicators. This relation will be described by Z-valued joint probabilities of the combined states[5]. In turn, construction of Z-valued joint probabilities requires to determine sign of dependence between the states of a DM h and the states of nature S. The determined sign of dependence is shown in Table 7.4.

Table 7.4. Dependence between S and h.

	$S_1 = (S_1^{(3)}, S_2^{(1)})$	$S_2 = (S_1^{(2)}, S_2^{(2)})$	$S_3 = (S_1^{(1)}, S_2^{(3)})$
$h_1 = (h_1^{(1)}, h_2^{(1)})$	negative	negative	positive
$h_2 = (h_1^{(1)}, h_2^{(2)})$	neutral	neutral	positive
$h_3 = (h_1^{(2)}, h_2^{(1)})$	neutral	neutral	negative
$h_4 = (h_1^{(2)}, h_2^{(2)})$	positive	positive	negative

Assume that the Z-valued joint probabilities determined on the base of the revealed dependence[5] are as it is shown in Table 7.5:

Table 7.5. Z-valued joint probabilities.

	$S_1 = (S_1^{(3)}, S_2^{(1)})$	$S_2 = (S_1^{(2)}, S_2^{(2)})$	$S_3 = (S_1^{(1)}, S_2^{(3)})$
$h_1 = (h_1^{(1)}, h_2^{(1)})$	About 0.18, sure	About 0.22, sure	About 0.05, sure
$h_2 = (h_1^{(1)}, h_2^{(2)})$	About 0.09, sure	About 0.1, sure	About 0.05, sure
$h_3 = (h_1^{(2)}, h_2^{(1)})$	About 0.014, sure	About 0.01, sure	About 0.0025, sure
$h_4 = (h_1^{(2)}, h_2^{(2)})$	About 0.22, sure	About 0.22, sure	About 0.02, sure

Let us now compute the Z-valued overall utilities for the alternatives on the base of (6.20). For example, for f_1 it has the following form:

$$U(f_1) = \left(\left| u(f_1(\omega_{14})) \right| -_h \left| u(f_1(\omega_{12})) \right| \right) \eta(\{\omega_{14}\}, \varnothing)$$

$$+ \left(\left| u(f_1(\omega_{12})) \right| -_h \left| u(f_1(\omega_{13})) \right| \right) \eta(\{\omega_{14}, \omega_{12}\}, \varnothing)$$

$$+ \left(\left| u(f_1(\omega_{13})) \right| -_h \left| u(f_1(\omega_{11})) \right| \right) \eta(\{\omega_{14}, \omega_{12}, \omega_{13}\}, \varnothing)$$

$$+ \left(\left| u(f_1(\omega_{11})) \right| -_h \left| u(f_1(\omega_{24})) \right| \right) \eta(\{\omega_{14}, \omega_{12}, \omega_{13}, \omega_{11}\}, \varnothing)$$

$$+ \left(\left| u(f_1(\omega_{24})) \right| -_h \left| u(f_1(\omega_{22})) \right| \right) \eta(\{\omega_{14}, \omega_{12}, \omega_{13}, \omega_{11}, \omega_{24}\}, \varnothing)$$

$$+ \left(\left| u(f_1(\omega_{22})) \right| -_h \left| u(f_1(\omega_{23})) \right| \right) \eta(\{\omega_{14}, \omega_{12}, \omega_{13}, \omega_{11}, \omega_{24}, \omega_{22}\}, \varnothing)$$

$$+ \left(\left| u(f_1(\omega_{23})) \right| -_h \left| u(f_1(\omega_{34})) \right| \right) \eta(\{\omega_{14}, \omega_{12}, \omega_{13}, \omega_{11}, \omega_{24}, \omega_{22}, \omega_{23}\}, \varnothing)$$

$$+ \left(\left| u(f_1(\omega_{34})) \right| -_h \left| u(f_1(\omega_{32})) \right| \right) \eta(\{\omega_{14}, \omega_{12}, \omega_{13}, \omega_{11}, \omega_{24}, \omega_{22}, \omega_{23}, \omega_{34}\}, \varnothing)$$

$$+ \left(\left| u(f_1(\omega_{32})) \right| -_h \left| u(f_1(\omega_{21})) \right| \right) \eta(\{\omega_{14}, \omega_{12}, \omega_{13}, \omega_{11}, \omega_{24}, \omega_{22}, \omega_{23}, \omega_{34}, \omega_{32}\}, \varnothing)$$

$$+ \left(\left| u(f_1(\omega_{21})) \right| -_h \left| u(f_1(\omega_{33})) \right| \right) \eta(\{\omega_{14}, \omega_{12}, \omega_{13}, \omega_{11}, \omega_{24}, \omega_{22}, \omega_{23}, \omega_{34}, \omega_{32}, \omega_{21}\}, \varnothing)$$

$$+ \left(\left| u(f_1(\omega_{33})) \right| -_h \left| u(f_1(\omega_{31})) \right| \right) \eta(\{\omega_{14}, \omega_{12}, \omega_{13}, \omega_{11}, \omega_{24}, \omega_{22}, \omega_{23}, \omega_{34}, \omega_{32}, \omega_{21}, \omega_{33}\}, \varnothing)$$

$$+ \left| u(f_1(\omega_{31})) \right| \eta(\{\omega_{14}, \omega_{12}, \omega_{13}, \omega_{11}, \omega_{24}, \omega_{22}, \omega_{23}, \omega_{34}, \omega_{32}, \omega_{21}, \omega_{33}, \omega_{31}\}, \varnothing),$$

where $\omega_{ij} = (S_i, h_j)$ is a combined state. The Z-valued bi-capacity $\eta(\cdot, \cdot)$ was computed as the difference of Z-valued capacities (see Section 6.4).

For the other alternatives $U()$ is determined analogously. The obtained Z-valued utilities $U()$ are shown in Figs. 7.1, 7.2, 7.3):

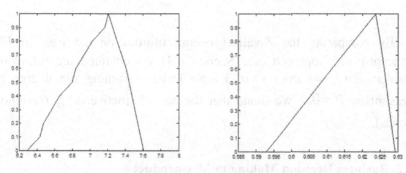

$$U(f_1) = (about\ 7.6, about\ 0.62)$$

Fig. 7.1. Z-valued overall utility for f_1.

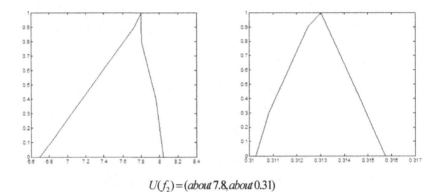

$$U(f_2) = (about\ 7.8, about\ 0.31)$$

Fig. 7.2. Z-valued overall utility for f_2.

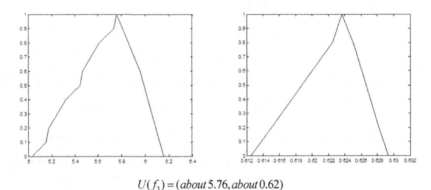

$$U(f_3) = (about\ 5.76, about\ 0.62)$$

Fig. 7.3. Z-valued overall utility for f_3.

By comparing the Z-valued overall utilities on the base of FO concept-based approach (see Section 4.3) we obtained the following results: $do(f_1) = 1$, $do(f_2) = 0.13$, $do(f_3) = 0$. Assuming the degree of pessimism $\beta = 0.3$ we found that the best alternative is f_1 (common bonds).

7.2. Business Decision Making in Mix-product

A manufacturing company produces products A, B and C and has six processes for production. A decision maker has three objectives:

maximizing profit, quality and worker satisfaction. Naturally, the parameters of objective functions and constraints are assigned by Z-numbers. Z-information on manufacturing planning is given in Table 7.6. Z-information on expected profit, index of quality and worker satisfaction index is given in Table 7.7.

Table 7.6. Z-information on manufacturing planning data.

Resource type	Product A (Z_{x_1})	Product B (Z_{x_2})	Product C (Z_{x_3})	Maximum available capacity per month (hours) (Z_{b_i})
1	$Z_{a_{11}} = (about\ 12, 0,9)$	$Z_{a_{12}} = (about\ 17, 0,9)$	$Z_{a_{13}} = (about\ 0, 0,9)$	$Z_{b_1} = (about\ 1400, 0,9)$
2	$Z_{a_{21}} = (about\ 2, 0,9)$	$Z_{a_{22}} = (about\ 9, 0,9)$	$Z_{a_{23}} = (about\ 8, 0,9)$	$Z_{b_2} = (about\ 1000, 0,9)$
3	$Z_{a_{31}} = (about\ 10, 0,9)$	$Z_{a_{32}} = (about\ 13, 0,9)$	$Z_{a_{33}} = (about\ 15, 0,9)$	$Z_{b_3} = (about\ 1750, 0,9)$
4	$Z_{11} = (about\ 6, 0,9)$	$Z_{42} = (about\ 0, 0,9)$	$Z_{a_{13}} = (about\ 16, 0,9)$	$Z_{b_4} = (about\ 1325, 0,9)$
5	$Z_{51} = (about\ 0, 0,9)$	$Z_{52} = (about\ 12, 0,9)$	$Z_{a_{53}} = (about\ 7, 0,9)$	$Z_{b_5} = (about\ 900, 0,9)$
6	$Z_{61} = (about\ 9,5, 0,9)$	$Z_{62} = (about\ 9,5, 0,9)$	$Z_{a_{63}} = (about\ 4, 0,9)$	$Z_{b_6} = (about\ 1075, 0,9)$

Table 7.7. Z-information on profits, quality, and worker satisfaction.

Type of objectives	Product A	Product B	Product C
Profit	$Z_{C_{11}} = (about\ 0, 0,8)$	$Z_{C_{12}} = (about\ 100, 0,8)$	$Z_{C_{13}} = (about\ 17,5, 0,8)$
Quality	$Z_{C_{21}} = (about\ 92, 0,8)$	$Z_{C_{22}} = (about\ 75, 0,8)$	$Z_{C_{11}} = (about\ 50, 0,8)$
Worker satisfaction	$Z_{C_{31}} = (about\ 25, 0,8)$	$Z_{C_{32}} = (about\ 100, 0,8)$	$Z_{C_{33}} = (about\ 75, 0,8)$

Taking into account Z-information given in Tables 7.6, 7.7, multi-criteria Z-LP model for multi-criteria planning decision may be formulated as follows.

$$Z_{f_1}(Z_x) = \big[(about\ 50, 0,8 \cdot Z_{x_1}) + (about\ 100, 0,8 \cdot Z_{x_2}) $$
$$+ (about\ 17,5, 0,8 \cdot Z_{x_3}) \to \max$$

$$Z_{f_2}(Z_x) = \Big[(about\ 92, 0,8 \cdot Z_{x_1}) + (about\ 75, 0,8 \cdot Z_{x_2})$$
$$+ (about\ 50, 0,8 \cdot Z_{x_3}) \to \max$$

$$Z_{f_3}(Z_x) = \Big[(about\ 25, 0,8 \cdot Z_{x_1}) + (about\ 100, 0,8 \cdot Z_{x_2})$$
$$+ (about\ 75, 0,8 \cdot Z_{x_3}) \to \max$$

$$(about\ 12, 0.9) \cdot Z_{x_1} + (about\ 17, 0.9) \cdot Z_{x_2} \le (about\ 1400, 0.9)$$

$$(about\ 2, 0.9) \cdot Z_{x_1} + (about\ 9, 0.9) \cdot Z_{x_2}$$
$$+ (about\ 8, 0.9) \cdot Z_{x_3} \le (about\ 1000, 0.9)$$

$$(about\ 10, 0.9) \cdot Z_{x_1} + (about\ 13, 0.9) \cdot Z_{x_2}$$
$$+ (about\ 15, 0.9) \cdot Z_{x_3} \le (about\ 1750, 0.9)$$

$$(about\ 6, 0.9) \cdot Z_{x_1} + (about\ 16, 0.9) \cdot Z_{x_3} \le about\ 1325, 0.9)$$

$$(about\ 12, 0.9) \cdot Z_{x_2} + (about\ 7, 0.9) \cdot Z_{x_3} \le about\ 900, 0.9)$$

$$(about\ 9.5, 0.9) \cdot Z_{x_1} + (about\ 9.5, 0.9) \cdot Z_{x_2}$$
$$+ (about\ 4, 0.9) \cdot Z_{x_3} \le about\ 1075, 0.9)$$

$$Z_{x_1}, Z_{x_2}, Z_{x_3} \ge 0.$$

This problem was solved by the approach suggested in Section 6.3.

7.3. Marketing Decision Making under Z-information

In this application we intend a problem of marketing decision making in the field of IT. Two new software products were introduced to the market by Techware Incorporated; the company has threealternatives related to these two products: it introduces product 1 only, product 2 only, or introduces both products.The costs for research and development for these two products are $180,000 and $150,000, respectively. The trend of the national economy and the consumers reaction to these products will affect the success of these products in the coming year.If the company introduces product 1, then it will have revenue of $500,000, $260,000 and $120,000 for strong, fair and weak national economy respectively. Similarly when product 2 is introduced, there will be a revenue of $420,000, $230,000 and 110,000 for a strong, fair and weak national economy, respecticely. Finally when introducing both products 1 and 2 the revenues will be $820,000, $390,000, $200,000 for strong, fair and weak national economy, respectively. The experts of the company are very sure that the probabilities of strong and fair economy are about 0.30 and about 0.50 respectively. The problem is to determine the best decision.

The analyzed data are obtained from Techware Incorporated in [140].

Let us proceed to formal description of the considered decision problem. The partially reliable linguistic decision-relevant information in the considered problem will be described by Z-numbers. The set of alternatives:

$$\mathcal{A} = \{f_1, f_2, f_3\},$$

where f_1 denotes introducing product 1 , f_2 denotes introducing product 2, f_3 denotes introducing both products (1 and 2). The set of states of nature:

$$\mathcal{S} = \{S_1, S_2, S_3\}$$

where S_1 denotes strong national economy, S_2 denotes fair national economy, S_3 denotes strong national economy. The probabilities of states of nature are $Z_{P(S_1)}$ = (about 0.3, quite sure), $Z_{P(S_2)}$ = (about 0.5, quite sure). The set of outcomes:

$$\mathcal{X} = \{(low, likely), (more\ than\ low, likely),$$

$$(medium, likely)\ (below\ than\ high, likely),$$
$$(high, likely)\}.$$

The partially reliable linguistic information for the probabilities of states of nature and the utilities of each alternative taken at different states of nature is shown in Table 7.8.

Table 7.8. The values of utilities for different alternatives and probabilities of states of nature.

	S_1	S_2	S_3
	(about 0.3, quite sure)	(about 0.5, quite sure)	(about 0.2, quite sure)
f_1	(*high; likely*)	(*medium; likely*)	(*low; likely*)
f_2	(*below than high; likely*)	(*medium; likely*)	(*low; likely*)
f_3	(*high; likely*)	(*more than low; likely*)	(*low; likely*)

The corresponding decision matrix with Z-number-based representation is shown in Table 7.9.

Table 7.9. Decision matrix with Z-number.

	S_1 Z_{41}	S_2 Z_{42}	S_3 Z_{43}
f_1	Z_{11}	Z_{12}	Z_{13}
f_2	Z_{21}	Z_{22}	Z_{23}
f_3	Z_{31}	Z_{32}	Z_{33}

The membership functions of the first and the second components of Z-numbers for probabilities and utilities from Table 7.9 are shown in Figs. 7.4-7.15.

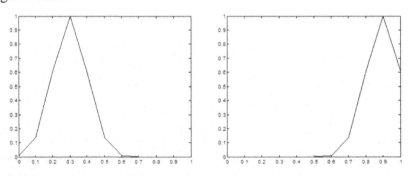

Fig. 7.4. Representation of the first state (Z_{41}) as a Z-number.

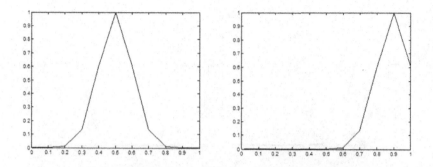

Fig. 7.5. Representation of the second state (Z_{42}) as a Z-number.

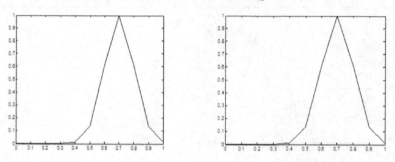

Fig 7.6. Representation of the first alternative in the first state (Z_{11}) as a Z-number.

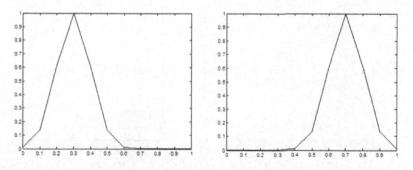

Fig 7.7. Representation of the first alternative in the second state (Z_{12}) as a Z-number.

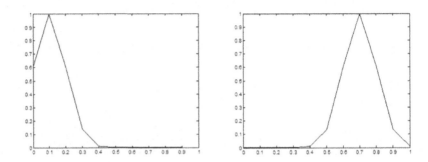

Fig 7.8. Representation of the first alternative in the third state (Z_{13}) as a Z-number.

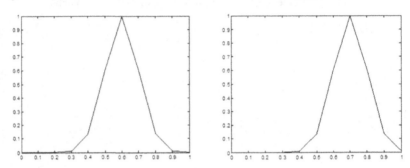

Fig 7.9. Representation of the second alternative in the first state (Z_{21}) as a Z-number.

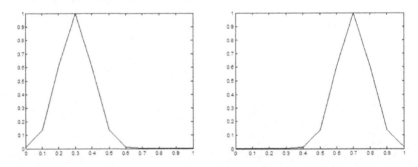

Fig. 7.10. Representation of the second alternative in the second state (Z_{22}) as a Z-number.

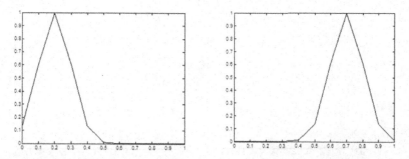

Fig. 7.11. Representation of the second alternative in the third state (Z_{23}) as a Z-number.

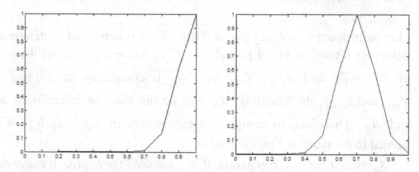

Fig. 7.12. Representation of the third alternative in the first state (Z_{31}) as a Z-number.

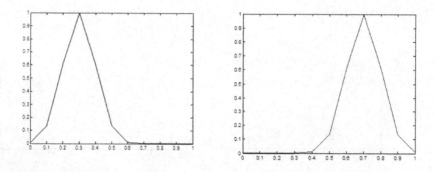

Fig. 7.13. Representation of the third alternative in the second state (Z_{32}) as a Z-number.

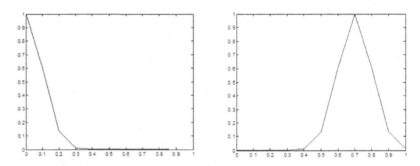

Fig. 7.14. Representation of the third alternative in the third state (Z_{33}) as a Z-number.

Let us proceed to solving the problem. First it is needed to determine unknown Z-number based probability $Z_{P(S_3)} = Z_{43} = (A_{43}, B_{43})$ on the base of $Z_{P(S_1)} = Z_{41}$ and $Z_{P(S_2)} = Z_{42}$. As $Z_{P(S_3)}$ is completely determined by $Z_{P(S_1)}$ and $Z_{P(S_2)}$, its reliability B_{43} will be the same as reliabilities B_{41} and B_{42}. Therefore, to complete determination of $Z_{43} = (A_{43}, B_{43})$ it is needed to compute A_{43} on the base of

A_{41} and A_{42}. For computation of A_{43} we used the approach suggested in [9]. The determined $Z_{43} = (A_{43}, B_{43})$ is shown in Fig. 7.15.

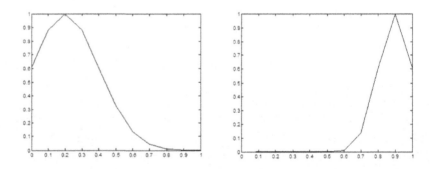

Fig. 7.15. Representation of the first state (Z_{43}) as a Z-number.

Based on the previous Z-number based data we compute the Expected Utility for each of the alternatives f_1, f_2, f_3 as follows:

$$Z_{U(f_1)} = Z_{11} \cdot Z_{41} + Z_{12} \cdot Z_{42} + Z_{13} \cdot Z_{43}$$

$$Z_{U(f_2)} = Z_{21} \cdot Z_{41} + Z_{22} \cdot Z_{42} + Z_{23} \cdot Z_{43}$$

$$Z_{U(f_3)} = Z_{31} \cdot Z_{41} + Z_{32} \cdot Z_{42} + Z_{33} \cdot Z_{43}$$

with multiplication and addition of Z-numbers described in Sections 4.1.6 and 4.1.3.

The results of computation of Expected Utilities for all the alternatives are shown in Figs. 7.16, 7.17, and 7.18.

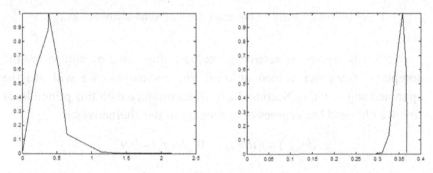

Fig. 7.16. The Expected Utility results for the first alternative $Z_{U(f_1)}$.

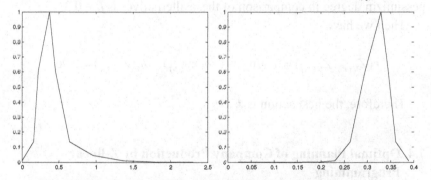

Fig. 7.17. The Expected Utility results for the second alternative $Z_{U(f_2)}$.

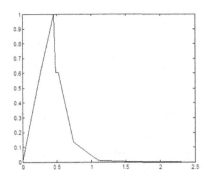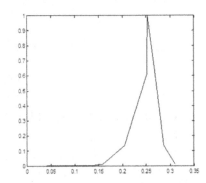

Fig. 7.18. The Expected Utility results for the second alternative $Z_{U(f_3)}$.

Now it is needed to determine the best alternative by comparing the computed Z-number valued utilities. For comparison we will use the approach suggested in Section 3.2.3. In accordance with this principle, at first we obtained the degrees of optimality of the alternatives:

$$do(f_1) = 1, do(f_2) = 0,\ do(f_3) = 0.92.$$

As one can see, the second alternative is not Pareto optimal. Now it is needed to compare the first and the second alternatives. Suppose that the pessimizm degree in comparison of these alternatives is $\beta = 0.3$.
Then we have

$$r(Z_{U(f_1)}, Z_{U(f_3)}) = 0.976 > \frac{1}{2}(do(Z_{U(f_1)}) + do(Z_{U(f_3)})) = 0.96.$$

Therefore, the best action is f_1.

7.4. Optimal Planning of Company Production by Z-linear Programming

Consider the following Z-LP problem with two decision variables[10]:

$$Z_{c_1} Z_{x_1} + Z_{c_2} Z_{x_2} \to \max$$

subject to

$$Z_{a_{11}}Z_{x_1} + Z_{a_{12}}Z_{x_2} \leq^Z Z_{b_1},$$

$$Z_{a_{21}}Z_{x_1} + Z_{a_{22}}Z_{x_2} \leq^Z Z_{b_2},$$

$$Z_{x_1}, Z_{x_2} \geq^Z Z_0,$$

where $Z_{x_1} = (A_{x_1}, B_{x_1})$, $Z_{x_2} = (A_{x_2}, B_{x_2})$ and $Z_{c_1} = (A_{c_1}, B_{c_1})$, $Z_{c_2} = (A_{c_2}, B_{c_2})$, $Z_{a_{11}} = (A_{a_{11}}, B_{a_{11}})$, $Z_{a_{12}} = (A_{a_{12}}, B_{a_{12}})$, $Z_{a_{21}} = (A_{a_{21}}, B_{a_{21}})$, $Z_{a_{22}} = (A_{a_{22}}, B_{a_{22}})$, $Z_{b_1} = (A_{b_1}, B_{b_1})$, $Z_{b_2} = (A_{b_2}, B_{b_2})$. The values of these Z-numbers are given below.

A Z-number $Z_{c_1} = (A_{c_1}, B_{c_1})$:

$$A_{c_1} = \frac{0.0}{0} + \frac{0.0}{1} + \frac{0.0003}{2} + \frac{0.01}{3} + \frac{0.14}{4} + \frac{0.61}{5} + \frac{1.0}{6} + \frac{0.61}{7}$$
$$+ \frac{0.14}{8} + \frac{0.01}{9} + \frac{0.0003}{10},$$

$$B_{c_1} = \frac{0}{0} + \frac{0}{0.1} + \frac{0}{0.2} + \frac{0.01}{0.3} + \frac{0.14}{0.4} + \frac{0.60}{0.5} + \frac{1}{0.6} + \frac{0.61}{0.7}$$
$$+ \frac{0.14}{0.8} + \frac{0.01}{0.9} + \frac{0}{1}.$$

A Z-number $Z_{c_2} = (A_{c_2}, B_{c_2})$:

$$A_{c_2} = \frac{0.0}{0} + \frac{0.0}{1} + \frac{0.0}{2} + \frac{0.0}{3} + \frac{0.0003}{4} + \frac{0.01}{5} + \frac{0.14}{6} + \frac{0.61}{7}$$
$$+ \frac{1.0}{8} + \frac{0.61}{9} + \frac{0.14}{10},$$

$$B_{c_2} = \frac{0}{0} + \frac{0}{0.1} + \frac{0.01}{0.2} + \frac{0.14}{0.3} + \frac{0.61}{0.4} + \frac{1}{0.5} + \frac{0.61}{0.6} + \frac{0.14}{0.7}$$
$$+ \frac{0.01}{0.8} + \frac{0}{0.9} + \frac{0}{1}.$$

A Z-number $Z_{a_{11}} = (A_{a_{11}}, B_{a_{11}})$:

$$A_{a_{11}} = \frac{0.01}{0} + \frac{0.14}{1} + \frac{0.61}{2} + \frac{1.0}{3} + \frac{0.61}{4} + \frac{0.14}{5} + \frac{0.01}{6} + \frac{0.001}{7}$$
$$+ \frac{0}{8} + \frac{0}{9} + \frac{0}{10},$$

$$B_{a_{11}} = \frac{0}{0} + \frac{0}{0.1} + \frac{0}{0.2} + \frac{0}{0.3} + \frac{0}{0.4} + \frac{0}{0.5} + \frac{0.01}{0.6} + \frac{0.14}{0.7}$$
$$+ \frac{0.61}{0.8} + \frac{1}{0.9} + \frac{0.61}{1}.$$

A Z-number $Z_{a_{12}} = (A_{a_{12}}, B_{a_{12}})$:

$$A_{a_{12}} = \frac{0.61}{0} + \frac{1}{1} + \frac{1.0}{2} + \frac{0.61}{3} + \frac{0.14}{4} + \frac{0.01}{5} + \frac{0.001}{6} + \frac{0}{7}$$
$$+ \frac{0}{8} + \frac{0}{9} + \frac{0}{10},$$

$$B_{a_{12}} = \frac{0}{0} + \frac{0}{0.1} + \frac{0}{0.2} + \frac{0}{0.3} + \frac{0}{0.4} + \frac{0}{0.5} + \frac{0.01}{0.6} + \frac{0.14}{0.7}$$
$$+ \frac{0.61}{0.8} + \frac{1}{0.9} + \frac{0.61}{1}. \quad \bullet$$

For simplicity, $Z_{a_{21}} = (A_{a_{21}}, B_{a_{21}})$ and $Z_{a_{22}} = (A_{a_{22}}, B_{a_{22}})$ are chosen as singletons:

$$A_{a_{21}} = 1, B_{a_{21}} = 1;$$

$$A_{a_{22}} = 1, B_{a_{22}} = 1.$$

A Z-number $Z_{b_1} = (A_{b_1}, B_{b_1})$:

$$A_{b_1} = \frac{0.14}{0} + \frac{0.61}{1} + \frac{1}{2} + \frac{0.61}{3} + \frac{1.0}{4} + \frac{0.61}{5} + \frac{0.14}{6} + \frac{0.01}{7}$$
$$+ \frac{0.001}{8} + \frac{0}{9} + \frac{0}{10},$$

$$B_{b_1} = \frac{0}{0} + \frac{0}{0.1} + \frac{0}{0.2} + \frac{0}{0.3} + \frac{0}{0.4} + \frac{0}{0.5} + \frac{0.01}{0.6} + \frac{0.14}{0.7}$$
$$+ \frac{0.61}{0.8} + \frac{1}{0.9} + \frac{0.61}{1}.$$

A Z-number $Z_{b_2} = (A_{b_2}, B_{b_2})$:

$$A_{b_2} = 0.01\big/_0 + 0.14\big/_1 + 0.61\big/_2 + 1.0\big/_3 + 0.14\big/_4 + 0.01\big/_5 + \big/_6 + \big/_7 + \big/_8$$
$$+ \big/_9 + \big/_{10},$$
$$B_{b_2} = \big/_0 + \big/_{0.1} + \big/_{0.2} + \big/_{0.3} + \big/_{0.4} + \big/_{0.5} + 0.01\big/_{0.6} + 0.14\big/_{0.7}$$
$$+ 0.61\big/_{0.8} + 1\big/_{0.9} + 0.61\big/_1.$$

By adding Z-valued slack variables, we obtain:

$$Z_{c_1} Z_{x_1} + Z_{c_2} Z_{x_2} \to \max$$

subject to

$$Z_{a_{11}} Z_{x_1} + Z_{a_{12}} Z_{x_2} + Z_{x_3} = Z_{b_1},$$
$$Z_{a_{21}} Z_{x_1} + Z_{a_{22}} Z_{x_2} + Z_{x_4} = Z_{b_2},$$

$$Z_{x_1}, Z_{x_2}, Z_{x_3}, Z_{x_4} \geq^Z Z_0.$$

Then we arrive at the equivalent form:

$$-(Z_{c_1} Z_{x_1} + Z_{c_2} Z_{x_2}) + (Z_{b_1} - (Z_{a_{11}} Z_{x_1} + Z_{a_{12}} Z_{x_2} + Z_{x_3} + Z_{x_4}))$$
$$+(Z_{b_2} - (Z_{a_{21}} Z_{x_1} + Z_{a_{22}} Z_{x_2} + Z_{x_3} + Z_{x_4})) \to \min$$

subject to

$$Z_{x_1}, Z_{x_2}, Z_{x_3}, Z_{x_4} \geq^Z Z_0.$$

We applied the suggested DEO algorithm-based method (Section 6.1) for solving this problem[10]. The following values of the parameters of the DE optimization algorithm were used: mutation rate $F = 0.8$, crossover probability $CR = 0.7$, population size is $PN = 80$. The obtained optimal solution and the optimal value of the objective function are given below[10].

The first decision variable $Z_{x_1} = (A_{x_1}, B_{x_1})$:

$$A_{x_1} = 1.0/_0 + 0.61/_1 + 0.14/_2 + 0.01/_3 + 0.0/_4 + 0.0/_5 + 0.0/_6 + 0.0/_7$$
$$+ 0.0/_8 + 0.0/_9 + 0.0/_{10},$$

$$B_{x_1} = 0.14/_0 + 0.61/_{0.1} + 1.0/_{0.2} + 0.61/_{0.3} + 0.14/_{0.4} + 0.01/_{0.5} + 0.0/_{0.6}$$
$$+ 0.0/_{0.7} + 0.0/_{0.8} + 0.0/_{0.9} + 0.0/_1.$$

The second decision variable $Z_{x_2} = (A_{x_2}, B_{x_2})$:

$$A_{x_2} = 0.01/_0 + 0.14/_1 + 0.61/_2 + 1/_3 + 0.61/_4 + 0.14/_5 + 0.01/_6 + 0/_7$$
$$+ 0/_8 + 0/_9 + 0/_{10},$$

$$B_{x_2} = 0/_0 + 0/_{0.1} + 0/_{0.2} + 0/_{0.3} + 0/_{0.4} + 0.0001/_{0.5} + 0.001/_{0.6} + 0.01/_{0.7}$$
$$+ 0.14/_{0.8} + 0.61/_{0.9} + 1/_1.$$

The third (slack) decision variable $Z_{x_3} = (A_{x_3}, B_{x_3})$:

$$A_{x_3} = 0/_0 + 0.01/_1 + 0.14/_2 + 0.61/_3 + 1/_4 + 0.61/_5 + 0.14/_6 + 0.01/_7$$
$$+ 0/_8 + 0/_9 + 0/_{10},$$

$$B_{x_3} = 0/_0 + 0/_{0.1} + 0/_{0.2} + 0.001/_{0.3} + 0.01/_{0.4} + 0.14/_{0.5} + 0.61/_{0.6}$$
$$+ 1/_{0.7} + 0.61/_{0.8} + 0.14/_{0.9} + 0.01/_1.$$

The fourth (slack) decision variable $Z_{x_4} = (A_{x_4}, B_{x_4})$ [10]:

$$A_{x_4} = 0/_0 + 0.01/_1 + 0.14/_2 + 0.61/_3 + 1/_4 + 0.61/_5 + 0.14/_6 + 0.01/_7$$
$$+ 0/_8 + 0/_9 + 0/_{10},$$

$$B_{x_4} = 0/_0 + 0/_{0.1} + 0/_{0.2} + 0.01/_{0.3} + 0.14/_{0.4} + 0.61/_{0.5} + 1/_{0.6}$$
$$+ 0.61/_{0.7} + 0.14/_{0.8} + 0.01/_{0.9} + 0/_1.$$

The optimal value of the objective function $Z_f (Z_{x_1}, Z_{x_2}) = (A_f, B_f)$:

$$A_f = \frac{0}{0} + \frac{0.61}{14} + \frac{1}{24} + \frac{0.61}{32} + \frac{0.14}{43} + \frac{0.14}{66} + \frac{0}{86}$$
$$+ \frac{0}{120} + \frac{0}{160},$$

$$B_f = \frac{0}{0.09} + \frac{0}{0.12} + \frac{0}{0.14} + \frac{0}{0.143} + \frac{0}{0.17} + \frac{0}{0.2}$$
$$+ \frac{0.0001}{0.22} + \frac{0.01}{0.224} + \frac{0.14}{0.25} + \frac{0.61}{0.28} + \frac{1}{0.3}.$$

For comparative analysis of results of this Z-LP example, the same LP problem from [87] which is stated in terms of GFNs is considered. A GFN is a modified trapezoidal fuzzy number $(a,b,c,d;w)$, where w is a maximal value of the membership function. The results obtained in [87] are as follows:

$$x_1 = 0, \quad x_2 = (1,2,4,7;0.7) \text{ and } f = (4,12,40,112;0.5).$$

The core of the first component in $Z_{x_1} = (A_{x_1}, B_{x_1})$ is equal to $core(A_{x_1}) = 0$ and the center of the interval with the highest membership values for the GFN x_1 is 3. The core of the first component in $Z_{x_2} = (A_{x_2}, B_{x_2})$ is $core(A_{x_1}) = 3$ and center of the interval with the highest membership values for the GFN x_2 is 2.45. The core of the first component of a Z-number $Z_f(Z_{x_1}, Z_{x_2}) = (A_f, B_f)$ describing optimal value of the objective function is $core(A_f) = 24$ and the rank of center of the interval with the highest membership values for the GFN $(4,12,40,112;0.5)$ is 21. At the same time, the difference in the reliability levels of the results obtained by the compared approaches is larger. However, one can see that the results obtained by both the approaches are close to each other. There are two basic differences between the approach suggested in [87] and our approach[10]. The first concerns structures of a Z-number and a generalized fuzzy number (GFN). A GFN is a modified trapezoidal fuzzy number $(a,b,c,d;w)$, where w is a maximal value of the membership function. Thus, in this formalization, belief related to an imprecise estimation is represented as a maximal value of membership function which may be lower than 1. In a Z-number, belief (reliability) to A_x is formalized as a value of probability measure of A_x. That is, a Z-number is a more structured formal construct and has a more expressive power. Moreover, in computation with Z-numbers, propagation of reliability is carried on a more fundamental level, and reliability is computed at each step. In contrast, when using GFNs, propagation of belief is more sketchy (min operation is used). From the other side, in a Z-number belief is described by a fuzzy number, whereas in GFN belief is a precise value which is counterintuitive.

Bibliography

1.   Abu Aarqob, O. A., Shawagfeh, N. T. and. AbuGhneim, O. A. (2008) Functions Defined on Fuzzy Real Numbers According to Zadeh's Extension. *International Mathematical Forum*, 3(16), pp.763 – 776.

2.   Aliev, R. A, Akif V. A. and Shirinova U. K. (2003). Fuzzy Chaos Approach to fuzzy linear programming problem, *Proc. 6th Int. Conf. on Soft Comp. and Comp. with Words in Syst. Anal., Decis. and Control*, ICSCCW, pp. 287-294.

3.   Aliev, R. A. (2013) *Fundamentals of the Fuzzy Logic-Based Generalized Theory of Decisions*. (Springer, New York, Berlin).

4.   Aliev, R. A. and Aliev, R. R. (2001) *Soft Computing and Its Application*. (World Scientific, New Jersey, London, Singapore, Hong Kong).

5.   Aliev, R. A. and Huseynov, O. H. (2014) *Decision theory with imperfect information*, (World Scientific, Singapoure).

6.   Aliev, R. A. and Pedrycz, W. (2009). Fundamentals of a fuzzy-logic-based generalized theory of stability, *IEEE T. Syst. Man CY. B.*, 39(4), pp. 971 – 988.

7.   Aliev, R. A. and Tserkovny, A. E. (1988). The knowledge representation inintelligent robots based on fuzzy sets, *Soviet Math. Doklady*, 37, pp. 541-544.

8.   Aliev, R. A. and Zeinalova, L. M. (2014). *Decision making under Z-information*, eds. Guo, P., Pedrycz, W., "Human-Centric Decision-Making Models for Social Sciences (Studies in Computational Intelligence)", (Springer), pp. 233-252.

9.   Aliev, R. A., Alizadeh A. V. and Huseynov O. H. (2015). The arithmetic of discrete Z-numbers, Inform. Sciences , 290(1), pp.134-155.

10. Aliev, R. A., Alizadeh, A. V., Huseynov, O. H. and Jabbarova, K.I. Z-number based Linear Programming. *Int. J. Intell. Syst.*, accepted.

11. Aliev, R. A., Alizadeh, A.V. and Huseynov, O.H. (2015). The arithmetic of discrete Z-numbers, *Inform. Sciences*, 290(1), pp. 134-155.

12. Aliev, R. A., and Liberzon M. I. (1987) *Methods and algorithms of coordination in integrated manufacturing systems,* (Radio i Svyaz, Moscow) (in Russian).

13. Aliev, R. A., Fazlollahi, B. and Aliev, R. R. (2004) *Soft Computing and itsApplication in Business and Economics*. (Springer-Verlag, Berlin, Heidelberg).

14. Aliev, R. A., Mamedova, G. A. and Tserkovny, A. E. (1991) *Fuzzy Control Systems*. (Energoatomizdat, Moscow).

15. Aliev, R. A., Pedrycz, W., Alizadeh, A. V. and Huseynov, O. H. (2013). Fuzzy optimality based decision making under imperfect information without utility, *Fuzzy Optim. Decis. Ma.*, vol. 12, issue 4, pp. 357-372.

16. Aliev, R. A., Pedrycz, W., Fazlollahi B., Huseynov O. H., Alizadeh A. V. and Guirimov, B. G. (2012). Fuzzy logic-based generalized decision theory with

imperfect information, *Inform. Sciences,* 189, pp.18-42.

17.   Aliev, R. A., Pedrycz, W., Huseynov, O. H. and Zeinalova, L. M. (2011). *Decision making with second order information granules.* In: "Granular computing and intelligent systems," (Springer-Verlag), pp. 327-374.

18.   Aliev, R. A., Pedrycz, W., Zeinalova, L.M. and Huseynov, O.H. (2014). Decision making with second-order imprecise probabilities, *Int. J. Intell. Syst.,* 29, pp. 137–160.

19.   Alizadeh A. V. and Huseynov O. H. (2014). Minimum and maximum of discrete Z-numbers. *Proc. 11th Int. Conf. on Appl. of Fuzzy Syst. and Soft Comp., pp.*

20.   Allahdadi, M. and Mishmast Nehi, H. (2013). The optimal solution set of the interval linear programming problems, *Optim Lett.,* 7, pp. 1893-1911.

21.   Ash, R. (2008) *Basic Probability Theory.* (Dover Publications, Mineola, N.Y).

22.   Azadeh, A., Saberi, M., Atashbar, N. Z., Chang E. and Pazhoheshfar, P. Z-AHP: A Z-number extension of fuzzy analytical hierarchy process. *Proc. of the 7th IEEE Int. Conf. on Digital Ecosystems and Technologies (DEST),* pp. 141-147.

23.   Baets, B. D. and Mesiar, R. (1999). Triangular norms on product lattices, Fuzzy Set. Syst., 104, pp. 61-75.

24.   Bashar, M. A. and Shirin, S. (2005). Squares and square roots of continuous fuzzy numbers. *Dhaka Univ. J. Sci.,* 53(2), pp.131-140.

25.   Baumfield, V. M., Conroy, J. C., Davis, R. A. and Lundie D. C. (2012). The Delphi method: gathering expert opinion in religious education, Brit. J. Relig. Educ., 34(1), pp. 5-19.

26.   Bede, B. and Gal, S. G. (2005). Generalizations of the differentiability of fuzzy-number-valued functions with applications to fuzzy differential equations, *Fuzzy. Set. Syst.,* 151, 581-599.

27.   Bede, B. and Stefanini, L. (2013). Generalized differentiability of fuzzy-valued functions, *Fuzzy Set. Syst.,* 230, pp. 119–141.

28.   Bellman, R. E. and Zadeh, L. A. (1970) Decision-making in a fuzzy environment, *Mgmt. Sci.,* 17, pp. 141-166.

29.   Benayoun, R., de Montgolfier, J., Tergny, J.and Laritchev, O. (1971). Linear Programming With Multiple Objective Functions: Step Method, *Mathematical Programming,*1, pp. 366-375.

30.   Bernardo, J. M., Bayarri, M. J., Berger, J. O. Dawid, A. P., Heckerman, D. Smith, A. F. M. and West, M. (1988). *Bayesian Statistics* 3, eds. West, M., "Modeling Expert Opinion," (Oxford University Press, UK) pp. 493-508.

31.   Bilal, M. A. (2001) *Elicitation of Expert Opinions for Uncertainty and Risks.* (CRC Press LLC, Boca Raton, Florida).

32.   Borges A. R.and Antunes C. H. (2002). A weight space-based approach to fuzzy multiple-objective linear programming, Decis. Support Syst., 34, pp. 427–443.

33.   Buckley, J. and Feuring, T. (2000). Evolutionary algorithm solution to fuzzy problems: fuzzy linear programming, *Fuzzy Set. Syst.,* 109, pp. 35-53.

34.   Buckley, J. J. (1992). Solving fuzzy equations,*Fuzzy Set. Syst.,* 50(1), pp. 1–14.

35. Buckley, J. J. and Leonard, J. J. (2008). *Monte Carlo Methods in Fuzzy Optimization,* Chapter 4 "Random fuzzy numbers and vectors in:, Studies in Fuzziness and SoftComputing 222, Springer-Verlag, Heidelberg, Germany.

36. Buckley, J. J.and Jowers, L. J. (2008). Solving Fuzzy Equations. *Stud. Fuzz. Soft Comp.*, 222, pp 89-115.

37. Buisson, J. C. (2008). Nutri–Educ, a nutrition software application for balancing meals, using fuzzy arithmetic and heuristic search algorithms, *J. Artif. Intell. Med.*, 42 (3), pp.213–227.

38. Burgin, M. (1995). Neoclassical analysis: Fuzzy continuity and convergence, *Fuzzy Set. Syst.*, 75(3), pp. 291-299.

39. Burgin, M. (2000). Theory of fuzzy limits, *Fuzzy Set. Syst.*, 115, pp. 433-443.

40. Burgin, M. (2010). Continuity in Discrete Sets. http://arxiv.org/abs/1002.0036.

41. Campos, L. and Verdegay, J. L. (1989). Linear programming problems and ranking of fuzzy numbers, *Fuzzy Set. Syst.*, 32, pp.1-11.

42. Carnap, R. (1942) *Introduction to Semantics* (Harvard University Press, Cambridge, MA).

43. Carnap, R. (1947). *Meaning and Necessity: A Study in Semantics and Modal Logic* 2d ed. (University of Chicago Press, Chicago, IL).

44. Casasnovas, J. and Riera, J. V. (2006). On the addition of discrete fuzzy numbers. *WSEAS Transactions on Mathematics*, 5(5), pp.549–554.

45. Casasnovas, J. and Riera, J. V. (2007). Discrete fuzzy numbers defined on a subset of natural numbers, *Adv. Soft Comp.*, 42, pp: 573-582.

46. Casasnovas, J. and Riera, J. V. (2009). Lattice Properties of Discrete Fuzzy Numbers under Extended Min and Max. *IFSA/EUSFLAT Conf.*, pp. 647-652.

47. Casasnovas, J. and Riera, J. V. (2011). Extension of discrete t-norms and t-conorms to discrete fuzzy numbers, Fuzzy Set. Syst., 167(1), pp.65-81. [doi>10.1016/j.fss.2010.09.016].

48. Charles, M., Grinstead, J. and Snell, L. (1997) *Introduction to Probability.* (American Mathematical Society, USA).

49. Chen, S., Liu, J., Wang, H., Xub, Y. and Augusto J. C. (2014). A linguistic multi-criteria decision making approach based on logical reasoning, *Inform. Sciences*, 258, pp. 266–276.

50. Cheng, C. H. et al (1999). Evaluating attack helicopters by AHP based on linguistic variable weight, *Eur. J. Opl. Res.*, 116, pp. 423-435.

51. Chuang, P. H. et al (1986) Plastic Limit Design Analysis With Imprecise Data. In: Pavlovic MN (ed). Steel Structures. Elsevier Applied Science Publishes: London, pp. 71-86.

52. Cloud, M. J.; Moore, R. E. and Kearfott, R. B. (2009). *Introduction to Interval Analysis,* (Society for Industrial and Applied Mathematics, Philadelphia).

53. Delgado, M., Duarte, O. and Requena, I. (2006). An arithmetic approach for the computing with words paradigm, Int. J. Intell. Syst., 21, pp. 121–142.

54.   Delgado, M., Verdegay J. L. and Vila M. A. (1989). A general model for fuzzy linear programming, *Fuzzy Set. Syst.*, 29, pp. 21-29.
55.   Diamond, P. and Kloeden, P. (1994) *Metric Spaces of Fuzzy Sets,Theory and Applications.* (World Scientific, Singapore).
56.   Dinagar, S. D. and Anbalagan, A. (2011). Two-phase approach for solving Type-2 fuzzy linear programming problem, *International Journal of Pure and Applied Mathematics*, 70, pp. 873-888.
57.   Dubois, D. and Prade, H. (1985). A review of fuzzy sets aggregation connectives, *Inform. Sciences*, 36, pp. 85-121.
58.   Farina, M., and Amato, P. (2004). A fuzzy definition of "optimality" for many-criteria optimization problems, *IEEE T. Syst. Man Cy. A: Systems and Humans*, 34(3), pp. 315-326.
59.   Fiedler, M., Nedoma, J., Ramik, J. and Zimmermann, K. (2006) *Linear optimization problems with inexact data*, (Springer Science+Business Media, New York).
60.   Fumika, O. (2004). A literature review on the use of expert opinion in probabilistic risk analysis, World Bank Policy Research Working Paper, no. 3201. http://www-wds.worldbank.org.
61.   Ganesan, K. and Veeramani, P. (2006). Fuzzy linear programs with trapezoidal fuzzy numbers, *Ann. Oper. Res.*, 143, pp. 305-315.
62.   Garcia, J. C. F. (2011). Interval type-2 fuzzy linear programming: Uncertain constraints. *IEEE Symposium on Advances in Type-2 Fuzzy Logic Systems*, T2FUZZ, pp. 94-101.
63.   Gilboa, I. (2009) *Theory of Decision under Uncertainty.* (Cambridge University Press, Cambridge).
64.   Gilboa, I. and Schmeidler, D. (1989). Maximin expected utility with a non-unique prior, *J. Math. Econ.*, 18, pp. 141-153.
65.   Glen, A. G., Leemis, L. M. and Drew, J. H. (2004). Computing the distribution of the product of two continuous random variables. *Comput. Stat. Data An.*, 44, pp. 451–464.
66.   Goetschell, R. and Voxman, W. (1986). Elementary calculs, *Fuzzy Set. Syst.*, 18, pp. 31-43.
67.   Grabisch, M., Murofushi, T., Sugeno, M., and Kacprzyk, J. (2000) *Fuzzy Measures and Integrals. Theory and Application* (Physica Verlag, Berlin, Heidelberg).
68.   Hahn, G. J. and Shapiro, S. S. (1967) *Statistical Models in Engineering.* (John Wiley and Sons, New York).
69.   http://thirteen-01.stat.iastate.edu/wiki/stat430/files?filename=Ch-2.2-trivedi.pdf.
70.   Hukuhara, M. (1967). Intégration des applications mesurablesdont la valeurest un compact convexe, *Funkcial. Ekvac.*, **10**, pp. 205–223 (in French).
71.   Ignizio, J. P. (1976) *Goal programming and extension*, (Lexington Books: Lexington, MA).

72.   Inuiguichi, M. and Ramik, J. (2000). Possibilistic linear programming: a brief review of fuzzy mathematical programming and a comparison with stochastic programming in portfolio selection problem, *Fuzzy Set. Syst.*, 111, pp. 3-28.

73.   Inuiguichi, M., Ichihashi, H. and Kume, Y. (1990). A solution algorithm for fuzzy linear programming with piecewise linear membership function, *Fuzzy Set. Syst.*, 34, pp. 15-31.

74.   Jabbarova, K. I. and Huseynov, O. H. (2014). A Z-valued regression model for a catalytic cracking process, *11th Int. Conf. on Appl. of Fuzzy Syst. and Soft Comp.*, ICAFS, pp. 165-174. (ozumetindeistinadetmek)

75.   Jaroszewicz, S. and Korzen, A. (2012). Arithmetic Operations On Independent Random Variables: A Numerical Approach. *SIAM J. SCI. Comput.* 34(3), pp. 1241-1265.

76.   Jiafu, T., Dingwei, W., Fung, R. Y. K and Yung, K. L. (2004). Understanding of Fuzzy Optimization: Theories And Methods, *J. Syst. Sci. Complex.*, 17, pp. 117-136.

77.   Kacprzyk J. (1983). A generalization of fuzzy multistage decision making and control via linguistic quantifiers. *Int. J. Control*, 38, pp. 1249-1270.

78.   Kacprzyk, J. and Zadrozny, S. (2010). Computing with words is an implementable paradigm: Fuzzy queries, linguistic data summaries and natural language generation, IEEE T. Fuzzy Syst., 18, pp. 461–472.

79.   Kang, B., Wei, D., Li, Y.and Deng, Y. (2012). Decision making using Z-numbers under uncertain environment, *J. Inf. Comput. Sci.*, 8, pp. 2807-2814.

80.   Kaufman, A. and Gupta, M. M. (1985) *Introduction to Fuzzy Arithmetic: Theory and Applications* (Van Nostrand Reinhold Company, New York).

81.   Khorasani, E. S., Patel, P., Rahimi, S. and Houle, D. (2011). CWJess: Implementation of an Expert System Shell for Computing with Words, *Proc. Federated Conference on Computer Science and Information Systems*, pp. 33–39.

82.   Khorasani, E. S., Patel, P., Rahimi, S.and Houle, D. (2012). An inference engine toolkit for computing with words, Journal of Ambient Intelligence and Humanized Computing.

83.   Kirkham, R. L. (1992) *Theories of Truth: A Critical Introduction* (MIT Press, Cambridge, MA).

84.   Klir, G. J. and Yuan, B. (1995) *Fuzzy sets and fuzzy logic, Theory and Applications* (NJ: PRT Prentice Hall).

85.   Kóczy, L. T.and Hirota, K. (1991). Rule Interpolation by α-Level Sets in Fuzzy Approximate Reasoning, *J. BUSEFAL*, 46, pp. 115-123.

86.   Kok, M. and Lootsma, F. A. (1985). Pairwise comparison methods in multiple objective programming with applications in along-term energy planning model, *Eur. J. Opl. Res.*, 22, 44-55.

87.   Kumar, A., Singh P. and Kaur, J. (2010). Generalized Simplex Algorithm to

Solve Fuzzy Linear Programming Problems with Ranking of Generalized Fuzzy Numbers. *TJFS*, 1, pp:80-103.

88.   Lai, T. Y. (1995). IMOST: Interactive Multiple Objective System Technique, *J. Opl. Res. Soc,* 46, pp. 958-976.

89.   Lai, T. Y. and Hwang, C. L. (1993). Possibilistic linear programming for managing interest rate risk, *Fuzzy Set. Syst.*, 54, pp. 135-146.

90.   Lai, Y. J. and Hwang, C. L. (1994) *Fuzzy Multi Objective Decision Making: Methods and Applications,* (Spinger –Verlag, Berlin).

91.   Lakoff, G. (1972). "Hedges: A study in meaning criteria and the logic of fuzzy concepts", *Papers from the Eighth Regional Meeting of the Chicago Linguistic Society,* pp:183–228.

92.   Lakshmikantham, V. and Mohapatra, R. (2003) *Theory of Fuzzy Differential Equations and Inclusions.* (Taylor and Francis, London, New York).

93.   Landeta, J. (2006). Current validity of the Delphi method in social sciences, *Technological Forecasting and Social Change,* Vol. 73, No. 5, pp. 467-482.

94.   Lawry, J. (2001). A methodology for computing with words, Int. J. Approx. Reason., 28, pp. 55–89.

95.   Lootsma, F. A. (1989) *Optimization with Multiple Objectives,* eds. Iri, M. and Tanabe K. "Mathematical Programming, Recent Developments and Applications," (KTKScientific, Publishers: Tokyo).

96.   Lorkowski, J., Aliev, R. and Kreinovich, V. (2014). Towards Decision Making under Interval, Set-Valued, Fuzzy, and Z-Number Uncertainty: A Fair Price Approach., *FUZZ-IEEE,* pp. 2244-2253.

97.   Lu, J., Zhang G., Ruan D.and Wu F. (2007) *Multi-objective group decision making. Methods, software and applications with fuzzy set techniques,* (Imperial college press, Series in electrical and computer engineering).

98.   Luhandjula, M. K. (1987). Linear programming with a possibilistic objective function, Eur. J. Oper. Res., 31, pp. 110-117.

99.   Maleki, H. R., Tata, M. and Mashinchi, M. (2000). Linear programming with fuzzy variables, *Fuzzy Set. Syst.*, 109, pp. 21-33.

100. Mamdani, E. H. (1977). Application of fuzzy logic to approximate reasoning usinglinguistic syntheses, *IEEE T. Comput.,* C-26(12), pp. 1182–1191.

101. Mathai, A. M. (1973). A Review of the Different Techniques used for Deriving the Exact Distributions of Multivariate Test Criteria., *The Indian Journal of Statistics,* vol. 35, series A, pt. 1, pp. 39—60.

102. Mendel, J. M. and Wu, D. (2010). Perceptual computing - Aiding people in making subjective judgements. (IEEE Press, N.J.).

103. Mendel, J. M., Zadeh, L. A., Trillas, E., Yager, R., Lawry, J., Hagras, H. and Guadarrama, S. (2010). What Computing With Words means to me?, IEEE Comput. Intell. M., 5(1), pp. 20–26.

104. Mizumoto, M. and Tanaka, K. (1979). Some properties of fuzzy numbers, eds. Gupta, M. M., Ragade, R. K.and Yager, R. R., *Advances in Fuzzy set theory and*

applications (North-Holland Publishing company).

105. Moore, R. C. (1985) Possible-World Semantics for Autoepistemic Logic, *Center for the Study of Language and Information,* (Stanford University), Report № CSLI-85-41.

106. Moore, R. E. (1966) *Interval Analysis. Englewood Cliff* (New Jersey: Prentice-Hall).

107. Negoita C. V. and Ralescu D. A. (1975) *Applications of Fuzzy Sets to Systems Analysis, Wiley* (John Wiley & Sons, New York).

108. Nguyen, H. T. and Walker, E. A. (2006) *A First Course in Fuzzy Logic,* (Chapman and Hall/CRC, Boca Raton, Florida).

109. O.Hagan, A., Caitlin, E. B., Daneshkhah, A., Eiser, J. R., Garthwaite, P. H., Jenkinson, D. J., Oakley, J. E. and Rakow, T. (2006) *Uncertain Judgments: Eliciting Experts' Probabilities* (Wiley).

110. Pal, S. K. and Banerjee R. (2013). An Insight Into The Z-number Approach To CWW. Fundamenta Informaticae, 124, pp. 197–229.

111. Pandian, P. and Jayalakshmi, M. (2013). Determining Efficient Solutions to Multiple Objective Linear Programming Problems,*Applied Mathematical Sciences*, 7(26), pp.1275 – 1282.www.m-hikari.com.

112. Papoulls, A. (1965) *Probability, Random Variables, and Stochastic Processes* (McGraw-Hill, New York).

113. Petrovic-Lazarevic, S. and Abraham A. (2003). Hybrid Fuzzy-Linear Programming Approach for MultiCriteria Decision Making Problems, Journal Neural, Parallel & Scientific Computations - Special issue: Advances in intelligent systems and applications, 11(1&2), pp. 53–68.

114. Ramik, J. (2005). Duality in fuzzy linear programming: some new concepts and results,*Fuzzy Optim. Decis. Ma.,* 4, pp. 25-39.

115. Ramsey, F. P. *Truth and Probability,* written 1926. Published 1931, The Foundations of Mathematics and other Logical Essays, pp. 156–198. (Chapter VII).: R.B. Braithwaite (Ed.), Kegan, Paul, Trench, Trubner & Co., Ltd, London. Harcourt, Brace and Co., New York.: Further Considerations written 1928.Published 1931 op. cit., pp. 199–211 (Chapter VIII). Probability and Partial Belief written 1929. Published 1931, op cit., pp. 256–257 (Chapter IX).

116. Reformat, M. and Ly, C. (2009). Ontological approach to development of computing with words based systems, Int. J. Approx. Reason., 50, pp. 72–91.

117. Roger, M. (1991) *Cooke Experts in Uncertainty: Opinion and Subjective Probability in Science* (Oxford University Press, New York).

118. Rommelfanger, H. (2007). A general concept for solving linear multicriteria programming problems with crisp, fuzzy or stochastic values, *Fuzzy Set. Syst.,* 158, pp. 1892-1904.

119. Roush, S. (2005) *Tracking Truth: Knowledge, Evidence, and Science,* (Oxford University Press, Oxford).

120. Sakawa, M. (1993) *Fuzzy Sets and Interactive Multiobjective Optimization*, (Plenum Press, New York). http://dx.doi.org/10.1007/978-1-4899-1633-4.

121. Sakawa, M. and Yano, H. (1985). Interactive fuzzy satisficing method using augmented minimax problems and its application to environmental systems, *IEEE Transactions on Systems, Man. and Cybernetics;* 15(6), pp. 720-729. http://dx.doi.org/10.1109/TSMC.1985.6313455.

122. Sakawa, M., Matsui, T. and Katagiri, H. (2013). An interactive fuzzy satisficing method for random fuzzy multiobjective linear programming problems through fractile criteria optimization with possibility. *Artificial Intelligence Research*, 2(4), pp. 75-86.

123. Sakawa, M., Nishizaki, I. and Katagiri, H. (2011) *Fuzzy Stochastic Multiobjective Programming*, (Springer, New York) http://dx.doi.org/10.1007/978-1-4419-8402-9.

124. Schmeidler, D. (1989). Subjective probability and expected utility without additivity, *Econometrita*, 57(3), pp. 571-587.

125. Seising, R. and González, V.S. (2012) *Soft Computing in Humanities and Social Sciences*. Stud.Fuzz. Soft Comp. (Springer-Verlag, Berlin, Heidelberg), 273, 519 p.

126. Springer M. D. (1979) *The Algebra of Random Variables*. (John Wiley and Sons Inc, New York).

127. Stefanini, L. (2008) *A generalization of Hukuhara difference*, eds. Dubois, D., Lubiano, M.A., Prade, H., Gil, M.A., Grzegorzewski, P. and Hryniewicz, O., "SoftMethods for Handling Variability and Imprecision", 48, (Springer-Verlag Berlin Heidelberg).

128. Stefanini, L. (2010). A generalization of Hukuhara difference and division for interval and fuzzy arithmetic, Fuzzy Set. Syst., 161, pp.1564-1584. 1564ñ1584,doi:10.1016/j.fss.2009.06.009.

129. Tadayon, S. and Tadayon, B. (2012). Approximate Z-Number Evaluation based on Categorical Sets of Probability Distributions, *Proc. 2nd World Conf. on Soft Computing*, WConSC.

130. Tanaka, H. and Asai, K. (1984). Fuzzy linear programming with fuzzy numbers, *Fuzzy Set. Syst.;* 13, pp.1-10.

131. Tarski, A. (1939). On Undecidable Statements in Enlarged Systems of Logic and the Concept of Truth, J. Symbolic Logic, 4(3), pp.105-112.

132. Trillas E., Moraga, C., Guadarrama S., Cubillo S., and Casticeira E. (2007). *Computing with Antonyms*, eds. Nikravesh M., Kacprzyk J., Zadeh, L. A., "Forging New Frontiers: Fuzzy Pioneers I, Studies in Fuzziness and Soft Computing,"(Springer-Verlag, Berlin Heidelberg), pp. 133–153.

133. Trivino, G. and Vander-Heide, A. (2008). An experiment on the description of sequences of fuzzy perceptions, *Proc. 8th International Conference on Hybrid Intelligent Systems*, pp. 228–233.

134. Ullmann, S. (1962) *Semantics: An Introduction to the Science of Meaning*,

(Barnes & Noble, New York).

135. Vander-Heide, A. and Trivino, G. (2010). Simulating emotional personality in human computer interface, *Proc. IEEE International Conference on Fuzzy Systems*, pp. 1–7.

136. Voxman, W. (2001). Canonical representations of discretefuzzy numbers, Fuzzy Set.Syst., 54, pp. 457–466.

137. Wang, G., Wu, C. and Zhao, C. (2005). Representation and Operations of discrete fuzzy numbers, *Southeast Asian Bulletin of Mathematics*, 28, pp. 1003–1010.

138. Williamson, R. C. and Downs, T. (1990). Probabilistic arithmetic. I. numerical methods for calculating convolutions and dependency bounds. *Int. J. Approx. Reason.*, 4(2), pp. 89–158.

139. Williamson, R. C. (1989). *Probabilistic Arithmetic*. Ph.D. dissertation, University of Queensland, Australia, http://theorem.anu.edu.au/~williams/papers/thesis 300.

140. Winston, W. L. and Albright, S.C. and Broadie, M. (2002) *Practical management science. Thomas Learning*, 2nd Ed., pp. 496-498.

141. Yager, R. R. (1998). *On measures of specificity*, eds. Kaynak, O., Zadeh, L. A.,Turksen, B. and Rudas, I. J., "Computational Intelligence: Soft Computing and Fuzzy-Neuro Integration with Applications," (Springer-Verlag, Berlin), pp. 94–113.

142. Yager, R. R. (2012). On a View of Zadeh's Z-Numbers, *Advances in Computational Intelligence, Communications in Computer and Information Science,* 299, pp. 90-101.

143. Yager, R. R. (2012). On Z-valuations using Zadeh`s Z-numbers, Int. J. Intell. Syst., 27, pp. 259-278.

144. Yang, R., Wang, Z., Heng, P.-A. and Leung, K.-S. (2005). Fuzzy numbers and fuzzification of the Choquet integral, *Fuzzy Set. Syst.* 153(1), pp. 95-113.

145. Yu, P. L. and Zeleny, M. (1975). The set of all non-dominated solutions in linear cases and a multicriteria simplex method, *Journal of Mathematical Analysis and Applications,* 49, pp. 430-468.

146. Zadeh L. A. (1975). *Calculus of fuzzy restrictions*, eds. Zadeh, L. A., Fu, K.S., Tanaka, K. and Shimura, M. "Fuzzy sets and Their Applications to Cognitive and Decision Processes," (Academic Press, New York), pp. 1–39.

147. Zadeh L. A. (1996). Fuzzy logic = Computing with words, IEEE T. Fuzzy Syst., 4(2), pp. 103–111.

148. Zadeh L. A. (2004). Precisiated natural language (PNL), AI Magazine, 25(3), pp. 74–91.

149. Zadeh, L. A. (1965). Fuzzy Sets, *Inform. Control,* 8, pp. 338-353.

150. Zadeh, L. A. (1968). Probability measures of fuzzy events, *J. Math. Anal. Appl.*, 23(2), pp. 421–427.

151.   Zadeh, L. A. (1972).A fuzzy-set-theoretic interpretation of linguistic hedges, J Cybernetics, 2(3), pp. 4–34.

152.   Zadeh, L. A. (1973). Outline of a new approach to the analysis of complex systemand decision processes, *IEEE T. Syst. Man. Cyb.* 3, pp. 28-44

153.   Zadeh, L. A. (1975). *Calculus of fuzzy restrictions*, eds. Zadeh L. A., Fu K. S., Tanaka K. and Shimura M., "Fuzzy sets and Their Applications to Cognitive and Decision Processes," (Academic Press, New York), pp. 1–39.

154.   Zadeh, L. A. (1975). Fuzzy logic and approximate reasoning. *Synthese* 30(3-4), pp. 407-428.

155.   Zadeh, L. A. (1975). The concept of a linguistic variable and itsapplications in approximatereasoning, *Inform. Sciences*, 8, pp.43–80, pp. 301–357; 9, pp. 199–251.

156.   Zadeh, L. A. (1979) *Liar's Paradox and Truth-Qualification Principle*, ERL Memorandum M79/34, (University of California, Berkeley).

157.   Zadeh, L. A. (1979). A theory of approximate reasoning, eds. Hayes J., Michie D. and Mikulich L. I., *Mach. Intell,*.9, (Halstead Press, New York), pp. 149–194.

158.   Zadeh, L. A. (1979). *Fuzzy sets and information granularity*, eds. Gupta, M., Ragade R. and Yager R. "Advances in Fuzzy Set Theory and Applications," (North-Holland Publishing Co., Amsterdam), pp. 3–18.

159.   Zadeh, L. A. (1982). Test-score semantics for natural language and meaning representation via PRUF, eds. Reiger B. "Empirical Semantics" (Broackmeyer University Press, Germany), pp. 281–349.

160.   Zadeh, L. A. (1983). A fuzzy-set-theoretic approach to the compositionality of meaning: propositions, dispositions and canonical forms, *Journal of Semantics*, 3, pp. 253–272.

161.   Zadeh, L. A. (1986). Outline of a computational approach to meaning and knowledge representation based on the concept of a generalized assignment statement, eds. Thoma M. and Wyner A. *Proc.of the Int. Seminar on Artificial Intelligence and Man–Machine Systems*, Springer-Verlag, Heidelberg, pp. 198–211.

162.   Zadeh, L. A. (1996). Fuzzy logic and the calculi of fuzzy rules and fuzzy graphs, *Multiple-Valued Logic 1*, pp. 1–38.

163.   Zadeh, L. A. (1999). From computing with numbers to computing with words – from manipulation of measurements to manipulation with perceptions, *IEEE T. Circuits-I*, 45(1), pp. 105-119.

164.   Zadeh, L. A. (2001). A new direction in AI — toward a computational theory of perceptions, *AI Mag.*, 22(1), pp. 73-84.

165.   Zadeh, L. A. (2005). Toward a generalized theory of uncertainty — an outline, *Inform. Sciences,* 172, pp. 1–40.

166.   Zadeh, L. A. (2006). Generalized theory of uncertainty (GTU) – principal concepts and ideas, *Comput. Stat. Data An.,* 51, pp. 15-46

167.   Zadeh, L. A. (2008). Is there a need for fuzzy logic? *Inform. Sciences,* 178, pp.

2751-2779.

168. Zadeh, L. A. (2010). A note on Z-numbers, *Inform. Sciences,* 181, pp. 2923–2932.

169. Zadeh, L. A. (2010). Foreword to the special section on Computing With Words, IEEE T. Fuzzy Syst., 18(3), pp. 437–440.

170. Zadeh, L. A. (2010). The Z-mouse—a visual means of entry and retrieval of fuzzy data, posted on BISC Forum, July 30, 2010. A more detailed description may be found in Computing with Words – principal concepts and ideas, Colloquium powerpoint presentation, University of Southern California, Los Angeles, CA, October 22.

171. Zadeh, L. A. (2011). The concept of a Z-number - A new direction in uncertain computation, *Proc. of the IEEE International Conference on Information Reuse and Integration,* IRI, pp. xxii-xxiii.

172. Zadeh, L. A. (2012) *Computing with words—principal concepts and ideas,* Studies in Fuzziness and Soft Computing, 277, (Springer, Berlin Heidelberg).

173. Zadeh, L. A. (2012) Outline of a restriction-centered theory of reasoning and computation in an environment of uncertainty and imprecision. http://trivent.hu/2012/ieeesofa2012/documents/presentation_zadeh.pdf.

174. Zadeh, L. A. (2012). Methods and systems for applications with Z-numbers, United States Patent, Patent No.: US 8,311,973 B1, Date of Patent: Nov. 13.

175. Zadeh, L. A. (2013). A restriction-centered theory of reasoning and computation, *Int. Conf.on Soft Computing and Software Engineering,* (PowerPoint presentation).

176. Zadeh, L. A. (2013). Z-numbers—a new direction in the analysis of uncertain and complex systems. 7th IEEE Int.Conf.on Digital Ecosystems and Technologies, IEEE-DEST. http://dest2013.digital-ecology.org/

177. Zadeh, L. A. (1981). *Possibility theory, soft data analysis,* eds. In: Cobb L. and Thrall R.M. "Mathematical Frontiers of the Social and Policy Sciences,"(Westview Press, Boulder, CO), pp. 69–129.

178. Zeleny, M. (1974) *Linear MultiObjective Programming,* (Springer-Verlag, Berlin, Heidelberg).

179. Zeleny, M. (1982) *Multiple Criteria Decision Making.* (McGraw-Hill, New York).

180. Zhang, D. (2005). Triangular norms on partially ordered sets, Fuzzy Set. Syst., 153, pp. 195-209.

181. Zimmermann, H. J. (1978). Fuzzy programming and linear programming with several objective functions, *Fuzzy Set. Syst.,* 1, pp. 45-55.

Index

Printed in the United States
by Bookmasters

Printed in the United States
By Bookmasters